Police Use of Force

Important Issues Facing the Police
and the Communities They Serve

Police Use of Force

Important Issues Facing the Police and the Communities They Serve

Edited by

Michael J. Palmiotto
Wichita State University
School of Community Affairs
Wichita, Kansas, USA

CRC Press
Taylor & Francis Group
Boca Raton London New York

CRC Press is an imprint of the
Taylor & Francis Group, an **informa** business

CRC Press
Taylor & Francis Group
6000 Broken Sound Parkway NW, Suite 300
Boca Raton, FL 33487-2742

First issued in paperback 2019

© 2017 by Taylor & Francis Group, LLC
CRC Press is an imprint of Taylor & Francis Group, an Informa business

No claim to original U.S. Government works

ISBN-13: 978-1-4987-3214-7 (hbk)
ISBN-13: 978-0-367-87374-5 (pbk)

Library of Congress Cataloging-in-Publication Data

Names: Palmiotto, Michael, editor.
Title: Police use of force : important issues facing the police and the communities they serve / Michael J. Palmiotto, editor.
Other titles: Police use of force (CRC Press)
Description: Boca Raton, FL : CRC Press, 2017. | Includes bibliographical references and index.
Identifiers: LCCN 2016006347 | ISBN 9781498732147
Subjects: LCSH: Police brutality--United States. | Police shootings--United States. | Police-community relations--United States. | Police misconduct--United States.
Classification: LCC HV8141 .P59353 2017 | DDC 363.2/32--dc23
LC record available at http://lccn.loc.gov/2016006347

Visit the Taylor & Francis Web site at
http://www.taylorandfrancis.com

and the CRC Press Web site at
http://www.crcpress.com

For my wife, Emily, for her unstinting love and support.

CONTENTS

PREFACE

This book on the *Use of Force* fills a void in a major issue facing American society. The use of force takes into consideration the social, criminal, and human rights issues important to a democratic country, such as the United States. The important aspect in dealing with the use of force is that it pits the police against the people they are sworn to protect and serve. It may not be the intent of either the police or the public they deal with to have a confrontation which could lead to deadly force being used.

Deadly force often has been used when an offender or citizen refuses to cooperate with a police request or refuses to listen to an order to perform a specific action. Sometimes, when the citizen refuses to cooperate, the officer, who has the authority to force the issue, may do so, which can lead to serious injury or death. This of course can escalate to demonstrations or riots.

In the early twenty-first century the use of force, especially deadly force, by the police has become a volatile issue that may cost police officers their lives or livelihood. There are activists and organizations that contend that the police are wrong when they use force, especially deadly force. It is generally held at the time of this writing that most police officers consider that they will be considered guilty until proven innocent when using force against a citizen. Along these same lines police officers hold the premise that they will not be supported and that people will do the politically correct thing to maintain the support of politicians and activists. Of course there are those that consider police actions generally wrong and abusive anytime the police resort to the use of force.

Police Use of Force provides a broader perspective than current books on the issue. Books in print include officer involved shooting, self-defense and the use of force, in the kill zone, a cop view of deadly force. A 1992 book published by the Police Executive Research Forum (PERF) on *What WE Know about Deadly Force* and several general books on the use of force all discuss the preceding issues.

The 10 chapters of this book are contributed by authorities in specific areas of the use of force. The contributors consist of those having law enforcement, academic, and research experience. They include technology experts, community psychologists, political scientists, legal scholars, training experts, and criminal justice personnel. With the use of force issue not going away anytime soon, this book should provide a good foundation for understanding the concern.

Chapter 1 by Professor Michael Palmiotto provides a review of social control, crime control, and the use of force from ancient times to modern day. After a look at "kin" police, ancient Roman, Greek, and Egyptian police are briefly examined. Policing in Europe and England is covered. The development of modern policing is discussed. Throughout history the use of force has been used in all societies and cultures and is primarily documented or integrated into the history of a specific society.

Chapter 2 on the "Use of Force" defines brutality and the use of force by the police. There are numerous definitions on what the use of force is when conducted by the police. This chapter addresses the issue when force is "necessary" and "reasonable" as used by the police. Also, covered in this chapter is the "improper" use of force which falls into two categories: "unnecessary" and "excessive." The emerging use of force issues are covered, the use of force continuum is discussed, and examples of excessive use of force by the police are provided, including the Abner Louima case and the Rodney King case, which received national attention.

Chapter 3 on deadly force defines the term and reviews when deadly force may be acceptable. The chapter explains when the police have the authority to use force and when it is not appropriate. For example, police can never use deadly force against someone committing a minor offense. Deadly force can be traced back to the middle ages when felony crimes were punishable by death. If an agent of the state killed someone committing a felony, the agent was considered to be doing the state a favor because the felony was punishable by death anyway. By comparison, in contemporary society, the only felony that can be punishable by death is first degree murder. In the United States, the use of deadly force by government officers can be traced back to colonial times and the Civil War. Most states have laws defining deadly force. When police officers use deadly force against a suspect or offender it usually involves firearms. However, neck holds by the police can also lead to death. The danger they create are discussed and an example is provided. The issue of deadly force acts committed by the police was as much a controversial issue in the last century as it is today.

Chapter 4 on "Nonlethal Weapons and Technology" written by Dr. Szde Yu reviews the controversial issue of nonlethal weapons. The primary concern has been that use of nonlethal weapons can still result in injury to the recipient. This chapter will discuss police use of force, Tasers, and other less lethal weapons.

The historical influence and impact of the police has been carefully reviewed by Dr. Laurence French in the "Militarization of the Police." Professor French traces the militarization of the police to early American history, noting that at times during American history, the military has functioned as the police. Currently, American society gives attention to the police on their strategies and actions that often reflect similar functions the military performs. Dr. French recommends that "law enforcement personnel especially chiefs, sheriffs, et cetera need to lose the military attire that attempts to present themselves as admirals and generals" (p. 78).

"Racism and Profiling" authored by Dr. Michael Birzer reviews theories about whether there is a problem of black crime and how the police relates to minorities. Does racism influence police behavior? If so, how? Do the police profile certain people? Is their profiling based on economic status, race, gender, or ethnic groups? Good profiling versus bad profiling is discussed.

Chapter 7, "Legal Issues," by Alison Brown deals with court decisions involving the use of excessive and deadly force. Court decisions pertinent to the United States Supreme Court, Federal Circuit Courts, and state courts are reviewed. Those uses of force and deadly force cases that have made an impact on police procedures are discussed.

Chapter 8, "Psychological Perspectives," by Jody Beeson reviews the cognitive decision-making process that influences the level of force applied by an officer in specific circumstances. The suspect's demeanor, the officer's personality, prior experience, and cognitive appraisal of the risk for harm to himself/herself and others are key factors that determine the cognitive processes that an officer will utilize in the decision-making process. Understanding this process is essential for preparing officers to make appropriate decisions when under pressure. This chapter discusses those processes.

Chapter 9, "Political Perspective," written by Carolyn Schmidt provides an insight to how activists and politicians view the use of force, specifically deadly force. Dr. Schmidt states that the political impact of police violence being viewed as reasonable or unreasonable depends upon the view of society. Views of police violence may depend upon race, ethnic background, religion, and economic class.

The last chapter, "Training and Prevention," authored by Professors Vladimir Sergevnin and Darrell L. Ross, deals with the important issue of training the police to prevent excessive force, examining when appropriate force can be used and emphasizing prevention of unnecessary use of force. Accordingly, this chapter discusses various prevention and training methods and recommends more than firearms training. Not only do officers need range training in using their firearms; they also need training in situations that teaches them when they may—and may not—use their firearms.

EDITOR

Michael J. Palmiotto, PhD, is a professor of criminal justice and undergraduate coordinator of the Criminal Justice Department at Wichita State University, Wichita, Kansas. He was formerly a police officer in New York, serving in White Plains and Scarsdale. He has experience establishing and operating a police training facility in Western Pennsylvania. Dr. Palmiotto earned a master's degree from John Jay College (CUNY) and a doctorate from the University of Pittsburgh. He has been a faculty member of several universities.

Dr. Palmiotto has published 12 books, 20 book chapters, and numerous articles on criminal justice and law enforcement. He has published in the areas of criminal investigation, community policing, police misconduct, police globalization, and police training among others. He is the recipient of two Fulbright awards.

CONTRIBUTORS

Jodie Beeson
School of Community Affairs
Wichita State University
Wichita, Kansas

Michael L. Birzer
School of Community Affairs
Wichita State University
Wichita, Kansas

Alison Brown
School of Community Affairs
Wichita State University
Wichita, Kansas

Laurence Armand French
Justice Works Institute
University of New Hampshire
Durham, New Hampshire

Michael J. Palmiotto
School of Community Affairs
Wichita State University
Wichita, Kansas

Darrell L. Ross
Department of Sociology,
    Anthropology and Criminal
    Justice
Valdosta State University
Valdosta, Georgia

Carolyn Speer Schmidt
Department of Criminal
    Justice
Wichita State University
Wichita, Kansas

Vladimir A. Sergevnin
Department of Law
    Enforcement
Western Illinois University
Macomb, Illinois

Szde Yu
School of Community Affairs
Wichita State University
Wichita, Kansas

CHAPTER 1

Use of Force Throughout History

Michael J. Palmiotto

☐ Introduction

Human beings establish governments for economic development; to maintain the safety of their citizens; and to control the natural environment. Governments are given or take social control for their state to maintain social order. A government without social order cannot protect its citizens and the country cannot economically prosper. There have been examples of countries in chaos that lack order or economic prosperity. "The idea of social control is often associated with the physical or coercive powers of the police. It is certain that a police force is an important and prominent example of social control" (Chriss, 2013: 36).

Since the early twentieth century social control has come to mean a concept that describes activities that involve the coordination, integration, regulation, or adjustment of individuals or groups to an ideal standard of conduct. Social control has come to mean regulation, either in terms of interpersonal relationships with other people; or regulating human behavior in terms of public safety; or enforcing laws and punishing violators of laws (Chriss, 2013: 23). Social control is often associated with the physical or coercive power of the police. The role of police has a great influence with social control in any culture. However, social norms can influence the behavior of people. For example, specific vocations and professions have specific values which informally control the behavior of fellow workers (Chriss, 2013: 36).

Walter Reckless associates social control as crime control, with the police in modern society having this responsibility. Crime control, according to Reckless, hopes to curb crime and hold it in check, stop it from spreading and provide society with protections from law violators (Reckless, 1955: 655). For decades the police have frequently been placed in situations in which they are given no choice but to use force. Often they are accused of brutality even when they had no other option than to use force to subdue the offender.

Law enforcement with its emphasis on social and criminal control can be traced to ancient times when the family, tribe, or clan assumed the responsibility for the safety of their members. The concept of "kin police" evolved with the idea that an attack against any member of the group was an attack on the entire group. In essence, the enforcers were the people who enforced their laws. Punishment was often inhumane and retaliatory. Branding and mutilation were often used, along with stoning, burning, and crucifixion. Unlike contemporary America, which has a formal process to maintain social control, ancient societies had an informal process to deal with violation against their kin group (Palmiotto, 2013: 11).

As mentioned in the previous paragraph policing can be traced to ancient times. Ancient policing utilized basic features which are still used to this day. This involves the approach of interpersonal mediation. The police were also expected to perform a wide variety of tasks, including firefighting, which had little to do with crime control. The first police organization was created in Egypt in around 3000 bc. Each administrative jurisdiction, there were 42 of them, had an official responsible for justice and security. In ancient Greece, policing duties were assigned to magistrates responsible for municipal upkeep (Britannica, 2014).

Throughout history those in authority have used force against those below them in status, power, and authority. Although specific information is lacking, abuses of authority most likely did occur in ancient societies. In ancient societies individuals addressed these violations themselves. Punishment or retaliation used such inhumane techniques as mutilation and branding. Stoning, burning, and crucifixion were also used as forms of punishment.

The killing of an Egyptian guard for abusing a Hebrew slave provoked Moses to perform the act of murder. This is an ancient example of

use of abusive force against an underling. Although there is little information on the abuse of lower status people in ancient times, it seems
likely that regular abuse of force took place. Realistically, it would appear
that slaves and criminals were recipients of the use of force. It should
be mentioned that governments would have to implement laws before
law enforcement could be established. The Babylonians, Assyrians,
Egyptians, Greeks, and Romans all had a system to maintain order.
From the time when some form of government existed, social control
was important for governments to function successfully. Governments or
those people in authority want to maintain their power and control over
the populace and often this requires that force be used.

Similar to ancient Greece, the Roman empire was not peaceful but
had crimes committed not only in Italy but also in the provinces of Rome.
Threats to the public order frequently occurred. The Roman empire, as in
modern society, had similar crimes. There were thefts, riots between sports
fans, travel was dangerous, and burglaries occurred. Unlike our modern
day, Rome did not have a police force that could compare to twenty-first
century police. As with the people of today, the Roman people desired
public order. The Romans had four forms of police, with the police coming
primarily from the military. The Roman provinces had the authority to
maintain order with civilian police who were Roman soldiers in the province under the control of the magistrates and municipal governments. The
local magistrates had the authority to use limited force to deter crime,
make arrests, and conduct trials for minor offenses (Fuhrmann, 2012: 9).

There were many types of Roman policing. It should be noted that
Roman military policing was carried out by soldiers. The types of Roman
police were the civilian police which functioned in the provinces.
These special troops were under the direct command of the emperor.
The emperor was the symbol of public order. The next level of policing
was at the provincial or gubernatorial level. Provincial governors were
responsible for security and public order and could activate the troops,
who functioned as police, under their command. The last level of Roman
military policing consisted of out posted soldiers who performed policing among civilians. Out posted soldiers often functioned without supervision (Fuhrmann, 2012: 10). It has been difficult to locate the use of
excessive force by the various levels of Roman military police but it seems
that excessive force was used by the military police, at least periodically.
A good example of excessive force at that time was the scourging of Jesus
at the pillar and the crowning with thorns.

Emperor Augustus made a number of contributions to law enforcement. He established the *Praetorian Guard* from the military legions to
protect the life and property of the emperor. The *urban cohorts*, units of
500–600 men, were created to keep the peace of Rome. The *praefectus*

urbi, the prefect of the city, was given responsibility to maintain order in the city. The *curators urbis* came under the direction of the *praefectus urbi* and were responsible for a specific area of the city. Augustine also established the *vigils of Rome* to assume firefighting duties. Rome was plagued with fires and a unit was needed to spot and fight fires. The *vigils of Rome* also had the responsibility for patrolling the streets (Palmiotto, 2013: 12). Although the literature is weak on the use of force by Roman military police; it would appear that police trained as soldiers would use force or even excessive force to enforce the laws of the Roman empire.

The French police can be traced to the middle ages but this section will only discuss the French police in the nineteenth century. Upon obtaining the leadership of France, Napoleon established law and order to eliminate the havoc caused by the French Revolution. Two police forces were inherited from the French Revolution: the gendarmerie, the model for police organizations in Europe during the nineteenth century and the administrative police, a civilian police unit. The two units were different from each other with the gendarmerie being a paramilitary unit primarily policing the countryside. The gendarmerie came under the control of the minister of war and was not accountable to civilian authorities. The administrative police or civilian police were assigned to policing in towns of over 5000 people and reported to the minister of general police in Paris. During periods of rebellion the gendarmerie proved to be very effective in repression, which has to be considered the use of excessive force to gain law and order (Broers, 1999: 27–35).

The British can trace their concept of policing to the Danish and Anglo-Saxon invaders. Originally citizens were responsible for peace keeping duties. The mutual pledge system was established by Alfred the Great, 870–901 and has been recognized as the initiating of modern policing. Under the mutual pledge system, every man was responsible not only for his own actions but also for the actions of his neighbor. It was every citizen's duty to raise the "hue and cry" when a crime was committed, to collect his neighbors, and to pursue a criminal who fled from the district. History is inundated with individuals who, when given the opportunity to apprehend offenders, would use their authority to abuse individuals arrested. It seems likely that that the conditions under the "hue and cry" made possible the use of excessive force against law violators.

In the thirteenth century, the constable system evolved as a rural form of policing. The constable maintained social order within the parish, the population center of worship. The constable was also a royal officer responsible for keeping the king's peace by the "hue and cry." In the urban area the "watch and ward" system was implemented and the duties of its officers were patrolling the streets, guarding the town's gates, arresting strangers at night, and preventing break-ins.

In 1789 the Gordon riots occurred. This was a Protestant protest against laws passed providing Catholics with special rights. King George ordered that the military be permitted to shoot the rioters at their own discretion. On the king's directive the soldiers killed or fatally wounded 300 persons and ended the riots (Reppetto, 2012: 4) The Gordon riots provide an example of excessive force being used by the British government as well as an example of deadly force.

On August 16, 1819 the Peterloo Massacre took place in Manchester, England when the cavalry charged into a crowd of 50,000 people who were protesting the economic conditions of that period. There was famine and unemployment and a lack of voting opportunities for the lower economic class. The protesters wanted the reform of parliamentary representation. Voting was restricted to adult male owners of land. The number of deaths or injured was not accurately determined. It is estimated that 11–15 people were killed, including women, and about 500 people were injured. The reaction to Peterloo was a crackdown on the reform the demonstrators wanted. A number of Peterloo leaders were tried for sedition. The government supported the cavalry charge. The army's action provides a good example of use of force. Since police forces were not designed to control demonstrations the army functioned in lieu of the police. The action of the army in their cavalry charge indicates a strong case of use of excessive force (Peterloo Massacre, 2016 [Spartacus-Education]).

During the late seventeenth century the policing system began to break down and corruption was rampant and the force unable to deal with social and economic upheaval. Crime in the seventeenth and early eighteenth century began to increase. It should be recognized that where ever corruption exists so does brutality. Corruption and brutality go hand in hand. In 1829, Sir Robert Peel established the Metropolitan Police of London as an answer to incompetence of the police and their corruption. The Metropolitan Police Act and the establishment of the London Police Department became the model for the United States. From the time when some form of government existed social control had to be put into place. Governments or those people in authority want to maintain their power and control over the populace. The putting down of riots forcefully by the police and military provides a good example of governments making every effort to maintain control over the populace.

In 1855, the Sunday Trading Riots lasted for four consecutive Sundays starting the last Sunday in June and continuing on the following three Sundays in July. Working men by the 1850s were allowed to make known their grievances but not allowed to riot. Two reasons for the riots were influenced by religious measures, with the passing of laws: first to close drinking establishments during specific hours on Sundays and second, to prohibit all Sunday trading, except for the selling of meat and fish, newspapers, and cooked meals. These laws created a stir among working people who did their shopping on Sundays, believing goods were cheaper on this day. In addition, many workers were paid on Saturday evening which gave them sufficient funds to shop on a Sunday (Harrison, 1965: 219–222).

On Sunday June 24 a meeting was held in Hyde Park with 200,000 people attending. The police attempted to prevent the public meeting. During the meeting wealthy people were arriving at Hyde Park. The crowd jeered, taunted, shouted, and used improper language for the time. Disorder was created which was condemned by the Monday papers. In the following weeks the Metropolitan Police Commissioner forbade a meeting for Sunday, July 1 in Hyde Park. The order was ignored and approximately 150,000 people gathered in Hyde Park. "The police endured great provocation, but could not restrain themselves when a large eel was removed from the Serpentine and was passed over the heads of the crowd on to a police detachment. In comparison with the previous Sunday, fewer promenading carriages arrived, but the police decided to clear the carriageway. With their truncheons they beat down opposition from the crowd and carried off 72 prisoners to the Vine Street police station" (Harrison, 1965: 223). The police used force on this Sunday and may have used excessive force to control the crowd and make the arrests. Because of the disorder in Hyde Park police brutality had become a preoccupation of the government. The government appointed a commission to look into the events of Sunday July 1 (Harrison, 1965: 224). The accusation of brutality was such a big issue that the government investigated the claim. Several police officers were fired and the incident faded away.

During the fall of 1887 radical demonstrations took place in London despite the government forbidding political meetings. On Sunday, November 13, 14,000 police with special constables and armed soldiers dispersed the crowd. The demonstrators were protesting being unemployed and were attempting to meet in Trafalgar Square. Bloody Sunday, which November 13 has been named, resulted in three fatal injuries, 75 people hospitalized and 50 people arrested (Keller, 2009). As previous writings indicate the police did use force to break-up demonstrations during the nineteenth century, and it could be said that they used excessive force.

☐ English Police: Political and Social History

The development of policing in America has its roots in England. The Eastern coast of the United States was settled predominately by English people who brought the English law enforcement system to the American colonies. As in England, American law enforcement developed slowly. It was not until the 1840s that the United States initiated a modern municipal policing concept. In 1844 the New York legislature provided funds for a night and day watch creating a consolidated police force. The New York model was adopted by other municipalities. With the creation of the modern police force, three issues came to the forefront. The first was the adoption of uniforms, the second arming the police, and third, the appropriate use of force by the police in making arrests. The first issue, the adoption of uniforms, was not highly contested. The second issue of arming the police was somewhat controversial with the talk of militarization of the police. The final issue dealing with the police has remained an issue from the 1840s and 1850s until today, the early decades of the twenty-first century.

The police have been given the authority to use force when necessary to maintain peace and order. The term enforcement actually means that force can be used. It is important to recognize that law enforcement have the legal authority to use force when offenders are threatening them or someone else or refuse to follow police commands. We as citizens have the responsibility to obey police orders. Citizens do not have the legal right to fight the police when requested to perform a specific action by the police.

Skolnick and Fyfe clearly state the important aspect of the issue when they write: As long as some members of society do not comply with law and resist the police, force will remain an inevitable part of policing. Cops, especially, understand that. Indeed, anybody who fails to understand the centrality of force to police work has no business in a police uniform (Skolnick and Fyfe, 1939).

Most rational people will acknowledge that society recognizes that the police have the legal authority to use force to protect themselves or another person who may be in danger. The issue pertaining to the use of force with regard to citizen upheaval occurs when the population believes that inappropriate force or excessive force was used unnecessarily. Of course it is at times difficult to be objective both on the part of the community and police if the use of force was inappropriate. More will be written about this issue in later chapters.

Although the police have authorization to use force, there have been times when an inappropriate use of force has been used in a cruel manner. The slave patrol of the south from colonial days until the mid-1860s provides an example of police brutality. Slave patrols walked into slave quarters and if met with resistance, the slaves would be punished. Slaves were beaten, and there were times when slaves who did not cooperate with slave patrols were beaten to death. At times slave patrollers would beat a slave without cause (Hadden, 2001: 106–114).

During the Civil War riots in New York City the city police used force to curb the riots. One police captain led 80 police officers in dispersing 2000 rioters, and on that same day clubbed a man to death (Reppetto, 2011: 48). Use of force continued in policing after the Civil War. Another captain known for his use of force was Captain Alexander "Clubber" Williams who was known for clubbing individuals. He stated "There is more law at the end of a policeman's nightstick than in a decision of the Supreme Court." He insisted until his death that he never clubbed anyone "that did not deserve it" (Ephemeral, 2009).

Thomas Byrnes who rose from detective to chief inspector, the number two position in the New York City police department, established a rogues' gallery containing pictures of criminals, had a daily lineup of arrested thieves, and required crooks to register at headquarters. He established a zone that forbids criminals from entering on physical punishment. Thomas Byrne was able to support his informal rules with a force not supported by the law. He was a practitioner of the third degree, using physical beatings and psychological torture. For example, he used a sweatbox, a small room where prisoners were kept for days without human contact. Byrnes had the support of political and business leaders and could get as tough as he wanted with criminals (Reppetto, 2011: 55–56).

The use of force or excessive use of force as used by Williams and Byrnes continued into the twentieth century. In 1929 President Herbert Hoover established the National Commission on Law Observance and Enforcement, known as the Wickersham Commission. The Commission submitted their *Report on Lawlessness in Law Enforcement* in 1931. The term "third degree" was defined by the Commission as used by the police to mean "the employment of methods which inflict suffering, physical or mental, upon a person, in order to obtain from that person information about a crime." The Report further states. "The third degree is a secret and illegal practice" (National Commission on Law Observance and Enforcement, 1931: 3). The use of the third degree or inappropriate force is illegal and prohibited by the American constitution. Specifically the following rights are violated: "personal liberty, bail, protection from personal assault and battery, the presumption of innocence until conviction of guilt by due process of law and the right to counsel ...." (National Commission on Law Observance and Enforcement, 1931: 3–4).

The Wickersham Commission found that the police's use of the third degree was widespread and common. Physical brutality, illegal detention, and refusal to allow those arrested access to counsel was common. Brutality and violence in making arrests was common but primarily used by urban police officers and not federal law enforcement personnel. The third degree was primarily used by patrol officers and detectives against arrested persons suspected of committing a crime. However, it is used on other persons suspected of committing a crime. *The Report on Lawlessness in Law Enforcement* came to three conclusions (National Commission on Law Observance and Enforcement, 1931: 7):

First, that they are the type of lawless enforcement of law which is especially liable to create resentment against law and government.

Second, that they may compel an appellate court to reverse the conviction of a guilty man, thus requiring additional trials and sometimes resulting in the escape of a guilty man from conviction.

Third, and perhaps the most seriously, that unfair practices may result in the conviction of the innocent.

The Wickersham Report found the "third degree" unacceptable behavior of the police. They emphasized that social order be controlled within the constitutional and legal framework established by the founding fathers and legislative bodies. The report strongly condemned the use of the "third degree" or police brutality for any reason. It cannot be justified on legal or moral grounds regardless of the seriousness of the offense. The Wickersham Report condemns the "third degree" as evil. The Supreme Court of Illinois has said: "To defend the third degree is to advocate lawlessness—often flagrant and habitual—committed by those who are specifically charged with the enforcement of the law" (National Commission on Law Observance and Enforcement, 1931: 181). The Commission specified four specific evils of the "third degree" (National Commission on Law Observance and Enforcement, 1931: 181–192):

1. The third degree involves the danger of false confessions.

2. The third degree impairs police efficiency.

3. The third degree impairs the efficient administration of criminal justice in the courts.

4. The third degree brutalizes the police, hardens the prisoner against society, and lowers the esteem in which the administration of justice is held by the public.

The "third degree" and police brutality provide the police with a negative image. It also provides the criminal justice process with a poor impression by the public and finally communication between the police and/or other criminal justice agencies lose their credibility with the community and public in general.

This chapter has dealt with the inappropriate use of force from ancient times to recent centuries. The following chapters deal with more specific topics and are relevant to the twenty-first century. These chapters include use of force, deadly force, legal issues pertaining to use of force, a psychological perspective, and training and prevention of excessive use of force.

☐ Summary

The use of force by those individuals representing government, whether the military or those responsible to maintain social order, has been permitted when individuals or groups of individuals have failed to follow the laws of the government. Violence can be traced from ancient times to our present day. Information on the maintaining of order in ancient times is somewhat sketchy and informal. Throughout history those in authority have used force against those below them in status, power, and authority. Although specific information is lacking, abuse of authority most likely occurred in ancient societies. In ancient societies individuals addressed these violations themselves.

Crimes were committed in ancient Egypt, Greece, and the Roman Empire and their provinces. Threats to public order frequently occurred. Unlike our modern day, Rome did not have police that could compare to twenty-first century police. Like the people of today the Roman people wanted public order. Similar to our modern times the Romans had many types of police.

The British began developing the concept of modern policing during the middles ages. Policing was evolving and continues to evolve in the twenty-first century. Modern American policing uses the British model as their policing foundation.

☐ References

Britannica. 2014. Ancient Policing, http://www.britannica.com/EBchecked/topic/46/467289/police/260916/P...

Broers, M. 1999. The Napoleonic police and their legacy, *History Today*, May, 49(5), 22–23.

Chriss, J. J. 2013. *Social Control: An Introduction*, Second Edition, Cambridge, UK: Polity.

Ephemeral New York. 2009. "The NYPD's infamous 'Clubber' Williams, http:// ephemeralnewyork.wordpress.com/2009/11/16/the-nypds-club.

Fuhrmann, C. 2012. *Policing the Roman Empire: Soldiers, Administration, and Public Order*, New York: Oxford University Press.

Hadden, S. E. 2001. Slave Patrols: Law and Violence in Virginia and the Carolinas, *Association for the Study of African American Life and history*.

Harrison, B. 1965. The Sunday Trading Riots of 1855, *The Historical Journal*, 8(2), 219–245.

Keller, L. 2009. Bloody Sunday demonstration, 1887. *The International Encyclopedia of Revolution and Protest*, Immanuel Ness (Ed.), Blackwell Reference Online, http://www.blackwellreference.com/public/tocnode?id=078140518.

National Commission on Law Observance and Enforcement. 1931. *Report on Lawlessness in Law Enforcement*, Washington, DC: U.S. Government.

Palmiotto, M. J. 2013. *Policing: Concepts, Strategies, and Current Issues in American Police Forces*, Kindle Publishing. www. amazon.com.

Peterloo Massacre. 2016. http://spartacus-educational.con/PRpeterloo.htm.

Reckless, W. C. 1955. *The Crime Problem*, Second Edition, New York, New York: Appleton-Century-Crofts.

Reppetto, T. 2011. *American Police: The Blue Parade 1845–1945*, New York: The Free Press.

Reppetto, T. C. 2012. *American Police: 1945–2012*, New York: Enigma Books.

Skolnick, J. H. and J. J. Fyfe. 1939. *Above the Law*, New York: The Free Press.

CHAPTER

Police Use of Force

Michael J. Palmiotto

A government, to be successful economically, needs and must maintain an orderly society and protect the safety of its citizens. Only when governments can provide a functional society based on social order can citizens and the country as a whole be productive. The peacekeepers who have been given the responsibility to maintain order in society are the police. Along with society giving the police the authority to maintain social order comes the use of force. Alpert and Smith (1994: 481) stated the following about the police: "The authority of the police to use force represents one of the most misunderstood powers granted to representatives of government. Police officers are authorized to use both psychological and physical force to apprehend criminals and solve crimes."

The authority and power of law enforcement officers is the biggest difference between them and the rest of citizens in society. The United States Civil Rights Commission (1981: 481–482) stated the following about the police: "Police officers possess awesome powers. They perform their duties under conditions with the public eye upon them. Police officers are permitted only a margin of error in judgment under conditions that impose high degrees of physical and mental stress. Their general responsibility to preserve peace and enforce the law carries with it the power to arrest and to use force—even deadly force" (v).

In this chapter we will review the controversial issue connected with the legitimate and illegitimate authority of the police to use force. The illegal, unacceptable, or excessive use of force has often been referred to as *police brutality*. "The lawless exercise of force employed in excess is popularly called police brutality" (Skolnick and Fyfe, 1993: xvi). Modern policing was initiated in the 1840s with the New York City Police Department. Since the beginning of modern policing the use of force, some claim excessive force, by police officers has been a controversial issue periodically receiving a great deal of attention.

The *use of force* by the police can be defined as occurring "any time the police attempt to have citizens act in a certain way" (Roberg et al., 2000: 310). Alpert and Dunham (2004: 20–21) provide definitions of the use of force: "The consensus among law enforcement officials and researchers is that force can be defined as physical action taken to control the movement or freedom of another individual. If there is no resistance to certain police actions, such as handcuffing or the use of firm grips and 'come-along' holds, the use of force may be inconsequential or negligible and no record of the activity need be made."

There are some who consider verbal abuse a form of police brutality while others consider this to consist solely of the excessive use of physical force. However, we begin to be concerned about such use of force used when it is seen as excessive or as an over-reaction to a given situation. For example, a highway patrol officer politely asks to see your driver's license after stopping you on the highway. While there is force involved, that is, you have no recourse but to comply, this is not seen as excessive. How about if the same highway patrol officer asks to see your license while hitting you with a flashlight and yelling obscenities? Here, the force used is definitely going to be seen as excessive, if there is nothing else that indicates violence or resistance on the part of the motorist.

Incidents of police use of excessive force have included beating civil rights protestors, deliberate kicking and choking someone while making arrests, and unprovoked use of deadly force when attempting to control riots and disturbances. Individual officers, a group of officers, or a large number of officers within the police department, thus pervading the culture of an entire police department, may carry out acts of excessive use of force. In the late 1990s in Los Angeles, such excessive force incidents even included officers who robbed banks, shot drug dealers, and then planted weapons on them (Time, March 6, 2000; Newsweek, 2000; Walker, 2000a,b).

It has been recognized that most occupations provide their members with opportunities for misconduct, and police agencies and their officers are no exception. There are three elements to occupational misconduct: "(1) opportunity structure and its accompanying techniques of rule violations, (2) socialization through occupational experiences, (3) reinforcement and encouragement from the occupational peer group, i.e., group support for certain rule violations" (Barker, 1977: 356). The opportunities for police officers to violate laws and departmental policies discouraging the excessive use of force are many. Techniques for accomplishing police operations often go hand in hand with the opportunities for such rule breaking. The socialization of police behavior begins in the recruit-training academy where the police recruit is instructed into the "us" versus "them" mentality. With this attitude the public becomes the enemy and the only friends of a police officer are his fellow police officers. Many cultures, including the United States, encourage group and peer support and police officers should not be considered any different from anyone else in this regard. From the initial day that the recruit enters training he or she quickly learns that the support of fellow police officers is important to his or her career success and future well-being as a police officer. The recruit quickly learns that it is generally best to look the other way when he or she sees fellow officers violating departmental rules and laws by using excessive force. The philosophy of "brother and sister" police officers in which the police subculture becomes a way of life can thus lead to police misconduct.

☐ Use of Excessive Force

Police officers hold a position of legal authority, control, and power over citizens. In our society, it is not unusual for citizens to challenge laws they consider unfair or unjust and thus challenge police authority. Examples of specific situations that police have to deal with which can lead to police misconduct or accusing the police of misconduct include mass demonstrations and sit-down strikes. Civil disobedience and direct confrontation with police authority may be encouraged or may even be a part of the strategy of groups who intentionally want to confront the police. The United States and other democratic countries offer citizens redress when they believe that the police have been involved in police misconduct or perceived misconduct. Citizens in an open society know they have rights and avenues of redress open to them when acts of police misconduct or perceived acts of police misconduct are committed by police officers. The foundations of citizen rights in American society are found in the U.S. Constitution, specifically in the Bill of Rights, which constitutes the first 10 amendments to the Constitution. In 1789, the Bill of Rights was adopted by the founding fathers to protect citizens from governmental abuses from the federal government and their agents. In the twentieth century the U.S. Supreme Court, to protect citizens from governmental abuses from the states and their agents, extended the Bill of Rights to be applicable to the states. The U.S. Supreme Court interpreted the "due process clause" of the Fourteenth Amendment as a protection for citizens against abuses by the state. Currently, the Bill of Rights protects citizens from both federal and state abuses and policing misconduct. It should be remembered that local police officers, city, village, town, and county officers, are agents of the state and the Bill of Rights applies to these police officers in their law enforcement authority.

When citizens directly challenge the authority of the police, it is often perceived by the latter as an attack on them. In confrontations between the police and citizens, the police often find themselves in many "no-win" situations. In such situations, the police are always open to criticism and formal charges of misconduct regardless of how they handled the situation. The police are often attacked for violating the legal rights of citizens in the manner they use in enforcing the law. Frequently police officers are accused of violating the civil rights of citizens under the U.S. Constitution and other relevant laws. Although some of these accusations may be erroneous, the police have the responsibility to use their legal authority within prescribed legal and constitutional restrictions. Further, in any society, the police can be successful in maintaining social order and solving crime only with the cooperation of citizens. When the police lose the confidence of those citizens because they are perceived as brutal or prone to unprovoked violence, the public will cease supporting the police in performing their law enforcement activities. This can include failing to providing information about crimes committed, refusing to serve as witnesses of crimes committed in their presence, or not supporting police when they want salary increase, and other benefits.

☐ Police Use of Excessive Force as Misconduct and Deviance

According to Thomas Barker (1978), the range of police misconduct includes the following activities: perjury, sex on duty, sleeping on duty, drinking and using drugs on duty, and police brutality. When a police officer abuses people physically, this is likely to be lamented and calls from observers for corrective action become loud. This, as we know, coincides neatly with how sociologists have defined the concept of deviance. The meaning of the term *"deviance"* is "conduct which the people of a group consider so dangerous or embarrassing or irritating that they bring special sanctions to bear against the persons who exhibit it," and that "the only way an observer can tell whether or not a given style of behavior is deviant, then, is to learn something about the standards of the audience which is responding to it" (Erikson, 1966: 3). Thus, police brutality can be defined as occurring when a police officer uses force in a way that the usual standards, as understood by the community, for such use are violated. Here are a few examples of police use of force:

- A police officer uses a threatening hand gesture and verbally intimidates a suspect who is being questioned regarding a crime.

- A police officer grabs hold of a motorist and shakes him or her for being slow in responding to a request to participate in a field sobriety test.

- A police officer beats and kicks an individual being interrogated about some discrepant information that he or she provided earlier.

- A number of police officers use pepper spray on an inebriated college student who refuses to obey their command to "move along."

As you can see, these examples run the gamut of possibilities in terms of use of force, from the possibly appropriate to the highly inappropriate. Are they all instances of police brutality? Without considering the situational factors in each of the above decisions to use force and without knowing what happened before each event, we are at a disadvantage in terms of judging whether the legal standards and police polices regarding the appropriate level of force used has been met.

Similar incidents of police use of excessive force in making arrests and in controlling disturbances have occurred throughout history. Such incidents may be carried out by individual officers, a group of officers, or even involve the entire police department or a large number of officers within the police department. Lundman (1980: 140–141) notes that five conditions must be met for police misconduct to be attributed to a dysfunctional police organization, that is, when occupational deviance becomes organizational deviance. Let us apply his ideas to the issue of excessive use of force by the police:

1. It must be contrary to norms or rules maintained by others outside of the police department. Here we should ask if such deviant actions of excessive force are formal violations of existing laws and expectations of police behavior.

2. The deviant action must be supported by internal operating norms that conflict with the police organization's formal goals and rules. To be considered a form of organizational deviance, fellow officers and higher-ups must be perceived as tacitly supporting the excessive use of force even though there may be official rules and policies forbidding it.

3. Compliance with the internal operation norms supportive of police misconduct must be ensured through recruitment and socialization. From this perspective, individuals who are apt to react with force and violence are sought and hired by the department.

4. There must be peer support of the misbehavior of colleagues. Officers are complicit in ignoring inappropriate uses of force by their colleagues and supportive of them when confronted by higher authorities or concerned members of the public.

5. For improper behavior to be organizationally deviant, it must be supported by dominant administrative coalition of the police organization. Those who are in command and those who have influence over the day-to-day operations of the department condone inappropriate or excessive use of force. One major reason for the acceptance of police use of inappropriate force is the "code of silence."

☐ Police Use of Excessive Force and the Code of Silence

As mentioned earlier, the code requires that police officers look the other way when they observe their fellow officers involved in acts of misconduct, in this case, brutality. Skolnick and Fyfe (1993: 110) write that the "code of silence" exists and that it "typically is enforced by the threat of shunning, by fear that informing will lead to exposure of one's own derelictions, and by fear that colleagues' assistance may be withheld in emergencies." Skolnick and Fyfe (1993) believe that, in reality, police officers will not deny assistance to fellow officers, even those who may have informed on fellow officers in emergencies. They suggest that the fear upon which the code of silence appears based is imagined, or that officers are paranoid when they believe that fellow police officers will not come to their aid when they need assistance. According to Skolnick and Fyfe (1993: 112), "The code of silence then, is not one that is enforced by assassins lurking in dark alleys or arranging for drug dealers to terminate cops who inform. The police code of silence is an extreme version of a phenomenon that exists in many human groups. It is exaggerated in some police departments and some police units because cops so closely identify with their departments, their units, and their colleagues, that they cannot even conceive of doing anything else."

☐ Forms of Police Excessive Use of Force

Incidents of the "use of excessive force" by police officers, or "police brutality," can be traced to early times in police history. In 1967, the President's Crime Commission (*Task Force: The Police*: 180) found that abuses in cities studied ranged from discourtesy to physical use of excessive force against people of all ages. The Commission further reported, "While allegations of excessive physical force receive the most attention, verbal abuse and discourtesy were probably greater irritants to community relations" (The President's Commission on Law Enforcement and Administration of Justice, 1967: 180). The same report found that many people, specifically minority groups, believe that the police are often engaged in excessive and unnecessary physical force. Similar to present day efforts, the Commission was unable to determine exactly how serious a problem the excessive use of physical force was in American police departments. However, although the Commission believed police brutality was a major problem, it was deemed to be not "systematic."

Barker (1978: 71) claims that when the public charges the police with excessive use of force, they are referring to any or all of the following actions by the police:

1. Profane and abusive language

2. Commands to move on or go home

3. Field stops and searches

4. Threats

5. Prodding with a nightstick or approaching with a pistol

6. The actual use of "physical force"

Most people would agree that it is inappropriate for police officers to use profanity and abusive language toward the general public. Although abusive language will not be good for police–community relations, should it be considered police brutality? The police have the authority to require people to move along or request they go home often for safety reasons. There are times when groups of individuals block entry into stores or the sidewalk making it difficult for people to pass. The police also have the authority to tell juveniles to go home when communities have curfews.

Third Degree

Some forms of "police brutality" have also been referred to as the *third degree*. The term "third degree" came into vogue during the early decades of the twentieth century and refers to the use of excessive force during the questioning of suspects. Apparently, the term "first degree" presumably means the arrest, the "second degree" the transportation to a place of confinement, and the "third degree" the interrogation, which often means brutality (Skolnick and Fyfe, 1993: 43). In 1930, the American Bar Association's Committee on the Lawless Enforcement of the Law reported, "We can only say that the 'third degree,' in the sense of rigid and severe examination of men under arrest by police officers or prosecuting attorneys or both, is in use almost everywhere if not everywhere in the United States" (Skolnick and Fyfe, 1993: 45). The National Commission on Law Observance and Enforcement (1931) (the Wickersham Commission) appointed by President Herbert Hoover reported, in 1931, that the third degree, which it defined as "the inflicting of pain, physical or mental, to extract confessions or statements" was widespread throughout the United States (Skolnick and Fyfe, 1993: 45). In 1947, the President's Commission on Civil Rights, appointed by President Truman, reported similar findings of excessive physical abuse by the police (181). The United States Civil Rights Commission (1961: 181) concluded, "Police brutality is still a serious problem throughout the United States."

Although it appears that the third degree or police brutality does not occur to the extent that it did in the early decades of the twentieth century, it would be unrealistic to assume that it does not occur at all. Incidents of third degree questioning have occurred not only in poorly administered police departments that lack concern about how their officers treat people, but also in departments that are managed well and concerned about the treatment of citizens they serve.

Major Incidents of Police Use of Excessive Force

The last decade of the twentieth century saw numerous incidents of excessive use of physical force by police officers. Such incidents have continued into the twenty-first century. The first event of excessive use of force that received national and international attention in the 1990s was the Rodney King incident. This event took place on March 3, 1991 in Los Angeles, California. The incident began at approximately 12:40 am when two California Highway Patrol (CHP) officers detected King speeding on the freeway. Apparently King's car passed the CHP car from the rear and passed the officers. The CHP officers paced the King vehicle. The officers activated their emergency equipment and signaled for King to stop. King failed to stop and continued to drive and ran a stop sign and a red traffic light. Later, King explained that he failed to stop because he was afraid of getting a traffic summons, which could result in his probation, for an earlier robbery conviction, being revoked. The CHP officers notified the LAPD (Los Angeles Police Department) that they were pursuing a vehicle at a high rate of speed. King finally stopped his automobile along a curbside where he was ordered out of his car. While this was taking place police officers from other agencies arrived at the scene. There were two passengers in King's vehicle who were ordered to get out of the car. They complied and were taken into police custody. Initially, King refused to leave the automobile and was struck with a Taser. When King finally came out, he was struck in the head with nightsticks and kicked several times by police officers. It appears that King was struck approximately 56 times by police officers. There were somewhere between 21 and 27 police officers who were witnesses or participants to the beating of King. The injuries King sustained consisted of a broken cheekbone, a fractured eye socket, missing teeth, kidney damage, skull fractures, external burns, and permanent brain damage (Christopher Commission, 1991).

What made the King-beating incident significantly different from earlier alleged occasions of police brutality was that a private citizen videotaped this incident. This videotape eventually fell into the hands of Cable News Network, which showed the King beating in the United States and throughout the world. The incident clearly shows excessive use of physical force by police officers at its worst. When brutality is alleged, often a police administrator investigates and takes appropriate actions based upon what is discovered. There is no doubt that the King beating gave the LAPD a black eye. Similar incidents, discussed later in this section that occurred in the 1990s, further damaged the reputation of the LAPD.

Several years after the King incident, another scandalous act of excessive use of force occurred on the eastern coast of the United States. On the morning of August 9, 1997, several New York City police officers responded to a fight taking place outside a club in Brooklyn. When the police officers arrived, one Abner Louima, in attempting to break up the melee, became drawn into the conflict. During the fight, one officer was punched and it was believed that Louima was the culprit. Louima was taken into custody. On the way to the 70th precinct police beat Louima with their fists in their patrol vehicle. While at the precinct, Louima, who was handcuffed, was taken to a restroom where a police officer rammed a 2–3 ft stick into Louima's rectum. Within a short period of time an ambulance was called and Louima was hospitalized. A nurse reported the incident to the Police Internal Affairs Unit. Within hours of the report, the Louima incident became a local and national sensation. Similar to the Rodney King incident, which affected the credibility of the LAPD negatively, the Abner Louima incident discredited the public image of the NYPD (New York City Police Department).

There are parallels and differences between the Rodney King beating and the Abner Louima case. Rodney King had a criminal history and failed to stop his vehicle when told to do so by police officers. The beating of King was a classic example of excessive use of physical force. The assault on Louima was bizarre; the lawyer of a codefendant of the officer who placed the stick up Louima's rectum condemned the act as defying "humanity" and labeled the officer who performed it as a "monster." Both the King and Louima cases were tried in federal court eventually and the police officers responsible were convicted of crimes.

King and Louima were both African American men who were brutalized by white police officers. The acts of brutality by white police officers against black men cannot fail to raise the question of racism. The LAPD chief and the NYPD commissioner both characterized these acts of police brutality as aberrations and denied that racism played a part in these incidents. Police critics agree that these acts were aberrations, but only in that white police officers used excessive physical force against blacks, which received wide publicity, and then were punished.

What We Know About Police Use of Force*

Bayley and Garofalo (1989) observed that it was quite rare in police–citizen encounters for police to be involved in use of force and injury.

---

* Taken from Use of Force, Kenneth Adams Chapter 1, U.S. Department of Justice 1999.

The International Chiefs of Police (IACP) in their study on the use of force found that force is used in less than one-half of 1% of dispatched calls for service (Adams, 1999: 3). The Bureau of Justice Statistics found the nearly 45,000 people had contact with the police during a 12-month period and that about 1% were subjected to the use of force or threat of force (Adam, 1999). The data indicate that the police rarely use force and the following information (1999) was recorded:

- Police use of force occurs at the lower end of the force spectrum, involving grabbing, pushing, or shoving. Relatively minor types of force dominate statistics on police use of force.

- Use of force typically occurs when police are to make arrest and the suspect is resisting. Research indicates that the police are most likely to use force when pursuing a suspect and attempting to exercise their arrest powers.

- A small number of studies suggests that use of force appears to be unrelated to an officer's personal characteristics, such as age, gender, and ethnicity.

- Police use of force is more likely to occur when police are dealing with persons under the influence of alcohol or drugs or with mentally ill individuals. More research needs to be done in this area. Police deal with a wide variety of situations in their work. They encounter minor to serious potentially dangerous deadly incidents.

- A small proportion of officers are disproportionally involved in use of force incidents. More research is needed.

- The incidence of wrongful use of force by police is unknown. Research is critically needed to determine reliability, validity, and precisely how often transgressions of use of force powers occur. We do not know how often police use force in ways that can be judged as wrongful.

- The impact of differences in police organizations, including administrative policies, hiring, training, discipline, and use of technology, on excessive and illegal force is unknown.

- Influences of situational characteristics on police use of force and the transnational nature of these events are largely unknown. Research on police–citizen encounters reveals that use of force by police is situational and transactional.

Use of Force Factors

Before a police officer decides to use force many factors should be considered which include a number of important factors. For instance is the use of force justified, did the officer receive proper training when legally appropriate to use force, and what liability will the police department be accountable for if force is used? The justification of the use of force must be considered the most important decision-making tool before the use of force takes place. Generally, the use of force can be justified when it is necessary to make an arrest, detain a suspect, or to protect the officer or a third party (Wittie, 2013).

The appropriate extent that the use of force can be considered reasonable is the degree necessary to obtain the compliance of a citizen. The determination of reasonable use of force is not an exact science since how and why the force was used against a citizen must be determined, and this is most difficult to evaluate after the fact. According to Wittie, a general definition of "reasonable in relation to the use of force" is any action that is reasonable in relation to the use of force and that a prudent person would believe to be necessary to complete the required task. "According to most experienced officers, reasonableness can be easily determined. However, in a civil or criminal case, the officer is not the one that has to determine if the force was reasonable, but rather, the citizens sitting on the jury will be tasked with determining the reasonableness of the force used by the officer" (Wittie, 2013: 17–18). Studies have indicated that police officers have often arrested people because of their demeanor and at times verbal confrontations have led to police using force against a person. O.W. Wilson, the renowned police administrator and innovator of the twentieth century had this advice to police officers:

> The officer … must remember that there is no law against making a policeman angry and that he cannot charge a man with offending him. Until the citizen act overtly in violation of the law, he should take no action against him, least of all lower himself to the level of the citizen by berating and demeaning him in a loud and angry voice. The officer who withstands angry verbal assaults builds his own character and raises the standard of the department. (The President's Commission on Law Enforcement and Administration of Justice, 1967: 181)

Use of Force Continuum

The use of force continuum was initiated to provide guidelines to police officers (Hampton, 2009). The guidelines were established to provide officers with information regarding the amount of force may be used against a subject resisting the commands of a police officer in a specific situation. The hope of the guidelines was to clarify for the officer and citizens the appropriate amount of force that an officer could legitimately use in a specific situation. It appears the use of force continuum that evolved in the 1980s and 1990s did not have one specific model for all police agencies. Police agencies established their own approach on a use of force continuum. The National Institute of Justice, in their outline of the use of force continuum, indicated that police agencies have policies to guide police officers to resolve use of force issues (The Use-of-Force Continuum 2009). The use of force continuum has several levels with officers instructed to respond to the level of resistance given to the officer. An example of the National Institute of Justice use of force continuum follows:

- *Officer presence*—No force used. Considered the best way to resolve a situation.

  - The mere presence of a law enforcement officer works to deter crime or diffuse a situation.

  - Officers' attitudes are professional and nonthreatening.

- *Verbalization*—Force is not physical.

  - Officer issues calm, nonthreatening commands, such as "Let me see your identification and registration."

  - Officers may increase their volume and shorten commands in an attempt to gain compliance. Short commands might include "Stop," or "Don't move."

- *Empty-hand control*—Officers use bodily force to gain control of a situation.

  - Soft technique. Officers' use grabs, holds, and joint locks to restrain an individual.

  - Hard technique. Officer's use punches and kicks to restrain an individual.

- *Less lethal methods*—Officers use less lethal technologies to gain control of a situation.

- Blunt impact. Officers may use a baton or projectile to immobilize a combative person.

- Chemical. Officers may use chemical sprays or projectiles embedded with chemicals to restrain an individual (e.g., pepper spray).

- Conducted energy devices (CEDs). Officers may use CEDs to immobilize an individual. CEDs discharge a high-voltage, low-amperage jolt of electricity at a distance.

- *Lethal force*—Officers use lethal weapons to gain control of a situation. Should only be used if a suspect poses a serious threat to the officer or another person.

  - Officers use deadly weapons such as firearms to stop an individual's actions.

It should be noted that there are various articulation of force continuum. According to Ken Wallentine (2009), the typical continuum generally progresses from "officer presence" to "deadly force" in specific steps. Wallentine's illustration follows:

Officer to	→	**Verbal to**	→	**Hand to**	→	**Impact to**	→	**Deadly**
Presence		**Command**		**Control**		**Weapon**		**Force**

Wellentine provides a common sense approach to police officers in their use of force. He recommends the best approach for police use-of-force decision making is a solid understanding of the law of force, linked with sound threat assessment skills. Wellentine recommends obtaining the advice of the department's legal counsel who can provide police officers with the legal understanding, risks of decision making, deficiencies in departmental policies, and in training pertaining to the use of force.

In a study of self-reported data by the Phoenix Police Department on the use of force continuum, Garner et al. found interesting information on the use of force. The authors of the study state, "This research emphasizes that force is a continuum and that understanding the use of force by and against the police requires systematically collected representative samples of incidents where different amount of force—including no force at all—are used" (Garner et al., 1995: 165). The authors provide an excellent recommendation on a use of force study by police officers. Several interesting points were reported by Gardner et al., for instance that the department and news media do not appear to appreciate the common absence of force by police officers. Their study also brings out that there are times when force may be used with no arrest being made. Another interesting point brought out by Gardner et al. is that arrests involving physical force are higher than reported in police–citizen encounters studies (Garner et al., 1995: 165).

In 1989 the *Graham v. Connor* case established guidelines on the use of force stating the "Fourth Amendment jurisprudence has long recognized that coercion or threat thereof effect it. Because the test of reasonableness under the Fourth Amendment is not capable of precise definition or mechanical application, however, its proper application requires careful attention to the facts and circumstances of each particular case, including the severity of the crime at issue, whether the suspect poses an immediate threat to the safety of officers or others, and whether he is actively resisting arrest or attempting to evade arrest by flight." The parameters of the *Graham v. Connor* require police officers to use reasonable force and inform officers when they can use force as the U.S. Supreme Court finds acceptable. To put it simply the courts evaluate the constitutional limits on the use of force on the Fourth Amendment of the U.S. Constitution.

After the *Garner v. Connor* decision, questions were raised as to the necessity of the use of force continuum. Defense attorneys, police trainers, and administrators became concerned that police officers, trainers, and administrators would be exposed to liability and this would be detrimental to police officers accused of using excessive force. Detractors of the use of force continuum claim that it confuses jurors and judges about the legal standard pertaining to excessive force. Additional complaints against the use of force continuum argue that some judges interpret the use of force continuum to equate to the Fourth Amendment's constitutional standard. Police unions report that officers have received inappropriate discipline, including being terminated when the use of force standard was inappropriately used as legal standards (Peters and Brave, 2006).

Many police departments have abandoned their use of force continuum (there are about 50) in favor of a "force option" model. In 2000, the San Jose Police Department became one of the largest police departments to move away from a continuum and toward a "force option" model. The "force options" are not ranked like the use of force continuum. The model considers that the "force options" provide the officers with more flexibility and discretion based on the total facts available to the officer. Use of force continuum models were developed several decades ago to provide officers guidance since the court system did not provide such direction. Detractors of use of force models claim that the continuum models were not based on law but in actuality many are in conflict with laws (Flosi, 2012).

A police officer may only use force when it is reasonable and necessary to make an arrest or detain someone. Anything beyond this guideline is excessive (*Payne v. Pauley*, 2003). The courts will consider the *Graham v. Connor* test and also the need to use force, the relationship between the need and amount of force used, and the extent of the injury on the suspect that the police officer inflicted. The previous sentence supports the "just be reasonable standard" in which advocates of this standard make arguments that the use of force continuum is dying. Fridell et al. argue that police departments should have the use-of-force continuum in departmental policies and officer training. The authors further claim that in the "just be reasonable" departments that police officers are trained that their use of force must be reasonable concerning the totality of the circumstances. Departments using the use of force continuum considers training in reasonableness that includes references to the continuum of several categories or levels of resistance of subjects (Fridell et al., 2015).

Fridell et al. do not support the "just be reasonable" standard and claim that critical analysis has not been conducted to validate the standard. Nevertheless, there are pros and cons.

Arguments for the "just be reasonable" standard (or against continuums) are presented below followed by Fridell et al.'s assessment.

• Continuums do not reflect the constitutional standard of reasonableness.

• Continuums are subjective and the "just reasonable" standard is objective.

• Continuums do not allow for consideration of the "totality of the circumstances."

• The profession will be well served by the added flexibility that "just be reasonable" provides to officers on the streets.

• The continuum is detrimental to quick decision making.

• Jurors cannot understand the nuances of continuums.

• Continuums must be eliminated because common definitions do not exist for the levels of resistance and force.

Fridell et al. counter the claims of the "just be reasonable" standard with the following:

- Continuums are designed to facilitate an officer's understanding of what "reasonable" means and represent the appropriate middle ground between (1) the impossible-to-achieve precise definition and mechanical application of reasonableness and (2) the very imprecise, ambiguous direction to "just be reasonable."

In May 2011 the IACP in cooperation with the Office of Community-Oriented Policing Services (COPS) sponsored a use of force symposium. The purpose of the symposium recognized by the organizations were the importance of research, the inquiry of use of force issues, and the findings of model policies and procedures for policing. Any findings from the study and findings on the use of force issues can assist police administrators to make decisions based upon facts pertaining to the use of force policy and provide a means of improving communications with the public (*Emerging Use of Force Issues*, 2012: 12). "It was suggested that the everyday attitude of officers during the course of their routine activities has as great an influence on perception as the actual use of force" (*Emerging Use of Force Issues*, 2012: 18). This symposium put forward several worthwhile recommendations. The following recommendations are found in the *Emerging Use of Force Issues* in 2012:

- Develop a model communications strategy for law enforcement on the topic on the use of force.

- Develop a national media guide to inform the public regarding the dangers of policing and the necessity to use appropriate force in furtherance of public safety.

- Develop a sustainable online resource library detailing programs and summaries of approaches that have proven to build better relationships between police and their communities (*Emerging Use of Force Issues* 2012: 18).

The symposium participants suggested that behavioral scientists should explore police responses to deadly encounters. The participants further mentioned that neither the police profession nor public understand the hundreds of factors that contribute to use of force incidents. It was brought out that the complexities involved in the decision of an officer to use force is not appreciated or understood. The IACP/COPS symposium made further recommendations as suggested by the participants of the symposium. The recommendations are:

- Propose national use of force reporting standards.

- Collect data and conduct annual national use of force analysis.

- Conduct evaluation of use of force issues for mid-size and small police agencies.

- Charge a single government-sponsored entity with responsibility for collection, analysis, and dissemination of real-time data describing violence directed at the police (*Emerging Use of Force Issues*, 2012: 20).

Police chiefs, according to symposium participants, need to be prepared for use of force issues. They need specialized training in maintaining the confidence of their police officers while communicating with the public. Planning has to be accomplished in advance before addressing an incident and not during an emotionally charged event. The IACP/COP symposium has the following recommendations for police leaders:

- Develop use of force management institute for police leaders.

- Develop use of force management publication for city officials.

Symposium participants indicated they were concerned with the training that officers were receiving in the use of force. Some participants wondered if training was ineffective since it was based on what officers could not do, and not on what they could do. The symposium recommended the following for training:

- Survey to determine nationally the current spectrum of use of force training.

- Develop model in-service use of force training.

- Validate use of force in-service training in pilot departments.

Participants of the symposium wanted access to actual violence used against the police. This information is important to police administrators. If police are subject to a large amount of violence then the use of force can be more readily justified. Also, what is the mindset of the police officers dealing with the public on a daily basis? Police administrators wanted information on the actual threat of violence toward officers and the state of mind of their officers. The recommendation on these questions is as follows:

- Survey to evaluate the use of force mindset of police officers.

- Support efforts such as LEOKA (law enforcement officers killed and assaulted) and the National Center for Prevention of Violence Against Police to collect, evaluate, and publish in real time, data that speaks of trends in violence against the police.

The IACP/COPS symposium provided excellent recommendations that need to be carried out but so far little or no action has taken place to put these recommendations in place. The use of force as an issue has been with American policing since the 1840s when the New York City Police Department was established. Over the decades the use of force has had high and low points as an issue. The IACP/COPS symposium has provided an excellent starting point to solve the use of force issue.

☐ Summary

Generally, a government to be successful must maintain social order and protect its citizens' safety. Governments to maintain social order provide for a peacekeeping force known as the police or law enforcement. The authority and power of the police are the biggest difference between them and the rest of citizens in society. The powers of the police have with it the responsibility to preserve peace and enforce the laws with the power to arrest and use force—even deadly force.

In this chapter controversial issues related to the legitimate and illegitimate authority of the police use of force was covered. The illegal, unacceptable, or excessive use of force often has been referred to as *police brutality*. According to Roberg et al. the use of force can be considered as any time a police officer attempts to force a citizen to behave in a specific way. Basically, a police officer uses force to control the free movement of an individual. The use of force has a broad definition from verbal abuse to excessive physical force being used.

There are numerous methods explaining police use of excessive force from beating civil rights protestors, deliberately kicking someone being arrested, and unprovoked use of deadly force while attempting to control disturbances. It has been recognized that most occupations provide workers with opportunities for misconduct and police departments and police officers are no different. The opportunities for police officers to violate laws and departmental police encouraging the excessive use of force are many.

The range of police misconduct includes activities such as perjury, sex on duty, drinking and using drugs on duty, and police brutality. When a police officer abuses people a call for corrective action can become loud. The use of force runs the gamut from the possibly appropriate to the highly inappropriate. There exists the claim that the police have a code of silence which means they look the other way when they observe their fellow officers involved in an act of misconduct.

Incidents of the "use of excessive force" by police officers or "police brutality" can be traced to early times in police history. In the 1930s the Wickersham Commission discovered that the "third degree," which can be considered police brutality, was commonly used by police officers during this period. The President's Crime Commission in the 1960s found that brutality still existed but not to the extent that occurred in the 1930s. Police brutality that occurred in the 1990s in the Rodney King incident was videotaped and shown worldwide. Approximately some 20 Los Angeles police officers gave King a broken cheekbone, fractured eye socket, missing teeth, skull fractures, external burns, and permanent brain damage. On the other coast, a case that parallels King's is the Abner Louima case. The assault on Louima was bizarre with a police officer placing a stick up Louima's rectum. Both of these cases were tried in federal court and the officers responsible for these incidents were convicted of crimes and sent to prison.

An officer must take into consideration many factors before he decides to use force. He must decide if the force is justified. Generally, the use of force can be justified when it is necessary to make an arrest, detain a suspect, or to protect the officer or a third party. To assist police officers when to use the appropriate amount of force a "use of force continuum" has been developed as a guide for police officers. The continuum functions as a guide as to the appropriate extent of force to be used by a police officer. During the last decade the "use of force continuum" has been challenged. With the Supreme Court *Garner v. Connor* decision of 1989 advocates against the continuum claim the guidelines should be the standards established by the Garner decision. At the time of this chapter's writing the final conclusion has not been reached.

☐ References

Adams, K. 1999. What we know about use of force, in *Use of Force by Police*, Washington, DC: National Institute of Police, p. 1.

Alpert, G. P. and R. G. Dunham 2004. *Understanding Police Use of Force*, New York, New York: University of Cambridge.

Alpert, G. P. and W. C. Smith 1994. How reasonable is the reasonable man? Police and excessive force, *Journal of Criminal Law and Criminology*, Volume 85, 481–501.

Barker, T. 1977. Peer group support for police occupational deviance, *Criminology*, Volume 15, No. 2, 356.

Barker, T. 1978. An empirical study of police deviance other than corruption. *Journal of Police Science and Administration*, Volume 6, No. 3, 264–272.

Bayley, D. and J. Garafolo 1989. The management of violence by patrol officers, *Criminology*, February, Volume 27, No. 1, 1–25.

Christopher, W. 1991. *A Report of the Independent Commission on the Los Angeles Police Department*, Los Angeles: City of Los Angeles.

Cukan, A. 2000. Jurors: The Only Issue Was the Law: Say Race Had No Part in Diallo Verdict? *APBnews.com*. May 18.

Emerging Use of Force Issues: Balancing Public and Officer Safety. 2012. Washington, DC: IACP/COPS.

Erikson, K. T. 1966. *Wayward Puritans: A Study in the Sociology of Deviance*, New York, New York: Allyn and Bacon.

Fielding, N. 2005. *The Police and Social Conflict*, Second Edition, Portland, Oregon: Cavendish.

Flosi, E. D. 2012. Use of force: Downfalls of the continuum, http://www.policeone.com/use-of-force/articles/5643926.

Fridell, L., S. Ijames and M. Bekow, 2015. Taking the straw man to the ground: Arguments in support of the linear use-of-force continuum, *Police Chief*, http:// www.policechiefmagineazine.org/magazine/index.cfm?fuseaction=dispay_arch&article_2548&issue_id=12201.

Fyfe, J. J. 1981. Observations on police deadly force, *Crime and Delinquency*, Volume 27, No. 3, 376–389.

Garner, J. H., T. Schade, J. Hepburn and J. Buchanan 1995. Measuring the continuum of force used by and against the police, *Criminal Justice Review*, Volume 20, No. 2, 146–168. Retrieved from: https://www.ncjrs.gov/App/Publications/abstract.aspx?ID=167543.

Geller, W. A. and M. S. Scott 1992. *Deadly Force: What We Know*, Washington, DC: Police Executive Research Forum.

Hampton, R. E. 2009. *Use of Force Continuum: A Debate*, National Black Police Association.

Herzog, S. 2001. Deviant organizational messages among suspect police officers in Israel, *Policing*, Volume 23, No. 4, 416–438.

Herzog, S. 2002. Police violence in Israel: Has the establishment of a civilian complaints board made a difference? *Police Practice and Research*, Volume 3, No. 2, 119–133.

Kolber, E. 1999. The Peril of Safety: Did Crime-Fighting Tactics put Amadou Diallo at Risk? *The New Yorker*, p. 50 (March issue). Retrieved from http://www.newyorker.com/magazine/1999/03/22/the-perils-of-safety.

Lundman, R. J. 1980. *Police and Policing: An Introduction*, New York, New York: Holt, Rinehart, and Winston.

National Commission on Law Observance and Enforcement. 1931. *Report on Police*, Washington, DC: U.S. Government Printing Office.

Newsweek. 2000. L.A's bandits in blue: A shocked city investigates charges that its cops lied, stolen and shot suspects for sport, *Newsweek*, Volume 155, No. 18, 48.

Palmiotto, M. J. 1997. *Policing: Concepts, Strategies, and Current Issues in American Police Forces*, Durham, North Carolina: Carolina Academic Press.

Peters, J. and M. A. Brave 2006. Force continuums: Are they still needed? *P and S Police and Security News*, Volume 22, No. 1, 2.

Roberg, R., J. Crank and J. Kuykendall 2000. *Police and Society*, Second Edition, Los Angeles, California: Roxbury.

Skolnick, J. H. and J. J. Fyfe 1993. *Above the Law*, New York, New York: The Free Press.

Terrill, R. J. 1990. Alternative perceptions of independence in civilian oversight, *Journal of Police Science and Administration*, Volume 17, No. 2, 77–83.

The President's Commission on Law Enforcement and Administration of Justice. 1967. *Task Force Report: The Police*, Washington, DC: U.S. Government Printing Office, p. 181.

The Use-of-Force Continuum. 2009, August 4. Retrieved 2015, from http://www.nij.gov/topics/law-enforcement/officer-safety/use-of-force/pages/continuum.aspx.

Time. 2000. Time and again, I stepped over the line: If Rafael Perez is telling the truth, an L.A. Cop Scandal will the city millions and more," *Time*, March 6, Volume 135, No. 110, 25.

United States Civil Rights Commission. 1947. *To Secure These Rights*, Washington, DC: U.S. Government Printing Office.

United States Civil Rights Commission. 1961. *The 50 States Report*. Washington, DC: U.S. Government Printing Office.

United States Civil Rights Commission. 1981. *Who Is Guarding the Guardians*? Washington, DC: U.S. Government Printing Office.

Vaughn, M. S., T. W. Cooper and R. V. del Carmen 2001. Assessing legal liabilities in law enforcement: Police chiefs' views. *Crime and Delinquency*, Volume 47, No. 1, 3–27.

Wallentine, K. 2009. The risky continuum: Abandoning the use of force continuum to enhance risk management. *International Municipal Lawyers Association Journal*, 1–2. Retrieved 2015, from http://imla.org.

Walker, J. 2000a. Gangsta cops, *Reason*, January, Volume 31, No. 18, 13.

Walker, J. 2000b. Gangster cops, *Reason*, Volume 31, No. 119, 13.

Wilson, O. W. 1967. In The President's Commission on Law Enforcement and Administration of Justice. 1967. *Task Force Report: The Police*, Washington, DC: U.S. Government Printing Office.

Wittie, M. C. 2013. Police use of force, *PB and J*, Vol. 2, No. 1, 17.

3
CHAPTER

Use of Deadly Force

Michael J. Palmiotto

"Deadly force can best be described as a force capable of causing serious bodily injury or death. Generally, the police have the authority to use deadly force to save their lives or the lives of others." (Palmiotto, 2001: 27). The police use of deadly force can be traced back to the common law of England, the historical foundation of American law. In our contemporary society the police legal right to use deadly force no longer comes from common law, it comes from statutory law. Statutory law is legislative law that has its foundation in common law.

Generally, police officers have the authority to use deadly force, to cause death of another human being, when their life or the life of another person is jeopardized. The police can trace their legal authority to use deadly force to the common law of England, which was developed during the middle ages.

Under common law the police have the authority to use deadly force against someone who was suspected of committing a felony, which was and is still considered a serious crime. Law enforcement under English common law had few felonies compared to our modern law which has too many felonies to count. The police never could use deadly force against a suspect committing a misdemeanor, a less serious crime than a felony. Felonies under the common law legal system were punishable by death. The police could use deadly force against a suspect absconding from the scene of a crime. The rationale for this was simply that since felonies committed were punishable by death, the police in a sense were doing the state a favor if he killed the suspect.

Since the nineteenth century and the passing of statutory laws only first-degree murder is a capital offense, punishable by death. Felonies are no longer a capital offense, except for first-degree murder, under the statutory laws passed by the legislative branch. The police who use deadly force against a felony suspect while apprehending them are exercising more authority and power than a judge or jury.

There are various methods in which physical force by a police officer could result in deadly force. The most common deadly force method used by police is firearms. Another method that can cause death is neck holds that can cut off circulation and/or blood flow. An unusual method of using deadly force was used by the Philadelphia Police in 1985, when they dropped an incendiary bomb from a police helicopter onto a house killing 11 members of a militant group.

Most states would have laws describing deadly force. Kansas is one such state which states the "Use of deadly force means the application of any physical force which is likely to cause death or great bodily harm to a person. Any threat to cause death or great bodily harm, including but not limited to, by the display or production of a weapon, shall not constitute use of deadly force, so long as the actor's purpose is limited to creating an apprehension that the actor will if necessary, use deadly force in defense of such actor or to affect a lawful arrest" (Kansas Statute Annotated, Article 32, Chapter 21, supp. 21-5221).

The Model Penal Code specifies when the use of deadly force can and cannot be used. First, the arrest is for a felony, the person making the arrest is a peace officer or assisting the peace officer, the force used by the officers causes no risk to innocent people, the officer believes the arrest involved includes the use or threatened use of deadly force and the person being arrested may cause substantial risk of serious bodily injury or death if apprehension is delayed (Model Penal Code 3.07(2) (b)).

☐ Reason for Firearms

In the United States in the 1840s there was an increase in the use of firearms in individual disputes. In the late 1840s and 1850s, police officers were occasionally shot in the line of duty. In the 1850s, it was a matter of personal choice for an officer to carry firearms for protection. Eventually, carrying firearms became an acceptable practice for police officers. Generally, many Americans felt that law enforcement was for others and not for them, and so during periods of social turmoil when violence was acceptable behavior for a specific segment of society, the establishment found the use of force acceptable police behavior (Johnson, 1981: 28–31).

During the 1840s New York City initiated the modern municipal police concept in America. New York City combined its day and night force into one department. By the 1860s the New York model had been accepted by many cites with some modification. While the basic principles of the New York model were largely acceptable, the new police system confronted three issues:

1. A controversy over the adoption of the uniform

2. A concern about arming the police, and

3. The issue of appropriate force in making arrest (Johnson, 1981: 28).

The purpose of the uniform was to make police officers readily visible to the public and for them to avoid hiding. The uniform issue is nonexistent today. The other two issues, firearms and force, especially deadly force, have been controversial since the police have carried firearms and were given legal authority to make arrest. The use of firearms and deadly force has led to violence in American streets. In the second decade of the twenty-first century violent mobs still take to the streets protesting police use of deadly force, usually with the use of a firearm. It appears that police using deadly force may be an issue that will never go away. The comments made by Anthony Bouza, former Minneapolis police chief in 1992 are as valid today as they were when he made them:

> The importance of police-involved shootings stems not so much from their frequency (they are rare compared with the hundreds of thousands of encounters each year between police and persons suspected of violating the law) but from their potential consequences. Any experienced police officer knows the potentially devastating effects of even justified shootings by police—loss of life and bereavement, risks to an officer's career, the government liability to civil suits, strained police–community relations, rioting and all the economic and social crisis that attend major civil disturbances (Geller and Scott, 1992: 1).

The Police Foundation is in agreement with Chief Bouza when it reports that with the United States having more than 750,000 police officers and with the police contacting millions of citizens each year, shootings by police are of a low frequency. They provide the reason that police officers are limited to specific circumstances as to when they can use deadly force (Klinger, 2005). Fyfe agrees with Bouza and the Police Foundation that the frequency of the use of deadly force is quite small. He indicates that most shooting occurs in large cities (Fyfe, 1982: 8).

The following studies reveal that the issue of deadly force and firearms use by the police began from the time the police became armed in the mid-nineteenth century up to our present day. Our first study of police shootings from the years 1875–1920 indicates that the police have had a long history of violent behavior. This violent behavior can be traced when police were nicknamed "clubbers" when they used their nightsticks against citizens until now when they have used deadly force, usually with firearms against unarmed citizens. Between 1875 and 1920, Chicago police officers killed 307 people (Adler, 2007: 233–237). From 1910 to 1920, African Americans made up only 3% of the population but comprised 21% of deaths by the police. These figures seems to parallel our modern day. More African Americans are killed by police than any other racial or ethnic group. During the period of this study death by police officers accounted for 85% to either defend themselves or arrest fleeing felons (Adler, 2007: 246). Police shootings in the twentieth century have fueled social unrest in the United States and were the cause of major race riots including Detroit (1943), Harlem (1943), Miami (1980, 1982, 1984), Washington, D.C. (1991), and New York City (1992) (Adler, 2007: 233). Demonstrations, if not riots, are continuing into the first decades of the twenty-first century because of police shooting. Ferguson, Missouri, a suburb of St. Louis had demonstrations and looting after a Ferguson police officer shot an unarmed black teenager.

☐ Fleeing-Felon Rule

Historically, police officers could use deadly force when a suspect was fleeing from a crime. A Tennessee statute provided that if a police officer has given notice of an intent to arrest a criminal suspect and the suspect flees or forcibly resists, "the officer may use all the necessary means to make an arrest." On October 3, 1974 at 10:45 p.m. Memphis police officers Elton Hymon and Leslie Wright responded to a prowler call. Upon arriving on the scene the officers observed a woman pointing to an adjacent house stating that someone was breaking in next door. While Wright was notifying the dispatcher that they had arrived at the scene, Hymon went to the back of the house. Hymon heard a door slam and observed someone run across the backyard. The runner, later discovered to be Edward Garner, stopped at a 6' link fence. Hymon had his flashlight on and was able to see Garner's face and hands. There was no sign of a weapon and Hymon thought Garner was unarmed. Garner, according to Hymon, was about 17 or 18 and about 5'5"–5'7 " tall. Hymon told Garner to halt but he began climbing the fence. If Garner got over the fence he would not be apprehended. Hymon shot Garner who eventually died in hospital. Hymon's actions were reviewed by the Memphis Firearms Review Board and presented to the grand jury with neither body taking any action. Gardner's father brought a civil suit in the Federal District of the Western District of Tennessee, seeking damage under 42 U.S.C. 1983 for violating Edward Gardner's constitutional rights. The complaint alleged that the shooting violated the Fourth, Fifth, Sixth, Eighth, and Fourteenth Amendments of the U.S. Constitution. The district judge held that Hymon's actions were authorized by the Tennessee statute, which was constitutional. The judge held Hymon's actions were reasonable and a practical means of preventing Gardner's escape. Gardner had recklessly attempted to vault over the fence to escape and thereby assumed the risk of being fired upon.

In 1983 the Court of Appeals reversed the District Court's decision. The Court of Appeals held that the killing of a fleeing suspect is "seizure" under the Fourth Amendment and is constitutional only if reasonable. The court further held that the facts did not justify the use of deadly force under the Fourth Amendment and is constitutional only if reasonable. Police officers cannot resort to deadly force unless they have probable cause to believe the suspect poses a risk to the safety of police officers or the community. The U.S. Supreme Court in 1985 affirmed the judgment of the Court of Appeals *Tennessee v. Garner et al.* (1985).

The impact of the Gardner decision influenced police homicides. The number of police homicides decreased substantially. The Gardner decision not only reduced the number of police shootings of fleeing felons but all shootings. As a result of the Gardner decisions all police shootings not related to protecting life seems to be decreasing (Tennenbaum, 1994: 258–259).

The Gardner case is limited to deadly force, and only in the context of the fleeing felon. Longo writes that the *Graham v. Connor* case pertains to all use of force, including deadly force. The Graham decision, according to Longo, established a loose framework that can be used to determine reasonableness of force (Longo, 2011: 267). Longo writes that the courts consider three fundamental questions in assessing use-of-force scenarios:

1. What is the nature or severity of the offense?

2. Did the suspect pose an immediate threat to the officer or others?

3. Is the suspect actively resisting or attempting to escape? (Longo, 2011: 267).

As mentioned in Chapter 2 there seems to be disagreement between the use of force continuum and "just be reasonable" standard as set forth in the U.S. Supreme Court in *Graham v. Connor* (1989). The U.S. Supreme Court stated that an arrest by using force has to be "objectively reasonable in view of all the facts and circumstances of each particular case, including the severity of the crime at issue, whether the suspect poses an immediate threat to the safety of officers or others, and whether he is actively resisting arrest or attempting to evade arrest by flight" (Alpert and Dunham, 2004: 21).

Fyfe (1981: 376), a recognized scholar on police use of deadly force, asserts that a hullabaloo over deadly force can be attributed to "Presidential Commissions, police practitioners, radical criminologists, traditional academics, social activists, law reviews and popular writers." As previously mentioned in this chapter there are a variety of ways the police can use deadly force against an individual.

The decision as to when police officers should draw their weapons has never been clearly defined nor has the question of when they should fire them. While both actions depend upon the discretion of the officer, there exists a difference between drawing and firing their firearms. Police officers who are well trained draw their firearm only when circumstances present a reasonable expectation that they will encounter life-threatening violence. Police officers working in busy police stations will draw their weapons more frequently than officers from slow police stations, since they have a greater chance of being fired upon. At times, police officers draw their firearm whey they respond to a violent crime. Officers who make arrests for serious crimes may have their weapons drawn to obtain quick response from suspects. Competent officers understand that it may be unwise to have their weapons visible to the mentally disturbed or those individuals acting in an illogical manner. It has not been determined as to whether the display of an officer's weapon may stimulate violence rather than discourage it. The police officer and the general public should be aware that every year there are officers who are shot with their own weapon (Skolnick and Fyfe, 1993: 41–42).

At times, shootings by police officers results in major unrest in the community they serve. On February 4, 1999, in the Soundview section of the Bronx, four New York City police officers, who were members of the Street Crime Unit, shot and killed Amadou Diallo, an immigrant from Africa. Forty-one rounds were fired, while 19 struck Diallo. Diallo was unarmed and standing by himself in the lobby of his apartment building. The victim was only 20 ft away from the officers who shot him. The death of Diallo became an outrage with racism as an outcry because four white police officers killed an African man. Following Diallo's death the building became a memorial, with messages of condolence and flowers lining the hallway (Kolber, 1999: 50). The four police officers on February 25, 2000 were found not guilty of second-degree murder, reckless endangerment, and manslaughter and criminal negligence in the death of Diallo by a mixed-race jury of seven men and five women. The jury concluded that the four officers feared for their life and acted in self-defense (Cukan, 2000: 2–4). The jury's verdict was poorly accepted and for several days, demonstrations occurred in New York City. The parents of Diallo petitioned the U.S. Justice Department to investigate the shooting for potential civil rights violations. The Justice Department decided in 2001 that the civil rights of Diallo were not violated and that federal charges would not be brought against the police officers.

There have been demonstrations and rioting in America for decades, even going back to the Civil War and colonial America. Some of the incidents that set off demonstrations and riots in earlier decades are mirrors for some of the demonstrations and rioting in the early decades of the twenty-first century.

The 1964 Harlem riots were initiated like so many violent incidents over a minor situation. You might say they were initiated when a white superintendent of an apartment building turned a water hose on some young black men who were loitering on the front steps of the apartment building and refused to move. Fifteen-year old James Powell chased him into the building. An off duty police lieutenant heard the commotion and was confronted by Powell who had a knife. Powell slashed the lieutenant on his forearm. The lieutenant drew his revolver and warned Powell who again lunged at him. The officer shot Powell and killed him. Some members of the community could not understand why the lieutenant could not have disarmed the young man without shooting him. Community activists motivated the crowd to march on the 123rd police precinct and make demands. The police were waiting for the crowd which was a hostile mob. The police informed the crowd that the shooting incident was being investigated by the district attorney's office. The crowd would not accept this information and the police soon had bricks and bottles coming from the roof at them. The riot police went after the crowd with their nightsticks and voices in the crowd called out "killer cops" and "murders." The angry mob went down the street breaking windows and looting. They began throwing Molotov cocktails at the police. Rioting spread to Bedford-Stuyvesant across the river in Brooklyn then to Rochester, New York. On July 22, there were 1000 people attacking the police (*Harlem—The Backlash Begins*). The 6 days of rioting left a large number of people arrested and injured. During the 1960s there were many riots in American cities and the reasons are for the most part similar today as in the 1960s. There exists a lack of respect toward the police by minorities. Also, Afro-Americans believe the police are abusive toward them and that they are treated in an inferior manner when compared to whites.

The use of deadly force appears to be an issue in many cities and states throughout the United States. One such state which has a history of deadly force, racially tinted police confrontations is Florida. Many of the police confrontations have involved unarmed men, which resulted in protests, riots, and hostility between minorities and the police. No police officer in the last 20 years has been charged with using deadly force improperly. Even getting a decision in Florida to seek charges is problematic. An example of such a case is a 2011 memorial day weekend shooting in South Beach, when 12 officers fired 110 rounds at a 22-year old young man whose car was stopped. In addition, four bystanders received wounds. This shooting was one of 42 cases involving the use of deadly force by the police (Alvarez, 2014: 1).

Another area of the country that overlooks police shooting is Clark County, specifically Las Vegas, Nevada. One 31-year-old, 8-year veteran Las Vegas police officer had shot two men in 21 months and was disciplined for dating a prostitute while off duty. He shot a third man; all three under peculiar circumstances and not one had a witness. The police officer was exonerated by the coroner's inquest and the department's internal Use of Force Review Board. The officer had several weeks off and returned to work cleared of any wrongdoing. In the last 20 years, the Las Vegas police had 310 shootings. Since 2000 the Las Vegas police on an average fired their weapons 17 times (Mower et al., 2011: 1–6).

A knife-wielding man was killed in Times Square, New York by two police officers who fired 12 shots at the man. The man was waving a kitchen knife scaring tourists. Experts on police procedures said the police did what they were trained to do. The New York City Police Commissioner and Mayor both said the police officers acted appropriately (McGeehan, 2012: 1).

Shooting by the Philadelphia police increased in 2012 while violent crimes decreased. The 2012 shootings by police was at the highest level in 10 years. The Philadelphia police shot 52 suspects with 15 of those being shot dying in 2012. Similar to Florida and Las Vegas, the Police Internal Affairs investigators and the district attorney's office had no concerns about the shootings (Wood, 2013: 1).

On Sunday morning on April 1, 2012, the Wichita Police shot an unarmed 24-year old black man, named Troy Lanning Jr., after a car chase. The police reported that after the car chase Lanning reached into a bag of belongings and the police reported he appeared to aim it against an officer in a threatening manner. Lanning was told by the police officer to stop looking into the bag but Lanning continued to reach into the bag. The officer claims Lanning continued pointing the bag at him. After several warnings the officer shot Lanning killing him. No weapon was found in the bag or in the vehicle Lanning was driving. Lanning's father believes the Wichita Police could have used a Taser on his son or a K-9 dog to catch him, rather than shooting him (Wenzl, 2012: 1).

Lanning's shooting led to demonstrations and a march on the police department. The demonstrators mentioned that since October 2011 five people were killed by the police under dubious circumstances with the Wichita police not being transparent and being disrespectful toward families of the victims (Stephenson and Shatz, 2012: 1). Stephenson and Shatz state, "Police killings are not an anomaly. In the United States, police kill over 7000 citizens each year. Activists from Anaheim and Baltimore announced through social media that their police force have killed their citizens unjustly, and their police departments continue to defend the actions of their police forces" (Stephenson and Shatz, 2012: 2). The authors quote Wichita police chief Norman Williams who stated in a press conference on July 11, "When you look at each one of these situations, the police gave commands for people to obey, to drop their weapon, to comply with what's going on, and they choose not to" (Stephenson and Shatz, 2012: 2). Stephenson and Shatz respond "In other words: blame the victim" (Stephenson and Shatz, 2012: 2).

On August 9, 2014 an incident occurred in Ferguson, Missouri which has occurred often in America: A police officer shoots a citizen. As history has shown more often than not the citizen being shot is a black man. The shooting of blacks by specifically white police officers have led to a lack of trust of Afro-Americans toward the police. Evidence indicates that throughout American's history blacks have been treated poorly and in an unjust manner. History reveals that they have been treated more unjustly than any other racial or ethnic group. It seems realistic to expect that Afro-Americans have a distrust of the police. The police have functioned at times as an "occupational army" rather than protectors of the community they police. The night of August 9, 2014 in Ferguson, Missouri was a night which led to looting, rioting, and demonstrations. This night lead to confrontation between the police and citizens. A scene not considered uncommon in the United States. You may say generations matured watching confrontation between police and citizens on television. It may have come to the point that the police may never be considered justified in shooting a black man regardless of the circumstances or evidence.

The fatal shooting by Ferguson, Missouri police officer Darren Wilson of 18-old Michael Brown, a black man, created attention not only in America but also throughout the world. The hullabaloo resulted from a simple incident of Michael Brown walking down the middle of the street with Dorian Johnson when Officer Wilson drove up to them and ordered them to walk on the sidewalk. Reports indicate a struggle occurred between Officer Wilson and Brown through the car window and somehow Wilson's revolver was fired. It is undermined whether the weapon was fired accidentally or intentionally. Brown and Johnson fled from Wilson in different directions with Wilson in pursuit of Brown. Officer Wilson fired his weapon 6 times killing Brown. A controversy exists as to whether Brown had his hands up or was approaching Wilson when he was shot.

St. Louis County police chief made the following comment about the incident. "When the officer tried to exit his vehicle, Chief Belmar said one of the two pushed the officer back into the cruiser. The suspect allegedly assaulted the officer in the car and the two struggled over his gun. At least one shot was fired inside the vehicle. A few moments later, Chief Belmar said, the officer allegedly fired multiple shots outside the vehicle that killed the suspect, about 35 feet from the cruiser" (Kesling et al., 2014).

When the news of Michael Brown's death reached the community, peaceful protests took place but eventually escalated to looting, vandalism, and confrontations with police officers that lasted for several days. With the police having difficulty maintaining order a curfew was established. Not only was the community of Ferguson and St. Louis County involved in the Brown shooting, but also the state and federal government became involved. For example, President Obama offered his condolences to the Brown family, Attorney General Holder made a visit to Ferguson and ordered a civil rights investigation of the Ferguson police department. The Governor of Missouri placed a Missouri State Highway Patrol captain in charge of maintaining order in Ferguson. Even the Secretary-General of the United Nations got into the act. He requested that all protestors' rights to peaceful assembly and freedom of expression be ensured (McAllister and Carey, 2014; U.N. Chief, 2014).

Several months after the interview, Darren Wilson, the police officer who shot Michael Brown, gave his account of the incident to federal civil rights investigators who were assigned by the Department of Justice. Officer Wilson said he was pinned in his vehicle and was fearful for his well-being. Wilson reported he struggled with Brown over his gun. He informed the investigators that Brown reached for his gun which was fired twice in the car as verified by forensic tests conducted by the Federal Bureau of Investigation. Michael Brown was struck in the arm by the first bullet while the second bullet missed. Forensic tests revealed Brown's blood was on the gun, the interior door panel, and on Officer Wilson's uniform. Officer Wilson informed investigators that Brown had punched and scratched him repeatedly leaving cuts on his neck and swelling on his face. This first account of Officer Wilson does not explain why he emerged from the car and fired several shots at Brown. Darren Wilson's account of the incident contradicts several witness accounts. The information provided by Wilson will not calm those who want to know why an unarmed man was shot 6 times (Schmidt et al., 2014).

On August 22, 2014 the St. Louis Post Dispatch published the autopsy report of the St. Louis Medical Examiner's Office. The report stated the following: "The deceased body sustained multiple gunshot wounds; three (3) wounds to his head, one was to the top of his head, right eye and right central forehead area. There were two (2) wounds to his chest, one wound to his upper right chest near his neck and the other was just right to his breast. Three (3) wounds to his right arm, one wound in his upper right arm, one wound in his upper right arm, middle of the arm and one to his forearm. One (1) wound to the inside of his right hand near his thumb and palm." The report further stated "The deceased had abrasions to his right side of his face and on his left hand. The deceased hands were bagged with paper bags to save any trace evidence." The medical examiner found marijuana in Brown's body (St. Louis County Health, 2014).

The forensic pathologists hired by the family of Michael Brown questioned the St. Louis County medical examiner's finding. The medical examiner concluded that Brown had gunshot residue on him after he had been fatally shot. Michael Baden, the forensic pathologist, hired by the Brown family in August, claims that the teen could have been shot from a distance of 30 ft. A leaked copy of the medical examiner's report, by the St. Louis Post Dispatch reported that microscopic particles of gunshot residue were found in a deep layer of skin, revealing that the teen was shot once in his thumb at close range. Baden claims he want to testify before the grand jury. He further reported that dirt can appear similar to gunshot residue. Further, Baden stated he wanted copies of the microscopic slides that show what the medical examiner claims is gunshot residue (Alcindor, 2014: 3A).

Traditionally, when a police officer is involved in a shooting, including the killing of a person, the investigation is sent to the grand jury by the district attorney. The police officer either has to be indicted and the case goes to trial or the officer is exonerated. Police officer Wilson's shooting of Michael Brown was sent to the St. Louis County grand jury. On November 21, the grand jury of St. Louis County after months of deliberation exonerated Officer Wilson from any wrongdoing in the death of Michael Brown.

The U.S. Government, through the Department of Justice, conducted an investigation of Officer Wilson's shooting of Michael Brown (Darren Wilson resigned November 30, 2014 from the Ferguson Police Department prior to the Justice Department's findings). The Justice Department's investigation of the shooting incident of Michael Brown was made public by the Attorney General Eric Holder on March 5, 2015. The law provides the government the authority to investigate the Brown shooting, or for that matter any shooting by a law enforcement officer. The investigative powers fall under the criminal statute that enforces the constitutional limitations that pertains to the use of force by police officers. The Federal law 18 U.S.C. 242 states the following "Whoever under color of any law,…willfully subjects any person…to the deprivation of any rights, privileges, or immunities secured or protected by the Constitution or laws of the United States [shall be guilty of a crime]." This law allows federal investigators to determine if a police officer had violated an arrested person or deceased person's civil rights. The Justice Department's investigation concluded that Darren Wilson shot and killed Michael Brown as a defensive act to save his life (Memorandum, 2015).

Approximately 2 months after the Ferguson shooting, another shooting occurred a short distance away. On October 8, 2014 an off duty St. Louis police officer in uniform working as a security guard shot an 18-year old black man. The black man fired three shots at the police officer before his weapon jammed. The officer returned fire with 17 shots at the black man and killed him. The parents of the man claimed their son was carrying a sandwich and not a weapon. The police found a weapon at the scene and three projectiles found at the scene of the incident (Muskal, 2014: 7A).

On Monday, October 13, 2014 demonstrators attempted to shut down a street in front of Emerson Electric in St. Louis holding signs reading, "Black lives do matter." Other demonstrators marched on City Hall, while attempting to hang a banner reading "What side are you on?" Nineteen people were arrested by St. Louis police according to a St. Louis County spokesman (Fiona, 2014). Since the Ferguson incident there have been numerous incidents of police shootings of black males usually followed by demonstrations. These shootings followed by demonstrations have occurred during the writing of this book and are expected to continue long after this book is published.

Delroy Burton, chairman of the Washington DC police union said the following, "People want to make generalizations that cops get away with stuff most of the time. No they don't. Most of the time their use of force is appropriate. But now, every single case of deadly use of force, particularly where race is a factor, it automatically becomes racism, and that's just not true.... The fact that officers are now guilty until proven innocent, or the force is inappropriate until an investigation is done—I think that sends a message to police officers, and I think it's a waste of resources for society in general" (Drehle, 2015: 27).

☐ Summary

The use of force and specifically deadly force had been an issue since the police began arming themselves in the 1840s. It has become a major issue in the second decade of the twenty-first Century. The use of deadly force by the police can be traced back to the middle ages when common law was the law of England. During the middle ages deadly force could be used by law enforcers against anyone committing a felony. Since, during this period of time, felonies were punishable by death a law enforcer killing a felon was considered doing the state a favor.

Unlike the middle ages, our modern society has many crimes considered a felony and only one punishable by death. First-degree murder is the only crime punishable by death. The police who use deadly force against a felony suspect while apprehending them are exercising more authority and power than a judge and jury.

Most states have laws describing deadly force. The Model Penal Code specifies when the use of deadly force can and cannot be used. Since the police are armed and have the authority to use deadly force to protect their lives or another person they will resort to deadly force when they consider it appropriate. Often, deadly force is used against an offender who refuses to cooperate with the police. If the offender is unarmed this can create a major issue for the police officer. The shooting of an unarmed offender can lead to demonstrations and rioting. Family members of offenders and those not police supporters often claim that the police could or should have subdued the offender without using deadly force. They make this claim even when the offender is bigger than the officer or has a weapon, such as a knife.

Demonstrations and rioting can be traced to colonial times and the Civil War. It has continued into the first decades of the twenty-first century. Riots were serious in the 1940s and 1960s and have been somewhat severe this second decade of the twenty-first century. However, as long as police shoot offenders it should be expected that demonstrations and rioting may be the outcome.

☐ References

Adler, J. 2007. Shoot to kill: The use of deadly force by the Chicago police, 1875–1920, *Journal of Interdisciplinary History*, Autumn, XXXVIII(2), 38(2), 233–254.

Alcindor, Y. 2014. Brown family's pathologist wants to testify, *USA Today*, October 31, 3A.

Alpert, G. P. and R. G. Dunham 2004. *Understanding Police Use of Force*, New York: Cambridge University Press.

Alvarez, L. 2014. Florida prosecutors face long odds when police use lethal force, *International New York Times*, September 3, www.nyti.ms/1r2UkzJ

Bouza, A. 1992. Introduction, In: Geller, W. and M. Scott (Eds.), *Deadly Force, What We Know*, Washington, DC: PERF, p. 1.

Cukan, W. 2000. Jurors: The only issue was the law: Say race had no part in Diallo verdict? *APBNews.com*, May 18.

Drehle, D. V. 2015. Line of fire, *Time*, April 20, 24–28.

Fiona, O. 2014. Protesters demonstrate in St. Louis area over police shooting of blacks, *Reuters*, http:://www.reuters.com/article/2013/10/13/us-usa-misso uri-shooting-idUSKCN01201520141013

Fyfe, J. J. 1981. Observations on police deadly force, *Crime and Delinquency*, 27(3), 376–389.

Fyfe, J. J. 1982. *Readings on police use of deadly force*, Washington, D.C.: Police Foundation.

Geller, W. A. and M. S. Scott 1992. *Deadly Force: What We Know*, Washington, DC: Police Executive Forum.

Harlem, R. 1964. (n.d.) *Harlem—The Backlash Begins*, www.detroits-great-rebellion.com/harlem-riot.html

Johnson, D. R. 1981. *American Law Enforcement: A History*, St. Louis: Forum Press.

Kansas Statute Annotated Article 32, Chapter 21, supp. 21-5221.

Kesling, B., M. Peters and D. Barrett 2014. FBI probes Missouri teen's shooting, *The Wall Street Journal*, (August 12) http://online.wsj.com/articles/missouri-teenager-killed-by-police-after-fight-1407698036

Klinger, D. 2005. Special theory and the street cop: The case of deadly force, *Ideas in American Policing*, Number 7, Police Foundation.

Kolber, E. 1999. The perils of safety: Did crime-fighting tactics put Amadou Diallou at risk, *New York Times*, May 22, p. 50.

Longo, T. 2011. Defining instrumentalities of deadly force, *Touro Law Review*, 27(2), 261.

McAllister, E. and N. Carey. 2014. Michael Brown remembered in Missouri with calls for peace, justice. *Reuters*, (August 26). Retrieved 2015, http://www.reuters.com/article/usa-missouri-shooting-idUSL1N0QV0Q220140826

McGeehan, P. 2012. Officials defend fatal shooting of a knife-wielding man near times Sq., *New York Times*, August 12, www.nytimes/2012/08/nyregion/police-fire-12-shots-in-killing-near-times-square.html-square.html

Memorandum 2015. Department of Justice Report Regarding the Criminal Investigation into the Shooting Death of Michael Brown by Ferguson, Missouri Police Officer Darren Wilson, March 4.

Mower, L., A. Maimon and B. Hayes 2011. Analysis: Many Las Vegas police shootings could have been avoided, *Las Vegas Review Journal*, November 27, www.reviewjournal.com/news/deadly-force/always-justified/analysis-many

Muskal, M. 2014. St. Louis braces for weekend of protests over Michael Brown killing. *Reuters*, (October 9). Retrieved 2015, http://www.reuters.com/article/us-usa-missouri-shooting-idUSKCN0HY08H20141009

Palmiotto, M.J. (eds.) 2001. Police misconduct: What is it? In: *Police Misconduct: A reader for the 21st century*, Upper Saddle River, N.J.: Prentice-Hall, p. 27.

Schmidt, M. S., M. Apuzzo and J. Bosman 2014. Police officer in Ferguson is said to recount a struggle, *New York News*, October 17. http://nyti.ms/1qtLBnC8

Skolnick, J. H. and J. J. Fyfe 1993. *Above the Law*, New York, New York: The Free Press.

Stephenson, R. and M. Shatz 2012. Wichitans take a stand against police shooting, August 13, http://www.occupy.com/article/wichitans-take-stand-against-police-shootings

St. Louis County Health. 2014. Narrative report of investigation, Exam case 2014–5143, Office of Medical Examiner, August 8.

Tennenbaum, A. 1994. The influence on the Gardner decision on police use of deadly force, *Criminology*, 6(1), 241–260.

Tennessee v. Garner et al. 1985. Supreme Court of the United States, 471 U.S 1; 105 S.Ct. 1694; 85 L.Ed2d 1; 1985 U.S. LEXIS 195; 53 U.S.L.W.4410.

U.N. Chief calls for protection of Rights in Missouri protests, *Reuters*, August 18. http://www.reuters.com/article/2014/08/usa-missouri-shooting-un-idSKBN0D11MF20140818

Wenzl, R. 2012. Wichita police give details of weekend shooting, April 2, http://www.kansas.com/news

Wood, S. 2013. Exclusive shootings by Philly police soar as violent crime plummets, *Philly Com*, May 14, www.philly.com/philly/news/Police_shootings_soar_as_violent_crime_falls.html

CHAPTER 4

Nonlethal Weapons and Technology

Szde Yu

☐ Introduction: Police Use of Force

Police use of force has always been a controversial subject. Ideology aside, the reality is the police must be allowed to use force when necessary and they must be allowed to exercise discretion in deciding what force is necessary under the circumstances. The controversy stems from such discretion for the most part. Admittedly, some people simply make bad decisions, and wearing a police uniform does not guarantee better decision making. When the police make a decision to use force, especially deadly force, the consequences are often irrevocable even when it turns out to be a bad decision. A simple search for "police brutality" on You Tube can bring up a variety of examples. We will not dwell on that in this chapter. Instead, the focus is on how the use of nonlethal weapons may or may not help reduce controversies surrounding police use of force.

☐   Nonlethal Weapons

Police officers have to deal with dangerous criminals on a daily basis. When they are under attack, they need to subdue the attackers by any means necessary not only to save their own lives but also to ensure the public's safety. Using a gun should be fairly reasonable in a situation like this, considering how many criminals have firearms. The use of lethal weapons is justified by the police even if the criminal does not have a firearm, as long as the threat is imminent. So, why do the police need nonlethal weapons? This is because at their discretion sometimes the officers do not feel the need to kill but they do need some leverage to control the situation. Firing a gun at someone could easily result in death even without the intention to kill.

There are many factors that influence police discretion, such as departmental policy, personal belief, experience, politics, and so on. The availability of alternative means is another factor. When the situation calls for the use of force but it is not really life threatening, less than lethal options should be available as an alternative to guns. Without such options, officers might be compelled to use lethal weapons, or they might be hesitant to use lethal weapons and in turn endanger themselves. Hence, while most people automatically think of guns when it comes to police force, nonlethal weapons actually play a crucial role in police work as well. To be exact, nonlethal weapons do not mean they cannot be used to inflict fatal wounds. Rather, the term "nonlethal" simply suggests the weapon is not designed to end a life. Just like a car is not designed to kill, but it is not incapable of killing.

There are a variety of nonlethal weapons that have been invented, and quite a few of them have been widely adopted in the police force. Generally, weapons other than firearms can all be considered nonlethal. Oleoresin capsicum (aka pepper spray), stun guns, tear gas, beanbag guns, rubber bullets, and plastic bullets are the commonly seen nonlethal weapons or less-than-lethal weapons. Some nonlethal weapons are not aimed at stopping people. Instead, they are designed to stop vehicles such as caltrops. Impact weapons, such as batons, are not usually included in the discussion of nonlethal weapons, but essentially they are not designed to kill, either. Regardless of the variety, the concept of nonlethal weapons is simple, that is, demobilizing the target without directly inflicting fatal wounds. Indirectly, however, as mentioned the use of nonlethal weapons could still result in a fatal outcome.

Although sufficient evidence is not yet in place to prove that nonlethal weapons can reduce justifiable citizen killings by the police (Bailey, 1996), the use of nonlethal weapons seems to have reduced death rates in suicide-by-cop incidents (Homant and Kennedy, 2000). Further, research has found that the use of nonlethal weapons lowers the likelihood of the suspect sustaining an injury (MacDonald et al., 2009). Likewise, the odds of injury to police officers are also significantly lower when nonlethal weapons are used, compared to the use of other physical force (MacDonald et al., 2009). On July 17, 2014, the death of Eric Garner in Staten Island, New York stirred controversies when Garner was ruled to have died from a chokehold put on him by a New York City Police Department officer. In that event, which was video recorded by eyewitnesses, Garner appeared to be resisting arrest although he did not attack the officer trying to handcuff him. In response, the officer used his arms to place a headlock which resulted in a chokehold on Garner's neck, according to the medical examiner. Although the officer was not indicted by a grand jury, which implies a crime was not committed, there is definitely room for discussion regarding how the situation could have been handled differently. For starters, it might have not been necessary for the officer to engage in such physical restraint, when Garner's physical resistance was minimal. Besides, there were multiple other officers on the scene, so there was no need for that one officer to overpower the suspect in such a manner. If force was needed in that situation, the use of nonlethal weapons or even batons would have been more appropriate to restrain Garner's movement, compared to choking him with bare hands. It would have been safer for the officers as well. Hence, it is important to note that the availability of nonlethal weapons is supposed to be beneficial to both the suspect and the officer involved in an incident where the use of force is warranted but death is unnecessary.

Another scenario where nonlethal weapons such as caltrops are preferred is when the suspect is fleeing in a vehicle but there are other people in the vehicle. In this case, shooting at the vehicle greatly endangers the innocent passengers, and therefore using caltrops, if available, to stop the vehicle is a less lethal option and thus preferable. In a riot or a protest, the police also often resort to nonlethal weapons, such as plastic bullets or beanbag guns, to quell the unrest or to compel protesters to move away. Certainly when violence escalates and becomes a threat to the safety of the police and the public, sometimes firearms are necessary to control the situation. Nevertheless, nonlethal weapons first used in these situations could signify a gesture that suggests the police have no intention to really hurt the people while maintaining order. A less hostile gesture may often prevent the need for further use of force when the crowd was not seeking violence in the first place. On the contrary, the display of deadly force prematurely in a peaceful protest could easily instigate violent reactions.

☐ Controversies

Although nonlethal weapons are meant to reduce unnecessary injuries and deaths, they have had their fair share of criticism regarding injuries and deaths caused by their use. Oleoresin capsicum (OC) spray and conducted energy devices (CEDs) are the most widely used nonlethal weapons nowadays, so they are at the center of these controversies. CEDs such as a stun gun or Taser are generally safe when they are tested in experiments because most people in the experiments are healthy people and the experiments are usually conducted in controlled environments. However, when they are used on the street in the line of duty, there are more variables that are unknown and uncontrollable to the officer. For instance, the subject's heath condition is a big risk factor. Strong electric currency could trigger a heart attack on a person with preexisting heart conditions (Zipes, 2014). It could also exacerbate existing injuries especially head injuries. Some drug use factors might also come into play and cause damages that would not be otherwise seen in a healthy person. As for OC spray, in theory it could cause asphyxia if the recipient had respiratory conditions, such as asthma. Although these are plausible claims, currently empirical data are rather limited in proving them (Sheridan, 2014), in part because it is highly unethical to intentionally test these weapons on people who are known to have these risk factors. It is also because current studies in this regard usually failed to control for circumstantial variables, such as the level of resistance from the suspect and the involvement of illicit drug use (MacDonald et al., 2009). However, tentative evidence does suggest that the likelihood of severe injuries resulting from these common nonlethal weapons is pretty small. Moreover, using CEDs could reduce the rate of injury to officers (Alpert et al., 2011), and therefore they are generally seen as a favorable addition to police weaponry.

Nonetheless, the low rates of injury are actually another cause for concern. Some police officers may feel too comfortable using these nonlethal weapons since they are less likely to result in severe injuries. On November 18, 2011, some demonstrators in an Occupy Wall Street movement at the University of California, Davis were pepper sprayed by a campus police officer John Pike, while they were peacefully sitting on a paved path on campus. UC Davis Chancellor later apologized for this incident and said the police were acting against her orders. This incident spawned heated debate on the propriety of using pepper spray on a peaceful demonstration, a right that many believe is protected by the First Amendment to the U.S. Constitution. In December 2014, a Texas police officer used a Taser on a 76-year-old man in a traffic stop regarding driving a car with an expired inspection sticker. As the incident was video recorded, it soon became clear that such use of force, albeit non-lethal, was uncalled for because the old man did not initiate any physical resistance that would warrant this level of police force. In 2015, this officer was fired. These incidents show that sometimes the use of nonlethal weapons can be controversial even when they do not cause permanent injury physically. Accordingly the police should be mindful that the availability of nonlethal weapons is not to be misconstrued as a loosened standard for police use of force. In other words, the police should not feel they can use nonlethal weapons any time they want because probably no one will die from it. On the New Year's Day in 2009, Oscar Grant III was shot by a police officer working for Bay Area Rapid Transit in Oakland, California. Grant was lying face down and handcuffed when he was shot by Officer Johannes Mehserle, who was convicted of involuntary manslaughter later in 2010. Mehserle claimed he was intending to use his Taser on Grant but mistakenly withdrew his pistol instead. The incident was video recorded and the video suggests there was no reason for the officer to either shoot or tase a man who was already handcuffed on the ground face down. Had the officer used Taser correctly, it would still have been excessive force. Oscar Grant died the next day.

☐ Body Cameras

The Eric Garner incident, the UC Davis incident, the Texas officer Taser incident, and Oscar Grant's death mentioned above all had one thing in common, that is, the incident was video recorded. When there is a recording, the truth is usually easier to be revealed even though different people may interpret the moral of it differently as some people would believe the police are simply doing their job and justify the use of force, while others assert that there is abuse of power. Nonetheless, we will know what happened and draw our own conclusion accordingly. In contrast, some events involving police use of force are not accompanied by a video or the video fails to record the full context of the event. In these cases, the truth becomes elusive as a 'he says she says' situation tends to produce many versions of story. Worse yet, in some events the participants could be dead and have no say in the revelation of the truth. Without a video showing what really happened, it is especially difficult for an agreement on accountability to be formed. As society does not typically have much trust in the police's ability to admit their wrongdoing, visual evidence becomes more crucial than ever for the public to expose police misconduct. On the other hand, the police need visual evidence to free themselves from wrongful or malicious accusations.

On August 9, 2014, in Ferguson, Missouri, Michael Brown, an 18-year-old black man, was fatally shot by Darren Wilson, a white police officer. Darren Wilson was responding to a police dispatch's call for the search for a robbery suspect. When he encountered Michael Brown and another black man, he believed they matched the description of the robbery suspect. An initial confrontation occurred on the street and led to an altercation in which Michael Brown allegedly engaged in physical struggle with the officer through the window of the police vehicle until Wilson's gun was fired. Brown and his friend then fled. Darren Wilson's pursuit of Michael Brown ended in the fatal shooting that later became the center of national controversies. One version of the story suggests Brown was moving toward the officer and hence was perceived as a threat even though he was unarmed. Another version of the story depicts Brown as surrendering himself with both hands raised. Due to the lack of a video recording the entire happening and the different eye-witness accounts, naturally people in the nation chose whatever they were inclined to believe as the truth. Fueled by a longstanding racial tension in the area, this equivocal event involving a dead black man and a white police officer quickly ignited social unrest in Ferguson as well as in other cities across the country. The way the Ferguson Police Department responded to the protests and riots entailed more criticisms. The militarized response suggests the police were not only willing to use deadly force but also employing lethal weapons that are deemed excessive by critics. The debate on militarization of the police force is ongoing, but it is beyond the scope of this chapter.

The truth about the shooting of Michael Brown remains open to discussion. To avoid such incidents, many police agencies responded by requiring their officers to wear a body camera on duty so as to record their interaction with citizens. The concept is similar to the one behind dashboard cameras installed on police vehicles. In the 1990s, allegations about racial profiling in traffic stops were rampant. A dashboard camera thus became a solution as it records the car being stopped and the interaction between the officer and the driver. One benefit of dashboard cameras is increasing officer safety, because officers could review the recordings and learn from others' mistakes, such as turning back on a potentially dangerous situation. These videos could also reduce civilian complaints, and most of time they can prove the officer was not at fault in the complaint. Early studies found that 96.2% of the time, the recording from a dashcam exonerates the officer (Westphal, 2004; IACP, 2004). Moreover, they can have a positive impact on public perception of the police, and the videos can be used as crucial evidence in a trial or sources of information on homeland security issues. With funding provided by the Department of Justice's Office of Community-Oriented

Policing Services (COPS), the majority of major police agencies in the United States now have this type of camera installed on their police vehicles. Ironically, the Ferguson Police Department did not install dashboard cameras on their vehicles (CNN.com, 2014).

Despite the benefits of dashboard cameras, most police–citizen interactions actually take place outside the view of a dashboard camera. Hence, the call for body cameras gains a louder voice in the wake of recent police shooting incidents. The belief is wearing body cameras can be useful for documenting evidence, preventing complaints from the public, resolving complaints, and strengthening police transparency and accountability (COPS, 2014). Basically the benefits of this implementation are expected to be similar to those of dashboard cameras, but it is believed body cameras can offer a more complete perspective on the interaction in question, assuming the cameras are being used properly.

The concern, however, is with respect to privacy and trust. When recording an event, participants may be captured by the camera unwillingly. For example, the victims of an incident may not want to have their identity revealed on a video, or they may not want the event to be recorded and become a permanent trauma that could be revisited anytime in the future especially when such videos end up on the Internet. The people in the video may have very little control over who can view the video and under what circumstances the video will be used. Police officers may also perceive this as a sign of distrust because they may feel the purpose of the body camera is to monitor their every move. To be fair, these concerns are not really new, nor are they specific to body cameras. In modern days, cameras are already prevalent in one's daily life, such as traffic cameras, surveillance cameras, or a random person's cell phone. Nevertheless, to officially adopt this implementation in the police force requires a thorough evaluation of its pros and cons. The storage and management of such videos produced by police body cameras need comprehensive planning. Otherwise, it could result in a waste of taxpayers' money when it fails to resolve the issues of public trust, and it could bring about more controversies about the use of digital evidence. For example, why should the public trust the police-generated video if the video does not fully show the officer's action because the camera is worn on the officer's body? When the police claim the footage is not available, how do the public know if the camera was not functioning or the police are simply trying to hide the evidence? Can the video be digitally altered? Should the videos follow the chain of custody as a form of digital evidence? Should these videos be used for any purposes other than resolving a citizen complaint? Should these videos be released to the press without all participants' permission? All these potential issues need to be given some forethought before implementation, instead of waiting for incidents where we realize these cameras do not really help strengthen a better relationship between the public and the police.

Some research endeavors funded by the federal government have been underway to address some of these issues in an attempt to offer evidence for the presumed benefits of police body cameras. For instance, the National Institute of Justice in 2014 has announced a few grants dedicated to the study of police body cameras. It is too soon now to draw conclusions. A policy of this scale should not be based on anecdotal evidence, and scientific evaluation takes time. However, police departments should still proceed to enact sensible policies regulating the use of these cameras since implementation is already underway. Some additional benefits or drawbacks may be less straightforward and require more exploration. In the meantime, both the public and the police ought to be more patient and give each other some time to get used to this new implementation. The police should be mindful of the concerns the public might have especially when they are not yet familiar with body cameras, whereas the public should understand the success of this implementation lies in sound policies and the police may need to go through some trial and error before perfect policies, if existent, can be reached.

☐ Technology

The implementation of body cameras in police work is a salient example that shows how technology is expected to improve police performance. The concept of using a camera to garner visual evidence has been long-standing. Besides dashboard cameras and body cameras, some agencies now have installed a camera on Taser guns, so as to evaluate how police officers use these nonlethal weapons and their effect on controlling a potentially dangerous situation. These videos can work both ways. They can protect officers from false complaints or they can expose inappropriate use of such weapons. As technology advances, most of the videos produced from these various types of cameras can offer high-resolution recording and clear audio. Many of them allow for filming in lowlight. Some manufacturers have developed software to help manage and analyze the videos, such as adding GPS stamps to connect the videos to a map. Some cameras even have the capacity to offer live stream so that a real-time visual can be provided for people who are not on the scene. This can be seen as a useful weapon at the police's disposal that not only generates solid forensic evidence but also keeps officers safer. Hence, it is not too far-fetched to imagine that one day perhaps a camera on lethal as well as nonlethal weapons will become a common standard in the police force.

Certainly technology utilized by the police is not limited to cameras. Other technologies, such as thermal imaging, drones, lasers, language translators, crime mapping, license plate recognition, global positioning systems, and record databases that provide instant comparison, can all be contributive to police work. Technically they may not be categorized as weapons, but there is no doubt they can greatly enhance efficiency in crime fighting when used properly. The downside is often related to the cost. Before police agencies purchase these technologies, a cost-benefit analysis is warranted. Such analysis should be aimed at determining whether the money spent on these technologies is worthwhile. To this end, police agencies must clearly define their goals first. Without knowing what to accomplish and without clear measurement of this accomplishment, there is no way to know if it is worth spending taxpayers' money on new technologies that may or may not improve police work in spite of the sales pitch. Moreover, ethical issues regarding civil rights also need to be addressed in case these technologies are misused for ulterior purposes.

☐ Policy Implications

As mentioned earlier, the police must be allowed to use weapons in the line of duty. It is equally critical, however, that the police use of force is under control and guidance. The delicate balance depends on two main factors: discretion and policy. This is true for both lethal and nonlethal weapons.

First, police discretion is inevitable. It refers to the officer's decision making given the circumstances. It is impossible to train police officers like a computer which reacts to a situation in the exact same way by following a set protocol. Although the police do have many protocols regarding what procedures should be taken in a given situation, there are still many factors that cannot be fully covered in the protocol. We call these factors variables, because they vary from case to case. When faced with variables, police officers must exercise discretion to decide the best action needed to be taken. When it comes to discretion, it means different officers could make very different decisions in the same situation. For instance, when an officer perceives a threat, the officer must make a quick decision to eliminate the threat. Personal discretion will dictate exactly what action is taken by the officer, because personal discretion also affects how the threat is perceived in terms of severity and urgency. Thus, when an encounter between the police and the public turns into a confrontation, police discretion will determine what force is used. With nonlethal weapons being a viable alternative, the officer can afford to exercise discretion more liberally. On the other hand, without these alternatives, police discretion could be trapped between two extremes, that is, no force or deadly force. Hence, to say the least, police officers should be equipped with these nonlethal alternatives, and training should be in place to guide officers about the proper use of these nonlethal weapons. As mentioned, the use of nonlethal weapons can be excessive and controversial as well. Besides, in some situations lethal weapons are actually more suitable than nonlethal weapons. Either way, better decisions result from better discretion. Education and training are the two main methods to ensure better discretion. Contrary to what is often portrayed in movies, the quality of police work is usually defined by the decisions officers make (i.e., discretion), instead of their physical strength or the speed of their bullets.

Second, departmental policies help guide police discretion. Research found that the type of police use of force is associated with departmental policies in that less restrictive policies on the use of nonlethal weapons could reduce the number of fatal shootings by police (Ferdik et al., 2014). This is to say police officers are more likely to adopt less than lethal options when the agency policies allow them more room to do so. On the other hand, no evidence suggests that adopting nonlethal weapons will expose the officer to more danger because research supports that the police use of the Taser is closely related to the resistance presented more than other situational factors (Crow and Adrion, 2011). This follows that most police officers would not put themselves in harm's way for the sake of using nonlethal weapons.

Nevertheless, less restrictive policies on the use of nonlethal weapons may cause abuse of such weapons. One salient concern is that some officers might resort to the use of nonlethal weapons, such as the Taser, too quickly instead of trying to defuse tension with personal skills (Ready and White, 2011). Hence, it seems departmental policies ought to put some restrictions so as to avoid such abuse. Research found that the level of Taser usage is largely affected by departmental policies (Crow and Adrion, 2011), which means if the department's policy aims to reduce Taser use, it generally would be effective in achieving this goal. Given existing research findings, there seems to be two somewhat contradictory implications. On the one hand, the officers should be allowed more leeway to use nonlethal weapons because by doing so it reduces fatal shootings by police. In turn, it reduces controversies surrounding situations in which deadly force may not be called for. On the other hand, the officers ought to be restricted in their use of nonlethal weapons to avoid excessive use. Is there a way to enact perfect policies that can accomplish both ends? Perhaps there is but the solution certainly is not obvious, considering all the controversies regarding police use of force in these years.

There are few universal policies that can adequately apply to every agency. Each police agency needs to create policies that serve the agency's needs in line with the agency's mission, while the agency's mission must reflect public interest within the jurisdiction. Many controversies arise from the discrepancy between the public's anticipation and the police's self-image. Sometimes the public and the police are actually aiming for the same goal, but public perception somehow suggests otherwise. In this regard, police agencies need to be more transparent in policy making by putting more effort into explaining the rationale behind their policies to the public. The public need to know the police policies about use of force, and understand why such policies are in place. The public need to know that some policies are necessary to ensure the safety of police officers, even though it means that with hindsight, the use of force may seem unnecessary. When the public is more informed, the benefit is twofold. First, it is less likely the public would overreact to a situation in which police use of force is involved. Second, police officers are less likely to find excuses to abuse power and engage in excessive force. Mutual understanding is the key. The public understand the police must use force under some circumstances according to departmental polices so that there is no need to respond to an incident emotionally before all facts are clear, whereas the police understand the public are aware of what action is just and what action is unjust according to the policies so that officers would be less likely to resort to excessive force for the sake of intimidation or manipulation.

Certainly, police agencies cannot expect that the public will actively seek to understand policies. Just because you make something public record, it does not mean most people would pay attention to it. This is why more proactive effort is warranted. Similar to the concept of community policing, police agencies may look for or even create opportunities to communicate with the public about their policies, especially the policies regarding police use of force. When should the public expect to see the police use deadly force? When should the public expect to see nonlethal weapons be employed? To what extent should the officers use such force? Why are they using such force? What should the public do in these situations, either as a participant or a bystander? What are the consequences when officers abuse power or misuse weapons? How will unjust police use of force be determined? Who is overseeing these issues? All these questions ought to be clearly addressed in departmental policies, and then they should be clearly conveyed to the public. An open discussion should be welcome when necessary. Listening to the public does not mean police agencies must give in to every demand from the public. It is always beneficial to know what the public's expectation is even if sometimes the expectation is unrealistic.

Besides written policies, police agencies need to constantly explore better training and screening methods in terms of strengthening police officers' discretion. As mentioned, policies cannot cover all possible scenarios. On a daily basis, officers are making decisions based on personal discretion. Policies not only should guide police discretion but also need to define how poor discretion will be judged and penalized. When it comes to the use of nonlethal weapons, in addition to regulating the timing of using these weapons, policies should encourage officers to exercise better discretion in assessing the manner of using these weapons, since nonlethal weapons are supposed to be used in a non-life-threatening situation in which there is usually more room for different approaches to work.

In addition to nonlethal weapons, the use of technology also needs to be guided by sound policies. Almost every new technology applicable to police work comes with privacy issues. To dispel public doubts on the application of these new technologies, police agencies need clear policies that illustrate the purpose, the procedure, and the safeguard. For instance, a secretive police technique has recently been brought to light, namely, StingRay. It is a device that is intended to track a suspect's cell phone activities, such as texts, emails, phone calls, and location, by functioning like a cell phone tower (Business Insider, 2015). Supposedly this technology should be of great help to the police in tracking criminals and terrorists. The problem is this device may capture data from not only the target but also everyone around the target. Hence, the privacy issue is in question, to say the least. In the absence of public polices, no one knows exactly how the data captured from this device would be used. In fact, no one knows for sure how many agencies have adopted this device in their daily practice. When there is no policy explaining the purpose, the procedure, and the safeguard with respect to the use of such technologies, it is only fair for the public to have doubts on the propriety of applying these spy technologies to police work. Doubt is not something beneficial to police agencies as it further weakens the mutual trust that is essential to a healthy public–police relations.

☐ Summary

In this chapter, we discuss the use of nonlethal weapons and technology in police work. As stressed, the police need to be allowed to use force, so there is no need to automatically assume that the police are in the wrong every time police use of force occurs. The real issue lies in the timing and extent of force. Nonlethal weapons provide an alternative to deadly force when the situation does not involve imminent threat to life. This is not to say nonlethal weapons are not capable of resulting in death. It simply means these weapons are not designed to kill, but they might still induce a fatal outcome. Hence, some people prefer to call them less-lethal weapons instead. Nevertheless, what we call them is nothing more than a label. The important thing to consider is how to make sure these weapons can be used properly. They not only should be helpful in reducing unnecessary killing by the police, but also should provide officers sufficient protection.

The abuse of nonlethal weapons is a distinct possibility, especially since they are perceived as less likely to inflict fatal injuries. Some controversial cases are discussed in this chapter. Even if in some of those cases the officers might not have done anything wrong technically, there definitely is room to examine how the situation could have been handled differently to avoid controversies. Certainly, the police should not be doing their job in fear of controversy all the time. Officers must do what is necessary in response to a situation, without worrying about how their actions may be misinterpreted in the aftermath. There are two factors that may alleviate such worries: discretion and policy. First, police officers need to be trained and encouraged to exercise better discretion. In other words, they need to possess the capacity to make proper decisions that can be effective in resolving a conflict and can be justified under scrutiny. The importance of training needs no further explanation, but simply knowing what they should do is not enough. Officers must be encouraged to make better decisions, rather than doing whatever is more convenient. For instance, losing your temper is more convenient than maintaining patience; using a Taser on someone verbally belligerent is more convenient than talking them down. The convenient solutions may not be the most appropriate. This is where policy comes in as the second factor. Agency policies need to aim not only at regulating police conduct but they should also aim at emphasizing the individual ability to make a better decision when policies do not offer detailed instructions. Moreover, agency policies need to be transparent from the public perspective. The public should be made aware of how policies are in place to regulate police use of force and what the public should anticipate to avoid unrealistic expectations.

This is also true for the police use of technologies. These technologies are often costly, and a lot of them have not been comprehensively tested for their benefits and potential downsides. Evaluation is warranted before spending tax dollars on expensive new gadgets. Agency policies ought to proactively provide safeguards against misuse and dispel public doubts. Because technology is advancing rapidly and can be new to everyone, both the police and public should give each other time to adjust. More importantly, the implementation of such new technologies should not be seen or used as a political stunt. It is not just about looking good or sounding good. If it works, the accomplishment should be clearly defined and publicized, whereas changes need to be made if it does not work. Scientific evidence should be constantly solicited so as to make sure whatever the police are doing with tax dollars actually benefit both the police and the public in the most cost-effective way.

☐ References

Alpert, G.P., Smith, M.R., Kaminski, R.J., Fridell, L.A., MacDonald, J., and Kubu, B. 2011. Police use of force, Tasers and other less-lethal weapons. *National Institute of Justice Research in Brief.* Retrieved on February 12, 2015 from https://www.ncjrs.gov/pdffiles1/nij/232215.pdf

Bailey, W.C. 1996. Less-than-lethal weapons and police-citizen killings in US urban areas. *Criminology & Penology*, 42(4), 535–552.

Business Insider. 2015. Police are using a secret gadget that can track your phone, and they can't talk about it. Retrieved March 16, 2015 from http://www.businessinsider.com/stingray-phone-tracker-used-by-police-2015-3

CNN.com. 2014. No dashcams in Ferguson: One less tool in Michael Brown shooting investigation. Retrieved on February 19, 2015 from http://www.cnn.com/2014/08/14/us/ferguson-dashcams/

COPS. 2014. Implementing a body-worn camera program: Recommendations and lessons learned. Retrieved on February 19, 2015 from http://www.justice.gov/iso/opa/resources/472014912134715246869.pdf

Crow, M.S. and Adrion, B. 2011. Focal concerns and police use of force: Examining the factors associated with Taser use. *Police Quarterly*, 14(4), 366–387.

Ferdik, F.V., Kaminski, R.J., Cooney, M.D., and Sevigny, E.L. 2014. The influence of agency policies on conducted energy device use and police use of lethal force. *Police Quarterly*, 17(4), 328–358.

Homant, R.J. and Kennedy, D.B. 2000. Effectiveness of less than lethal force in suicide-by-cop incidents. *Police Quarterly*, 3(2), 153–171.

IACP. 2004. The impact of video evidence on modern policing. Retrieved on February 19, 2015 from http://www.theiacp.org/Portals/0/pdfs/WhatsNew/IACP%20In-Car%20Camera%20Report%202004.pdf

MacDonald, J.M., Kaminski, R.J., and Smith, M.R. 2009. The effect of less-lethal weapons on injuries in police use-of-force events. *American Journal of Public Health*, 99(12), 2268–2274.

Ready, J.T. and White, M. 2011. Exploring patterns of Taser use by the police: An officer-level analysis. *Journal of Crime and Justice*, 34(3), 190–204.

Sheridan, R.D. 2014. Letter by Sheridan regarding articles, "Taser electronic control devices can cause cardiac arrest in humans" and "TASER electronic control devices and cardiac arrests: Coincidental or causal?" *Circulation*, 130, 167.

Westphal, L.J. 2004. The in-car camera: Value and impact. Retrieved on February 19, 2015 from http://www.policeone.com/police-products/police-technology/articles/93475-The-in-car-camera-Value-and-impact/

Zipes, D.P. 2014. TASER electronic control devices can cause cardiac arrest in humans. *Circulation*, 29, 101–111.

Militarization of the Police

Laurence Armand French

☐ Introduction

There is much concern and consternation within America today concerning what many perceive to be the excessive use of force by law enforcement personnel especially when encountering threatening, yet unarmed, suspects, usually minority males. Part of this problem can be traced to the type of equipment available to law enforcement agencies, notably the increased firepower of modern military-style weapons. Also pertinent to this discussion is the continued undercurrent of racial/ethnic, sectarian, and class biases that are inherent in a complex multicultural environment such as the United States. Add to this the proliferation of high-capacity handguns and assault rifles within the general population, a situation worsened within the twenty-first century by *Second Amendment advocates* such as the National Rifle Association. While better training in the use of nonlethal weapons is a desired outcome for the prevention of the advent of deadly force, the disharmonious relations existing between law enforcement and those perceived by the police to be "troublemakers" also need to be addressed. A common social-psychological principle is that reciprocal antagonism involving members of polarized groups tends to fuel mutual antipathy. Georg Simmel explained this phenomenon as such: "Out-group hostility increases in-group cohesion."[1] Consequently, in divided societies where there this sense of polarized antagonism prevails, such as between white police officer and minority young-adult males, an otherwise minor incident can mushroom into a serious crisis. These situations often lead to elevated emotional states among those involved in the altercation, kicking in the participant's autonomic reactions of the sympathetic nervous system. This results in an increased adrenal response that, at this stage, is difficult to regulate with a rational override, hence resulting in mutual "fight or flight" responses where the better-armed party usually prevails—such as a police officer emptying his/her weapon at the "perceived" threat. This phenomenon is clearly illustrated with the November 29, 2012 Cleveland, Ohio case in which more than 100 police officers in 60 cruisers chased two unarmed blacks, because their car backfiring was mistaken for gunfire, for 22 miles ending when the car stopped and 12 officers on the scene fired 137 shots into the vehicle with one officer, Michael Brelo, firing 49 of those bullets, 15 while standing on the car's hood firing directly at the black male and female through the windshield. Brelo was subsequently charged with voluntary manslaughter but acquitted by a judge at his trial in May 2015. Although the United States now is known for its highly decentralized law enforcement apparatus, there is a long history of the symbiotic relationship between the military and police in enforcing U.S. laws. In addressing these issues we need to look at the interactions between the military and police in American society from its colonial roots to the present day situation.

☐ A Brief History of Police–Military Connection

British common laws prevailed in the 13 colonies along with the concept of county sheriffs and justices-of-the-peace. The sheriff and his deputies were considered to be "officers of the court," a system that continued after independence, making the county sheriff a constitutional law enforcement officer. This system, along with state militias, continued following independence. It is important to recognize the nature of the legal system during this time. Laws did not apply to all members of society but instead were made to protect the privileged class. Even the *Bill of Rights*, notably the first 12 amendments to the U.S. Constitution, pertained only to franchised white males. Women and children held no legal standing and had to rely on church officials for any redress for serious abuse. Blacks and American Indians, on the other hand, were not even considered to be "people" under the Constitution's preamble, "We the people of the United States... ." Indeed, the new U.S. republic's laws were based on the concept of *Divine Rights* under the term, *Manifest Destiny*. Hence, these laws were based on the concept of white supremacy, a political philosophy that encouraged the widespread practice of *ethnic cleansing* in addressing the *Indian Problem*. The new U.S. republic, like many nations at the time, relied on the military as the major national police force giving it overall jurisdiction over state militias and county sheriff's departments.[2]

American Indian tribes posed the greatest obstacle to whites reaping the riches of America and considerable efforts were made to reduce their influence mainly through their removal from lands and resources desired by whites. Colonial militias were organized as a form of local *homeland security* force within each colony with the original function of providing protection from Indian raids or retaliation. This model carried over to the new republic following independence. Hence, the earliest form of policing in American involved a paramilitary organization that had a solid link with the U.S. military. In 1803, the United States not only doubled its size and eliminated French colonial influence; the Louisiana Purchase also provided a dumping ground for unwanted Indian tribes with the creation of *Indian Territory* (Oklahoma). This set the stage for legal, forceful, removal of Indian tribes, a job initiated by the U.S. Army. Clearly, the major law enforcement task of the nineteenth century was policing American Indians. In addition to aiding the militias in fighting Indian flare-ups, the U.S. Army first played a significant policing role in the forceful removal of Indian tribes from the original 13 states west of the Mississippi River to *Indian Territory*. This action is best illustrated by the removal of the Five Civilized Tribes, notably the Cherokees in 1838, known as the *Trail of Tears*. This police action began in May 1838 under Congressional authorization via the 1830 *Indian Removal Act* and was conducted under the direction of the head of the U.S. Army, Major General Winfield Scott. Cherokees were forced at gunpoint and bayonets to leave their homes and placed into makeshift military stockades. By the end of June Scott's men had detained more than 10,000 Cherokees. In all some 20,000 Cherokees were rounded up and forced west to Indian Territory under army guard. More than 4000 died due to this police action, some while in the stockades and many more along the forced march to Oklahoma. Hundreds more died upon arrival in Indian Territory as a result of illnesses, and exposure during the 1000 mile forced march.[2]

The U.S. Army played a significant role in policing states and territories throughout the nineteenth century, mainly policing American

Indians that incidentally involved the United States longest war—the *Indian Wars* (1860s to the 1890s). The long military police action against American Indians in the west coincided with the advent of the U.S. Civil War. The war effort served to mitigate deplorable conditions on the Indian reservations leading to outbreaks by Sioux, Navajo, and Apache, among others. The Great Sioux Uprising, for example, occurred in the fall of 1862 whereby the Santee Sioux, on the verge of starvation, was led by Little Crow in attacks on white settlers occupying their former tribal lands. In June 1863, the U.S. Army, under the command of Colonel Kit Carson, began a punitive expedition against the Navajo resulting in their forceful removal known as the *Long Walk*. As with the removal of the Five Civilized Tribes 25 years earlier, herds, crops, and villages were destroyed and those who refused to be removed were hunted down and killed by the U.S. Army. Eight thousand Navajo were eventually removed to Fort Sumner in New Mexico where many more died due to the poor living conditions in the military concentration camp. Only in 1868 were the Navajo allowed back to their greatly reduced tribal lands.[3]

These police actions using the U.S. Army as the primary law enforcement backup to the U.S. marshals changed dramatically following the end of the U.S. Civil War. Now the Indian campaign became the main focus of the U.S. Army where the west was divided into military regions. Those battles fought from 1865 until 1891 qualified servicemen, both white and black (Buffalo Soldiers) with the *Indian Campaign Medal* thus making the Indian Wars the longest U.S. military campaign, longer than the current war on terrorism in Afghanistan. The *Indian Campaign Medal* provided the forerunner for the *Silver Star* given that a silver citation star was attached to the medal for meritorious or heroic conduct. The highest U.S. military award, the *Congressional Medal of Honor,* established during the Civil War, was also awarded during the Indian campaigns.[4]

Interestingly, the current contentious argument surrounding the Second Amendment has its roots in the British colonial era. The *right to bear arms* was actually a colonial requirement for local policing. During the colonial era, the 13 British colonies maintained militias (Provincial Defense Forces, the forerunner of both the current National Guard system and state police agencies) mainly for protection from the French and Indian forces. The Provincial Defense Force consisted of all able-bodied, Protestant males between the ages of 16 and 60. They were required to own their own musket, a bayonet, knapsack, and cartridge box, with 1 lb of black powder, 20 bullets, and 20 flints. They mustered 4 times yearly and were on-call the remainder of the time. Each regiment was headed by a colonel (commanding officer), and a lieutenant colonel (executive officer), with majors heading battalions and captains in charge of companies. A New England colonial militia captain (later major) Robert

Rogers, created a "commando unit patterned after the Indian fighters, living off the land and making hit-and-run strikes into enemy territory. More companies were added forming a ranger battalion with major Rogers in charge. Rogers "28 Rules of Ranging" provided the foundation for both the Queen's York Rangers of the Canadian Army and the U.S. Army Rangers.[5] Other local protection included night watchmen until the advent of municipal police in the mid-1800s. State police forces came about with the advent of automobiles and state highways that transcended county lines. Again they based their organizational structure on the British colonial "Provincial Defense Force" with a colonel in charge and barracks (companies) headed by captains distributed throughout the state jurisdiction.

Federal law enforcement agencies in the United States, on the other hand, trace their origin to 1789 when Congress authorized the Revenue Cutter Service, now the U.S. Coast Guard, and the U.S. federal marshals. The U.S. marshal is the federal counterpart to the county sheriff, both being officers of the court. The new U.S. republic was now divided into a two-tier law enforcement system based on state/local jurisdictions and the federal jurisdiction. Much of the federal legal system dealt with international relations, including interaction with Indian tribes that initially held the status of independent nations which were dealt with via treaties. George Washington appointed the first 13 U.S. marshals on September 24, 1779, one for each of the states, making them the first "officers of the court" with the responsibility of carrying out the death sentence imposed by the federal courts. The U.S. marshal was also responsible for taking the census in his jurisdiction (state) every 10 years for the annual tally.

The U.S. marshal's office was the civilian federal law enforcement for Indian Country beginning with the Louisiana Purchase. On July 1, 1870, the U.S. Congress created the Department of Justice giving it authority over federal law enforcement, including the U.S. marshals making them the first police agency authorized to enforce federal laws in the states and territories. Given this authority, the U.S. marshals and their deputies played a significant role in Indian Territory during the Indian Wars up until the beginning of the twentieth century. That is why the U.S. marshal and not the FBI is portrayed in western lore, movies, and television shows. Later, in 1908, U.S. Attorney General Bonaparte created the Bureau of Investigation as the investigative arm of his office. In 1932, it was renamed the U.S. Bureau of Investigation, and, finally, in 1935, the Federal Bureau of Investigation or the FBI. Hence, the FBI emerges at about the same time as state police agencies. The "Bureau," however, had its influence in federal Indian Country beginning in 1908 primarily due to passage of the Major Crimes Act of 1885, now sharing these responsibilities with the long-established U.S. marshal's office.

Today the FBI, perhaps best known worldwide, is but one of many federal law enforcement agencies that have emerged over the past century, each with its own special jurisdictional authority established by Congress. All four major branches of the U.S. military (Army, Navy, Air Force, Marines) have their own law enforcement agencies under the Department of Defense (DOD) while the U.S. Coast Guard acts as a law enforcement agent under the newly created Department of Homeland Security (DHS) following the September 11, 2001 terrorists attacks along with numerous other law enforcement agencies including Customs and Border Protection (CBP); Office of Border Patrol (OBP); United States Secret Service (USSS); and the Transportation Security Administration (TSA). Other federal agencies with law enforcement authority include the U.S. Department of Agriculture (USDA); Department of Commerce (DOC); Department of Education; Department of Energy (DOE); Department of Health and Human Services; U.S. Department of the Interior (USDI) with the Bureau of Indian Police (BIA Police) and Bureau of Land Management and U.S Park Rangers; Department of Justice (USDOJ) which includes the U.S. Marshals Service (USMS); the FBI; the Bureau of Prisons (BOP); Bureau of Alcohol, Tobacco, Firearms, and Explosives (ATF); U.S. Drug Enforcement Administration (DEA); and Office of Inspector General (DOJOIG); Department of State (DoS); Department of Labor; Department of the Treasury; and the Department of Veteran Affairs.

☐ The Evolution of Firearms and Deadly Force

During the colonial era and the time of the Second Amendment (1791), muzzle-loader, flintlock firearms prevailed, notably the musket which had a smoothbore like that of shotguns today. This limited the effective range of these weapons often requiring close combat involving bayonets. The advent of the Kentucky rifle during the early 1800s now made the muzzle-loader more accurate and at a greater range. The addition of "lands and groves" in the barrel of rifles and pistols along with a firing cap replacing the flintlock provided greater accuracy but still limited these to a single-shot action. The bow and arrow used by most American Indian tribes provided greater firepower and equal accuracy as the early muzzle-loaders. It was the advent of the rapid-fire revolver, and later the rifle–carbine, that transformed both the U.S. military and law enforcement. Samuel Colt developed a muzzle-loader, black powder, single-action revolver in the 1830s, but its widespread fame came from the Texas Rangers.

The Texas Rangers emerged as the militia for the breakaway Republic of Texas following the disbandment of both the regular army and navy. And the Texas Rangers are closely linked to the Colt revolver. Indeed, the Republic of Texas became the proving grounds for this innovative weapon. Texas was Colt's first customer, ordering 180 .36-caliber holster-model, five-shot, Paterson Colt revolvers for its navy in August 1839. The Texas Rangers, on the other hand, had been ordering them individually since they first became available in 1837. Once President Sam Houston disbanded the Texas navy, these Colts were reassigned to the Texas Rangers. The Texas Rangers often carried three or more revolvers with loaded extra cylinders, greatly increasing their firepower thus enhancing the Texas Rangers' image as a deadly force. Once Texas was annexed to the United States in 1845 as a slave state, the Texas Rangers became one of the most deadly forces during the Mexican War (1846–1848). With modifications suggested by the Texas Ranger (trigger guard, six-shot capacity...), the United States adopted the revolver now called the Colt 1851 Navy Revolver. As such, it became a popular sidearm for both Union and Confederate forces during the U.S Civil War (1861–1865).[6]

The development of the self-contained (integrated) cartridge (bullet) further enhanced the firepower of repeating weapons, both rifles and pistols, and allowed for more rapid firing breech-loading single-shot rifles such as the Sharps Military Carbine, widely used during the Indian Wars. Prior to the self-contained cartridge, both long guns (smoothbore or rifles) and handguns (including the revolver) required the additional step of activating the "cap-and-ball" sequence whereby black powder had to be packed into each cylinder (muzzle loading) along with the installation of a firing cap at the hammer. The early cartridges had the powder held together in a cardboard bullet that was either rim- or center-fired by a firing pin that ignited the percussion cap. The French were the first to invent the cartridge which soon evolved from a cardboard to a metallic shell (shotgun shells still use the cardboard format). Indeed, the .22 caliber percussion cap soon became a bullet in itself with the .22 LR (long rifle) one of the most popular calibers today.

The advent of the bullet led to new adaptations to the revolver, notably the Colt Single Action Army Revolver introduced in 1873. The civilian model of this .45 caliber six-shooter was commonly known as the *Peacemaker*. It was used by both the military during the Indian Wars and by law enforcement, notably U.S. Marshals and county sheriffs, as well as being popular with outlaws. The .45 Colt saw action in all military actions from 1873 including World War I. It was replaced with the semiautomatic, single-action .45 caliber M1911, 7-shot pistol which itself served the U.S. military through three wars (World War II, Korea, and Viet Nam). It fired a shorter ACP (automatic Colt pistol) round than the Colt revolver that was also in submachine guns like the Thompson and its various adaptations. The M1911 semiautomatic pistol was unique in that it was gas-operated so that the slide extracted the spent round and cocked the hammer on the back stroke while chambering another round from the magazine on its return. The M1911 was single-action in that the initial round needed to be manually fed which, in turn, cocked the hammer. It replaced the double-action .38 caliber military revolver that proved ineffective against the Moros during the Philippine resurrection early in the twentieth century. Later modified to double-action, the .45 automatic continues to be popular with military (USMC, Navy, Delta Force) units and with federal (FBI, etc.), state (New Mexico, etc.) and local police (LAPD, SWAT, etc.) in the United States as well as in other countries. The M1911 was the prototype for later semiautomatic pistols, foreign and domestic, that now come in a variety of calibers. When the U.S. military replaced the .45 pistol with the M.9 mm Beretta, many local law enforcement agencies followed suit but the trend in both law enforcement and the military is to go back to the more powerful .45 caliber pistol.

The cartridge (bullet) was used by the U.S. military in its Sharps rifles which eventually led to the popular .45–70 caliber. The single-shot, breech loaded, falling block design provided a rate of fire of 8–10 shots per minute. The carbine model was used by both Union and Confederate cavalry troops during the Civil War and was used throughout the Indian Wars. During this same era, Christopher Spencer created the lever-action repeating rifle that was also used during the Civil War and throughout the Indian Wars. It used copper rim-fire bullets stored in a removable 7-round tube magazine. The bullet (aka cartridge, round) led to the development of repeating rifles and carbines with lever, bolt, or pump actions. Winchester lever-action rifles and carbines were built on this model and became even more popular in the U.S. west following the Civil War up into the early twentieth century. Indeed, the Winchester Model 1873 became known as "the gun that won the west." Models 1873 and 1876 (centennial model) were widely used during the Indian Wars and the Spanish-American War as well as by the Texas Rangers and the Canadian North-West Mounted Police. The 1876 model also introduced smokeless powder that replaced the black powder round. Lever-action .30–30s remains a popular hunting rifle to this day.

The introduction of a rapid-fire weapon, the *machine gun* also has its origin with the Civil War with the *Gatlin Gun*. The Gatlin gun was used by Union forces during the Civil War and during the Indian Wars, the Spanish-American War, Philippine-American War, Boxer Rebellion, and the Russo-Japanese War, and other conflicts. The Gatlin gun used a cyclic multibarrel design that synchronized the firing-reloading sequence keeping the barrels from overheating. Just as the U.S. Civil

War provided the incentive for better military firearms, World War I provided the testing ground for submachine guns, two American models that saw action in both military and civilian operations. The M1918 Browning Automatic Rifle (BAR) was designed in 1917 and saw limited action during the World War I, yet remained the light machine gun for both the U.S. Army and the U.S. Marine Corps up through the Viet Nam War where it was replaced by the M60 machine gun. The BAR used the powerful 30–06 caliber bullet and came with 20-round magazines and a bi-pod for prone firing. The M1928A1 Thompson submachine gun (Tommy gun) was developed at the end of the World War I (1921) and chambered the .45 ACP round that the military 1911-model .45 pistol used. It came with a variety of magazines holding from 30 to 100 rounds. It was widely used during World War II, Korea, and Vietnam. It was widely used by law enforcement agencies in both the United States and Israel and by U.S. gangsters and the Irish Republican Army (IRA) during the 1969–1998 conflict known as *The Troubles*. The BAR was good up to 500-yards making it a versatile military weapon and was issued as the automatic weapon among USMC squads. The Thompson, on the other hand, had a limited effective range like its .45 pistol of about 50–60 yards.[7] Indeed, these two weapons were often stolen from National Guard Armories and used by criminals like Pretty Boy Floyd, the Barrow Gang, the Barker-Karpis Gang, the Baby Face Nelson Gang, the Dillinger Gang, and Bonnie and Clyde during America's *Great Crime Wave* during the Depression Era. This use of deadly force by these gangs armed with Thompsons and BARs provided J. Edgar Hoover the incentive he needed to petition the U.S. Congress to finally arm the FBI which up to that time remained unarmed and had to rely on either local law enforcement agencies or the U.S. Marshals for backup.[8]

The .30 caliber M1 carbine was also one of the first gas-operated assault weapons with the M2 having the option for semiautomatic or fully automatic fire. The M1 carbine was widely used in World War II, Korea, and Vietnam as well as by British forces in Northern Ireland during *The Troubles*. It remains a popular weapon among law enforcement agencies in both the United States and abroad. The more powerful M1 rifle (Garand) is a gas-operated, semiautomatic rifle using the 30–06 caliber round like its BAR counterpart. It was widely used during the World War II and in Korea. It was replaced by the M14 which was of a similar design as the M1 Garand but instead of using an 8-round clip, it used a magazine like the BAR and M1/M2 carbine and had the capacity for fully automatic fire. It also used the 7.62 NATO round (US 308 caliber) which was similar to the 30–06 round. The M14 is still the NATO preferred long-distance rifle. However, the jungle warfare in Vietnam required another type of weapon hence the M16 rifle in caliber 5.56 mm.

Used selectively by the U.S. Army beginning in 1963, it became the standard service rifle for the U.S. military in 1969 and was later modified to fire 3-round burst per trigger pull. The smaller version, M4 carbine, is used as well.[9] The M16 rifle/M4 carbine played a significant role in the militarization of U.S. law enforcement in that they coincided with the advent of Special Weapons and Tactics (SWAT) teams devised during the 1960s in Los Angeles for riot control, and with the creation of the Law Enforcement Assistance Administration (LEAA) each state began creating its own SWAT teams for potential riot control as well as to participate in the national *war on drugs*. An even more intense militarization effort followed the 9/11/01 terrorist attacks and the new *war on terrorism*. Clearly, a major factor in the militarization of law enforcement in the United States was the creation of SWAT teams and their federal support through programs such as LEAA and Homeland Security.[10]

☐ The Contemporary Scene

Federal training of police included law enforcement agencies within the United States and beyond, began in earnest in an effort to curtail the influx of illicit drugs into America. The focus turned to Mexico following the successes in Colombia, resulting in the recent militarization of the U.S./Mexico border. The *war on terrorism* that began following the 9/11/01 attacks in New York and DC led to another round of federal funding for state and local law enforcement through grants made available through the newly created DHS. Here, the Border Patrol, National Guard units, state, country, and local law enforcement act in unison against perceived threats against the United States. Granted these coordinated efforts are needed and the end result has contributed toward better law enforcement coordination and standards, nonetheless, some feel that these achievements have been at the expense of traditional community policing. The effectiveness of these coordinated efforts was clearly demonstrated with the manhunt subsequent to the 2013 Boston Marathon terrorist attack on April 15 which included both federal and state (Massachusetts and New Hampshire) law enforcement personnel.

Police: The Civilian Military—Authority and Status

An interesting outcome of the militarization of law enforcement is the corresponding rank/status phenomenon. Anthropologists and sociologists have long recognized that authority and privilege are associated with a person's status within the society. In this sense, all organized societies define the status hierarchy. Ralph Linton noted that cultures usually subscribe to two types of status, *ascribed* based mainly on sex, age, and family/clan affiliation; and *achieved,* based on individual accomplishments or elective processes such as occupation, marriage, and the like. I would add two subcategories to the latter—*enhanced* and *fabricated* status. Enhanced status is when an obviously legitimate status is elevated to something higher while fabricated status is when someone creates a status far removed from their actual position.

In societies like the United States where there are no inherited titles, military status ranks high. The military is based on a caste system that divides commissioned officers from enlisted personnel. The officer ranks (O-1to O-10), in turn, are divided into two echelons with "field-grade" ranks, that is major and above, being the most prestigious. Within this system, a captain (O-3) is the commanding officer (CO) of a company or battery while a battalion has a lieutenant colonel (O-5) as the CO and a major (O-4) as the executive officer (XO). Colonels generally head regiments, while brigadier generals are CO's of brigades and major generals lead divisions and so on. Thus, a field-grade officer can command anywhere from 1,000 to 10,000 military personnel, including entire armies or navies. The United States did not have a permanent four-star general until 1866 when this status was awarded to U.S. Grant. The Confederate Army, however, created the four-star rank during the Civil War. When U.S. Grant became president, the sole four-star rank was passed on to William T. Sherman and then to Philip H. Sheridan who led the Indian Wars in the west. This permanent rank was not allocated again until 1919 when it was given to John (Black Jack) Pershing. World War II not only saw the proliferation of four-star generals and admirals but also the creation of the five-star generals; even then, only nine men held this rank; four admirals and five generals. This was a lifelong position and was retired in 1981 with the death of General Omar Bradley. George Washington was added to the list posthumously on July 4, 1976. Today, the head of the Joint Chiefs-of-Staff, the heads of the four military services (Army, Navy, Air Force, and Marines), and the head of NATO forces, are four-star generals or admirals, albeit superior to other four-star officers serving under their command.

Civilian superiors, such as the Secretary of the Army, Navy, and Air Force, do not hold military rank. Yet, the use of military rank predominates within U.S. society especially within the paramilitary police organizations. The military structure at the state level, on the other hand, occurs with the National Guard which follows the regular military rank structure with the governor appointing the commanding general. Using

New Hampshire as an example, the commanding general until recently was a brigadier general. However, the prolonged *war on terrorism* in Iraq and Afghanistan, with greater reliance on the federalized National Guard, resulted in an upgrade to the rank with a major general in command of the overall National Guard and brigadier generals as heads of the two components, the Army National Guard and the Air National Guard. This inflation at the higher echelon of military rank has also afflicted the U.S. military in general.

Within the civilian criminal justice systems, both federal and state, the top law enforcement officer is the Attorney "General." Within the state system, the state police is the law enforcement agency assigned to the attorney general's office with statewide jurisdiction. At the federal level, the U.S. Marshal's office was designed in 1789 to act as the law enforcement for U.S. Courts with a high marshal appointed to each state and territory. State police agencies, on the other hand, usually follow the military rank structure with the director using holding the rank of O-6 colonel acting under the direction of the AG (attorney general). State police forces often have "troops" located throughout the state's jurisdiction, again using the military rank model with a captain heading the troop.

When looking at the largest municipal police department in the United States, New York City with a population of over 8 million and covering 468.9 square miles in five boroughs, it becomes evident that a well-organized police force is justified. In the New York Police Department (NYPD) we again see the five-star rank, this time for the police commissioner who supervises up to 40,000 personnel. Clearly, this falls under the enhanced status category while the basic rank hierarchy below the commissioner's office clearly follows a reasonable paramilitary format: chief of department holds four stars; bureau chief, three stars; assistant chief, two stars; and deputy chief, one star. Inspectors are full-bird colonels; deputy inspectors, lieutenant colonels; while captains head precincts. Below captains are lieutenant, sergeant, and patrolmen. Captains head the 76 precincts. The Los Angeles Police Department (LAPD) has jurisdiction for a similar geographic area as the NYPD but with half the population. The LAPD's (third largest U.S. police agency—Chicago is second largest), rank structure has the politically appointed (by the mayor) chief of police holding four-star general status with the assistant chief (Deputy Chief II) holding three-star general rank while the Deputy Chief I is a two-star general, and police commanders hold one-star status. The intermediate field-grade military ranks (O-4 major/lieutenant commander; O-5 lieutenant colonel/commander; and O-6 colonel/captain) are omitted with the next highest rank being that of captain and then lieutenant, police sergeant II/police detective III (staff sergeants), police sergeant I/police detective II (buck sergeants); police detective I/ police officer III (corporals) with police officers I and II having no military insignia.

Other police departments soon picked up on this military-style ranking, assigning themselves the rank of general regardless of the size or jurisdiction of their department. The proliferation of this fabricated status was soon demonstrated with heads of departments putting on general's stars (including four or five stars) regardless if their legal status was high sheriff or chief of police. This practice clearly speaks of the "arrogance of position" raising serious questions concerning their commitment as public servants, who are licensed to use lethal force, in their role in securing public safety. Law enforcement represents a public service agency, one licensed to use deadly force in protecting the public at large. Enhanced and inflated status has little to do with carrying out law enforcement functions. Instead, it can lead to a self-fulfilling prophecy whereby the chief or high sheriff comes to believe that they are, in fact, far superior to their fellow officers, an image conveyed to the public as well. Law enforcement was not intended to be a high-status occupation. All that is necessary to convey their authority to the public is the uniform and shield or badge. The standard for any state should be the state police force which has the broadest jurisdiction.

☐ Conclusions

The issue of policing is not a simple matter where a single solution can solve all the issues confronting America and other societies. All societies have rules and enforcement agents whether they are a secular or sectarian dictatorship, or some form of representative government (parliament, legislature, executive committee, etc.). Indeed, law enforcement, by its definition, compels police to enforce the laws/rules promulgated by societal leaders. Unfortunately, given human nature, these rules are often biased to favor the majority or the group in control. Consequently, discrimination needs to be addressed at the leadership level (U.S. Supreme Court, federal–state legislative levels) first before we can adequately train and better regulate enforcement agencies such as the police. These issues are more complex within multiethnic, multisectarian societies including contemporary, developed societies such as the United States.

Good, viable solutions were offered by the numerous Presidential Blue Ribbon commissions/committees that followed the riots of the 1960s and 1970s. They included such concepts as hiring police officers with a minimum of a 4-year liberal arts college degree. Instead, police academies morphed into military-style boot camps (cop shops) providing the mind-set of an occupation force ready to face the perceived "enemies" of society. This was the antithesis of the concept of "community policing" whereby law enforcement is an integral component of the community within its jurisdiction (its patch/beat). Ideally, the police would be trained to be available to all members of the community regardless of race, ethnic origin, gender, or religion. And for this to be effective, the police would have to be attired for easy recognition without looking like a military occupational force.

Another recommendation at the time of the Omnibus Crime Control and Safe Streets Act was for civilian oversight in the form of "police commissions." Unfortunately in many instances these positions became politicized with civilian commissions, like the prosecution, often automatically siding with law enforcement when issues of excessive force or blatant discrimination surfaced. Toward this end, the states and federal government need to provide professionally trained omnibus personnel that are independent of any political or ideological influence. And as stated earlier, law enforcement personnel, especially chiefs, sheriffs, et cetera, need to lose the military attire that attempts to present themselves as admirals and generals. Law enforcement personnel also need to align with their community and not with the *Blue Brotherhood* (aka *Bubbahood*). Clearly, this is a profession where unions should be exempt if only because they instill a sense of "us versus them" within society, and yet another factor is the polarization of police and segments of the public.

Another critical factor is the screening process. Psychological scales can determine, to a fair accuracy, not only mental suitability (*mad cop*) but also problematic character logic flaws including serious personality disorders (*bad cop*). The machismo/macho image also needs to be addressed, especially if steroids are involved. At minimum, psychological reassessments need to be administered if a clique of officers falls into this group. This can be seen as a form of intimidation among members of society, notably minority members of the community. Moreover, training needs to focus on the use of nonlethal approaches to crisis situations where the subject does not have a viable weapon (firearm, machete, etc.). Psychological protocols can train officers to control their level of adrenal response to crisis situations (those situations where officers empty their clip of 15–17 rounds in their response to a perceived threat). These options have been available for over 40 years, yet seldom employed. Law enforcement is an integral part of any viable society, how it is used is often a political factor and as long as divisions are allowed and fostered within a society, so will police abuses.

☐ References

1. See, G. Simmel, *Conflict* (K.A. Wolff, trans.). New York, New York: The Free Press, 1955; L. Coser, *The Functions of Social Conflict*. New York, New York: The Free Press, 1956.
2. See, L.A. French, *Winds of Injustice: American Indians and the U.S. Government*. New York, New York: Garland Publishing, 1994; L.A. French, *Legislating Indian Country: Significant Milestones in Transforming Tribalism*. New York, New York: Peter Land, 2007; *Indian Removal Act* (May 28, 1830). U.S. Statutes at Large, 4:411–412.
3. *Op cited* #2; and C. Kluckhohn and D. Leighton, *The Navajo*. Cambridge, Massachusetts: Harvard University Press, 1946; G. Bailey and R.G. Bailey, *A History of the Navajo*. Santa Fe, New Mexico: School of American Indian Research Press, 1986; L.R. Baily, *The Long Walk*. Los Angeles, California: Westernlore Press, 1964.
4. See, F.N. Schubert, *Black Valor: Buffalo Soldiers and Medal of Honor, 1870–1898*. Wilmington, Delaware: Scholarly Resources, Inc. 1997; R.W. Stewart (ed.). Winning the West: The Army in the Indian Wars, 1865–1890 (Chapter 14). *The Unites States Army and the Forging of a Nation, 1775–1917, Vol. I* (*Army Historical Series*). Washington, DC: U.S. Government Printing Office, 2001.
5. See, J.R, Cuneo, *Robert Rodgers of the Rangers*. New York, New York: Oxford University Press, 1959; J.F. Ross, *War on the Run: The Epic Story of Robert Rogers and the Conquest of America's First Frontier*. New York, New York: Bantam Books, 2009.
6. See, L.A. French, *Running the Border Gauntlet: The Mexican Migrant Controversy*. Santa Barbara, California: Praeger, 2010; C.H. Harris, III and L.R. Sadler, *The Texas Rangers and the Mexican Revolution: The Bloodiest Decade, 1910–1920*. Albuquerque, New Mexico: University of New Mexico Press, 2004; C.T. Haven and F.A. Belden, *A History of the Colt Revolver*. New York, New York: Morrow, 1940; J.E. Parsons, *The Peacemaker and Its Rivals: An Account of the Single-Action Colt*. New York, New York: Morrow, 1985.
7. See, C. Bishop, *The Encyclopedia of Weapons of World War II*. New York, New York: Sterling Publishing, 2002; FM23–15, *Basic Field Manual—Browning Automatic Rifle, Caliber 30, M1918A2*. Washington, DC: U.S. Department of Defense, 1940; *M1 Thompson (Tommy Gun)—Submachine Gun, History, Specs and Pictures, Military Security and Civilian Guns and Equipment*, www.militaryfactory.com/smallarms/detail.asp?
8. See, B. Burrough, *Public Enemies: America's Greatest Crime Wave and the Birth of the FBI, 1933–34*. New York, New York: Penguin Books (2004).
9. See, E.D. Ezell, *The Great Rifle Controversy: Search for the Ultimate Infantry Weapon from World War II through Vietnam and Beyond*. Harrisburg, Pennsylvania: Halstead Press, 1984; D.R. Hughes, *The History and Development of the M16 Rifle and its Cartridge*. Oceanside, California: Armory Publications, 1990.
10. See, P.B. Kraska and V.E. Kaeppler, Militarizing American police: The rise and normalization of paramilitary units, *Social Problems*, 44(1):1–18, 1997.

6

CHAPTER

Racial Profiling: The Intersection of Race and Policing

Michael L. Birzer

☐ Introduction

On August 9, 2014, Officer Darren Wilson of the Ferguson, Missouri Police Department was on patrol when he observed Michael Brown, an 18-year-old African American male walking in the middle of the street. Officer Wilson pulled up beside Brown and requested that he get out of the middle of the street. Facts later reveal that Brown had robbed a convenience store minutes earlier. Brown allegedly took a package of cigarillos. What happened next is sketchy but witness reports say that Brown reached into Officer Wilson's police cruiser and which point an altercation occurred between him and Officer Wilson. A single gunshot was then heard. Within seconds, witnesses saw Brown running from the police cruiser with Officer Wilson chasing after Brown and yelling for him to stop. Brown turned around and charged at Officer Wilson. Officer Wilson fired several rounds with his handgun killing Brown.

The shooting prompted rumors throughout Ferguson, albeit inaccurate and largely fueled by the media that Officer Wilson executed Brown as he had his hands up and was attempting to surrender. A St. Louis area prosecutor announced that a grand jury had decided not to indict Officer Wilson and that no charges would be brought against Officer Wilson. A Department of Justice investigation also cleared Officer Wilson of wrongdoing in the shooting of Brown (United States Department of Justice, 2015a).

The shooting of Michael Brown and the decision not to indict Officer Wilson sparked several days of protests and riots resulting in millions of dollars of property damages to Ferguson's businesses. Since the Ferguson riots, unrest has erupted in many other cities across the United States as the result of what many perceive to be police abuse of African American citizens. More recently in Baltimore, following the death of Freddie Gray, an African American man who died while in police custody, large-scale rioting and unrest occurred. Six police officers were charged with crimes ranging from second-degree murder to unlawful arrest of Freddie Gray. The rioting in Baltimore resulted in property damages to businesses totaling nearly 10 million dollars.

Community activist groups such as Black Lives Matter contend that the recent shootings and other abuses of African Americans at the hands of the police are merely the tipping point of what they view as biased police practices and a criminal justice system in which they more often than not are treated unfairly. In Ferguson this appears to be the case. After the Michael Brown shooting incident the Department of Justice investigated the practices of the Ferguson Police Department in light of reports of biased practices against racial minority citizens (United States Department of Justice, 2015b). The investigation uncovered a systemic pattern of biased practices against African Americans by police authorities in Ferguson. Specifically, the Department of Justice found that the police department engaged a pattern or practice of

- Conducting stops without reasonable suspicion and arrests without probable cause in violation of the Fourth Amendment

- Interfering with the right to free expression in violation of the First Amendment

- Using unreasonable force in violation of the Fourth Amendment

The Department of Justice found that Ferguson Municipal Court has a pattern or practice of

- Focusing on revenue over public safety, leading to court practices that violate the 14th Amendment's due process and equal protection requirements.

- Court practices exacerbating the harm of Ferguson's unconstitutional police practices and imposing particular hardship upon Ferguson's most vulnerable residents, especially upon those living in or near poverty. Minor offenses can generate crippling debts, result in jail time because of an inability to pay and result in the loss of a driver's license, employment, or housing.

The Department of Justice found a pattern or practice of racial bias in both the Ferguson Police Department and the municipal court.

- The harms of Ferguson's police and court practices are borne disproportionately by African Americans and that this disproportionate impact is avoidable.

- Ferguson's harmful court and police practices are due, at least in part, to intentional discrimination, as demonstrated by direct evidence of racial bias and stereotyping about African Americans by certain Ferguson police and municipal court officials.

This chapter examines the intersection of race and the police through what many believe is racial profiling or bias-based policing. The chapter has three primary objectives. First, an examination of past abuses by the police on racial minorities will be discussed, providing the important context into why so many racial minority citizens have distrust of the police and equate the practice of racial profiling as a continuation of past injustices. Second, the chapter examines how racial minority citizens experience what they believe to be racial profiling. The chapter concludes with a discussion on strategies that the police and community can engage together in an attempt to begin to resolve racial profiling.

☐ A Fractured History

Racial minorities, particularly African Americans, have had a long and troubled history of disparate treatment by United States Criminal Justice Authorities. Some argue that the police, the law, the courts, and the correctional system, have all been used as instruments of oppression based on race, and if the nation is to complete the processes eliminating this subjugation, we "must move to eliminate all vestiges of racial bias" from the criminal justice system (Moss, 1990, p. 88).

The perceptions of racial profiling by the police of minority citizens may exist, in part, because of the long history of disparate treatment by the criminal justice system. Consequently, there is a race coding of sorts that takes place and which culminates in stereotyping that associates race to crime (Quillian and Pager, 2001, 2010). The symbolic criminal figure is often portrayed as a black male who is in turn subjected to increased surveillance, profiled, policed, adjudicated, and incarcerated disproportionately. Therefore, racially biased policing in law enforcement is merely a symptom of a more serious problem that afflicts the entire criminal justice system. Moreover, it represents one of the single most pressing issues that face fundamental criminal justice policy and practice which to date has only been addressed in a superficial manner.

Underpinning of Race

Race and policing, and for that matter, criminal justice are inextricably linked. To dismiss this fact is somewhat naïve. Consider that more than 60% of the individuals in prison are racial and ethnic minorities. In the case of black males the data are more alarming. One out of eight black males in their 20s are in prison or jail on any given day. While Black Americans represent between 13% and 14% of the general population, "they are disproportionally represented in every aspect of the criminal justice system, as victims, offenders, prisoners and arrestees" (Ogletree et al. 1995, p. 13). In federal prisons alone, blacks represent nearly 38% of inmates serving time. Similarly, over half the inmates incarcerated in our nation's jails is either black or Hispanic (United States Census Bureau, 2012).

The intersection of race and the criminal justice system from a historical lens reveals a pattern of the disparate treatment of racial minorities, especially of blacks. This includes of a legacy of Jim Crow laws and other injudicious acts. From the inception of the American police they were charged with upholding the status quo, a status quo that in some cases legally mandated inequality (Barlow and Hickman-Barlow, 2000). The following is a telling description of this legacy:

> The fact that the legal order not only countenanced but sustained slavery, segregation, and discrimination for most of our nation's history, and the fact that the police were bound to uphold that order, set a pattern for

police behavior and attitudes toward minority communities that has persisted until the present day. That pattern includes the idea that minorities have fewer civil rights, and the police have little responsibility for protecting them from crime within their communities. (Williams and Murphy, 1990, p. 2)

During slavery in the United States, slave catchers acting with police authority in many southern states were charged with the duties of returning runaway slaves to their masters. Every slave-owning state had active, established slave patrols, and though they had many functions within the community, their primary objective was to act as the first line of defense against a slave rebellion. Slave patrols caught runaway slaves, enforced slave codes, discouraged any large gathering of blacks, and generally perpetuated the atmosphere of fear that kept the slaves in line (Hadden, 2001).

Slave patrols were a unique form of policing. They worked closely with the militia and were virtually given free rein to stop, search, and when necessary, beat slaves all under the protection of the legal system. It is an uncomfortable fact that police forces in the south actively pursued slaves. Slave patrols proved to be an integral step in the development of southern police organizations (Wadman and Allison, 2004). Professor Samuel Walker referred to slave patrols as "a distinctly American form of law enforcement," and he went on to say that they were probably the first modern police forces in this United States (Walker, 1999, p. 22).

Slave patrols were made up of mostly poor whites that frequently brutalized slaves caught without passes after curfew (Genovese, 1976). The influence of slave patrols in the southern states is the cornerstone to what some contend is the institutional racism mentality that continues to plague some American police departments (Wadman and Allison, 2004).

At the conclusion of the radical reconstruction (the year 1877) in the south, the criminal justice system represented one of the major instruments of white supremacy (Walker, 1980). Some police agencies in the south maintained white supremacy through their brutal and discriminatory practices toward African Americans (Barlow and Hickman-Barlow, 2000). Slavery was officially abolished in 1865 but its dark shadow would continue to impact African Americans for many years to come (Patterson, 1998). Southern whites found ways to defy reconstruction, preserve their social order which subsequently limited economic growth (Lynch, 1968). The humiliation and subjugation of African Americans continued through the enforcement of Jim Crow laws, economic and educational segregation, and the acceptance of lynching as means of social control (Wadman and Allison, 2004).

If an African American found himself on the wrong side of the criminal justice system he had a mark even going into a trial. If he did go to trial, the deck was stacked against him.

> The standards of evidence in most court trials were so low, the means of obtaining damaging testimony so dubious, the importance of constituted authority so evident, that insurrection prosecutions at law must be seen as a religious more than a normal criminal process. By such means individual slaves, and sometimes the whites affiliated with them, were made sacrifices to a sacred concept of white supremacy. (Wyatt-Brown, 1982, p. 402)

Jim Crow laws (roughly 1880s through the 1960s) were passed throughout the south as a way to keep African Americans in inferior positions segregated from whites. Under Jim Crow laws it was permissible in Mississippi to require African Americans to pass literacy tests in order to vote. Other states throughout the south in unison fashion passed similar Jim Crow laws that mandated separate bathrooms for African Americans, forbade interracial marriage, prohibited African Americans from eating in the same room as white customers in restaurants, forbade black barbers from cutting a white man or woman's hair, and made it unlawful to bury African Americans in the same cemeteries as deceased whites.

In September 1962 a federal court ordered the University of Mississippi to accept James Meredith, a 28-year-old African American, much to the vehement opposition of segregationists. The Mississippi governor at the time said he would never allow the school to be integrated with African Americans. This outraged whites and set off several days of violence and rioting in Oxford, Mississippi. Meredith, accompanied by federal law enforcement officials enrolled on October 1, 1962. The point that is important here is that James Meredith was escorted into the University of Mississippi by U.S. marshals, with minimal or no protection by state or local police authorities (Hendrickson, 2003).

There are many cases throughout the 1960s, where police authorities refused to protect racial minorities. In her book *Mississippi Challenge*, Mildred Pitts Walter describes police practices in the State of Mississippi during the 1960s.

> Good citizens averted their eyes. Law-enforcement officers, if not actually involved, did nothing to prevent the seizure of jailed suspects, and no mob leader is known to have been punished. Police officials refused to launch investigations when ordered to do so. Some victims were seized in daylight hours and blowtorched immediately after their trials for murder. Yet no one was able to identify the mob leaders. (Pitts Walter, 1992, p. 79)

Law enforcement's refusal to protect citizens is further exemplified by the many civil rights protesters in the 1960s that were regularly pelted with rocks and bottles from hostile white crowds while police authorities offered minimal or no protection (Pitts Walter, 1992). In some cases the police were the aggressors. One such case occurred in Canton, Mississippi in the late 1960s. In this case the police used tear gas to disrupt a peaceful civil rights march (Katz, 1995). Images such as Birmingham, Alabama's public safety commissioner Eugene "Bull" Connor further exemplify how law enforcement was used by the power structure to maintain deplorable practices by any standards. Commissioner Connor was an outspoken proponent against racial integration and without hesitation ordered the brutal use of police dogs and fire hoses to disperse civil rights demonstrators in Birmingham (Nunnelley, 1991).

What follows is another example of law enforcement's tactics used against African Americans in the southern United States. This event took place in 1967. Neshoba County Mississippi's sheriff Lawrence Rainy and his deputy sheriff Cecil Ray Price were two of the 18 Mississippians convicted in 1967 of conspiring to violate the civil rights of three civil rights workers who were murdered in 1964. It was determined that the murders were carried out with the help of Neshoba County sheriff's officials and the Ku Klux Klan (Huie, 2000).

Let's examine a few more fairly recent cases. One incident occurred early one spring morning on March 3, 1991, in Los Angeles. That is when Rodney King, an African American man was pulled over for a traffic violation. He had been speeding and took police on about a 15-min car chase. According to police, King emerged from his automobile in an aggressive manner that suggested he might have been high on drugs. Numerous officers confronted King and before handcuffing him, they delivered over 50 blows with their batons, numerous kicks, and two 50,000 shock volts from a Taser stun gun. Twenty other police officers stood by and watched the beating. Here is how King (2012) described the beating in his official memoir:

> Suddenly I was being hit with multiple baton blows to every part of my body—my knees, ankles, wrists, and head. The beatings continued to rain down on me. (King 2012, p. 45)
>
> How many bones did they have to break, how many quarts of blood did I have to lose before their fear died down? After 40 plus baton blows, after a dozen kicks to the head, neck, and testicles, after not one but two Taser electrocutions, how could they possibly justify continuing to mutilate me because they were still afraid of me? (King, 2012, p. 95)
>
> Each baton hit and boot kick, each word I remembered the officers screaming at me, "you better run. We're going to kill you, nigger, run!" (King, 2012, p. 102)

A man named George Holliday, standing on the balcony of a nearby building, videotaped the incident. The next day, he gave his 81-s tape to Los Angeles TV channel 5. By the end of the day, the video was being broadcast by TV stations around the world. Four days later, all the charges were dropped on King and four officers were charged with felony assault and other beating-related charges.

The Independent Commission on the Los Angeles Police Department came out 3 months later documenting the "systematic use of excessive force and racial harassment in the LAPD." It also noted management problems and condemned the department's emphasis on crime control rather than crime prevention which served to isolate the police from the public (Christopher Commission, 1991).

On April 29, 1992, the four police officers were found not guilty of committing any crimes against Rodney King. After the announcement of the verdict, the local police were caught fleeing several south central Los Angeles neighborhoods where large-scale riots had erupted. The National Guard was called in and the riots ended 6 days after they began. The collateral damage was the deaths of 42 people, the burning of 700 structures, the arrest of nearly 5000 people, and almost $1 billion in property damage.

Almost a year after the riots, LAPD (Los Angeles Police Department) Sergeant Stacey Koon and Officer Laurence Powell were convicted by a federal jury for violating the civil rights of Rodney King. The other two officers involved in the incident were acquitted. The 1991 *Report of the Independent Commission on the Los Angeles Police Department* (also called the Christopher Commission Report) was published in the aftermath of the notorious beating of Rodney King. The report stated:

> Within minority communities of Los Angeles, there is a widely held view that police misconduct is commonplace. The King beating refocused public attention to long-standing complaints by African Americans, Latinos, and Asians that Los Angeles Police Department officers frequently treat minorities differently from whites, more often using disrespectful and abusive language, employing unnecessarily intrusive practices such as the "prone-out" (prone-out refers to the police practice of placing individuals who are being questioned on the street face down on the pavement), and engaging in the use of excessive force when dealing with minorities. (Report of the Independent Commission on the LAPD, 1991, p. 70)

An incident involving Malice Green and the Detroit police in 1992 is another case to consider. In this case four Detroit police officers beat to death a black motorist named Malice Green. Green was reportedly struck in the head numerous times by one of the officers with a heavy flashlight which resulted in his death. Four Detroit police officers were charged in Green's death.

One other case of police abuse occurred in New York City in 1997. This case involved Abner Louima, a Haitian immigrant who was brutalized by New York City police officers. Louima suffered a torn bladder and intestine which required several surgeries to repair the damage after New York police officers beat him and rammed the handle of a toilet plunger into his rectum and mouth at a Brooklyn police station. Several officers plead guilty or were convicted in federal court for violating Louima's civil rights.

In November 2011, Kenneth Chamberlain, Sr., an unarmed 67-year-old African American was shot to death by White Plains, New York, police officers. Mr. Chamberlain, a retired veteran of the U.S. Marine Corps, who suffered from a chronic heart condition and wore a pendant to signal Life Aid, had mistakenly triggered his medical alert, and although he told police he was OK and did not need assistance, he ended up in an hour-long standoff with the police. Witnesses report hearing the officers using the "N" word and screaming at Mr. Chamberlain to open the door. Police eventually broke in to Chamberlain's apartment and shot him with a stun gun and a beanbag shotgun. The police said they were acting in self-defense because Chamberlain was emotionally disturbed and pulled a knife on them. Only recently did the Westchester District Attorney's Office announce that they will present the case to a grand jury.

On July 17, 2014 New York City police officers investigated Eric Garner, a 43-year-old African American man who was suspected of selling single cigarettes on the street corner without a tax stamp. There were some words exchanged between Garner and the investigating officers and a physical confrontation ensued. One of the police officers placed a choke hold on Garner while pulling him to the ground in an attempt to handcuff him. Garner reportedly yelled that he could not breathe as several officers plummeted on him. During the altercation Garner lost consciousness. Police officers called for an ambulance and Garner was transported to a hospital where he later died. At no time did the officers attempt to administer CPR (cardiopulmonary resuscitation) or other lifesaving procedures. An autopsy by the medical examiner determined that Garner had died from the choke hold along with compression of the chest and positioning by the police officers while being arrested. A grand jury failed to indict the police officers involved in the incident. Once again, like many others, Garner's death at the hands of police authorities sparked national outrage.

You may question how these incidents, especially those occurring many years ago, are relevant to a discussion of racial profiling. The past injudicious treatment of minorities by the police is very relevant to the contemporary discourse centering on racial profiling. For many racial minority citizens, especially African Americans, the police represent a troubled part of their history. The police in many states enforced oppressive laws that resulted in devastation for many racial minorities. The not-so-glamorous portrait of history can help foster a better understanding of the perceptions and experiences of racial minority citizens with racial biased policing along with other concerns about the police by the minority community.

☐ Racial Profiling

Racial profiling represents one of the most pressing issues of our time. American Presidents have spoken about it and denounced it. Police authorities are trained not to engage in it. Laws have been passed criminalizing it, and reported cases have been the subject of endless hours of media stories. In spite of the considerable attention centering on racial profiling, a great many racial minority citizens say it happens frequently in their communities.

When black and white Americans are surveyed about the prevalence of racial profiling, they both believe it is a widespread phenomenon in the United States (Police Executive Research Forum, 2014). A 2004 Gallup poll of citizens found a substantial proportion of Americans believe racial profiling is widespread. Fifty-three percent of those polled think the practice of stopping motorists because of their race or ethnicity is widespread (Carlson, 2004). One other analysis of public opinion of racial profiling found 90% of blacks that were polled believed that profiling was widespread, followed by 83% of Hispanics, and 70% of whites (Weitzer and Tuch, 2005).

Experiencing Racial Profiling

A few years ago the author spent nearly two years interviewing racial minority citizens who believed that they had been racially profiled by the police. Fifty-three African American citizens, 33 Hispanic citizens, and one Asian citizen living in the midwestern United States were interviewed after they reported that they had been profiled because of their race and subsequently stopped while driving their automobiles. There were six common themes that appeared to weave through each of their stories of racial profiling. Because racial profiling is arguably one of the more contentious issues impacting the relationship between racial minority communities and police authorities, a summary of these themes are presented in the following pages. For a more detailed discussion of this study see Birzer (2013).

Theme 1: Emotional and Affective

In this theme, citizens talked about their emotional experiences as a result of being stopped by the police for what they believe to be based solely on their race. For many, these emotions had a lasting impact. This theme carried with it several subthemes such as embarrassment, heightened alertness upon seeing police, increased anxiety, anticipation of being stopped, frustration, anger, a sense of helplessness, and lasting emotional trauma.

Racial minority citizens spoke of the embarrassment of being stopped by the police. They told stories of being made to stand alongside the street while their vehicles were being searched. They spoke of the humiliation of having other motorists staring as they drove past. Finally, they felt a sense of embarrassment because they firmly believed that they did not do anything wrong, and that the sole reason they were stopped was for driving while being black or brown. This seemed to be exacerbated by the reason for the stop (e.g., cracked windshield, failure to use a turn signal within 100 ft of an intersection, cracked brake light, tinted windows, etc.). There was a pervasive feeling among participants that the police use, for example, a pretext such as a cracked windshield as a reason to stop them, when the real underlying motive may be that they suspect other criminality, which, according to participants, is perpetuated by race, appearance, type of car, and/or geographical area. In order to cope, many participants said they purposively avoid driving in areas where there is a high probability that the police will be present. Read how some of the citizens describe the feeling of embarrassment and humiliation when stopped by the police.

Sharla, a black female in her early 40s with a graduate degree and employed as a parole officer, recalls one memorable encounter that she and her family had with the police. Sharla and her family were stopped one summer morning at about 12:30 a.m. They had been playing cards at a friend's home and as they were driving back to their home they were stopped by the police. During the encounter, she questions the treatment her family received by the police. Sharla's husband was driving a 1987 Cadillac which he takes great pride in keeping in pristine condition. Sharla was sitting in the front passenger seat, and two of their friends along with their toddler grandson were sitting in the backseat. All were black with the exception of the grandson who Sharla described as biracial. Listen to Sharla tell the story.

My husband was driving and we noticed the police were following us for a long time. The police officer signaled his red lights and we heard the siren and we pulled over. He walked up to the car and asked for my husband's driver's license. My husband gave him the license. He [the officer] then asked where we were headed to. My husband said, well why do you need to know, why did you pull me over? Then the officer said do you have your registration? So my husband pulls it out and gives it to him. My husband asked the officer again why we were being stopped. And then my husband asked, "What did I do wrong?" The officer was like just stay right here, as if we were going to go somewhere. So he goes back to his car and he never told us what he stopped us for. Finally he walked back to our car and we noticed two other police cars drive up and I was like what the hell, what's going on? So he comes back to the car. Now I begin to question him and was asking like what is the problem? He says well your car is reported stolen. We were like what! What are you talking about! So then he tells us we need to get out of the car, first he tells my husband to step out of the car. So my husband steps out of the car and he [the police officer] says well I'm going to have everybody step out of the car.

By this time there were five other police cars that had driven up, so there were a total of like seven police officers. So he asks my husband to step back, does his procedure, and asks him if he can search the vehicle. I started talking then and said no, why do you need to search our vehicle? If it was reported stolen why are you searching the vehicle? And I want to know who made the report? So then he says, well ma'am, I'm not addressing you and you need to be quiet. I said No, I will not be quiet. This car is registered to us—you see who it is registered to, my husband. The owner is driving the car so how can it be stolen. The officer got really upset with me because I was arguing with him and asking him questions. He said that I was being argumentative and that if I did not shut up he was going to put me in the back of the police car. So now my husband is angry because he [the officer] just threatened to put me in the police car for trying to find out what's going on. My husband started yelling that you just pulled us over because we are Black. After several more minutes it was over, all of sudden the officer said we could get back in our car and were free to leave. We did not even get an apology. As we were walking back to our car one of the officers said, I suppose you are one of the ones that are going to say we racially profiled you too. We just got back in the car and got out of there.

My husband drove right down to the substation to file a complaint. He told the supervisor that we don't appreciate this and my family was embarrassed, all these people were watching us and they just randomly picked us. My husband told the police supervisor at the substation that he wanted to see the stolen car report. They never did produce the report.

Sharla describes how embarrassing it was for her as a parole officer to be standing alongside of the road while police officers searched the car. Sharla said, "There were cars driving by and slowing down to get a look." She said, "We were all standing out on the side of the street at 12:30 a.m." Sharla attributes it all to being black and driving a nice looking car at 12:30 a.m. A few days after the interview I received a follow-up email communication from Sharla. She wrote that she forgot to mention that after the stop, "they did not receive a ticket." She also related that "they [the police] never knew I was a parole officer until they asked for my driver's license and saw my badge." Sharla writes verbatim in her email.

> They [the police] wanted to know what the badge was for and I told them I was a parole officer. One of the officers must have recognized me and he told me that he asked me to issue a warrant over the phone a while back and he told the officer—the one that had stopped us, that that he remembered me from the parole office.

DeMarcus, a black male in his late 20s, who is college educated with a master's degree, employed as a youth care worker, describes the embarrassment he felt when he and his wife (who is white) and their small child were stopped while driving on a highway in the midwestern United States. DeMarcus began the interview by telling me that even though he has never been in trouble or arrested, being stopped by the police is just "part of his world," he said, "I have just gotten used to it."

DeMarcus along with his wife and their daughter were returning from a long trip one afternoon driving to their home when they were stopped by a highway patrol trooper. DeMarcus describes the incident.

> We were on the highway just on our way home. I saw the police car pass us going the opposite direction. I noticed that he immediately made a U-turn and started to follow us. He really followed us for a while, maybe a mile or two, and then stopped us. He was a young White trooper. He told me the reason he was stopping me was because I was following a semitruck too close. I thought to myself what! He asked for my driver's license—and then with no explanation he asked me and my wife to get out the car. He separated us at opposite ends of the car. He started going back and forth between us asking us questions. It seemed like he was purposively trying to mix up our stories. He kept asking where we were coming from and where we were going and this and that. He kept asking the same questions over and over. My daughter was still in the back seat and she was scared.
>
> After a while he asked me if he could search my car. I told him well you're not going to find anything in the car except my bag of clothing. He

then said, where did you guys say you were coming from again, did you say you were from Texas? I was like no! I told you Albuquerque, and he was like are you sure you didn't say Texas. I said no I didn't tell you Texas. So he kept trying to use that line over and over again and he had us out there for a good 45 min. My wife started getting irritated. She told him this is against the law—you can't do this. He didn't say anything. Yeah, he searched and the first thing he went for was my bag. I have a big Nike duffle bag, big duffle bag for school and you know he's digging through clothes and shoes. You know he searched the car, let us go, and no ticket, not nothing...Even though you're like I don't want him to search my car because you're not going to find nothing...This whole thing made me feel bad, I was upset, it was just, you know, really embarrassing. I have learned not to argue with them [police] when I get stopped. If you do they make it hard on you. There is just not a dammed thing you can do about it.

DeMarcus believes the reason he was stopped was because the officer saw a black male and white female driving along the highway and probably thought that they were drug smugglers. DeMarcus concluded that the trooper kept trying to trip them up on their story by saying, "are you sure you didn't say you were from Texas." DeMarcus is convinced that his race prompted the suspiciousness on the part of the trooper coupled with the fact that he was just leaving a rural and predominantly white community. He said the officer used the pretext of following the semitruck too close as the reason to stop him even though, according to DeMarcus "he [trooper] could probably care less about that charge." He explains, "It was embarrassing to be stopped like this and standing along the highway with my wife and little girl while he searched our car and asking if I had any guns or drugs in the car."

Jada, a Hispanic woman in her early 30s described it this way:

I was embarrassed that someone who knows me would drive by and see me standing along the street with the police searching my car. You know there must have been four or five police cars. You know that you haven't done anything and it hurt so badly and you can't do anything about it. You know what, this all boils down to being a Latina driving a customized car in America. You learn to expect this.

Many described increased anxiety while driving and seeing the presence of a police car. For example, one participant remarked, "I started driving really conscientiously when I saw the police car." Another participant, Javier, a Latino from Dodge City in his early 20s described it this way, "I noticed the officer pull a U-turn and start to follow me. When I first saw him I really got nervous and in the back of my mind I knew he was going to start following me."

Rodney, a college educated African American male in his late 20s provides further context to what many minority citizens experience while driving.

> For many of us, especially African American males we laugh and joke about it, but this is a serious matter. Whenever I drive past the police, I find myself getting nervous even though I've done nothing wrong. We get a scary feeling when driving past the police, even when we've done nothing wrong. There's something about driving past the police that makes you scared and it turns you into the perfect driver. Whenever I'm driving and I spot the police, I'm aware of where they're at. I'm constantly checking my mirrors to keep an eye on them.

The sense of anxiety that citizens described while driving and spotting a police car, led to the "anticipation of being stopped." There is a subconscious feeling they could be stopped. Rita, a Hispanic woman in her late 20s describes the anticipation of being stopped this way: "As I was driving, I saw the police officer sitting in the parking lot and I was mindful of his next potential move." One citizen said this:

> I saw him [the police officer] sitting in the parking lot and he stared at me as I drove by. I knew there was a good chance he would start following me. I was about maybe a block away and I saw him pull out and come in my direction. He followed me for about two more blocks and I remember thinking, OK he is going to stop me any minute. That's just a fact when you are Black and driving late at night.

Citizens described feeling frustrated and angry when stopped by the police for what they believe to be racial profiling. The frustration and anger is usually controlled because they know if they openly exhibit emotion, it will make matters worse. Many described a sense of helplessness, or as one participant put it, "there is not a damn thing I can do about it." One young African American male in his mid-20s said:

> They [the police] always ask if they can search my car; they let me know that I have a choice. So I let them search because I know I had nothing to hide. I knew if said no, he would have called more officers and it would have been worse. You know there is nothing you can do, and you better not say anything or they will make it tough on you.

Theme 2: Symbolic Vehicle

The second theme that emerged from the interviews highlight the frustration and anger of being stopped for what they say is for stereotyping because of their race coupled with in some cases the type of car they drive. This was the case with Ana, a 34-year-old college-educated Hispanic female and former correctional officer now employed as an advocate for crime victims. Ana describes the anger and frustration she felt and how she questioned the officer's motive.

> I was driving a 1985 Cutlass Supreme low rider. It had gold plates. My family is in the business of customizing cars. My brother borrowed my car that day because he had a job out of town and my car got better gas mileage. My son had a doctor's appointment and I had to get him there. I asked my brother if I could use his car because my son needed medicine. He said, no sweat, take my Cutlass, we just painted it, but it's ready. My brother said to take his wife's tag and put it on the car. That tag had not been registered because they were restoring the car and they hadn't used it in forever.

Ana recalls that this was a onetime thing and that she just wanted "to get from point A to point B and back with no problems." She continues her story.

> The car had very expensive rims and sits low to the ground...I saw the sheriff's car traveling in front of me. I was a behind him a little ways. I made a turn onto [location purposively taken out] and noticed that the sheriff's car made a U-turn and got behind me and started following me. Now I am a very good driver and I was thinking to myself that this can't be happening. I know from my friends that they will stop you if you're driving a low rider because they think you are just gang banging Mexicans. He followed me for a while, maybe a mile or so and then stopped me. By this time I was pretty upset about what was happening... When he came up to the car I told him you better have a good reason to stop me. He told me he was randomly running tags and that he ran my tag and it was not assigned to the vehicle. I remember thinking he is stopping me because I'm driving a low rider which they associate with Mexican gang members. I got upset and yelled at him. I was yelling that this is not a serious thing and why did you turn around and follow me in the first place. He told me to get out of the car because I was being verbally aggressive. I kept on questioning him about why he turned around and started to follow me. He then grabbed me and forcibly pulled me from my car and handcuffed me. I remember that he searched me in front of his video camera. He searched my car and impounded it and he refused to let my brother pick it up. I think that he was maxing out his authority because I was so angry and not very cooperative with him. I asked if I could pull it into a parking lot and he said no. I know my actions might have made this worse, but I watched the whole thing play out and I knew what was going on. He turned around to follow me just because I am Hispanic driving a low rider. I was embarrassed that someone I know would see me standing alongside of the road in handcuffs. I lived in the area where I was stopped.

Ana believes she was profiled because of her Hispanic ethnicity coupled with the fact she was driving a customized Cutlass Supreme low rider. She said, "We were traveling westbound and there is no way he could get behind me unless he intentionally braked to do so. That's why I feel I was profiled."

Many racial minority citizens that were interviewed believe police authorities hold stereotypical beliefs about the type of vehicle that minority citizens drive as well as the appearance of their vehicles. For example, they believe if you are, for example, black, and driving an expensive car, this will attract increased police suspicion because of the belief that the vehicle is too expensive for a black citizen to drive. One black male said, "They stopped me because I was Black and driving a nice car. They probably think I am not supposed to drive a nice car. If I was driving my Kia I would have never been stopped." Another black male in his early 30s, is convinced he was stopped by police and peppered with interrogating questions for simply being black, and driving a newer model Mercedes. In another interview, Rick, a 28-year-old black male said, "You know, it was just the type of car I was driving." During the interview with Rick, it was revealed he was driving a 1995 Chevy Caprice with customized rims and tinted windows. Another participant, Angela, who is a black female in her early 50s, talked about being stopped by police authorities for driving a nice car.

…It's like they think you are not supposed to driving this nice car. It's like we are still in slavery. They never issue me a ticket so I think it had to be because I was Black and driving that nice Jaguar. You know the thing is that I never got a ticket. They would just check me out and let me go.

Some racial minority citizens believe the make and model along with the appearance of their car will attract police attention because it is perceived as the type of car a minority would not drive. There is a belief that the police construct the "symbolic vehicle" based on stereotypes. The "symbolic vehicle" would include customized apparel such as wheel rims, nice paint job, sits low to the ground (low rider), window tint, gold around the tag, etc. Participants believe the police associate certain cars with black and Hispanic drivers.

An interview with Melvin, a black man in his early 20s reveals it was not necessarily a customized car that resulted in him being stopped, but rather for driving an expensive car. Melvin was stopped for a turn signal violation. Here is how Melvin describes it:

When the police officer walked toward my 2005 Cadillac CTS, he says is this your car? The officer didn't ask for my driver's license, instead he wanted my insurance. I think the reason for this is because he thought a young African American male can't drive a nice car. After he looked at my insurance, he then asked me for my driver's license. I thought it was fishy but being an African American sometimes you have to bite your tongue when it comes to certain situations.

Perhaps the story that most effectively illustrates the symbolic vehicle theme was one shared by a 62-year-old black male who is employed as a custodian. This story is especially important because the officer interjects the symbolic gesture of race and ethnicity along with the symbolic vehicle into the context of the stop.

> I was driving my Ford F-50 two-toned extended cab pickup truck. I noticed the police officer driving in the opposite direction. As we passed each other, I noticed he looked directly at me and seemed to be surprised. It was kind of strange. I just had a feeling I would be stopped. I watched in my rear-view mirror and sure enough, he did a U-turn and turned on the red lights. I immediately pulled over and stopped...There were two White police officers in the police car. They approached on each side of the truck. He asked for my driver's license. I asked him why I was being stopped and he said for having tinted covers over my headlights. Now listen, you know this was at 10 o'clock in the morning...I received a ticket for driving with covers over my headlights. I didn't realize this was even a violation because they're sold in just about every automotive store. As he was giving me the ticket he kind of looked my truck up and down and said your truck kind of looks like the kind of truck a Mexican would drive.

Theme 3: Nature of the Violation

Another common theme was named "Nature of the Violation." In this theme, participants describe the pre-textual basis of their being stopped by police authorities. In other words, they believe the police routinely use, in their words, "petty" or "minor" traffic violations to stop and "harass them" because of their race.

The U.S. Supreme Court decided that pre-textual stops by police authorities are legally permissible. The Supreme Court in the 1996 decision *Whren v. United States* decided that the police can stop motorists and search their vehicles if probable cause exists that the occupants are, for example, trafficking illegal drugs or weapons. Under the Whren decision, police can stop motorists for a traffic violation even though the traffic violation may not be the underlying motive for the stop. Regardless of the legality of this police practice, participants feel that they are routinely stopped for "minor traffic offenses" and that the police often use these minor traffic offenses as a reason to profile them.

Many citizens reported that they did not receive a traffic citation after they were stopped. The irony here is many citizens may view this as a desirable outcome, but to minority citizens this seems to reinforce the racialized aspect of being stopped. For example, the absence of a traffic citation seems to signal to minority citizens that their suspicions of a racially motivated stop are supported. Professor Karen Glover (2009) made note of this in her research on racial profiling. According to Professor Glover (2009, p. 97), "The traffic stop, innocuous as it appears to some and especially when no citation is issued, is a micro-level occurrence that demonstrates the state's reach on a macro-level."

In 60 (65%) stops reported by participants, traffic citations were not issued. While on the other hand, 32 (35%) stops resulted in a traffic citation or a fix-it ticket being issued. In 30 (35%) stops reported were for what participants described as "being suspicious" and/or for "tinted windows."

Theme 4: Officer Demeanor

Citizens felt like they were treated like criminals after being stopped by the police. This is how Peter, a Hispanic male in his middle 30s, and a former U.S. Army demolition expert who holds a master's degree, describes his experience. As a preface to Peter's story, he was traveling in Wichita on a major thruway at about 5:00 p.m. His children, both Hispanic, were in the backseat. He was driving a black 1998 Dodge Neon with tinted rear windows. The car also had a clear plastic film cover over the license plate. The officer stopped Peter for the tinted windows.

Peter was in a hurry when he left his residence because he had to pick his wife up from work. In his haste to get his children out the door and into the car, Peter left his driver's license at home. During the stop, the officer confirmed that Peter had a valid driver's license. Here is how Peter describes his experience.

> I didn't feel like I was doing anything wrong and I really think this was a racially motivated stop. He [the officer] acted superior, talking down to me and his voice, his words, the way he talked and acted was aggressive. He treated me like I was inferior...I thought the way he treated me was awful and if they are getting away with this with me, what else are they getting away with?

As Peter continues to tell his story the emotionally laden context of the stop is revealed. I sensed that this incident was emotionally charged for Peter. He continues:

> My kids were frightened and they thought something was going to happen to me. You know, he didn't have to talk to me like that in front of my kids. They were afraid and saw law enforcement as bad people because of this situation. I mean, I was angry, but I didn't want my kids to see me that way, they [police] are not all bad, even if I think this one was wrong.

Peter believes his incident was racially motivated. For Peter, this was reinforced by the police officer's comments about what Peter believes is his Hispanic heritage. Peter explains further in the following passage.

> When he [police officer] came back up to the car, he said that he wasn't going to give me a ticket for the tint being too dark, but instead he was going to give me a ticket for you know those plastic film covers you can get to put over your license plate. He was still asking about my driver's license. I think I asked him why he still thought I didn't have a driver license even after he confirmed it in the computer. He told me that usually when he pulls people over like me they usually don't have a driver's license, or it's suspended and they start coming up with excuses as to why they don't have a license on them.

After the officer used the term "people like me," Peter recognizes that he may have just been profiled because of his Hispanic heritage. Peter is upset and questions the officer regarding the statement. He continues:

> I said, wait a minute! People like me! I asked him what he meant by people like me? He seemed surprised that I was questioning him, and then he really tried to explain himself. I think he knew I caught him. I really believe that he didn't think I was going to challenge him on that statement. He really started to change his tune after that.

Peter was greatly bothered by this stop. He believes the officer was pushing his weight around. Peter has never been in trouble with the police and spent many years in the military. After his discharge from the military, he enrolled in college and earned a master's degree. Peter said, "The officer kept repeating to me that not having your driver's license on your person is an 'arrestable offense.'" I asked Peter to explain why he felt that this incident was racial profiling. Peter believes that when the officer used the term "people like me," that the officer was making an association to undocumented Mexicans living in the United States. He said that the officer knew he got caught and did not expect me to challenge him. Peter believes that the officer used the threats of arrest to make it seem like he (the officer) was doing Peter a favor or cutting him a break. The motive, Peter believes, is so that he (Peter) would not make an issue out of the racialized remark. Peter said what really surprised him about this incident was that the officer was black.

During one group interview session of African Americans the discussion was centered on the officer demeanor theme. One male in his middle 20s suggested if the police were polite and improved their communication skills when dealing with minority citizens it would minimize many negative perceptions of the police. He said, "It's all in the way they talk to us." He admits he has a past arrest history along with several what he referred to as "run-ins with the police." He said the officer's communication during the initial contact can go a long way. The participant suggested in some of his encounters the officer's demeanor escalated his reaction which in some cases resulted in him arguing with and challenging the police. Here are a few remarks of one other focus group participant.

> In the academy, if they were to train them to be polite and then take action, it would kill a lot of problems. None of them know how to communicate. They don't even talk to us right. You are automatically a threat to them. I think a lot of Black men get offended because they [the police] make them feel like less than a man, especially in front of other people. If you run from them you get a case, if you say something smart to them, you get a case. You can't talk smart to them or question or challenge them about anything. There is nothing you can do. If you try to, it makes the situation worse.

Theme 5: Normative Experiences

Many citizens that were interviewed accept racial profiling a normative part of their lives. The interviews revealed a pervasive feeling that the chances of being stopped by police authorities for the most minor traffic infraction is very real for minority citizens. This was especially prevalent among black male participants. For example, during one group interview session with eight African Americans (six males and two females), one participant, a black male in his early 60s, when asked about what he things of when he hears the term racial profiling replied, "I think about Black men." Another participant underscored this sentiment and said, "I've really gotten used to being stopped, it's just a part of life for a Black man." Another participant replied, "Getting stopped by the police is a reality in our neighborhood. White communities don't understand because they don't face this like we do. It's a matter of fact to us." Recall Arnold, the African American minister who shared the many incidents of being stopped in eastern Kansas. Arnold said, "It's just a routine fact of life, at first I really had a lot of rage built up inside, but as I have matured in life, I learn to accept it as the norm."

Perhaps the most revealing statement that underscored the normative experience is the one volunteered by Cory, a black male participant in his late 20s. Here is what Cory said:

> It's almost like we are in slavery. Every time we are driving around we got to watch out because we might get stopped. You know I have become so used to the possibility of being stopped it's like an everyday thing. You get used to it after a while. When I see a police officer, I automatically begin to think that I may be stopped. It is always there in the back of your mind, it's automatic, you just think about it when you see the police car.

Cory's narrative is troubling. Here we have an African American male in his late 20s, a productive citizen raising a family, equating the experience of potentially being stopped by police authorities to slavery. He captures how a great many minority citizens feel. Participants constructed an almost normative expectation of being stopped by the police. The "normative experience" theme was strong throughout this study and was often intertwined with the other themes.

Theme 6: Race and Place

Many citizens that were interviewed believe there is a greater likelihood of being stopped in certain geographical areas of the communities in which they reside. They describe this in two parts. First, there is a sense that as racial minorities they are more likely to be stopped in what they described as predominately white and affluent neighborhoods. Second, there is an increased chance of being stopped in economically disadvantaged areas including areas targeted by the police.

Racial minority citizens say they consciously avoid driving through some affluent white neighborhoods for fear that they will attract police attention. This theme was discussed during one focus group. One black male who is employed as a house painter recalls driving through an affluent, predominately white neighborhood and being followed for several blocks by the police. He believes it was simply because he was black and "out of place." He explained he had a paint job that he was finishing in the neighborhood. He makes it a habit of not driving through some neighborhoods in order to avoid police scrutiny, even if it means driving several blocks out of his way. Many citizens that were interviewed described altering their routes in order to avoid police attention.

The race and place theme not only reveals a heightened awareness among participants of being stopped in predominately white affluent neighborhoods, but also neighborhoods disproportionally impacted by crime including those that are economically disadvantaged. Citizens reported being stopped by police authorities for driving, for example, in lower income areas, many of which have high crime rates.

☐ Solving a Complex Problem

Racial profiling is a phenomenon that many white citizens will most likely never experience in their lifetimes. Racial profiling may be witnessed by white citizens, but not experienced. Even the basic interaction between the police and citizens living in black communities is most likely "completely foreign to White citizens" (Barlow and Hickman-Barlow, 2000, p. 86). What was striking about the interviews reported previously in this chapter is that for many racial minority citizens, profiling by the police remains prevalent in many parts of their lives. So what are the solutions to begin to resolve the perception or reality of racial profiling? Moreover, what has to be done in order to restore the trust between the police and minority community? As a start, there are six prongs that are important in order to address this complex problem: (1) training; (2) fostering mutual trust and respect; (3) professional motorist contacts; (4) building and sustaining community coalitions; (5) communication, and (6) community-oriented policing strategies.

Training

Police officers should be trained in bias-based policing and the dire consequences of engaging in this practice. Corollary training should focus on cultural diversity.

Racial Profiling Training

Racial profiling training should include the purpose and scope of the agency's data collection strategies. This training should ensure that both recruit training and in-service training for veteran police officers provide information regarding racial profiling laws in the jurisdiction and data collection mandates (mandatory or voluntary) involving the department. If a police agency collects stop data, training should include the proper procedure to record information regarding police stops.

The most effective racial profiling training is training that is made as hands on as possible. Police officers may benefit from having active role-playing and problem-centered learning exercises. These include scenarios where, for example, racial minority citizens allege the police department engages in racial profiling. Police officers could then work in small learning groups to tailor strategies addressing the allegations. It may be beneficial to have members of the racial minority community participate in racial profiling training. This may result in an understanding from both the police and the citizens. In other words, the police and citizens learn from one another. This may heighten a mutual understanding of why the police do what they do in certain situations.

In racial profiling training, it is important to engage officers in reflection, an internal audit of sorts, of his or her practices in the field. This is reflective learning which has long been touted as an effective educational and training technique. Reflective learning techniques propose that learning does not necessarily result from the experience per se, but rather from effective reflection on that experience. Thus, reflective learning is the process where law enforcement officers internally examine and explore racial profiling from different worldviews, perhaps from the worldview of minority citizens who claim they have been racially profiled and from the worldview of police officers themselves. This can be accomplished in training sessions or other community friendly forums by problem posing and dialog.

The following three-step technique may be beneficial in creating a more interactive training environment, and by engaging officers in reflection on their stop practices.

1. First, have officers think about an experience they have had with being accused of racial profiling. Officers then write down in bullet point fashion thoughts and reflections about that experience. Officers who have not been accused of racial profiling can write down in bullet point fashion thoughts and reflections about the racial profiling controversy.

2. The next step is to have officers think about ways they can deal with accusations of racial profiling and consider if there was anything they may have done differently during the stop to resolve the perception of racial profiling on the part of the citizen.

3. In the final step officers would discuss long held beliefs, assumptions, and values about the racial profiling controversy.

Cultural Diversity Training

It is unknown if multicultural training for the police would result in fewer perceptions among the racial minority citizenry of racial profiling, or actual incidents of racial profiling. Likewise, it is unknown if it would make a prejudiced officer less prejudiced. However, diversity training is essential for police officers. It sends a positive message to the community. It has only been in the recent past that police agencies have begun to include diversity training as part of the pre- and post-service training requirements. Training that assists in familiarizing officers with ethnic and cultural groups in their community is important. Training in culture and diversity has a number of potential benefits.

Multicultural training may potentially reduce the number of lawsuits. It may also reduce the possibility of civil disorder. Historically, strategies employed by police in dealing with racial minority issues have differed from other groups. While improvements in those strategies have occurred in the recent past, further improvements are needed. Although these improvements have often focused on African Americans, many cultural diversity issues have similar implications for other racial and ethnic groups. Coderoni (2002) writes:

> Cultural diversity training helps the police break free from their traditional stance of being "apart from" the community to a more inclusive philosophy of being "a part of" the community. Realizing the difficulty of becoming a part of something that they do not understand causes a desperate need for an intense and ongoing educational process for developing an understanding of cultural differences and how those differences affect policing a free and culturally diverse society. (Coderoni, 2002, p. 14)

Fostering Mutual Respect and Trust

An important objective in both racial profiling training and cultural diversity training is to provide police officers with information on the issue of mutual respect. In fact, the Department of Justice's Office of Community-Oriented Policing Services produced a training curriculum for police officers on mutual respect. They suggest that an important outcome of this training is to increase police officers' awareness of respectful police behavior. By doing so, their ability to work toward better community relationships will be strengthened. They further suggested interim performance objectives of this training should be to:

1. Recognize that we are all influenced by past experiences and that treating people with dignity and respect is the foundation of good communication.

2. Recognize that a police officer's actions and demeanor shape the image of their agencies and of law enforcement in general.

3. Recognize that good law enforcement practices involve investigating patterns of criminal behavior and the use of race as a reason to stop someone is illegal.

4. Recognize that gaining community support and acceptance requires mutual trust and respect between the citizenry and the police.

5. Recognize that establishing positive community partnerships is an effective use of police authority (United States Department of Justice, 2001, p. 6).

Professional Motorist Contacts

Police officers should never understate the impression that a motorist stop can have on citizens. Weitzer and Tuch (2002) made an important point when they suggested the perceptions that citizens have of police stops may be considered just as important as the actual objective reality of the stop. This is salient in this research. The traffic stop is, in many cases, the only contact a citizen may have with the police. The manner in which the police officer communicates can leave lasting impressions. Many participants perceived that the police are demeaning, hostile, and talk down to them during a stop. Police officers should always act in a professional and courteous manner during a stop of an individual. In some cases the officer may have to be stern but being stern is very different from being demeaning and hostile.

Building and Sustaining Community Coalitions

It is beneficial for police authorities to establish and/or enhance their involvement with local community organizations such as the NAACP (National Association for the Advancement of Colored People), Urban League, Boy's and Girl's Clubs, Hispanic coalitions, and Asian or Indo-Chinese community centers and coalitions. Because the faith community provides a leadership role in many racial minority communities, increasing contact with them may be advantageous too. Coalitions should be formed to not only address issues centering on racial profiling but also to achieve better police community relations. When the police have good relations with the racial minority community it is much easier to tailor solutions to underlying causes of friction between the police and the community. It is critical that community input should be solicited during this review, including requests for public comment and discussion. Likewise, the police should inform the community of the various options that are available to report racial profiling at the federal, state, and local levels.

Developing coalitions and contacts in organizations such as these will keep management informed about the minority community's issues and concerns centering on not only racial profiling but also other important issues. Many racial minority citizens revealed that often their voices are not included in coalitions and boards, and their voices are sometimes represented by persons who are dubbed as leaders in the minority community. They suggested that citizens "from all walks of life" be included in boards and coalitions to ensure their voices are heard and they have input.

Communication

Regular communication between the police and the community can dispel rumors and resolve potential misunderstandings. The police and the community have to engage in productive dialog about racial profiling. This can be accomplished through holding regular or semi-regular community forums and town hall meetings. In order to avoid complaining sessions, the community forum or town hall meetings should not be held only when hot button issues have caused unrest in the community. Dialog between the community and police may include the following:

• Sessions with the police chief advisory boards (either one board with members from several minority communities, or several boards, one for each community)

• Chaplain or faith programs involving minority clergy

• Radio and TV shows with calls

• Beat meetings that are integral to joint community problem solving

• Facilitated discussions (with a neutral, third-party moderator), which increase police and resident accountability for following up on agreed upon actions

• Study circles, which are structured to include three steps: (1) organization of the community; (2) identification of areas of mutual police-citizen concern; and (3) agreement and action taken by both the police and minority groups (Fridell et al. 2001, pp. 105–106)

Community-Oriented Policing

Police agencies may find it beneficial to implement or expand existing community-oriented policing strategies as a way to enhance public safety and interaction through collaborative partnerships with the minority community. Community-oriented policing may also be beneficial in improving police relations with racial minority communities. Moreover, community-oriented policing strategies could result in resolving the sometimes mistaken perception of racial profiling.

Community policing strategies call for an increased emphasis on the service aspect of policing as opposed strictly to crime reduction. Police agencies solely committed to crime reduction strategies are more likely to be accused of racial profiling. On the other hand, agencies that are steeped in crime reduction strategies pose a far greater potential for officers to develop an operating mentality to reduce crime by any means necessary. A large extent of crime reduction strategies are carried out in economically disadvantaged neighborhoods (often minority neighborhoods) where large numbers of stops are conducted. These practices by themselves have the potential to lower trust in law enforcement and minimize cooperation of the minority community.

It is certainly not suggested that law enforcement desist from crime reduction strategies in economically disadvantaged areas, but rather they be augmented with a significant service orientation that is built as an operational strategy. Community policing with its emphasis on service orientation actually includes proactive policing strategies. For example, under community policing the police would focus increased attention on small disorder problems that usually would not be expected, or for that matter, result in a police response under a crime reduction model. Some examples of small disorder problems are minor vandalisms, public drinking, neighborhood blight, abandoned property and vehicles, and the like. Focusing on small disorder problems inherent in neighborhoods will bring the police into more frequent interaction with citizens in order to discuss and tailor solutions to these problems. By addressing small disorder problems, more serious crime-related problems may be prevented. It should be underscored that working to resolve small order problems should be done with affected citizens living in affected neighborhoods. Moreover, small disorder problems should be addressed by a well-planned problem solving approach that does not include aggressive and unequal enforcement activities which will further fracture the relationship between the police and the minority community.

☐ Conclusion

As the conclusion to this chapter was being written, another allegation of police abuse in Chicago was reported in the national news. A video recording, taken from a police cruiser's dash cam, was released to the public showing the October 2014 shooting death of Laquan McDonald, a 17-year African American male by a white Chicago police officer. The video depicts Laquan walking in the middle of street appearing to carrying a knife but presenting no threat to officers before he was shot. There were 16 rounds fired at the victim. The release of the video sparked large-scale protests in Chicago. Protesters contend that this is another example of racial bias in policing. Many are questioning why it took over a year to release the video. The Chicago police officer involved in the shooting has been charged with first-degree murder. African American leaders in Chicago have called for the resignation of police superintendent and a federal investigation into the practices of the Chicago Police Department.

The intersection of race and policing in the United States has a complex and troubled history. The troubled history impacts modern day police operations and presents a host of challenges for the police when addressing allegations of racial profiling, and in the mending of strained relations with racial minority communities. In short, there are no easy answers or solutions. Police agencies will increasingly be required to practice procedural justice of sorts. Procedural justice that includes transparency, fairness, and allowing citizens to have a voice. In order to mend strains in their relationship with the minority community, it will increasingly be important to allow minority citizens to collectively have the opportunity to explain their situation or tell their side of the story regarding their neighborhoods and/or communities. This includes having the opportunity to have their voices heard before the police make decisions about how their neighborhoods are policed.

☐ References

Barlow, D.E. and Hickman-Barlow, M. 2000. *Police in a Multicultural Society: An American Story.* Prospect Heights, Illinois: Waveland Press.

Birzer, M.L. 2013. *Racial Profiling: They Stopped Me Because I'm—!* Boca Raton, Florida: CRC Press.

Coderoni, G.R. 2002. The relationship between multicultural training for police and effective law enforcement. *FBI Law Enforcement Bulletin*, 71(11), 16–18.

Carlson, D.K. 2004. Racial profiling is seen as widespread, particularly among young Black men. Gallup. Retrieved from Gallup website: http://www.gallup.com/poll/12406/racial-profiling-seen-pervasive-unjust.aspx.

Christopher Commission. 1991. Report of the Independent Commission on the Los Angeles Police Department, Los Angeles.

Fridell, L., Lunney, R., Diamond, D. Kubu, B, Scott, M., and Laing, C. 2001. *Racially Biased Policing: A Principled Response*. Washington, DC: Police Executive Research Forum.

Genovese, E.D. 1976. *Roll Jordon Roll: The World of Slaves Made*. New York: Vintage Books.

Glover, K.S. 2009. *Racial Profiling: Research, Racism, and Resistance*. Lanham, Maryland: Rowman & Littlefield Publishers, Inc.

Hadden, S.E. 2001. *Slave Patrols: Law and Violence in Virginia and the Carolinas*. Cambridge, Massachusetts: Harvard University Press.

Hendrickson, P. 2003. *Sons of Mississippi: A Story of Race and its Legacy*. New York: Alfred A. Knopf.

Huie, W.B. 2000. *Three Lives for Mississippi*. Jackson, Mississippi: University Press of Mississippi.

Katz, W.L. 1995. *Eyewitness: A Living Documentary of the African American Contribution to American History*. New York: Touchstone.

King, R. 2012. *The Riot within: My Journey from Rebellion to Redemption*. New York: Harper.

Lynch, J.R. 1968. *Facts of Reconstruction*. New York: Arno Press.

Moss, E.Y. 1990. African Americans and the administration of justice. In W. L. Reed (Ed.), *Assessment of the Status of African Americans* (pp. 79–86). Boston: University of Massachusetts, William Monroe Trotter Institute.

Nunnelley, W.A. 1991. *Bull Connor*. Tuscaloosa: University of Alabama Press.

Patterson, O. 1998. *Rituals of Blood: The Consequences of Slavery in Two American Centuries*. New York: Basic Civitas Books.

Pitts Walter, M. 1992. *Mississippi Challenge*. New York: Bradbury Press.

Police Executive Research Forum. 2014. *Legitimacy and Procedural Justice: A New Element of Police Leadership*. Washington, DC: Police Executive Research Forum, U.S. Department of Justice, Bureau of Justice Assistance.

Ogletree, C.J., Prosser, M., Smith, A., and Talley, W. 1995. *Beyond the Rodney King Story: An Investigation of Police Conduct in Minority Communities*. Boston, Massachusetts: Northeastern University Press.

Quillian, L. and Pager, D. 2001. Black neighbors, higher crime? The role of racial stereotypes in the evaluation of neighborhood crime. *American Journal of Sociology*, 107, 117–167.

Quillian, L. and Pager, D. 2010. Estimating risk: Stereotype amplification and the perceived risk of criminal victimization. *Social Psychology Quarterly*, 73, 79–104.

United States Census Bureau. 2012. Law enforcement courts and prisons: Jail inmates by sex, race, and Hispanic origin. U.S. Census Bureau. Retrieved from: http://www.census.gov/compendia/statab/cats/law_enforcement_courts_prisons.html.

United States Department of Justice. 2015a. *Department of Justice Report Regarding the Criminal Investigation into the Shooting Death of Michael Brown by Ferguson, Missouri Police Officer Darren Wilson.* Washington, DC: U.S. Department of Justice. Retrieved on November 25, 2015 from: http://www.justice.gov/.

United States Department of Justice. 2015b. *Investigation of the Ferguson Police Department.* Washington, DC: U.S. Department of Justice. Retrieved on November 25, 2015 from: http://www.justice.gov.

U.S. Department of Justice. 2001. *Mutual Respect in Policing: Lesson Plan.* Washington, DC: Office of Community Oriented Policing Services.

Wadman, R.C. and Allison, W.T. 2004. *To Protect and Serve: A History of Police in America.* Upper Saddle, NJ: Prentice Hall.

Walker, S. 1980. *Popular Justice: A History of American Criminal Justice.* New York: Oxford University Press.

Walker, S. 1999. *The Police in America: An Introduction,* (2nd ed). Boston: McGraw Hill.

Williams, H. and Murphy, P.V. 1990. *The Evolving Strategies of Police: A Minority View.* Washington, DC: National Institute of Justice. Retrieved from https://www.ncjrs.gov/ pdffiles1/nij/121019.pdf.

Weitzer, R. and Tuch, S.A. 2005. Racially biased policing: Determinants of citizen perceptions. *Social Forces,* 83, 1009–1030.

Weitzer, R. and Tuch, S.A. 2002. Perceptions of racial profiling: Race, class, and personal experience. *Criminology,* 40(2), 435–456.

Whren v. United States. (1996). 517 U.S. 806.

Wyatt-Brown, B. 1982. *Southern Honor: Ethics and Behavior in the Old South.* New York: Oxford University Press.

CHAPTER **7**

Understanding the Law of Police Use of Force to Arrest

Alison Brown

☐ Introduction

The law is not emotional: it is analytical. To convict, the criminal law requires proof beyond a reasonable doubt of every component of a crime as that crime is written, not as the crime may be generally perceived. These basic truths of the criminal law often create a conflict between the public's perception of a fair and just outcome in a criminal case, and the actual outcome of a case based upon legal precedent that has developed over the last 1000 years. Nowhere is this conflict more apparent than in cases involving police use of force to arrest. While this conflict between the law and public perception has always existed, today it seems to be even more present in the endlessly increasing media reports from radio, television, newspapers, newsmagazines, and the internet streaming live 24/7 from computers, smart phones, tablets, and even watches. It is now almost impossible to escape the stories fighting for our attention.

Police using their authority to commit bad acts, or just over responding to a situation based on their emotions rather than their training, is not a new phenomenon. In 1963, a few horrific pictures filtered out of Selma, Alabama showing white police officers using the tools of their profession, including dogs, clubs, and other weapons, to suppress a civil-rights march. In 1991, a video of Rodney King being beaten by police with department issued clubs was played on the nightly news for months. With the advent of YouTube, every cell phone video capturing questionable police interaction with the public is available for instant replay by the media and the general public. Videos like the 2008 incident involving a Baltimore, Maryland officer screaming and ranting at young teens are likely to go viral, passed from person to person through social media until everyone in the country views it multiple times. Whether purposeful criminal acts, or just momentary loss of control, today it is likely the public will see the bad act and is not willing to tolerate it.

Following the 2014 shooting death of Michael Brown by a Ferguson, Missouri police officer trying to take Brown into custody, people from across the nation went to Ferguson to protest. Most of the protesters were marching to draw attention to concerns that police routinely use excessive force when arresting people of color. The protests were large enough, and garnered enough attention across the country, to cause politicians to promise to find answers to the protesters' questions. When the answers came, however, the public was not satisfied, just as they have not been satisfied with the answers provided by criminal justice professionals in most of the cases in which the police were investigated for use of excessive force, whether or not racial bias is perceived to be at issue. In many, although not all, of these types of events it is difficult to develop an understandable response to these questions because the answers are based upon the laws and rules concerning police use of force. This chapter will provide an explanation of the principal laws related to police use of force in connection with arrest. Specifically, this chapter will analyze the primary state and federal criminal law, as well as the federal civil law, which control an officer's criminal and civil liability for use of force during an arrest.

☐ Prosecuting Excessive Force under State Criminal Codes

Although every state independently determines which acts that it wishes to criminalize, most states have adopted laws prohibiting conduct outlawed by common law, including murder, manslaughter, battery, and assault. The common law is the body of law that began creation more than 1000 years ago in England, under the direction of William the Conqueror. It continued to evolve and expand over time to incorporate the changing needs of English society and was brought to America as part of the colonization process. When the United States broke away from England, however, both the new federal government, as well as the states, kept the common law and many of the customs and practices of English society so that citizens of the brand new nation would have some form of legal regulation that was both understandable and accepted.

Murder, rape, kidnapping, battery, and assault are generally understood within the United States to be terms for illegal acts. For example, every child in the United States learns at some point during their early childhood that taking a human life is murder and it is wrong. Similarly, while the criminal designations that the various states adopt to proscribe hitting, holding someone against their will, and forcible sexual contact may differ, every child knows that hitting another person, capturing another person, or improperly touching another person are bad acts. At the same time that children learn to identify bad acts, however, they also learn that sometimes bad acts are justified. So, children understand that taking a human life is bad but sometimes it is necessary to kill another person if one is acting to save their own life. In the same way, hitting another person is bad, but sometimes smacking a hand is the only way to teach a 3-year old not to touch a hot stove. This basic understanding that sometimes it is OK do bad things is written into every state criminal code under the general heading of "defenses to criminal acts." These defenses are some of the oldest parts of the criminal law, and versions fairly similar to those promulgated hundreds of years ago continue to be followed today.

Defenses can be categorized as: justification, excuse, alibi, and no crime. Except for the alibi defense, each of these types of defenses recognizes that the actor did the act. The "no crime" defense is used when the actor believes that the act is not an unlawful act under the law. The various excuse defenses are used when an actor admits he committed the act but asks to be excused from criminal responsibility by virtue of special circumstances which negate the actor's intent to act criminally. An accused using an excuse defense may claim to be legally insane or a juvenile. The final category of defenses are called justifications. Justification defenses are used when the actor admits to having committed a wrongful act, but claims the act was necessary to avoid a greater evil. Self-defense and defense of others are two types of justification defenses.

In common law "use of force to effect an arrest" was a justification defense available to anyone acting to stop and detain a felon. This defense recognized that an actor could use as much force as was necessary to effect the arrest, up to and including, deadly force. As common law evolved into statutory law, and designated law enforcement officers began to replace citizen vigilantes, most states accepted the legitimacy of the rationale behind the use of force doctrine and adopted legislation recognizing the common law defense of "use of force to effect an arrest."*

The public policy behind the use of force defense is clear. Policing is by definition a dangerous profession. Officers are sent to multiple calls for help during every shift. Citizens do not usually ask for help until the situation has arisen to a level where danger may occur, or has already occurred. If the police tried to do their jobs while fearing prosecution for carrying out an arrest, they may choose to walk away from individuals who refuse to cooperate with an arrest, rather than force the individual to submit. Additionally, officers have reason to believe that individuals will act dangerously during an arrest if given an opportunity. Although failing to cooperate with an arrest, and resisting arrest, are additional offenses in every state, an arresting officer must know that the law will back him up if he needs to enforce these, or any other, laws. Thus, because of the nature of the policing and the nature of arrests, both police and the community must understand that police are legally empowered to take control of a situation, and to remain in control of a situation until the situation no longer exists.

The common law rules regarding use of force to arrest have changed slightly over time, mostly as the result of judicial decisions. Cases dating back to the earliest state courts provide examples of police officers being prosecuted by the state or sued by an arrestee or their next of kin for using more force than was necessary to accomplish the arrest. Law enforcement officers have been able to defend their actions by relying upon the state's authorization to use that amount of force necessary to complete an arrest, and prevent the arrestee from defeating the arrest and escaping. A 1894 California case involving the prosecution of a law enforcement officer for homicide arising from an attempt to arrest provides a clear example of how state courts have applied the use of force defense to allegations of criminal conduct. In that case, the Supreme Court of California held that if an officer had probable cause to believe that a felony crime had occurred, and probable cause to believe that an individual had committed that felony crime, the law allowed the officer to take reasonable steps to stop the fleeing felon, even if it turned out that the individual was not the offender but "an innocent and respectable citizen."†

---

* *People v. Kilvington*, 104 Cal. 86, 37 P. 799, 1894.
† Ibid, at 93, 801, and 11.

A 1919 case heard by the Supreme Court of Washington was also asked to review a police officer's right to use the use of force defense. That court stated that Washington operated under the common law, and that under the common law a law enforcement officer making an arrest based upon probable cause could make an arrest. In making that arrest the officer was authorized by the law to use "that degree of force the circumstances of the case warrant; that is to say, if the crime is a misdemeanor he may use the force the law permits in making arrests for misdemeanors, and if it be a felony he may use the force the law permits in making arrests for felony."* If that officer is later prosecuted for assault, battery, or homicide he has the right to explain to the jury the circumstances surrounding the arrest, as well as his perception and understanding of those circumstances. Then, unless the jury finds that the officer was lying, or the response was too egregious to be justified, the jury must accept the officer's defense.† In short, this means that when a regular citizen is prosecuted for a crime, the state need only prove that the person committed the act with the requisite intent. When a law enforcement officer is prosecuted for a crime associated with having used force during an arrest, however, the prosecution must not only prove that the officer used that amount of force that rises to the level of a criminal act, but must also prove that the officer's use of that amount of force was not permitted by and justified by the use of force defense. This sets a very high standard for convicting an officer of a criminal act for having used force during an arrest.

States were largely unguided in their application and interpretation of the defense of "use of force to effect an arrest" until 1984, when the Supreme Court decided the case of *Tennessee v. Garner*.‡ The facts underlying the Garner case involved a 1974 shooting death of a 15–year-old, unarmed teenager, Edward Eugene Garner, by a Memphis police officer. Garner's father filed a lawsuit, but the state defended the officer's actions under the provisions of that state's use of force defense. At that time the Tennessee law provided that "[if], after notice of the intention to arrest the defendant, he either flee or forcibly resist, the officer may use all the necessary means to effect the arrest.'"§ Acting under the authority of this statute, a Memphis police officer shot and killed Edward Garner after Garner refused to comply with an order to halt, and attempted to flee over a fence at night in the backyard of

---

* *Coldeen v. Reid, Sheriff, et al.*, 107 Wash. 508, at 516, 182 P. 599, at 601, 1919 at 112.
† Ibid. See also, *Schumann v. McGinn*, 307 Minn., at 458, 240 N. W. 2d, at 533; *Holloway v. Moser, supra*, at 187, 136 S. E., at 376, 1927.
‡ *Tennessee v. Garner et al.*, 471 U.S. 1, 105 S. Ct. 1694, 85 L. Ed. 2d 1, 1985.
§ Ibid, at 4, 1698, and 5. Tenn. Code Ann. § 40–808, 1974.

a house he was suspected of burglarizing. The officer admitted that he used deadly force despite being reasonably sure the suspect was unarmed, and despite thinking that the suspect was a slightly built 17 or 18 year old.[*] The officer shot at Garner because he believed that the juvenile would be able to climb over the fence and outrun him, thereby escaping arrest. The officer believed that the only means to effect the arrest of Garner was to shoot to kill.[†]

The Federal District Court for the Western District of Tennessee reviewed the state's law permitting the police officer to use "all necessary means" to carry out an arrest, and found it to be constitutional based upon all legal precedent up to that time. The U.S. Court of Appeals for the Sixth Circuit upheld the District Court's decision, again based upon all legal precedent up to that time.[‡] Garner's father appealed that decision to the U.S. Supreme Court. The Supreme Court determined that the common law was superseded by the law of the U.S. Constitution. The Fourth Amendment encompassed the law regarding search and seizure. An arrest is, by definition, a seizure. Therefore, under the Fourth Amendment the Tennessee use of force rule was unconstitutional to that degree that it authorizes the use of deadly force to prevent the escape of an apparently unarmed suspected felon.[§]

The Garner decision restricts a state's ability to authorize law enforcement officers to use an unlimited amount of force to carry out an arrest, but it did not prevent states from protecting officers' use of *reasonable force* to carry out an arrest. So, the Garner case specifically held that using deadly force to shoot at an unarmed suspect to stop the suspect from fleeing is unconstitutional and therefore unreasonable. The majority of states, however, continue to maintain some form of statutory authority for police to use force to carry out an arrest (see Table 7.1). For example, Tennessee's current law uses the language provided within the Garner case.

> A law enforcement officer, after giving notice of the officer's identity as an officer, may use or threaten to use force that is reasonably necessary to accomplish the arrest of an individual suspected of a criminal act who resists or flees from the arrest.[¶]

---

[*] Ibid.

[†] Ibid.

[‡] *Garner v. Memphis Police Department, City of Memphis, Tennessee and Jay W. Hubbard and E.R. Hymon* in their official capacities, 6.

[§] *Tennessee v. Garner et al.*, 471 U.S. 1, 105 S. Ct. 1694, 85 L. Ed. 2d 1, 1985.

[¶] Tenn. Code Ann. 40-7-108(a), 2015. Resistance to officer.

TABLE 7.1 State Law Citations to Use of Force Regulations

State	State Code Abbreviations	Citation Authorization of Use of Force to Arrest	Citation Prohibition to Resist Arrest	Citation Tort Claim Protection for Use of Force	Citation Parameters for Use of Deadly Force
Alabama	Ala. Code	§ 13A-3-27(a)	§ 13A-3-28	§ 6-5-338	§ 13A-3-27(b)
Alaska	Alaska Stat.	§ 11.81.370	§ 11.81.400	*	§ 11.81.370
Arizona	Ariz. Rev. Stat. Ann.	§ 13-409	§ 13-2508	§ 13-413	§ 13-410
Arkansas	Ark. Code Ann.	§ 16-81-107	§ 5-6-612	*	§ 5-2-607
California	Cal. [Penal] Code	§ 835 and § 835a	§ 834a	Cal Gov. Code § 820.2	*
Colorado	Colo. Rev. Stat. Ann.	§ 18-1-707	§ 18-8-103	*	§ 18-1-707(2)
Connecticut	Conn. Gen. Stat.	§ 53a-22	§ 53a-23	*	§ 53a-22(c)
Delaware	11 Del. Code Ann.	§ 467	§ 1257	*	467(c)
Dist of Columbia	D.C. Code Ann.	§ 5-123.02	§ 22-405(b)	*	*
Florida	Fla. Stat.	§ 776.05	§ 776.051	§ 776.05	§ 776.05

(Continued)

TABLE 7.1 (*Continued*) State Law Citations to Use of Force Regulations

State	State Code Abbreviations	Citation Authorization of Use of Force to Arrest	Citation Prohibition to Resist Arrest	Citation Tort Claim Protection for Use of Force	Citation Parameters for Use of Deadly Force
Georgia	Ga. Code Ann.	16-3-20	§ 16-10-24	*	§ 17-4-20(b)
Hawaii	Haw. Rev. Stat.	§ 703-307	§ 803.7	*	§ 703-307(3)
Idaho	Idaho Code	§ 19-602	§ 19-610	*	§ 18-4011
Illinois	Ill. Comp. Stat.	§ 720 ILCS 5/7-5	§ 720 ILCS 5/7-7	*	§ 720 ILCS 5/7-5
Indiana	Ind. Code	§ 35-41-3-3(b)	§ 35-41-3-3	§ 34-13-3-3	§ 35-41-3-3(b)
Iowa	Iowa Code	§ 804.8	§ 804.12	§ 670.4 & 670.12	§ 704.1
Kansas	Kan. Stat. Ann.	§ 21-5227	§ 21-5229	§ 75-6101 et seq.	§ 21-5227
Kentucky	Ky. Rev. Stat. Ann.	§ 431.025 and § 503.090	§ 503.085 & 520.090	*	§ 503.090(3)
Louisiana	La. C.Cr.P.	Art. 220	Art. 220	*	La.R.S. § 14:20

(*Continued*)

TABLE 7.1 (*Continued*) State Law Citations to Use of Force Regulations

State	State Code Abbreviations	Citation Authorization of Use of Force to Arrest	Citation Prohibition to Resist Arrest	Citation Tort Claim Protection for Use of Force	Citation Parameters for Use of Deadly Force
Maine	Me. Rev. Stat. Ann.	17-A.M.R.S. § 107	*	15-A.M.R.S. § 704	17-A.M.R.S. § 107(2)
Maryland	Md. Crim. Law. Code Ann.	*	§ 9-408	*	*
Massachusetts	Mass. Gen. Laws	*	Ch. 268. § 32B.	*	*
Michigan	Mich. Comp. Laws	§330.1427A	§ 750.479 & § 750.81D	*	*
Minnesota	Minn. Stat.	§ 609.06	§ 609.06	*	*
Mississippi	Miss. Code Ann.	*.	§ 97-9-73	§ 11.46.9	*
Missouri	Mo. Rev. Stat.	§ 563.046	§ 575.150	*	*
Montana	Mont. Code Ann.	§ 46-6-104	§ 45-3-108	*	*

(*Continued*)

TABLE 7.1 (*Continued*) State Law Citations to Use of Force Regulations

State	State Code Abbreviations	Citation Authorization of Use of Force to Arrest	Citation Prohibition to Resist Arrest	Citation Tort Claim Protection for Use of Force	Citation Parameters for Use of Deadly Force
Nebraska	Neb. Rev. Stat.	§ 28-1412	§ 28-1409 & § 28-904	*	*
Nevada	Nev. Rev. Stat.	*	§ 28-1409	§ 41.032 et seq.	§ 171.1455
New Hampshire	N.H. Rev. Stat. Ann.	§ 633:7	§ 633:5	§ 633:6 and 633:7	§ 633:8
New Jersey	N.J. Stat. Ann.	§ 2C:3-7	§ 2C:29-2	*	*
New Mexico	N.M. Stat. Ann.	*	§ 30—22-1	§ 41-4-4	*
New York	NY CPL	§ 120.80. & § 140.15	§ 35.27	*	*
North Carolina	N.C. Gen. Stat.	§ 15A-401d	§ 14-223	*	*
North Dakota	N.D. Cent. Code	§ 12.1-05-07	§ 12.1-05.03	*	§ 12.1-05-07(2)

(*Continued*)

TABLE 7.1 (*Continued*) State Law Citations to Use of Force Regulations

State	State Code Abbreviations	Citation Authorization of Use of Force to Arrest	Citation Prohibition to Resist Arrest	Citation Tort Claim Protection for Use of Force	Citation Parameters for Use of Deadly Force
Ohio	Ohio Rev. Code Ann.	§ 2935.12 & § 2935.03	§ 2921.33	*	§ 2917.05
Oklahoma	Okla. Stat.	§ 21 Okl. St. 643	§ 21 Okl. St. 748	§ 21 Okl. St.748	§ 21 Okl. St. 732
Oregon	Or. Rev. Stat.	§ 161.235	§ 162.315	*	§ 161.239
Pennsylvania	Pa. Cons. Stat.	18 Pa.C.S. §	34 Pa.C.S. § 904	*	*
Rhode Island	R.I. Gen. Laws	§ 12-7-8	§ 12-7-10	*	§ 12-7-9
South Carolina	S.C. Code Ann.	*	§ 16-9-320	§ 15-78-70	*
South Dakota	S.D. Codified Laws	§ 22-18-3	§ 22-11-4	*	*
Tennessee	Tenn. Code Ann.	§ 40-7-108	§ 40-7-108	*	§ 39-11-620 & § 40-7-108

(*Continued*)

TABLE 7.1 (*Continued*) State Law Citations to Use of Force Regulations

State	State Code Abbreviations	Citation Authorization of Use of Force to Arrest	Citation Prohibition to Resist Arrest	Citation Tort Claim Protection for Use of Force	Citation Parameters for Use of Deadly Force
Texas	Tex. Code Crim. Pro.	TCCP Art. 14.05 & Tex. Penal Code § 9.51	Tex. Penal Code § 9.52	*	Tex. Penal Code § 9.51(d)
Utah	Utah Code Ann.	§ 77-4-1	§ 76-8-305	*	§ 76-2-404
Vermont	Vt. Stat. Ann.	*	§ 13 VSA 1028	*	13 VSA § 2305
Virginia	Va. Code Ann.	*	§ 18.2-460	*	*
Washington	Wash. Rev. code	RCW § 10.31.050	RCW § 9A.76.020	*	*
West Virginia	W.Va. code	*	*	*	*
Wisconsin	Wis. Stat.	§ 939.45	*	*	*
Wyoming	Wyo. Stat. Ann.	*	§ 6-5-204	*	*

Note: The asterisk is used to denote no specific statute available in that state.

The Garner decision also impacted the "fleeing felon" rule. At common law a fleeing felon was by definition someone who was very dangerous. As the understanding of the term "felon" has evolved, though, it encompasses people who have committed nonviolent acts as well as violent acts. The Court in Garner recognized that the meaning of the word "felony" had changed, which meant that the rule which developed to prevent dangerous offenders from escaping capture had been expanded to include both dangerous and non-dangerous offenders. The Garner Court stated that

> It has been pointed out many times that the common law rule is best understood in light of the fact that it arose at a time when virtually all felonies were punishable by death. . . Neither of these justifications makes sense today. Almost all crimes formerly punishable by death no longer are or can be. And while in earlier times "the gulf between the felonies and the minor offences was broad and deep" today the distinction is minor and often arbitrary. Many crimes classified as misdemeanors, or nonexistent, at common law are now felonies. These changes have undermined the concept, which was questionable to begin with, that use of deadly force against a fleeing felon is merely a speedier execution of someone who has already forfeited his life. They have also made the assumption that a "felon" is more dangerous than a misdemeanant untenable.*

The Garner case forced states to reevaluate the authority that they granted to officers to use any amount of force in carrying out an arrest, but it is best known for limiting the legal right of officers to use deadly force. Today, in most states statutory authorization to use deadly force is addressed separately from non-deadly force (see Table 7.1). For example,

---

* *Tennessee v. Garner,* at 13–15, 1702–1703 and 11–12, citing "American Law Institute, Model Penal Code § 3.07, Comment 3, p. 56 (Tentative Draft No. 8, 1958) (hereinafter Model Penal Code Comment)." The full quote reads, "Neither of these justifications makes sense today. Almost all crimes formerly punishable by death no longer are or can be. See, e.g., *Enmund v. Florida,* 458 U.S. 782, 1982; *Coker* v. *Georgia,* 433 U.S. 584, 1977. And while in earlier times "the gulf between the felonies and the minor offences was broad and deep," 2 Pollock & Maitland 467, n. 3; *Carroll v. United States, supra,* at 158, today the distinction is minor and often arbitrary. Many crimes classified as misdemeanors, or nonexistent, at common law are now felonies. Wilgus, 22 Mich. L. Rev., pp. 572–573. These changes have undermined the concept, which was questionable to begin with, that use of deadly force against a fleeing felon is merely a speedier execution of someone who has already forfeited his life. They have also made the assumption that a "felon" is more dangerous than a misdemeanant untenable. Indeed, numerous misdemeanors involve conduct more dangerous than many felonies.

Tennessee adopted a separate law regarding use of deadly force following the Garner decision. The Tennessee law currently provides:

a. A law enforcement officer, after giving notice of the officer's identity as such, may use or threaten to use force that is reasonably necessary to accomplish the arrest of an individual suspected of a criminal act who resists or flees from the arrest.

b. Notwithstanding subsection a, the officer may use deadly force to effect an arrest only if all other reasonable means of apprehension have been exhausted or are unavailable, and where feasible, the officer has given notice of the officer's identity as such and given a warning that deadly force may be used unless resistance or flight ceases, and

1. The officer has probable cause to believe the individual to be arrested has committed a felony involving the infliction or threatened infliction of serious bodily injury.

2. The officer has probable cause to believe that the individual to be arrested poses a threat of serious bodily injury, either to the officer or to others unless immediately apprehended.[*]

The Tennessee law is very similar to the laws adopted by most other states, and has been found to be constitutional when reviewed.

While court decisions have brought about changes in state laws, no court decision has changed the basic precepts accepted since the advent of the common law: police officers are treated differently by the law. When prosecuting a nonpolice officer for a crime involving use of force, the prosecutor needs to show that the actor used force, because nonpolice are generally prohibited from using force against others. When prosecuting a police officer, however, there is no question that the officer used force, and maybe a lot of force. The prosecution must be able to prove that the amount of force used by the officer to complete the arrest was greater than permitted by law. "This rule takes into account the special situation of the police defendant."[†] Unlike private citizens, police officers

---

[*] Tenn. Code Ann. 39-11-620. Use of deadly force by a law enforcement officer.

[†] *Edson v. City of Anaheim*, 63 Cal. App. 4th 1269, 74 Cal. Rptr. 2d 614, 1998. (See also, *Graham v. Connor*, 490 U.S. 386, 109 S. Ct. 1865, 104 L. Ed. 2d 443, 1989).

act with the authority granted by the law to protect the public interest.* Law enforcement officers are directed to use force as part of their duties. No one seriously questions that "the right to make an arrest or investigatory stop necessarily carries with it the right to use some degree of physical coercion or threat thereof to effect it."† This means that police officers are not analogous to similarly situated ordinary battery defendants.‡ For these reasons, when a "defendant police officer is in the exercise of the privilege of protecting the public peace and order he is entitled to the even greater use of force than might be in the same circumstances required for self-defense."§ For all of these reasons, it is very difficult to prosecute a police officer for a state level crime arising out of an excessive use of force to arrest.

While it is difficult to meet the legal standards to bring state level criminal charges against police officers, it is certainly not impossible.¶ In 2015, a state prosecutor announced that her office would prosecute six Baltimore, Maryland, police officers who participated in the arrest of Freddy Gray. The state crimes filed against the officers included manslaughter, assault, misconduct in office, and false imprisonment. The State's Attorney for Baltimore City stated that after reviewing the evidence in the case, the officers acted outside the law by arresting Mr. Gray, as he had committed no crime, and therefore the officers had no probable cause to support his arrest. Charging an officer with a crime is just the first step, however. A jury will have to find that the officers committed the acts alleged and that the law of reasonable force to carry out an arrest did not act to shield the officers' actions from criminal liability.

☐ Prosecuting Excessive Force under Federal Law

In 1992 four police officers were charged by the Los Angeles District Attorney with the state crimes of assault with a deadly weapon and excessive use of force by a police officer. After a trial, a jury found all four

---

* Ibid.
† Ibid (citing *Graham v. Connor*, at 396, 1273, 616, 8).
‡ Ibid.
§ Ibid (at 1273, 616, 8).
¶ Alan Blinder and Richard Perez-Pena, 6 Baltimore Police Officers Charged in Freddie Gray Death. *New York Times* May 1, 2015. C., Doug. Many obstacles to prosecuting police. *The Baltimore Sun* July 12, 2015.

officers not guilty beyond reasonable doubt.* Because federal prosecutors perceived that the acts of the four officers as shown in the video violated federal criminal law, federal indictments were sought against the four officers. On August 4, 1992, a federal grand jury returned indictments against all four officers.†

The federal government's decision to prosecute the four officers was not double jeopardy. Under the legal concept of "dual sovereignty" every jurisdiction may prosecute an individual for crimes committed within its jurisdiction, even if the criminal acts are made criminal by another jurisdiction. Thus, for example, the U.S. Government could prosecute Terry Nichols for the federal crimes of conspiracy and use of a weapon of mass destruction, as well as other crimes arising out of his participation in bombing the Murrah Federal Building in Oklahoma City, Oklahoma in 1995, after which the State of Oklahoma prosecuted him for 161 counts of murder.

Federal criminal liability for excessive force used in an arrest typically arises under 18 U.S.C. § 242 ("§ 242").‡ This is a relatively old law, as the precursor of the modern day § 242 was adopted by Congress in the

---

* *Koon v. U.S.* and *Powell v. U.S.*, 518 U.S. 81, 88, 116 S. Ct. 2035, 2042, 135 L. Ed. 2d 392, 406, 1996. Koon, Powell, Briseno, and Wind were tried in state court on charges of assault with a deadly weapon and excessive use of force by a police officer. The officers were acquitted of all charges, with the exception of one assault charge [*88] against Powell that resulted in a hung jury. The verdicts touched off widespread rioting in Los Angeles. More than 40 people were killed in the riots, more [**2042] than 2,000 were injured, and nearly $ 1 billion in property was destroyed. New Initiatives for a New Los Angeles: Final Report and Recommendations, Senate Special Task Force on a New Los Angeles, December 9, 1992, pp. 10–11.
† Ibid.
‡ 18 USCS § 242, 2015. Based on title 18, U.S.C., 1940 ed., § 52, March 4, 1909, ch. 321, § 20, 35 Stat. 1092. Deprivation of rights under color of law. "Whoever, under color of any law, statute, ordinance, regulation, or custom, willfully subjects any person in any state, territory, commonwealth, possession, or district to the deprivation of any rights, privileges, or immunities secured or protected by the Constitution or laws of the United States, or to different punishments, pains, or penalties, on account of such person being an alien, or by reason of his color, or race, than are prescribed for the punishment of citizens, shall be fined under this title or imprisoned not more than one year, or both; and if bodily injury results from the acts committed in violation of this section or if such acts include the use, attempted use, or threatened use of a dangerous weapon, explosives, or fire, shall be fined under this title or imprisoned not more than ten years, or both; and if death results from the acts committed in violation of this section or if such acts include kidnapping or an attempt to kidnap, aggravated sexual abuse, or an attempt to commit aggravated sexual abuse, or an attempt to kill, shall be fined under this title, or imprisoned for any term of years or for life, or both, or may be sentenced to death."

years following the Civil War. Section 242 was passed to allow the federal government to prosecute a state official for using state authority to deny a citizen of the United States any right secured by the Constitution of the United States.* Section 242 reads in pertinent part:

> Whoever, under color of any law, statute, ordinance, regulation, or custom, willfully subjects any person in any State, Territory, or District to the deprivation of any rights, privileges, or immunities secured or protected by the Constitution or laws of the United States, or to different punishments, pains, or penalties, on account of such person being an alien, or by reason of his color, or race, than are prescribed for the punishment of citizens," shall be subject to specified criminal penalties.†

This law also provides penalties ranging in severity based upon the severity of harm suffered by the victim of the constitutional violation. If the harm is categorized as a kidnapping, sexual assault, or murder, the penalty may be as great as life imprisonment.‡ It was, in fact, § 242 under which the four officers in the Rodney King beating case were prosecuted by the federal government in 1992.

There are essential elements that the government must prove beyond reasonable doubt to secure a conviction under § 242 for police

---

* *Screws v. U.S.*, 325 U.S. 91, 98–100. 65 S. Ct. 1031, 1035, 89 L.Ed. 1495, 1501–1502, 1945. "Sec. 20 was enacted to enforce the Fourteenth Amendment. It derives from § 2 of the Civil Rights Act of April 9, 1866. 14 Stat. 27. Senator Trumbull, chairman of the Senate Judiciary Committee which reported the bill, stated that its purpose was "to protect all persons in the United States in their civil rights, and furnish the means of their vindication." *Congressional Globe, 39th Congress, 1st Session,* 211pp. In origin it was an antidiscrimination measure (as its language indicated), framed to protect Negroes in their newly won rights. See Flack, The Adoption of the Fourteenth Amendment, 1908, p. 21. It was amended by § 17 of the Act of May 31, 1870, 16 Stat. 144, and made applicable to "any inhabitant of any State or Territory." The prohibition against the "deprivation of any rights, privileges, or immunities, secured or protected by the Constitution and laws of the United States" was introduced by the revisers in 1874. R. S. § 5510. Those words were taken over from § 1 of the Act of April 20, 1871, 17 Stat. 13 (the so-called Ku-Klux Act) which provided civil suits for redress of such wrongs. See *Congressional Record, 43rd Congress, 1st Session,* 828pp. The 1874 revision was applicable to any person who under color of law, etc., "subjects, or causes to be subjected" any inhabitant to the deprivation of any rights, etc. The requirement for a "willful" violation was introduced by the draftsmen of the Criminal Code of 1909. Act of March 4, 1909, 35 Stat. 1092. And we are told "willfully" was added to § 20 in order to make the section "less severe." 43 Congressional Record, 60th Congress, 2nd Session, 3599pp.
† Ibid (18 USCS § 242, 2015).
‡ Ibid.

use of excessive force.* Typically, courts break the required elements of the crime of use of excessive force to arrest into four elements: (1) the defendant was acting under color of law when he committed the acts charged in the indictment; (2) the defendant deprived the arrestee of his right to be free of unreasonable seizures secured by the Fourth Amendment to the Constitution of the United States; (3) the defendant acted with a willful intent to deprive the arrestee of the constitutional right; and (4) the offense resulted in bodily injury to the arrestee or the offense included the use, attempted use, or threatened use of a dangerous weapon.†

The first of the four elements requires that the actor be "acting under color of law." This element recognizes that the authority to carry out the official duties of a governmental office, whether elected or appointed, is authority provided by the law. So, an individual acts under color of state law when exercising authority held by virtue of a state government office or position. Courts must evaluate evidence to determine whether the defendant was exercising power bestowed by state law or was acting only as a private individual.‡ The Supreme Court has clearly stated that § 242 excludes acts committed by persons carrying out their personal pursuits, even when that person is a law enforcement officer. Specifically, § 242 only encompasses overstepping or abusing the authority of a State office.§ Just because a police officer was rude, unpleasant, or mean while wearing a governmental uniform is not enough to support a § 242 contention that harm to a person arose out of an officer's legal authority. For example, in § 242 of a Florida sheriff, the court recognized that the sheriff, while wearing her uniform, used her handcuffs for the private ends of assaulting and scaring a young man she caught in a compromising situation with her daughter. The assault happened in the sheriff's home when she was returning from a duty shift. The court in that case stated:

> If the allegations are true, Collier's treatment of Butler was badder than old King Kong and meaner than a junkyard dog. She might even have acted like the meanest hunk of woman anybody had ever seen. Still, the fact that the mistreatment was mean does not mean that the mistreatment was under color of law.¶

---

* See *Tarver v. City of Edna*, 410 F.3d 745, 752, 5th Cir. 2005.
† *U.S. v. Rodella*, 2015 U.S. App. LEXIS 19275, November 4, 2015.
‡ *Screws v. United States*, 325 U.S. 91, 111, 65 S.Ct. 1031, 1040, 89 L. Ed. 1495, 1945.
§ *Butler v. Sheriff of Palm Beach County et al.*, 685 F.3d 1261, 1265 2012.
¶ *Butler v. Sheriff of Palm Beach County*, at 1269.

The second element of a § 242 charge arising out of excessive force to arrest is the "act" element. This element requires evidence that the defendant did some act(s) that deprived the arrestee of his right to be free of unreasonable seizures secured by the Fourth Amendment. Unreasonable seizures include the right to be free from unlawful arrests and the right to not be subjected to excessive force. Federal prosecutors use the facts of the interaction between the law enforcement officer and the arrestee to support the allegation that the arrestee was subjected to an unreasonable seizure. For example, Sheriff Thomas Rodella was alleged to have unreasonably seized an individual whom he arrested. However, it was not just the limited interaction of the arrest that supported the § 242 charge, it was the entire interaction between Rodella and the victim. Rodella began the interaction by aggressively following the victim's vehicle. Rodella was in an unmarked vehicle, and the victim was not alleged to have committed any traffic violations at this point. The victim was so frightened by Rodella's aggressive driving that he began to drive in excess of the speed limit to get away from Rodella's threatening driving behavior. Eventually, Rodella forced the victim off the road, leapt into the individual's passenger side seat, and displayed a firearm. Rodella's son pulled the victim from his vehicle, forced him to the pavement, after which Rodella picked the victim's head up by the hair and hit him in the face with his badge.* Rodella's actions were deemed to be carried out under color of law as he was "pursuing" the individual, and seized the individual under his authority as a law enforcement officer.

The third element of § 242 is the element that requires that the government prove that the amount of force was unreasonable and the officer knew it to be unreasonable. This element is the element of "willful intent" to deprive the arrestee of rights guaranteed by the Fourth Amendment. To be "willful" the government must be able to show that the accused either knew or should have known that the acts would be considered an unreasonable amount of force. In 2014, the Second Circuit Court of Appeals specifically analyzed this element in relation to police use of excessive force during an arrest. The accused officer in that case, Cossette, was charged with using force without provocation or need, specifically, with "assaulting a detainee who was already handcuffed in a holding cell and compliant with the police.† The court stated that Cossette could not truthfully argue that the state failed to prove this element. Every police officer in the country knows that "gratuitously assaulting a detainee, without provocation or need, constituted an unreasonable use

---

* *U.S. v. Rodella*, 2015 U.S. App. LEXIS 19275, November 4, 2015.
† *U.S. v. Cossette*, 593 Fed. Appx. 28, 30, 2014.

of force."* In another case out of Tennessee, a district court judge was prosecuted under § 242 for sexually assaulting women employees of the court. On appeal, the defendant judge claimed that although the federal court found that sexually assaulting women of the court was a violation of the due process rights of the victims, the defendant judge had no way of knowing that in advance as no court had ever before stated that standard. The sixth Circuit accepted this argument and overturned the judge's § 242 conviction. The U.S. Supreme Court, however, overturned the sixth Circuit.† That Court held that defendants are on notice of the wrongfulness of their action is either a preexisting case, or preexisting law has made the action illegal.‡

The fourth element of a § 242 alleging excessive force associated with an arrest is the "harm" element. This element requires that the government prove that the offense resulted in bodily injury to the arrestee or the offense included the use, attempted use, or threatened use of a dangerous weapon. The level of force alleged must result in an actual physical or emotional harm. The mere act of using some force to carry out an arrest does not rise to the level of harm necessary to support this element of a § 242 claim. Clearly, some level of force, usually minimal, is necessary to complete any arrest.§ Additionally, the seriousness of the injury is not necessarily equated to amount of force used by the officer.¶ While a greater injury provides stronger evidence that an arresting officer used an unlawful amount of force under the Fourth Amendment, smaller injuries may still convince the fact finder that excessive force was used to arrest.** In short, this standard requires that a harm be suffered, but cannot be read to permit injuries and harms that do not leave a mark upon the victim's body. Such a restrictive standard would encourage and approve the development of tortures that do not photograph well.

The federal government has effectively used § 242 to prosecute many officers for acts of unreasonable use of force to arrest. A well-known example is the 1992 case against the four officers who beat Rodney King during an arrest.†† Three of the officers, Powell, Briseno, and Wind, were charged with willful use of unreasonable force in

---

* Ibid.
† *U.S. v. Lanier,* 520 U.S. 259, 272, 117 S. Ct. 1219, 1228, 137 L. Ed. 2d 432, 446, 1997.
‡ Ibid.
§ *Cortez v. McCauley,* 478 F.3d 1108, 1112, 10th Cir. 2007.
¶ *Hudson v. McMillian,* 503 U.S. 1, 112 S. Ct. 995, 1000, 117 L. Ed. 2d 156, 166, 1992.
** *U.S. v. Rodella,* 2015 U.S. App. LEXIS 19275, ___, November 4, 2015.
†† *Koon v. U.S.* and *Powell v. U.S.,* 518 U.S. 81, 88, 116 S. Ct. 2035, 2042, 135 L. Ed. 2d 392, 406, 1996.

arresting King. The fourth officer who had been in charge that night, Stacey Koon, was charged with willfully permitting the other officers to use unreasonable force during the arrest. The federal jury convicted Koon and Powell but acquitted Wind and Briseno. During the sentencing hearing of Koon and Powell, the federal district judge provided a clear review of the criminal law as applied to the facts.* The judge stated that much of the officers' conduct that night was lawful, although at the end of the arrest their behavior crossed the law into unlawfulness. The court recognized that while the officers were found guilty of using the batons as weapons to violate King's constitutional rights, the fact that weapons were present or used was not in itself the unlawful act. The court stated that "police officers are always armed with 'dangerous weapons' and may legitimately employ those weapons to administer reasonable force." In the King case, King admitted that he had been driving while intoxicated, had tried to outrun the police, and had initially failed to obey officers' commands. In arresting someone for those acts police may need to use force, and in this case the officer's initial use of force was deemed to be "provoked and lawful." But, at some point the officers' conduct crossed the line from a legal use of force to arrest into an unlawful deprivation of civil rights.†

Unfortunately, media stories at the time depicted the decision by the federal court as proving that the jury in the state case was biased and wrong when, in fact, the two cases involved different laws with different legal standards. It is entirely possible that the state jury would have found Koon and Powell guilty beyond a reasonable doubt for violation of the federal crime of violating § 242, but the state jury was not asked that question. The state jury was asked whether the state had proven that the state law which permitted the use of force to arrest was violated beyond reasonable doubt. Applying the evidence presented in the case to the elements of the state crimes, the state jury found the officers not guilty beyond reasonable doubt. The federal jury was asked a different question: whether the amount of force used to arrest Rodney King was unreasonable under the Fourth Amendment to the Constitution beyond a reasonable doubt. That jury found two of the four officers guilty beyond a reasonable doubt of violating that legal standard. Regrettably, the consequences of asking two juries to review the same set of facts to make different legal decisions is poorly understood by noncriminal justice professionals. When juries make decisions that the public views as

---

* *Koon v. U.S.* and *Powell v. U.S.*, at 103, 2049, and 416.
† Ibid.

conflicting, the jurors themselves may be cast as acting out of bias rather than merely having reviewed and applied different laws.*

A more recent § 242 analysis was conducted by the U.S. Department of Justice when it investigated the facts of the 2014 shooting death of Michael Brown by a Ferguson, Missouri police officer.† In an 86-page report outlining all of the evidence, and reviewing the applicable legal standards, the report concludes that the "matter lacks prosecutive merit and should be closed."‡ In applying the § 242 legal standards, the Department of Justice concluded:

> Darren Wilson has stated his intent in shooting Michael Brown was in response to a perceived deadly threat. The only possible basis for prosecuting Wilson under Section 242 would therefore be if the government could prove that his account is not true—i.e., that Brown never assaulted Wilson at the SUV, never attempted to gain control of Wilson's gun, and thereafter clearly surrendered in a way that no reasonable officer could have failed to perceive. Given that Wilson's account is corroborated by physical evidence and that his perception of a threat posed by Brown is corroborated by other eyewitnesses, to include aspects of the testimony of Witness 101, there is no credible evidence that Wilson willfully shot Brown as he was attempting to surrender or was otherwise not posing a threat. Even if Wilson was mistaken in his interpretation of Brown's conduct, the fact that others interpreted that conduct the same way as Wilson precludes a determination that he acted with a bad purpose to disobey the law.

---

* See, for example, *State v. Simpson*, No. BA-097211 (Cal. Super. Ct., L.A. County June 17, 1994). Uelmen, Gerald F., Jury-Bashing and the OJ. Simpson Verdict. 20 Harv.J.L.& Pub. Pol'y 475, 196.
Satterberg, William, Tales from the Interior: Voir Dire, 24 AK Bar Rag 18 (July/August, 2000). "The crowning touch is my O.J. Simpson trilogy. I ask the jurors whether or not they believe what they read in the newspaper, hear on the radio, or watch on television. By then, all hands are flying up quickly indicating that they do not believe any of those three news sources. I next ask the jurors to raise their hands if they can keep an open mind. Once again the hands fly up. By then, the trap is set. I then ask the jurors for a show of hands if they believe that "O.J. did it." Usually, but not always, a chuckle will arise in the courtroom. It is a valid technique, which goes to impress upon the jurors their need to keep an open mind, and judge a case only on the evidence presented, and not upon public opinion, sentiment, or press releases."
† Memorandum: Department of Justice Report Regarding the Criminal Investigation into the Shooting Death of Michael Brown By Ferguson, Missouri Police Officer Darren Wilson, U.S. Department of Justice. March 4, 2015. http://www.justice.gov/sites/default/files/opa/press-releases/ attachments/2015/03/04/doj_report_on _shooting_of_michael_brown_1.pdf
‡ Ibid, at 86.

While the findings of this investigation may not have resulted in the politically popular or emotionally satisfying outcome that was hoped for, this investigation did exactly what the law requires. The report clearly applies the law as it has developed over a long time, to the facts as they occurred on that day and time, to determine if the officer's actions constituted a federal crime under § 242.[*]

☐ Federal Civil Liability for Excessive Use of Force

Criminal prosecution is not the only remedy available to persons who believe that they have suffered harm. Victims themselves may sue the officer seeking damages in a civil court. Just as criminal wrongs are called "crimes," civil harms are known as "torts." The standard of proof to prove a tort is "preponderance of the evidence," which means "to be more sure than not." This standard of proof used in civil cases is much lower than the "beyond a reasonable doubt" standard of proof required to prove a crime, which means that it is easier to prove a civil wrong than it is to prove a crime. It is not unusual for someone to be found not guilty beyond a reasonable doubt in a criminal court, but then be found liable for the harms of the act in a civil court. A well-known example of this was seen in the O.J. Simpson cases.[†]

---

[*] Ibid. On March 4, 2015, the U.S. Department of Justice (U.S.D.O.J.) released its report ("U.S.D.O.J. Report") into the shooting death of 18-year-old Michael Brown by Officer Darren Wilson of the Ferguson, Mo. Police Department. The U.S.D.O.J. Report begins with an overview of the investigation into the shooting death of Michael Brown on August 9, 2014. The report provides an overview of the prosecutorial standard that federal prosecutors must meet before seeking an indictment against an individual. First, a federal prosecutor must be convinced that a federal crime occurred and that the accused committed that crime. Second, the prosecution must be in possession of that quantum of admissible evidence that could reasonably be expected to convince a jury beyond a reasonable doubt. After reviewing all of the available evidence the U.S.D.O.J. concluded that "Darren Wilson's actions do not constitute prosecutable violations under the applicable federal criminal civil rights statute, 18 U.S.C. § 242, which prohibits uses of deadly force that are "objectively unreasonable," as defined by the United States Supreme Court. The evidence, when viewed as a whole, does not support the conclusion that Wilson's uses of deadly force were "objectively unreasonable" under the Supreme Court's definition."

[†] *State v. Simpson*, No. BA-097211 (Cal. Super. Ct., L.A. County June 17, 1994). Uelmen, Gerald F., Jury-Bashing and the O.J. Simpson Verdict. 20 Harv.J.L.& Pub. Pol'y 475, 196.

While States recognize torts associated with excessive use of force, such as wrongful death, wrongful imprisonment, and assault, most civil lawsuits against officers are filed under the federal civil-rights statute codified at 42 U.S.C. § 1983. Whereas state torts are historically difficult to apply to police who are recognized to have a right to use force to carry out an arrest, the federal law creates a different form tort liability that seeks to address those specific harms suffered by persons who are deprived by state government officers of "'rights, privileges, or immunities secured' to them by the Constitution."* For the sake of brevity, litigation under 42 U.S.C. § 1983 is usually referred to as a "§ 1983" action.† While money damages are awarded to plaintiffs who win a § 1983 suit, the actual amount of damages is ordinarily determined according to principles derived from the common law of torts.‡

A § 1983 civil lawsuit, like a § 242 criminal action, requires evidence that an individual has acted under "color of law" granted by a state, territory, or the District of Columbia to cause a deprivation of a right guaranteed by the United States Constitution. But, the two laws are different, and dealt with very differently within the federal courts. A significant difference between the two laws is that § 242 extends to "any person" in any state, while § 1983 specifically protects "citizen[s]" of the United States.§ A second major difference is that § 242 is a criminal action requiring proof beyond a reasonable doubt to convict, while § 1983 is a civil lawsuit. That means that proving a § 1983 allegation requires the much lower standard of proof of preponderance of the evidence, and the individual claiming the harm may file the lawsuit directly without involving a criminal prosecutor.

---

* *Memphis Community School Dist, et al. v. Stachura*, 477 U.S. 299, 306, 106 S.Ct. 2537, 2542, 91 L.Ed.2d 249, 258, 1986 (quoting, *Carey v. Piphus*, 435 U.S. 247, 253, 1978, quoting *Imbler v. Pachtman*, 424 U.S. 409, 417, 1976).

† 42 U.S.C. § 1983. Civil action for deprivation of rights. "Every person who, under color of any statute, ordinance, regulation, custom, or usage, of any State or Territory or the District of Columbia, subjects, or causes to be subjected, any citizen of the United States or other person within the jurisdiction thereof to the deprivation of any rights, privileges, or immunities secured by the Constitution and laws, shall be liable to the party injured in an action at law, suit in equity, or other proper proceeding for redress, except that in any action brought against a judicial officer for an act or omission taken in such officer's judicial capacity, injunctive relief shall not be granted unless a declaratory decree was violated or declaratory relief was unavailable. For the purposes of this section, any Act of Congress applicable exclusively to the District of Columbia shall be considered to be a statute of the District of Columbia."

‡ Ibid. (See *Smith v. Wade*, 461 U.S. 30, 34, 1983; *Carey v. Piphus*, 435 U.S. 247, at 257-258, 1978; *Monroe v. Pape*, 365 U.S. 167, 196, and n. 5, 1961).

§ Ibid.

42 U.S.C. § 1983 does not include officers acting under authority granted by the federal government. In 1971, however, the U.S. Supreme Court found that federal officials who violate the Fourth Amendment may be sued for damages.* This authority to seek legal redress against *federal law enforcement officers* has been subsequently expanded to include other constitutional rights, and is known as a "Bivens action."† The rules for proving a § 1983 violation and a Bivens violation are virtually identical. In both types of lawsuits a plaintiff may be awarded money damages from government officials who have violated constitutional or statutory rights.

To establish a cause of action under § 1983 or Bivens action, the individual claiming to have suffered harm, known as the plaintiff, must show that the defendant, an identified actual person acting under color of law, caused the plaintiff to suffer a violation of a clearly established constitutional right. The phrase "under color of law" has the same meaning in 18 U.S.C.S. § 242 as it does in 42 U.S.C.S. § 1983.‡ Any private citizen can commit an illegal act. By imposing the requirement that the actor has acted "under color of law" private conduct is excluded, and cases are limited to abuse of official powers.§

A § 1983 or Bivens requires that an identified "person" has acted to violate the citizen's rights. According to the Supreme Court based upon the clear language of the Eleventh Amendment granting states immunity from certain lawsuits, states are not "persons" subject to suit under § 1983.¶ The Court also determined that the Eleventh Amendment "bars suits not only against the State when it is the named party, but also when it is the party in fact."** "Its applicability is to be determined not by the

---

* *Bivens v. Six Unknown Fed. Narcotics Agents*, 403 U.S. 388, 91 S. Ct. 1999, 29 L. Ed. 2d 619, 1971.

† See, for example, *Carlson v. Green*, 446 U.S. 14, 100 S.Ct. 1468, 64 L.Ed.2d 15, 1980. (Eighth Amendment cruel and unusual punishment); *Davis v. Passman*, 442 U.S. 228, 99 S.Ct. 2264, 60 L.Ed.2d 846 (1979) (Fifth Amendment due process).

‡ *Butler v. Sheriff of Palm Beach County et al.*, 685 F.3d 1261, 1269, 2012.

§ Ibid.

¶ *Will v. Michigan Dept. of State Police*, 491 U.S. 58, 105 L. Ed. 2d 45, 109 S. Ct. 2304, 1989. USCS Const. Amend. 11. Suits against states—restriction of judicial power. The Judicial power of the United States shall not be construed to extend to any suit in law or equity, commenced or prosecuted against one of the United States by citizens of another state, or by citizens or subjects of any foreign state.

** *Scheuer v. Rhodes*, 416 U.S. 232, 237, 94 S. Ct. 1683, 1687, 40 L. Ed. 2d 90, 98. (Citing to: *Edelman v. Jordan*, 415 U.S. 651 1974); *Poindexter v. Greenhow*, 114 U.S. 270, 287 (1885); *Cunningham v. Macon & Brunswick R. Co.*, 109 U.S. 446, 1883).

mere names of the titular parties but by the essential nature and effect of the proceeding, as it appears from the entire record."*

A municipality does not have the same protections as a state government, which is notable as the majority of law enforcement officers are employees of municipal governments. In *Monell v. New York City Dept. of Social Services*, the Court held that municipalities are "persons" subject to damages liability under § 1 of the Ku Klux Act of 1871, 42 U.S.C. § 1983, for violations of that act visited by municipal officials.† The court narrowly defined municipal liability, however. It held "that municipal liability could not be premised on the mere fact that the municipality employed the offending official," but instead, "municipal liability could only be imposed for injuries inflicted pursuant to government 'policy or custom'."‡

To establish the liability of a municipality, the "causal" standard is understood as "deliberate indifference." " 'Deliberate indifference' is a stringent standard of fault, requiring proof that a municipal actor disregarded a known or obvious consequence of his action."§ The court clearly explained this standard in the 1989 case of Canton, *Ohio v. Harris*. The court held that a municipality can be found liable under 42 U.S.C.S. § 1983 only where the municipality itself causes the

---

* Ex parte New York, 256 U.S. 490, 500, 41 S. Ct. 588, 590, 65 L.Ed. 1057, 1062 (1921). See also, *Hafer v. Melo*, 502 U.S. 21, 25, 112 S.Ct. 358, 361-362, 116 L.Ed.2d 301, 309, 1991 "In *Kentucky v. Graham*, 473 U.S. 159, 87 L. Ed. 2d 114, 105 S. Ct. 3099, 1985, the Court sought to eliminate lingering confusion about the distinction between personal- and official-capacity suits. We emphasized that official-capacity suits "generally represent only another way of pleading an action against an entity of which an officer is an agent." *Kentucky v. Graham*, at 165 (quoting *Monell v. New York City Dept. of Social Services*, 436 U.S. 658, 690, n. 55, 56 L. Ed. 2d 611, 98 S. Ct. 2018, 1978). Suits against state officials in their official capacity therefore should be treated as suits against the State. 473 U.S. at 166. Indeed, when officials sued in this capacity in federal court die or leave office, their successors automatically assume their roles in the litigation. Because the real party in interest in an official-capacity suit is the governmental entity and not the named official, "the entity's "policy or custom" must have played a part in the violation of federal law." *Kentucky v. Graham*, at 166 (quoting Monell, at 694). For the same reason, the only immunities available to the defendant in an official-capacity action are those that the governmental entity possesses. *Kentucky v. Graham* at 167."

† *City of Oklahoma City v. Tuttle*, 471 U.S. 808, 105 S.Ct. 2427, 85 L Ed.2d 791 (1985) (quoting *Monell v. New York City Dept. of Social Services*, 436 U.S. 658, 1978).

‡ *City of Oklahoma City v. Tuttle*, 471 U.S. 808, 810, 105 S.Ct. 2427, 2429, 85 L Ed.2d 791, 796 (1985). See also, *Brd. Of County Commr's of Bryan County, OK v. Brown*, 520 U.S. 397, 117 S.Ct. 1382, 137 L.Ed.2d 626, 1997.

§ *Brd. of County Commr's of Bryan County, OK.v. Brown*, at 410, 1391, and 643.

constitutional violation at issue. Respondeat superior or vicarious liability will not attach under § 1983. It is only when "the execution of the
government's policy or custom inflicts the injury that the municipality
may be held liable under § 1983."[*] The Canton decision also clearly set
forth the standard for holding a municipality liable under § 1983 for
failure to train. That Court held that if certain employees are assigned
specific duties that require those performing such duties to be provided
more or different training in order to carry out those duties, and a
municipality decides not to provide the employees such training, "the
policymakers of the city can reasonably be said to have been deliberately indifferent to the need."[†]

Qualified immunity shields federal and state officials from money
damages unless a plaintiff pleads facts showing (1) that the official violated a statutory or constitutional right and (2) that the right was "clearly
established" at the time of the challenged conduct.[‡] Qualified immunity
is only a defense in lawsuits against an official in their personal capacity.[§]
The only immunities that can be claimed in an official-capacity action
are forms of sovereign immunity, such as those immunities provided by
the Eleventh Amendment.[¶]

The standard that actionable conduct involves violation of a clearly
established statutory or constitutional right of which a reasonable person
would have known protects officers from being required to know laws

---

[*] *City of Canton, Ohio v. Harris*, 489 U.S. 378, 385, 109 S.Ct. 1197, 1204, 103 L. Ed.2d
412, 424, 1989.

[†] *City of Canton, Ohio v. Harris*, 489 U.S. 378, 396, 109 S.Ct. 1197, 1208, 103 L. Ed.2d
412, 431 (1989).

[‡] *Ashcroft v. al-Kidd*, 563 U.S. 731, 131 S. Ct. 2074, 2080, 179 L. Ed. 2d 1149, 1155,
2011. *Pearson v. Callahan*, 555 U.S. 223, 231, 129 S. Ct. 808, 172 L. Ed. 2d 565, 2009.
(Quoting *Harlow v. Fitzgerald*, 457 U.S. 800, 818, 102 S. Ct. 2727, 73 L. Ed. 2d 396,
1982).

[§] Ibid. (Citing to: *Owen v. City of Independence*, 445 U.S. 622, 1980; see also *Brandon v.
Holt*, 469 U.S. 464, 1985).

[¶] Ibid. See also, *Hafer v. Melo*, 502 U.S. 21, 25, 112 S.Ct. 358, 362, 116 L.Ed.2d 301,
309–310, 1991. "Personal-capacity suits, on the other hand, seek to impose individual liability upon a government officer for actions taken under color of state law.
Thus, "on the merits, to establish personal liability in a § 1983 action, it is enough
to show that the official, acting under color of state law, caused the deprivation
of a federal right." *Kentucky v. Graham*, p. 166. While the plaintiff in a personal-
capacity suit need not establish a connection to governmental "policy or custom,"
officials sued in their personal capacities, unlike those sued in their official capacities, may assert personal immunity defenses such as objectively reasonable reliance
on existing law. *Kentucky v. Graham*, pp. 166–167."

or judicial decisions before they occur.* "A clearly established right is one that is 'sufficiently clear that every reasonable official would have understood that what he is doing violates that right.'"† So, if an officer was acting in reasonable reliance upon an existing law or policy, the officer is granted qualified immunity from liability in the case.‡

Whether a method of arrest or detention, or the amount of force used to complete an arrest, is reasonable is an objective legal inquiry.§ Objective reasonableness is a legal standard. Objective reasonableness evaluates whether at the time of the challenged conduct any reasonable officer in the same situation would have known that his actions would be in violation of a constitutional right.¶ Understanding how objective reasonableness applies in any case depends upon the "facts and circumstances of each particular case."** "A court must make this determination from the perspective of a reasonable officer on the scene, including what the officer knew at the time, not with the 20/20 vision of hindsight."†† In an attempt to clarify this standard in the Kingsley case, the Court reviewed case law precedent to provide a nonexclusive list of considerations that may have applicability in a determination as to whether an officer's use of force was objectively reasonable.

> Considerations such as the following may bear on the reasonableness or unreasonableness of the force used: the relationship between the need for the use of force and the amount of force used; the extent of the plaintiff's

---

* *Camreta v. Greene*, 563 U.S. 692, 131 S. Ct. 2020, 2031, 179 L. Ed. 2d 1118, 1132, 2011. *Scott v. Harris*, 550 U.S.372, 377 127 S. Ct. 1769, 1774, 167 L. Ed. 2d 686, 692, 2007. In resolving questions of qualified immunity, courts are required to resolve a threshold question: taken in the light most favorable to the party asserting the injury, do the facts alleged show an officer's conduct violated a constitutional right? This must be the initial inquiry. If, and only if, the court finds a violation of a constitutional right, the next, sequential step is to ask whether the right was clearly established in light of the specific context of the case. Although this ordering contradicts the U.S. Supreme Court's policy of avoiding unnecessary adjudication of constitutional issues, such a departure from practice is necessary to set forth principles which will become the basis for a future holding that a right is clearly established.
† *Mullenix v. Luna*, 2015 U.S. Lexis 7160, November 9, 2015. (Quoting *Reichle v. Howards*, 566 U.S. ___, ___, 132 S. Ct. 2088, 182 L. Ed. 2d 985, 989, 2012).
‡ *Kentucky v. Graham*, 473 U.S. 159, 166–167, 105 S. Ct. 3099, 3105–3106, 87 L. Ed. 2d 114, 122, 1985. (Citing to: *Imbler v. Pachtman*, 424 U.S. 409, 1976 (absolute immunity); *Pierson v. Ray*, 386 U.S. 547, 1967 (same); *Harlow v. Fitzgerald*, 457 U.S. 800, 1982 (qualified immunity); *Wood v. Strickland*, 420 U.S. 308, 1975).
§ *Ashcroft v. al-Kidd*, 563 U.S. 731, 131 S. Ct. 2074, 179 L. Ed. 2d 1149, 2011.
¶ Ibid.
** *Graham v. Connor*, 490 U.S. 386, 396,109 S. Ct. 1865, 1872, 104 L. Ed. 2d 443, 455, 1989.
†† *Kingsley v. Hendrickson*, 135 S. Ct. 2466, 2473, 192 L. Ed. 2d 416, 426, 2015.

injury; any effort made by the officer to temper or to limit the amount of force; the severity of the security problem at issue; the threat reasonably perceived by the officer; and whether the plaintiff was actively resisting. We do not consider this list to be exclusive. We mention these factors only to illustrate the types of objective circumstances potentially relevant to a determination of excessive force.[*]

It is important to understand phrases such as "objectively rea-sonable" are legal terms of art, and cannot be understood to have the meaning they might have in ordinary conversation. For example, media stories covering prosecutorial investigatory reports in the shooting death of a 12-year-old boy by a Ohio police officer, seized on that phrase to sug-gest that the prosecutor found the shooting to be "reasonable."[†] Instead, the prosecutor was specifically required to use that phrase to describe the legal evaluation conducted.

While plaintiffs in § 1983 and Bivens cases may dislike the broad protections of the concept of the qualified immunity, the public policy justifications for it have long been accepted. Official immunity developed hundreds of years ago based upon two mutually dependent rationales: (1) the injustice, particularly in the absence of bad faith, of penalizing an officer for performing those acts of his job which require use of physical force and individual discretion; and (2) "the danger that the threat of such liability would deter his willingness to execute his office with the decisiveness and the judgment required by the public good."[‡] In a society that expects the government to actively work to protect the individual's safety and individual's property rights against those who would wrong-fully harm either, society's defenders, the police must be confident that if they carry out their duties in conformance with existing laws, rules, and policies, the government that employs them will protect them.

The media have reported that the family of Michael Brown has filed a § 1983 civil suit against the City of Ferguson, Missouri.[§] If that case proceeds, a federal jury will eventually be asked to decide, if whether by a preponderance of the evidence, the City of Ferguson, Missouri was aware of, and deliberately indifferent to, obvious consequences of that city's policy or custom, which resulted in the shooting death of Michael

---

[*] *Kingsley v. Hendrickson*, 135 S. Ct. 2466, 2473, 192 L. Ed. 2d 416, 426, 2015.

[†] Graham, David, Yet Another Report Excuses Police in Tamir Rice's Death. The Atlantic. November 12, 2015. http://www.theatlantic.com/politics/archive/2015/11/report-vindicates-police-in-tamir-rices-death/415731/

[‡] Ibid.

[§] Robert Patrick, St. Louis federal judge dismisses several counts of Brown family lawsuit, *St. Louis Post-Dispatch*, July 14, 2015; Matt Pearce, Michael Brown's family sues Ferguson, Mo., for wrongful death. *Los Angeles Times*, April 23, 2015.

Brown. If the jury answers that question in the affirmative, the family of Michael Brown may be awarded money damages from the City of Ferguson. Just as importantly, the jury will have identified those specific acts which municipalities must recognize and change, effectively notifying all cities and police officers of those policies and procedures that must be changed to comply with the requirements of the constitution.

☐ Conclusion

If Michael Brown's family wins their § 1983 civil suit against the City of Ferguson, Missouri, many will be left with the impression that the Department of Justice report was wrong, and Darren Wilson escaped justice when prosecutors failed to prosecute him. The law is not that simple, however. Decisions by juries in civil suits are only a finding of financial liability, and cannot be compared to a legal determination of criminal guilt, whether under state law or § 242.

For both police officers, and those sitting in judgment of police officers, it can never be forgotten that the law is not emotional: it is analytical. An arrest should never devolve into an officer's irrational fear response, or a vengeful rage. At the same time, when reviewing an officer's conduct for criminal or civil liability, the standard cannot be emotional. The criminal law requires proof beyond a reasonable doubt of every component of a crime as that crime is written, not as the crime may be generally perceived. It is incumbent upon all citizens of the United States to do more than call the police for law enforcement service and judge the police for the manner of providing that law enforcement service. Americans should make an effort to understand the laws, as least generally, that dictate how an officer performs his duties and the protections accorded to him by the law for performing those duties within the permitted parameters. Real choices about changing the law require understanding it. Learning to differentiate between permitted and prohibited use of force is an important step in eliminating injustices perpetrated by law enforcement officers.

Psychological and Social Factors in the Use of Force

Jodie Beeson

☐ Introduction

Psychologists have played a role in the selection of law enforcement recruits since the early 1900s. One of the first uses of psychology in police selection occurred in 1917 with the use of the Stanford-Binet Intelligence Scale in the pre-employment screening of potential candidates (Terman et al., 1917). Since that time, the use of psychological principles and police psychologists has steadily increased. Psychologists have addressed issues in the field of law enforcement and the health of law enforcement professionals from many directions.

By the 1960s, issues such as corruption, racial bias, coercion, and inappropriate use of force became key concerns in the field of psychology. In 1965, funding was made available by the Law Enforcement Assistance Administration to improve the services delivered by law enforcement professionals and to reduce corruption and abuse of power. By the 1970s, the use of pre-employment personality tests to assess the fitness of a candidate became a widespread practice. In 1973, the Police Task Force Report of the National Commission on Criminal Justice Standards and Goals recommended that all law enforcement agencies enlist help from those in the behavioral sciences to address issues in law enforcement (Bartol, 1996).

While the impact of excessive use of force by law enforcement professionals is great, the frequency of events where excessive use of force occurs are fortunately rare. Currently, psychologists approach the issue of excess use of force by law enforcement professionals from many angles. A law enforcement candidate's appropriateness for a law enforcement career is assessed with pre-employment screening for personality traits that may contribute to overly aggressive approaches to conflict and critical situations. In addition to pre-employment screening, various approaches to understanding excessive use of force by law enforcement professionals have been researched. Those areas include; the social learning process of officers during the career span, the impact of police culture on decision-making in critical instances, the cognitive decision-making process of officers in the line of duty, and the effects of intensity and stress on the behavior of law enforcement professionals in citizen interactions.

☐ Personality and Individual Characteristics

Understanding what officer characteristics are associated with instances of an excessive use of force is central to devising pre-employment screening protocols and post-employment policies to reduce the occurrence of inappropriate uses of force. In a study, police psychologists were asks to identify individual characteristics common among the officers they treated in association with an inappropriate use of force. The psychologists identified the following elements (Scrivner, 1994):

• Personality disorders including lack of empathy, narcissism, and anti-social disorders

• Individuals with early career issues such as impulsiveness, impression-ability, low tolerance for frustration, and need for strong supervision

• Officers who utilized a more dominant policing style and were sensitive to challenges and provocation

• Individuals who were experiencing major life events such as divorce or a change in job situation or status

The use of pre-employment screening is the first step in reducing incidences of excessive use of force by law enforcement professionals. Pre-employment screening is used to identify individuals who may be at increased risk for aggressive or inappropriate behavior prior to employment. There is no widespread standardized process for the pre-employment screening of law enforcement officer candidates. Each agency constructs an independent screening process. While some agencies utilize an extensive battery of physical, cognitive, psychological tests, interviews, background checks, and polygraph tests prior to making hiring decisions, others make hiring decisions based on less information. Typically, larger agencies have more rigorous screening procedures. The following personality assessments are frequently used to make hiring decisions (Detrick and Chibnall, 2013; Surrette et al., 2003; Twersky-Glasner, 2005):

- Minnesota Multiphasic Personality Inventory 2—revised Form (MMPI-2-RF)

- Revised NEO Personality Inventory (NEO PI-R)

- California Personality Inventory (CPI)

- Edwards Personal Preference Schedule (EPPS)

- Big Five Inventory (BFI)

- Inwald Personality Inventory (IPI)

In an effort to evaluate the usefulness personality traits to predicted job performance in law enforcement officers, a study based on the big five personality traits as measured by the BFI as well as a measure of attitude and age, was conducted (Sanders, 2008) The BFI evaluates for the presence of five major personality traits. The five personality traits are the following:

- Extroversion

- Neuroticism

- Agreeableness

- Conscientiousness

- Openness

Generally, traits such as conscientiousness and extroversion are highly related to satisfactory job performance, while neuroticism may be associated with unsatisfactory job performance. For the study, satisfactory job performance was measured according to the following characteristics:

- Job knowledge

- Quality of work

- Cooperation

- Responsibility

- Initiative

- Quantity of work

- Dependability and

- Interaction with public

However, in the analysis of law enforcement officers, the association between these personality traits and satisfactory job performance was not a strong predictor of satisfactory performance. The age of the officer and his/her attitude toward the job were stronger predictors of performance quality.

One of the most commonly used assessments is the MMPI-2-RF. The MMPI-2-RF consists of scores on multiple personality scales. In a study of law enforcement officers that had passed pre-employment screening, the scales that related to personality traits associate with the excessive use of force are: thought dysfunction (disordered thinking), persecutory ideation (feeling misunderstood or blamed), and stress/worry (anxious apprehension or preoccupation with disappointment) (Ben-porath and Tellegen, 2011; Tarescavage et al., 2014; Tarescavage et al., 2015). Of those traits, thought dysfunction was the only trait that was significantly correlated with a higher risk for the use of excessive force. Thought dysfunction is characterized by disordered or unusual thought patterns. A person with thought dysfunction may not perceive or interpret events accurately (Alan et al., 2014). For example, an officer with thought dysfunction may perceive an interaction with a citizen as threatening, even if objective evidence would indicate otherwise.

In another study, a comparison of personality between candidates who were not recommended for hire, those who were considered to be "marginal" upon hire, and those who were recommended for hire (Fischler, 2004). The candidates who were not recommended for hire exhibited higher levels of unusual or disordered thinking, obsessive thinking, suspiciousness, impulsivity, aggressiveness, hostility, cynicism, alcoholism, and other traits indicating instability or psychological problems. When a comparison of candidates who were recommended for hire with candidates that were deemed marginal upon hire; the candidates that were recommended for hire experienced lower levels of sustained serious complaints. A factor analysis in the study identifies three basic groups of officer characteristics based on scores from their personality assessments:

- Well adjusted, agreeable, and possessing a high work ethic

- Antisocial, impulsiveness, and alcohol problems

- Disordered (unusual) thinking and suspiciousness

Individuals who scored higher in the disordered thinking factor had higher levels of sustained complaints. This can likely be attributed to an officer's inability to properly assess situations and respond accordingly as well as a tendency to assess a situation as more negative than objective reality would indicate.

☐ The Impact of Social Factors on Use of Force Decisions

Social Learning Theory

Social learning is a theory first proposed by Albert Bandura in 1971 that learning takes place through social modeling. In his experiment, he modeled aggressive behavior with a doll, Bobo, in front of children. He then allowed those children to play with the doll and observed their behavior. The children witnessing the aggressive behavior exhibited more violent behavior toward the doll than the children who had not witnessed this modeling (Bandura, 1971). In order for social learning to take place, following four conditions must be met:

- Attention: the learner must observe the behavior and the behavior must capture the learner's attention over all other stimuli

- Retention: the learner must distinctly remember the behavior and have the mental ability to rehearse the behavior

- Reproduction: the learner must be able to perform and practice the behavior

- Motivation: the learner must be motivated to perform the behavior

Differential Association Theory

Differential association theory is a social theory that suggests that deviant behaviors occur in social environments with close social groups. When individuals are exposed to groups that are exclusive and deviant behaviors are widely accepted and reinforced in a group where acceptance is highly desired, a motivation for social learning is created. In the case of police officers, the police subculture may create an environment where social learning paired with differential association may create the perfect stage for the development of behaviors that lead to an excessive use of force (Burgess and Akers, 2015; Chappell and Piquero, 2004; Maskaly and Donner, 2015).

Research indicates that attitudes toward deviant behavior in law enforcement are influenced by the subculture of the group and that it is necessary to "override" those behaviors with training to change the normative attitudes of the group (Chappell and Piquero, 2004). Law enforcement professionals may be particularly vulnerable to this type of social learning due to the awareness of the risk of death associated with working in law enforcement.

Terror Management Theory

Coping with the constant threat of mortality is referred to as terror management (Maxfield et al., 2014). In an individual with healthy psychological adaptive skills many strategies are utilized to address the anxiety associated with high-risk occupations. Those strategies may include cultural perspectives, social attachments, religion, cognitive reappraisal, and humor. Cognitive reappraisal is the regulation of thought processes to reduce anxiety by restructuring one's appraisal of a threat situation. For example, an officer may recognize the threat of mortality, but decide that he or she is extremely unlikely to face that event due to high levels of professional proficiency. One coping mechanism that persons associated with law enforcement professionals often recognize is the use of humor and even black humor to address stressful working environments. The use of humor to deal with stressful conditions allows for individuals to reframe conditions in order to relieve the tension created by an emotional closeness to the situation. The use of humor is also associated with social bonding (Long and Greenwood, 2013; Rowe and Regehr, 2010; Wilkins, 2014).

In the absence of effective strategies to cope with the threat of mortality, law enforcement officers may resort to maladaptive strategies, experience increased anxiety, and potentially develop a psychological dysfunction that would increase the risk for using excessive force (Maxfield et al., 2014). In a condition where the salience of the presence of the threat of mortality is particularly high, individuals are more likely to respond in a more punitive and more defensive manner.

Integrating Social Theories

Maskaly and Donner propose the integration of terror management theory and social learning theory to understand instances where officers use deadly force against unarmed individuals. This integration of theories is used to explain cases such as the shooting of Tamir Rice on November 22, 2014 in Cleveland, Ohio. Six days prior to that event an officer was killed in the line of duty in Akron, Ohio. The death of the officer in close geographic proximity may have increased the officer's awareness of the threat of mortality. If the subculture in the department was favorable toward authoritarian and aggressive reactions to threats, the officers may be more likely to utilize a more aggressive approach to ambiguous situations than at other times (Maskaly and Donner, 2015).

☐ Cognitive Decision-Making Factors

In a perfect world, law enforcement officers would make decisions regarding the level of force that should be used in any given situation according to a clear set of objective criteria. Officers are instructed to use deadly force only in situations where there is not another reasonable option. Many officers receive extensive training in tactical decision making. Yet, in practice, the decision to use force is not always made in an objective manner. There are many factors that influence the cognitive decision-making processes of an officer in the line of duty. In a meta-analysis of 44 analyses regarding event characteristics and factors where a use of force decision was made, specific characteristics fell into four categories: encounter characteristics, suspect characteristics, officer characteristics, and community characteristics (Bolger, 2014).

Encounter Characteristics

Encounter characteristics are factors that relate to the interchange between the officer and/or officers at the time when a decision was made on the level of force to be used. Of the four sets of characteristics, the characteristics of the encounter had the highest effect on the level of force used. The significant factors associated with an increased level of force were the following:

• Offense seriousness

• Suspect resistance during the course of an arrest of suspect

• Level of conflict at scene

• Number of officers at scene

Of those factors, the level of resistance of the suspect had the greatest impact on the level of force decision, followed by whether or not the encounter occurred during the course of an arrest. Interestingly, the presence of a weapon was not a significant factor.

Suspect Characteristics

Suspect characteristics are characteristics of the suspect that were evident at the time of the encounter. The following factors had a significant effect on the level of force used:

- Suspect race

- Suspect sex

- Suspect demeanor

- Suspect social class

- Suspect intoxication

Of the above listed factors, the demeanor of a suspect was by far the factor that had the greatest impact on the level of force used. This is logical, as there would be a greater need to use force in a situation where the suspect was uncooperative or out of control. The sex and the race of the suspect were significant factors in most studies.

Officer Characteristics

Officer characteristics relate to the officer most directly related to the suspect in the encounter. The only factor associated with a direction in the level of force used in an encounter was sex. Female officers were less likely to use force.

Community Characteristics

The factors related to community characteristics included in the study were: economy, racial makeup of community, and the crime rate in the community. None of these characteristics had a significant influence on the decision regarding the level of force used.

The Impact of Emotional Factors and Anxiety

In a society where television shows and YouTube videos about law enforcement officers are so prevalent, there is a tendency for citizens to overestimate their understanding of the emotional and cognitively demanding situations law enforcements officers are in while making decisions regarding the use of force. While watching videos taken by bystanders during a police encounter, it would seem that all of the pertinent information is available right there on the monitor. However, there are several factors that would impact the officer's ability to make a clear decision that are not apparent from a video. Decisions are made through cognitive processes in the frontal lobe of the brain. This is a process that occurs throughout one's waking hours without much awareness of the process. However, when an individual has other processes running at the same time, decision-making processes have to share the available cognitive resources. Other processes can include distractions, emotions, anxiety, or any other process that would use cognitive resources.

In a study, designed to evaluate the effect of anxiety on performance while shooting a gun during a simulation exercise (Nieuwenhuys et al., 2012), participants were exposed to situations where either a suspect with a gun would appear or a suspect without a gun would appear. If the suspect had a gun, the participant was to shoot at the suspect. If the suspect did not have a gun, the participant was to shoot at a black square. The participants were also presented with a high-anxiety situation and a low-anxiety situation. In the high-anxiety situation, a "blowback" gun would shoot plastic pellets at the participant's feet if they did not shoot an armed suspect on time. In the low-anxiety situation the suspect would shoot back on the video, but the participant would receive no physical punishment.

The results of the study clearly indicated that the correct decision on whether or not to shoot a subject based on whether they were armed or not, the time to make a decision, and accuracy of shooting were all effected by the high-anxiety condition. Participants were more likely to shoot an unarmed suspect and take less time to decide whether to shoot or not in the high-anxiety condition. The accuracy was slightly lower in the high-anxiety condition.

In a phenomenological study of police academy cadets, cadets were placed in a variety of reality-based training scenarios that were both physically and emotionally taxing. The cadets were then asked to report on their experiences (Broomé, 2011). The results indicated that, while the scenarios were simulated, they each experienced physiological, emotional, and cognitive reactions to the simulated events. In more stressful events, participants experienced "flight, fight, posture, and freeze" reactions to the events in the simulation. These are typical parasympathetic nervous system responses humans and animals exhibit when exposed to perceived or actual danger. Their responses became more automated and less complex when exposed to high-intensity situations. The study indicates that officers involved in an actual encounter most likely experience the same symptoms and that their responses may be more automatic and less capable of distinguishing nuances in situations.

Working memory is also a factor in officers' decision-making processes regarding the decision to shoot or not to shoot, based on whether a suspect has a weapon or a nonthreatening object such as a cell phone. One study found that participants with lower working memory capacities tended to make more wrong decisions in both conditions. This effect was enhanced when either negative emotions or heightened arousal was factored into the equation (Kleider et al., 2010).

The aforementioned studies illustrate the limitations of the cognitive processes necessary for decision making under intense, ambiguous situations. This presents definite implications for training officers. While most officers receive tactical training and training regarding the ethics and policies of training, these studies indicate that this approach would not change an officer's ability to respond appropriately in a high-intensity situation. Practice and rehearsal can improve the ability to function in high-intensity situations. While practice and rehearsal are not practical solutions for such high-impact low-frequency events, simulation trainings may offer an answer. In Canada, researchers studied the effects of using simulated exercises to recreate the physical and emotional intensity of real-world use of force incidents (Armstrong et al., 2014). Research also supports situational awareness (SA) training as an effective approach to improving an officer's ability to make decisions in high-intensity situations. SA training utilizes the technology of virtual reality to create and manipulate simulated environments and situations that would be similar to the environment an officer would face in the line of duty. The benefit of virtual reality is that the simulation can be stopped and restarted on demand to allow for reflection and input by trainers (Saus et al., 2006). With the chance to break the scenarios into different parts, participants become more aware of how different responses change the entire scenario. Benefits of this training include increased awareness of the factors leading up to a use of force incident and the ability to practice reacting under stressful circumstances.

☐ Conclusion

The issues relating to the use of force by law enforcement professionals are complicated and require input from many disciplines. Personality psychology offers insights to the selection of police officer candidates with the intellectual and psychological stability and the qualities that are best suited for the work required of a law enforcement professional. Social psychology and the theories of social learning, differential association, and terror management offer insights into the socialization and learning of law enforcement officers after employment and initial training that may influence an individual officer's ability to make appropriate decisions regarding the use of force. Cognitive psychology offers insight to the decision-making processes and the limits of officers in making decisions in high-intensity situations, as well as training approaches to improve the cognitive performance of officers. Together, these insights offer pieces to the puzzle of addressing issues related to the problem of excessive use of force by law enforcement professionals, while understanding the absolute necessity for an officer to act in a manner that reduces risk for officers while on duty.

☐ References

Alan F. F., Bolinskey, P. K., Levak, R. W., and David, S. N. 2014. *Psychological Assessment with the MMPI-2/MMPI-2-RF* (Third Edition). Abingdon: Routledge.

Armstrong, J., Clare, J., and Plecas, D. 2014. Monitoring the impact of scenario-based use-of-force simulations on police heart rate. *Evaluating the Royal Canadian Mounted Police Skills Refresher Program*, 15(1), 51–59.

Bandura, A. 1971. *Social Learning Theory*. Englewood Cliffs, New Jersey: Prentice-Hall. Doi:10.1111/j.1460-2466.1978.tb01621.x.

Bartol, C. R. 1996. Police psychology: Then, now and beyond. *Criminal Justice and Behavior*, 23(1), 70–89.

Ben-Porath, Y. S. and Tellegen, A. 2011. *Manual for Administration, Scoring, and Interpretation*. Minneapolis: University of Minnesota Press.

Bolger, P. C. 2014. Just following orders: A meta-analysis of the correlates of American police officer use of force decisions. *American Journal of Criminal Justice*, 40, 466–492. Doi:10.1007/s12103-014-9278-y

Broomé, R. E. 2011. An empathetic psychological perspective of police deadly force training. *Journal of Phenomenological Psychology*, 42(2), 137–156. Doi:10.1163/156916211X599735.

Burgess, R. L. and Akers, R. L. 2015. A differential association-reinforcement theory of criminal behavior. *Social Problems*, 14(2), 128–147.

Chappell, A. T. and Piquero, A. R. 2004. Applying social learning theory to police misconduct. *Deviant Behavior*, 25(December 2013), 89–108. Doi:10.1080/01639620490251642.

Detrick, P. and Chibnall, J. T. 2013. Revised NEO personality inventory normative data for police officer selection. *Psychological Services*, 10(4), 372–377. Doi:10.1037/a0031800.

Fischler, G. L. 2004. Identifying psychological predictors of police officer integrity problems. Community Oriented Policing Services (COPS) Office of the United States Department of Justice (US DOJ) CFDA No. 16.710, "Creating a Culture of Integrity."

Kleider, H. M., Parrot, D. J., and King, T. Z. 2010. Shooting behaviour: How working memory and negative emotionality influence police officer shoot decisions. *Applied Cognitive Psychology*, 24(5), 707–717. Doi:10.1002/acp.

Long, C. R. and Greenwood, D. N. 2013. Joking in the face of death: A terror management approach to humor production. *Humor*, 26(4), 493–509. Doi:10.1515/humor-2013-0012.

Maskaly, J. and Donner, C. M. 2015. A theoretical integration of social learning theory with terror management theory: Towards an explanation of police shootings of unarmed suspects. *American Journal of Criminal Justice*, 40(2), 205–224. Doi:10.1007/s12103-015-9293-7.

Maxfield, M., John, S., and Pyszczynski, T. 2014. A terror management perspective on the role of death-related anxiety in psychological dysfunction. *The Humanistic Psychologist*, 42(1), 35–53. Doi:10.1080/08873267.2012.732155.

Nieuwenhuys, A., Savelsbergh, G. J. P., and Oudejans, R. R. D. 2012. Shoot or don't shoot? Why police officers are more inclined to shoot when they are anxious. *Emotion*, 12(4), 827–833. Doi:10.1037/a0025699.

Rowe, A. and Regehr, C. 2010. Whatever gets you through today: An examination of cynical humor among emergency service professionals. *Journal of Loss and Trauma*, 15(5), 448–464. Doi:10.1080/15325024.2010.507661.

Sanders, B. A. 2008. Using personality traits to predict police officer performance. *Policing: An International Journal of Police Strategies and Management*, 31(1), 129–147.

Saus, E.-R., Johnsen, B. H., Eid, J., Riisem, P. K., Andersen, R., and Thayer, J. F. 2006. The effect of brief situational awareness training in a police shooting simulator: An experimental study. *Military Psychology*, 18(sup3), S3–S21. Doi:10.1207/s15327876mp1803s_2.

Scrivner, E. M. 1994. The role of police psychology in controlling excessive force, 1, 30. Retrieved from https://books.google.com/books?hl=en&lr=&id=_VJF9QyA5SsC&pgis=1.

Surrette, M. A., Ebert, J. M., Willis, M. A., and Smallidge, T. M. 2003. Personality of law enforcement officials: A comparison of law enforcement officials' personality profiles based on size of community. *Public Personnel Management*, 32(2), 279–286.

Tarescavage, A. M., Corey, D. M., and Ben-Porath, Y. S. 2014. Minnesota multiphasic personality inventory-2-restructured form (MMPI-2-RF) predictors of police officer problem behavior. *Assessment*, 22(1), 116–132. Doi:10.1177/1073191114534885.

Tarescavage, A. M., Corey, D. M., Gupton, H. M., and Ben-Porath, Y. S. 2015. Criterion validity and practical utility of the Minnesota multiphasic personality inventory-2-restructured form (MMPI–2–RF) in assessments of police officer candidates. *Journal of Personality Assessment*, 97(4), 382–394. Doi:10.1080/00223891.2014.995800.

Terman, L. M., Otis, A. S., Dickson, V., Hubbard, O. S., Norton, J. K., Howard, L., and Cassingham, C. C. 1917. A trial of mental and pedagogical tests in a civil service examination for policemen and firemen. *Journal of Applied Psychology*, 1(1), 17–29.

Twersky-Glasner, A. 2005. Police personality: What is it and why are they like that? *Journal of Police and Criminal Psychology*, 20(1), 56–67. Doi:10.1007/BF02806707.

Wilkins, J. 2014. The use of cognitive reappraisal and humour as coping strategies for bullied nurses. *International Journal of Nursing Practice*, 20, 283–292. Doi:10.1111/ijn.12146.

CHAPTER 9

Police Violence, Public Response
The Public Gets What It Tolerates

Carolyn Speer Schmidt

☐ Police Violence, Public Response: The Public Gets What it Tolerates

The United States is a representative democracy where the will of the people indirectly but eventually finds its voice in public policy. This tie between what "the people" want and what they get is real and is supported by what scholars call a "living constitution" along with a dynamic legal landscape. In the years since the Industrial Revolution in the United States, the subsequent growth of urban areas, and the establishment of a professional police force, public opinion has grown in importance. In the last several decades, and in particular recently in light of the events flowing from the Ferguson unrest of 2014, it has become clear that the public and political response to police violence are intimately linked. Ultimately, it comes down to how police violence, and any public violence that might happen as a result, is perceived by the middle and upper classes in the United States, especially as represented by older, better-educated, white voters. In fact, it is this group, and not necessarily the groups most directly impacted by police violence, that has the most political power to effect change in the country. When the larger society views police violence as justified, the political response is muted or nonexistent. But when the violence offends established middle class social norms, politicians are more likely to respond with public statements, policy initiatives, or other responses that will bring real change to communities.

The issue of police violence is one that has been with the United States for well over 100 years. Called alternatively "police brutality," "police violence," and "use of force," the general concept has remained the same throughout the years:

> The relationship between police perpetrators and their victims has remained roughly the same. Like criminal suspects generally, victims of police brutality were mainly poor and working class, often immigrants or newcomers to the city. Jews and other southeastern Europeans were common complainants at the turn of the century, while African Americans and Latinos gradually replaced them by the mid-twentieth century. The overrepresentation of these groups was not just a result of economic and demographic trends; it was also aggravated by racial tensions and bias ... Such conflicts were usually between police and lower class immigrants or African Americans, but on occasion—as in the clashes between police and antiwar demonstrators in the 1960s—they also flowed upward (Johnson, 2003: pp. 3–4).

The excessive use of police violence has been an important research area in the United States for many decades. Writing in 1970, Gamson and McEvoy called police violence an accepted norm in the United States where for many, "there is apparently a thin blue line between order and chaos. Breach it and untold furies lie beyond. The police require unconditional support when they are in combat; sins are understandable and forgivable when they occur in the stress of battle" (Gamson and McEvoy, 1970: p. 98). Three decades later, Ross found that while people do not condone "excessive" police violence, what actually constitutes excessive varies by person, and in fact most people do not tend to see any police violence as being excessive (Ross, 2000).

The issue of police treatment of civilians is more complicated than the specific instance of police violence. According to the Pew Research Center, few Americans now believe the police treat different racial and ethnic groups equally, with most Americans believing that racial minorities are treated less well by the police. Only 30% of Americans believe that officers are held accountable when police exhibit misconduct, and 70% of African Americans believe that police departments do a poor job of punishing police misconduct. This issue becomes particularly stark with regard to the treatment of Americans by race/ethnic group. Overall, 32% of Americans believe the police do an "excellent" or "good" job at treating all Americans equally. Only 10% of African Americans hold that opinion. The issue of the use of force makes a particularly striking example of how these two group of Americans differ: 41% of whites believe the police use the "right amount" of force for each situation whereas only 6% of African American hold the same view (Pew Research Center, 2014a, b).

On every measure, there is a stark difference between how African Americans view the police and how whites do. Even in the case of local policing, where most Americans express "at least a fair amount of confidence … [that] forces avoid using excessive force and treats blacks and whites equally," there remains significant racial divides in opinion (Pew Research Center 2014a, b, para. 2). Overall, whites are twice more likely to believe the police treat different racial groups equally than are African Americans, and the number of African Americans who have "very little" confidence in the police has increased from 34% in 2009 to 46% in 2014. Police departments' use of military style equipment is of particular concern to African Americans, with 68% having very little or no confidence in the police's ability to use these resources appropriately; 60% of whites have a great deal or "fair" amount of confidence that these resources are being used appropriately by the police (Pew Research Center, 2014a, b).

These stark differences in opinion are likely due to the very different experiences subgroups of Americans have when coming into contact with the police. Taking a historical view of police violence, Johnson finds that excessive use of police force and police brutality has consistently impacted racial and ethnic minorities and the working class disproportionately (Johnson, 2003). Gabrielson et al. point out the problem has become markedly more noticeable in recent years, and today, "[y]oung black males … [are] at a far greater risk of being shot dead by police than their white counterparts" (Gabrielson et al., 2014, para. 1). The federal data are shocking: between 2010 and 2012 there were 1217 deadly police shootings in the United States, with black males being 21 times more likely to be killed at the hands of the police than are white men. For blacks between the ages of 15 and 19 the rate of death was 31.17 per million. Whites died at the rate of 1.47 per million in that same time frame. To put it in perspective, ProPublica calculated how many whites would be killed if they were the victims of police violence at the same rate: 185 additional deaths over the 2-year period would make the rates equal (Gabrielson et al., 2014).

Unfortunately, the nature of recordkeeping makes getting complete data for deaths by police action impossible in the United States. The FBI (Federal Bureau of Investigation) statistics provide the minimum count for these deaths, because reporting is voluntary. There are 17,000 police departments in the country, and several of them have never filed reports regarding police shootings and other uses of force. Other departments have filed reports for some years and not for others. Departments in the state of Florida, for example, have not filed reports since 1997. Yet even with the incomplete data available to researchers, "the disparity between black and white teenage boys'" chances of being killed at the hands of the police is so significant that it the rates are clearly not an artifact of the poor recordkeeping (Gabrielson et al. (2014, para. 11). Regardless of the age of the victim, the vast majority of police officers involved in violence of this kind are white officers, although slightly more than 10% of this violence is committed by African American officers. Many of those who were killed by police between 2010 and 2012 were fleeing or resisting arrest, and a disproportionate number of these killed for this reason were African American. There is no wonder that the data between the views held by African Americans and whites is so vastly different. Their experiences are very different as well.

Clearly, then, most of those killed by police are engaged in formal interactions with law enforcement. Those people who live in high-crime neighborhoods or who are otherwise exposed to crime at a rate that is higher than that for the larger society tend to have more negative views of the police, and those people who come into formal contact with law enforcement in any capacity are significantly more likely to have negative views of the police than do those whose contact remains informal. Those with no actual contact with the police have the most positive view of them. Being the victim of a crime is especially likely to lead to a negative view of the police, regardless of race or ethnicity (U.S. Department of Justice, 2003). Given these data, it comes as no particular surprise that 76% of African Americans see problems with the United States justice system with regard to racial issues and law enforcement while only 33% of whites hold the same view (Pew Research Center, 2015a, b). Disturbingly, Pew polling indicates that a majority of African Americans anticipate relations between the police and minorities to worsen in the future.

These statistics may not seem particularly surprising post Ferguson. Statistics such as these have been regularly discussed on the media, but what remains a question is why such strong opinions on the part of African Americans appear to have had so little impact on public policy. To understand this problem, it is important to understand voting rates in the United States. The "voting rate" is the measure of the number of voters as a proportion of the overall number of people in a particular population or subpopulation in a community. Historically, voting rates in the United States are well below those in other countries with free and fair elections. While many reasons for this trend in the United States have been posited, generally political scientists agree that the nature of the two-party system combined with relative social stability combine to give the United States such low voting rates. For example, in 1978, only 48.9% of eligible voters participated in the national election, and while the statistics bounced around slightly over the years, the general trend was toward lower participation over time. In 2014, only 41.9% of the eligible voting population participated in the election (File, 2015).

The full impact of American voting rates does not come into focus until the numbers are broken down by race and ethnicity. Since voting was expanded to include African American men after the Civil War and then to include women in the early twentieth century, whites have voted at higher rates than any other racial or ethnic category in almost every national election. In the last 30 years, only the 2008 and 2012 presidential elections, both of which had Barack Obama on the ballot, saw blacks vote at a higher rate than whites, and even in those years, the rates were very close with about 70% of the eligible African American voting population voting in each year. But in previous presidential election years whites outvoted African Americans by approximately 10 percentage points, and outvoted Hispanics and other racial minorities at rates that ranged between 15 and 20 percentage points (United States Elections Project, 2015). Other measures of social status and class are also significant in this discussion. Across all federal elections in the last 30 years, eligible voters over age 60 are significantly more likely to vote than any other age category, and vote at rates that are 30 percentage points higher than eligible voters 18–29 years of age. Similarly, voters with a postgraduate education outvote those with less than a high school education by 25 percentage points (United States Elections Project, 2015).

Taken together, then, we find that whites are almost always more likely to vote than are African Americans in the United States, but further, those people who are younger, less well educated, and a member of a minority are significantly less likely to vote than are those who are older, better educated, and white (United States Elections Project, 2015). That is, precisely the same people who have higher rates of formal interactions with law enforcement, more negative views of law enforcement, and higher rates of death at the hands of law enforcement are those who are statistically least likely to vote and therefore least likely to have the ability to impact public policy in the direction of their views. And while voting is technically within the grasp of most non-felon American citizens, in reality such things as distrust of government and a feeling of nonrepresentation means that minorities in general, and poorer members of minority communities specifically are least likely to connect voting behavior with public policy results.

As a consequence, police violence has historically been met with occasional acts of public violence such as rioting. As Conyers argued in 1981, "[t]he evidence shows that unequal treatment in the criminal justice system and political powerlessness add to the anger of those who riot. The evidence shows that a pattern of police violence makes a city prone to a riot. And clearly, undeniably, and unequivocally, the evidence shows that police brutality precipitates riots" (Conyers, 1981: p. 5). In fact, while the current social climate links racial and ethnic minorities with these public acts of discontent, historically speaking, the link between police violence and public rioting is more a function of groups feeling powerless than it is about race specifically. It may seem surprising, but:

> Large-scale disorder and riots were commonplace in the American cities of the mid-1800s. The business elites and middle class of American cities increasingly feared for the stability of society .... Elites' fear of riots and civil disorder, combined with their interest in protecting property, prompted the desire for a mechanism to control those seen as threats to the stability of society. Their fear of the dangerous classes was the major factor motivating the establishment of city police departments (Holmes and Smith, 2008: pp. 21–2).

Labor unrest in the late nineteenth and early twentieth centuries tended to be bloody conflicts between first the Pinkertons who broke 77 strikes between 1869 and 1892 (as in the Battle of the Monongahela in 1892) and later the police and even the military as in the Pullman strike in 1894 (Ladd and Rickman, 1998; Websdale, 2001). The political response to these conflicts tended to rest solely on the middle and upper classes' perception of the reasonableness of the violence overall, and the police violence specifically. When the strikers were seen as being in the right, society tended to side with them, and when they were seen as being in the wrong, society sided with the police, regardless the amount of violence used to quell riots or break strikes. Police violence surrounding labor unrest was not the only concern at this time; "[m]iddle class, native-born whites became increasingly incensed by frequent corruption scandals and accounts of brutality, motivating a political movement to reform the police" (Holmes and Smith, 2008: p. 23).

Similarly, with the 1968 Chicago riots, the nation was "horrified" to watch the violence unfold each night on the news, and as with the labor unrest from decades before, the anger and feelings of disaffectedness came not from racial minorities (Grossman, 2012). Instead, the 1968 Chicago riots involved discontented young people of a variety of social, racial, and ethnic backgrounds. Yet, in retrospect, it is striking to look at the language of the officers who were engaged in the Chicago police violence: Len Colsky, a former Chicago police officer recalls, "Things became very confusing. I remember well in 1968 where it was hard to distinguish the hippies from the criminals; they all looked the same. And the ones who were causing trouble and promising to do damage looked and dressed like hippies" (as quoted in Kusch, 2004). That is, the very act of political protest served to signal to police that all discontented young people they encountered protesting were potential physical threats and should legitimately be treated with a violent response. Certainly, similar arguments were made about the enraged crowds protesting in Ferguson, Missouri in 2014, and because the crowds were disproportionately African American, the visual signaling of "otherness" from the police was equally as clear.

Of course what links riots such as the ones in Chicago in 1968 and in Ferguson in 2014 was the extensive media coverage of the events. In contrast, the Stonewall riots of 1969, which were important enough to have sparked the gay rights movement, were treated at the time as a local issue and were covered only on the local news in New York City (Rothman, 2015). Clearly, not all acts of police or public violence are treated equally by the media. Yet there is absolutely no question that media coverage of these events is a critically important element in their political impact. On the one hand, when media accounts emphasize social violence and the risk that police officers face in the line of duty, regular media reporting of these events can "promote public and official tolerance for police violence" (Hirschfield, 2010). Ross (2000) argues there is no clear reason why some acts of police violence excite media attention while others do not. In fact,

> The majority of incidents of police violence receive little media attention. Unless the case is "sensational," articles about police abuse are often relegated to the "metro" or back portion of the newspaper and/or given little space, becoming almost lost among other, well-covered "news events" (e.g., entertainment and sports). On the other hand, those events that receive considerable media attention do raise people's concerns regarding controversial police practices which, in turn, may lead to public unrest (Ross, 2000: p. 120).

But when the media does cover acts of police violence, and when it does so in a critical manner, it can directly impact both public opinion of the events and public policy changes that can flow from them.

The 2014 Ferguson unrest illustrates this point very well. Images of police in military gear excited the public imagination across the country, not only in the small Missouri town where the violence was taking place. As the unrest continued throughout the late summer, and national media attention grew, local and national politicians, and even the President of the United States spoke out against racial injustices in Ferguson. Without the media attention, it is difficult to believe there would have been a Justice Department investigation and a finding that the protestors' free speech rights had been violated by the local police (Bora, 2015). But what is notable from the perspective of the political impact of and response to police violence in Ferguson is that prior to the 2014 unrest, "the uneasy relationship between its growing black population and its mostly white police force barely registered in local headlines" (Breitbart, 2015). It certainly never broke into the national consciousness before the police donned military gear and the population protested in the streets.

Over a year after the initial Ferguson unrest, Breitbart (2015) reported that the political landscape for the town changed. The city has a new police chief, city manager, and municipal judge, and they are all African Americans. The city council has three African American members as well. And even though a U.S. Justice Department report found no grounds to prosecute the officer involved in the shooting of Michael Brown, it was so critical of Ferguson's municipal government and police department that most of the top leaders resigned as a result. The police department is now wearing body cameras as well, and it is initiating a community policing effort to get the police out of their patrol cars and onto the city streets. These are real changes, both in policy and in action, and they came as a direct result of the events surrounding the unrest and the police violence that precipitated it. But again, none of these outcomes would have been likely had the media coverage been lacking.

It is also important to note that while there have been some positive changes in Ferguson, the racial divide regarding the events is still stark. For example, 23% of whites thought the decision not to charge Darren Wilson, the officer who shot Michael Brown, was the wrong decision, and 80% of African Americans thought so. African Americans were also more likely to believe that race was a factor in that decision (Pew Research Center, 2014a, b). Yet public opinion is changing in ways that might be surprising. Today, 59% of Americans overall believe that the United States needs to continue to make changes in order to achieve racial equality between African Americans and whites. And while there is a racial divide on the issue, with 86% of African Americans having that view and 53% of whites agreeing, in 2014 only 39% of whites held that view (Pew Research Center, 2015a, b). This is a likely consequence of the Ferguson unrest and the media coverage that accompanied it.

Within the current political realities of the United States, what whites, and particularly older and better educated whites believe about issues has real policy implications for the country. Because whites vote at higher rates and more regularly than any other racial or ethnic group in the United States, changing their opinion is more likely to impact public policy than even the strengthening of opinions in the African American and other racial minority communities. As Ross argued, "Although it is difficult to determine whether police violence will increase in the future, unless we break the pattern of apathy, obedience/deference to authority, and sublimated frustration, which is periodically vented through protest only after a sufficient number of events have taken place, we cannot realistically lessen and control police violence. If the public, government, and law enforcement officials remain complacent, it may well be business as usual for police departments, the government, and citizens alike" (Ross, 2000: p. 126).

Public opinion has the power to influence political policies that go well beyond police violence as well and reach into many other aspects of the criminal justice system. For example, in Ferguson attention is now being paid to municipal fines and the crippling cost they bring on the poor community in the city. Across the country, public opinion has driven crime policies in many arenas and in the last few decades these policies have contributed to a huge growth in the prison population (Hetey and Eberhardt, 2014). Today, the United States has the highest incarceration rates in the world with a rate of 500 prisoners per 100,000 residents (Tsai and Scommenga, 2012). This explosion in the prison population has had a particular impact on young (20–34) African American men, 11.4% of whom are incarcerated (Tsai and Scommenga, 2012).

Clearly, many issues surrounding police violence and other aspects of the criminal justice system are not "fair." But in a representative democracy like the one that functions in the United States, "fairness" is measured largely by those who make policies, and those people are chosen by those who vote. The dangerous irony is that when groups of people become, or feel that they have become, socially disenfranchised and marginalized, they are less likely to vote, and are left with avenues of political self-expression that are likely to be less effective and more violent. At this point, those groups lose much of the ability to control their own message and are left with the whims of a media that sometimes covers police violence and a community's response to it, and sometimes does not. Even when these issues break onto the national agenda through sufficient media coverage, the nature of the coverage itself has an outsized impact on how the larger society will judge the event. When, as happened in the last few decades, the middle and upper classes perceive these events are threatening the peace and safety of the community, these voters respond by supporting increasingly oppressive policies that have the ultimate impact of making matters worse for those communities that have resorted to nonstandard modes of political expression. It is possible, in the wake of the Ferguson unrest, however, that media coverage has changed enough to impact the consciousness of the larger community. It has long been clear that African Americans and other racial minorities have seen significant social problems that whites have not. But the most recent data indicate the opinion gap between the races may be closing in the United States.

☐ References

Bora, K. June 30, 2015. Ferguson riots: Justice department says police response violated citizens' rights. *International Business Times*. Retrieved from http://www.ibtimes.com

Breitbart N. August 8, 2015. Ferguson still recovering from riots one year after Michael Brown's death. *Breitbart News*. Retrieved from http://www.breitbart.com/

Conyers, J. 1981. Police violence and riots. *The Black Scholar*, 12(1), 2–5. Retrieved from http://www.jstor.org/stable/41067960

File, T. 2015. Who votes? Congressional Elections and the American Electorate: 1978–2014. U.S. Department of Commerce Economics and Statistics Administration, U.S. Census Bureau.

Gabrielson, R., Jones, R. and Sagara, E. October 10, 2014. *Deadly Force, in Black and White*. ProPublica. Retrieved from http://www.propublica.org/

Gamson, W. and McEvoy, J. 1970. Police violence and its public support. *The Annals of the American Academy of Political and Social Science*, 391, 97–110. Retrieved from http://www.jstor.org/stable/1040028

Grossman, R. April 29, 2012. For five days and nights in August 1968, Chicago was a war zone. *Chicago Tribune*. Retrieved from http://articles.chicagotribune.com

Hetey, R. and Eberhardt, J. August 5, 2014. Racial disparities in incarceration increase acceptance of punitive policies. *Psychological Science*. Retrieved from http://pss.sagepub.com

Hirschfield, P. May 2010. Legitimating police violence: Newspaper narratives of deadly force. *Theoretical Criminology*, 14(2), 155–182.

Holmes, M. and Smith, B. 2008. *Race and Police Brutality: Roots of an Urban Dilemma*. New York: State University of New York Press.

Johnson, M. 2003. *Street Justice: A History of Police Violence in New York City*. Boston: Beacon Press.

Ladd, K. and Rickman, G. 1998. The Pullman Strike: Chicago 1894. *Kansas Heritage*. Retrieved from http://www.kansasheritage.org/pullman/

Kusch, F. 2004. *Battleground Chicago: The Police and the 1968 Democratic National Convention*. Retrieved from http://www.press.uchicago.edu/Misc/Chicago/465036.html

Ross, J. I. 2000. *Making News of Police Violence: A Comparative Study of Toronto and New York City.* Westport, Connecticut: Praeger.

Rothman, L. September 25, 2015. How TIME covered the Stonewall riots. Retrieved from http://time.com/4042859/stonewall-inn-history-time/

Pew Research Center. August 25, 2014a. Few say police forces nationally do well in treating races equally. Retrieved from http://www.people-press.org/

Pew Research Center. December 8, 2014b. Sharp racial divisions in reactions to Brown, Garner decisions. Retrieved from http://www.people-press.org/

Pew Research Center. April 28, 2015a. Divide eetween blacks and whites on police runs deep. Retrieved from http://www.people-press.org/

Pew Research Center. August 5, 2015b. Across racial lines, more say nation needs to make changes to achieve racial equality. Retrieved from http://www.people-press.org/

Tsai, T. and Scommenga, P. 2012. U.S. has world's highest incarceration rate. *Population Reference Bureau.* Retrieved from http://www.prb.org/

United States Elections Project. 2015. Voter turnout demographics. Retrieved from http://www.electproject.org/home/voter-turnout/demographics

U.S. Department of Justice. 2003. Factors that influence public opinion of the police. Research for Practice. NCJ 197925.

Websdale, N. 2001. *Policing the Poor: From Slave Plantation to Public Housing.* Boston: Northeastern University Press.

Prevention and Training

Vladimir A. Sergevnin and Darrell L. Ross

Incidents where excess force is used are preventable. There are many preventative measures that reduce the risks of excessive force, such as preemployment screening, education/training, appropriate psychological and social support services, and organizational structure. This chapter will discuss the various approaches used in law enforcement to reduce the excess use of force.

☐ Introduction

Law enforcement personnel are constantly striving to promote and preserve a positive, moral image of their departments to the public they are sworn to serve and protect in democratic society. However, the community's perception is influenced by multiple variables and use of force has one of the strongest impacts on it. Continuously honorable and conscientious police work of hundreds of thousands of law enforcement officers across the nation can be discredited by one story of excessive force.

Due to several recent controversial use of force incidents, use of force phenomena has moved into the public, academic, and even political spotlight. A sharp rise in rulings nationwide that law enforcement officers violated departmental policies and procedures in using deadly force has prompted a review of use of force prevention and training concepts. The training concept has to be reassessed in a broader scale from recruitment and hiring to discretion and ethical dimensions. Nationwide efforts have been undertaken by law enforcement institutions to confront and reevaluate the use of force paradigm. While the scope of existing publications addresses many use of force prevention and training issues, a comprehensive law enforcement approach has not been available. The importance of a comprehensive and coordinated use of force prevention and training approach for law enforcement officers, along with other proactive and reactive measures such as recruitment, hiring, and enhanced policies and protocols, are emphasized in this chapter. This chapter is an exploratory assessment and an overview of the nature and extent of the law enforcement prevention and training response to use of force issues.

☐ Challenges of Use of Force Training

To clearly understand the role of use of force training in today's world and to ensure that basic recruit training and in-service training use of force realistic programs are the rule rather than the exception, training planners and administrators should start from comprehensive job task analysis efforts to define exactly what use of force training is in place and how much of it is needed. For many peace officer standards and training (POST) units, this has proved to be a very challenging task.

For decades, professional and research associations, such as the International Association of Chiefs of Police (IACP), the Police Executive Research Forum (PERF), the Police Officers Safety Association (POSA), have tried to provide standards and guidelines for use of force training. Despite these efforts police practitioners and academicians believe that use of force training is inadequate or insufficient (IACP, 2012; PERF, 2015).

The traditional model of use of force training for decades has been focused on perfecting technical skills and their speedy application. The majority of training materials and certification tests are focused predominantly on these two parameters. On the other hand, developing a knowledge base and skills in the rational, emotional, and psychological dimensions of use of force was not a priority for agencies and training institutions. When law enforcement trainers are dealing with police tools and weapons, a paramilitary training philosophy seems applicable and valid. Unsatisfactory training or an absence of training is considered by the courts to be organizational negligence and deliberate indifference (Birzer, 2003; Martinelli, 2015). In response, majority of law enforcement agencies and well-recognized training institutions have developed a variety of approaches.

☐ Recruiting, Selecting, and Evaluating

Use of force by law enforcement officers is not an isolated issue in law enforcement actions. It is connected to all dimensions of police work, management, and organization. When law enforcement administrators have concerns about the use of force practices in the agency it is imperative to approach this critical issue as a whole phenomenon and start with recruitment, selection, and retaining personnel who will use powers and force appropriately and will minimize any potential problems with community on these grounds. The new era of policing requires appropriate strategies and methods of recruitment and selection.

For several decades' personnel practices emphasized enforcement capabilities of the candidates, recruiting and selecting futures warriors on the American streets. The recent trend toward a general community policing approach has transformed the focus to service-related profiles of the recruits. This remarkable change initiated the slow movement toward recruiting and selecting to law enforcement agencies individuals predisposed to solving social and psychological problems among members of the community applying intellectual and emotional skills rather than crime fighters armed with the traditional technical skills of police work. Because of that according to PERF's recent discussion on use of force training, it is imperative for the police agency to provide potential applicants with a sense of how the department sees its mission ("warriors vs. guardians"). Articulating respect to human life and rights, concern to democratic ideals and liberties, partnership, collaboration, and commitment to communities provides a proactive message and clear expectations of the desired qualities to potential candidates.

Some researchers have concluded that a relatively small number of officers are responsible for the majority of complaints about excessive force (Lersch and Mieczowski, 1996; Brandl et al., 2001). Multiple studies have tried to identify some personal characteristics of individuals predisposed to use excessive force and use them as a basis for selection decisions. There are several factors that should be taken into account in developing recruitment and selection strategies which have some proven indications in possible prevention of excessive use of force.

Increased educational standards are viewed as one of the factors which can contribute to diminish potential problems with excessive use of force. Law enforcement and correctional institutions across the nation through selection standards are searching for college-educated candidates under the assumption that college-educated officers will not use force extensively. Early research on the relationship between education and use of excessive force in particular, has produced inconsistent and conflicting findings (Brandl et al., 2001). Current research indicates that only officers receiving the benefit of a 4-year degree were significantly less likely to rely on physical forms of force in their daily encounters with the public but simply attending college is not enough when it comes to less reliance on physical force. In this respect, actually completing a 4-year program is most beneficial (Paoline and Terrill, 2007; McElvain and Kposova, 2008; Rydberg and Terrill, 2010, Paoline et al., 2015).

Research has shown that female officers are less likely to use physical force and are more effective communicators. Additionally, female officers are better in de-escalating and defusing potential use of force confrontations before those encounters turn deadly. A 2002 study by the National Center for Women and Policing illuminates the differences in the way that men and women perform their policing duties and found that the male officer is several times more likely than his female counterpart to have an allegation of excessive force or to be named in a complaint of excessive force (Longsway, 2002) These findings highlight the importance of hiring women as a strategy for reducing problems of excessive force.

It is beneficial for a law enforcement agency to conduct a self-assessment and determine the agency's recruitment, selection, and retention goals in the use of force area. The essential step in designing an effective recruitment and selection process is to determine whether the agency has incorporated any specific tools to select individuals which are conservative in application of force and generate fewer complaints from the public. The purpose is to identify competencies during selection such as problem solving and judgment, stress reaction, integrity, self-control, visual acuity, perception, and emotional health which assist in selecting satisfactory candidates. Law enforcement recruits need to display a strong service orientation that fosters goodwill within their communities (Stanard and Associates, 2015). In addition, an agency should conduct a community assessment to determine citizens' view, criticism, or support toward use of force practices. It is important to determine the "degree" of community satisfaction with use of force policies and practices.

A proactive system of personnel reviews and follow-up can address individual problems in use of force practices and can reduce the need for a law enforcement agency to deal with excessive use of force investigations. Evaluations enable supervisors to meet with an officer, discuss his or her use of force practice, and formally record frequency, strengths, weaknesses, complaints, and community expectations. Early identification of unacceptable behavior in use of force application should be communicated to the officer along with offering assistance, additional training, and thorough explanation of agency and community expectations. Citizen complaints on officers' use of lethal and LTL (less than lethal) forces is a critical problem. Citizen complaint reports is one of several ways researchers can obtain data on the use of force issue (Ross, 2005). According to Hickman, during 2002 large state and local law enforcement agencies, representing 5% of agencies and 59% of officers, received a total of 26,556 citizen complaints about police use of force: about a third of all force complaints were not sustained (34%), 25% were unfounded, 23% resulted in officers being exonerated, and 8% were sustained; and using sustained force complaints as an indicator of excessive force resulted in an estimate of about 2000 incident of police use of excessive force among large agencies in 2002 (Hickman, 2006).

Early intervention systems (EISs) (also known as early warning programs) have been used by many agencies for more than two decades, and the recent evolution of EIS is having increased success in addressing and preventing various personnel issues, including excessive use of force. According to Alpert and Walker (2000), the three main elements of an early warning system are: identification of officers with problematic behavior; intervention to correct the problem; and follow-up with those who have received assistance. The early intervention system (EIS) is a key element in the strategy to address at-risk behavior. Once an officer exceeds an established number of risk factors (such as reaching the top percentage of officers who have used force or received a complaint within a certain time period, officer-involved shooting, preset number of complaints, etc.), an early intervention assessment will be conducted. This kind of assessment may also be conducted at the discretion of a supervisor. The rationale behind EIS is to intervene and provide assistance by identifying possible problematic behaviors before they result in actions that are contrary to the use of force policy and protocol, and ethical standards. Identification of problematic officers leads to the development of various types of assistance or mentoring programs focused on the critical area. The Miami-Dade police department has established one of the earliest EIS in the United States, and demonstrated some success. Its approach clearly indicates that since 1981 the number of officers identified for excessive use of force has substantially diminished (Rothlein, 2015). While the CALEA (The Commission on Accreditation for Law Enforcement Agencies) guidelines provide a basic outline of what an EIS or early warning system should entail, at this time, there are no consistent standards for identifying problem officers.

☐ Training Framework and Limitations

Failing to provide ongoing training to officers commensurate with their duties can increase the agency's exposure to civil liability. In *City of Canton v. Harris* (1989) the U.S. Supreme Court ruled that a local government can be held liable under § 1983 when it fails to provide training to agency personnel. Failure to train may serve as a basis for § 1983 liability when the failure amounts to "deliberate indifference" to the rights of persons with whom the police may come into contact. The degree of fault is fundamentally related to the policy requirement noted in *Monell v. New York Department of Social Services* (1978). Moreover, *Monell* will not be satisfied by a mere allegation that a training program represents a policy for which the city is responsible. The Supreme Court stated that "in light of the duties assigned to specific officers or employees, the need for more or different training is so obvious, and the inadequacy so likely to result in the violation of constitutional rights, the policy makers of the city can reasonably be said to have been deliberately indifferent to the need." Addressing the need for use of force training in light of these cases on a regular basis places an agency in compliance with the *Canton* decision. In addition the Court's decision in *Graham v. Connor* (1989) should be reviewed with officers and supervisors in order for agency personnel to understand what criteria the court establishes and uses to examine a claim of excessive force and further explain how the decision integrates into the agency's force policy. To protect an agency from potential claims of a failure to train its use-of-force training system, and to increase officer safety and survival in the field, a pattern of providing documented training needs to be developed. Annually, a total of 32–40 h of training is recommended which can be presented in 8–10 h blocks each quarter, or a 16- to 18-h block semiannually. This assists in maintaining officer certification, competency, and proficiency. Additionally the *Canton* decision outlines that officers should "receive ongoing 'realistic training' commensurate to their job tasks." Thus training that is designed to replicate field stressor variables and environmental conditions confirms the court's admonition to provide realistic training. Providing realistic training on a frequent basis will place the agency in compliance with the *Canton* decision and assures the best method of developing and retaining skills that improves officer safety. Police administrators confirmed that training needed to be focused on situations based in reality as opposed to training that simply provides certification (IACP, 2012).

Some court cases stress the necessity for dynamic scenario-based training to provide imitation of a level of threat and improve use of force decision making. For example, in *Zuchel v. City and County of Denver, Colorado (1993)*, the court ruled that simply watching a film regarding lethal force decision making did not meet realistic training objectives and held the agency liable for failing to train (Sergevnin and Ross, 2012). At the same time many police administrators questioned if training had become ineffective because it was based on what an officer could not do rather than a positive format focused on what an officer could do or in fact must do with respect to the use of force (IACP, 2012).

Present day use of force training utilizes adult learning principles as well as problem-based training, role-play, lectures, and demonstrations to provide the recruits and officers with the skills needed to be successful in critical situations. The use of force training was traditionally developed, directed but also limited by the POST boards, agency administrators, the financial abilities of an agency, and various state statutes. POST agencies update basic training curriculum infrequently, agency administrators are not interested in increasing training hours thus the amount of training does not match the need, and state statues are not "catching up" with new technological realities and law enforcement practices (Sergevnin and Ross, 2012).

Use of force training traditionally has been rather disjointed and technical skills oriented rather than decision-making focused. Officers learn the use of firearms, the Taser, baton, pepper spray, handcuffing, and others as isolated skills (Arnspiger and Bowers, 1996). Training focuses on the efficiency of an isolated element in the force spectrum gradually increasing general military-like aggressiveness of total use of force tools application.

Law enforcement trainers use the military-like methods to condition their personnel to overcome natural reluctance to use deadly force (Williams, 1999). Traditional training techniques are used to dehumanize "suspects." Instructors refer to suspects in various derogatory terms conditioning officers to think of suspects as less than human and who deserve the application of force (Williams, 1999; Wittie, 2011). This type of conditioning contradicts humanity ideals expressed in mission statements and helps to develop dangerous stereotypes which can lead officers to unnecessary force.

Computerized technological advances in scenario-based training present other new challenges: some smaller law enforcement agencies do not have funds to purchase rather expensive equipment. Those departments which got the machinery face other limitations such as the fact that officers are trained without real life stressors. Also various use of force training equipment does not allow enhancing communicating and de-escalating skills.

Recently many law enforcement administrators felt that due to negative public perception and fear of lawsuits, some officers were inadvertently being trained to return fire only when fired upon rather than using that force reasonably necessary to prevent injury or death (IACP, 2012).

☐ Training Models and Needs

Generally, law enforcement agencies around the nation are utilizing three types of use of force training: (a) basic training which focuses on common minimum standards of use of force and basic skills; (b) in-service training which is oriented on knowledge and skills updates, and (c) specialized training as a channel to develop and provide unique skills. Law enforcement administrators have noted that use of force recruit training is not sufficient and in-service training has not been validated in the same rigorous fashion as academy training, and that the level of accountability is far different for officers when approaching in-service training—as they do not fear failure or loss of job based on poor performance during these exercises (IACP, 2012).

Traditional models of use of force training rely on static repetitions of standard defensive tactics and techniques which can prepare officers to some degree to deal with resistance on the street (Ashley, 2003). According to Newstrom (1993), 40% of skills learned in training are transferred immediately; 25% remain after 6 months; and only 15% remain 1 year later. Roughly 20% of the critical skills needed to do a job are provided by training programs; 80% are learned on the job.

In the past, training was mainly focused on the development of isolated technical skills (such as firearms target practices and defensive tactics), rather than decision-making practice. This traditional approach generally dominates the use of force training realm in recruit training. According to a recent PERF national survey of 280 law enforcement agencies on current recruit training practices, the major segments are still firearms training (58 h) and defensive tactics (49 h), while use of force scenario-based training is only 24 h, communication skills—10 h, de-escalation—8 h, and crisis intervention—8 h. Similar distribution of training effort can be found in in-service training: firearms training 18% of training time, defensive tactics 13%, while use of force scenario-based training is only 9%, communication skills—5%, de-escalation—5%, and crisis intervention—9% (PERF, 2015). Traditional use of force model has substantial setbacks: focus on one of the element(s) of the possible situation, unrealistic "slow motion" or light impact techniques, no imitation of physical resistance, and unrealistic environment.

Since 2000, law enforcement agencies have started an active search for new training models. In 1999, the COPS office provided funding to PERF and the Reno (Nevada) police department to develop an alternative national model for training new officers that would incorporate community policing and problem-based learning techniques. The resulting police training officer (PTO) program addresses the traditional duties of policing in the context of specific neighborhood problems and includes several segments on the use of force. Many agencies are using the outlines of the PTO program to develop their own in-house programs adapted to their particular needs.

Recent demands in professionalizing law enforcement activities enlarged simulation training that utilizes the environment reconstruction approach to closely approximate actual confrontations, by creating model situations and allowing the trainee the use of near true intensity force. This method of training can enhance officers' behavior and develop realistic expectations regarding specific methods of use of force effectiveness, while enhancing officer abilities in actual physical confrontation. Many law enforcement administrators suggest that video and audio recordings should be used more routinely as tools to manage and train officers. Use of audio–video will allow first-line supervisors to critique use of tactics or communication meant to manage conflict (IACP, 2012).

Use of force training should reflect the needs of law enforcement agencies and individual police officers in pursuing the functional balance between institutional goals, the agency's current position, and personal expectations. The training needs has to be identified in such a way that it demonstrates the officer's comprehension and confidence level in the skill required, using the authorized techniques and equipment in accordance with agency policy. There are three major levels at which training needs should be identified: (a) at the state level; (b) at the agency level; and (c) at the individual level.

At the state level, use of force training needs analysis involving the POST boards acting as a sponsor in cooperation with the state law enforcement associations, and other stakeholders (such as basic training academies) to carry out training needs analysis. Training needs analysis often occurs as a result of political and mass media attention to certain downfalls (e.g., excessive use of force), new legislation, enhanced technology, and changes in law enforcement practices. Police training boards and police academies should be becoming increasingly proactive in recognizing the training needs through intensifying research efforts, organizing, updating, and evaluating use of force curriculum.

At the agency level, some police departments have strategies, which can be instrumental in the development of training needs. Clear objectives should be identified at this level. Outside consultants should be hired because most law enforcement administrators do not have the skills to identify training needs. The absence of an accurate system to update training needs often results in wasted resources by repeated training.

To ensure effective use of force policy implementation, training must address force decision-making review; proper application of physical control techniques; competency in using force tools, including all restraints, impact weapons, aerosols, conducted energy devices (CEDs), and all firearms; knowledge of medical assessment requirements and summoning emergency medical personnel; summoning back-up; summoning supervisory personnel; transportation protocols; report writing requirements, and conducting use of force investigations. Providing training on agency policy should be done on many levels: FTO (field training officer) program, roll call, firearms training, subject control training, and any use-of-force equipment training (i.e., handcuffs and other restraints, aerosols, CEDs, impact weapons, and other authorized equipment) (Sergevnin and Ross, 2012). Use of force training should also include frequent review of agency policy, state statutes, and federal guidelines concerning its application. According to Schlosser and Gahan (2015) the implications of the research findings suggest that officer training should emphasize ground control/ground fighting as a larger part of the training than the use of the baton. The use of the baton seems to be diminishing, and it could be conceivable that one day officers will no longer carry them. The use of OC (oleoresin capsicum) spray and the advent of Tasers could be what are affecting the minimal use of batons. Also, it is possible that the use of batons, even when appropriate, appears to be more aggressive, and officers are concerned about public opinion. Also, they suggest that the display of Tasers should be addressed through scenario-based training at a greater level at the same time some police administrators are concerned that too much technology and too many choices in weapons systems degraded an officer's operational awareness and slowed reaction times (IACP, 2012).

Addressing the individual level of training needs is crucial for the development of use of force training. Identification of individual training needs performance evaluation, current levels of skills measured against required levels of individual performance, changes of functions brought about as a result of in service training, individual plans of filling the gaps in skills, knowledge, and experience. Some law enforcement administrators are concerned that more training needed to be focused on communication and command presence. Often later in their careers, officers did not look prepared, while younger officers relied too much on physicality as opposed to using verbal tactics to de-escalate and mitigate confrontational situations (IACP, 2012).

According to Schlosser and Gahan (2015) officers who work for smaller departments should be provided more training with single officer arrest situations as they are less likely than larger departments to have back-up. Also, they stress that the importance of verbal tactics should continue to be emphasized as one of the most important training skills for law enforcement officers. Recent media headlines have been filled with upsetting stories of minorities allegedly suffering injuries, and even death at the hands of police officers. As a result, there has been a reactive trend to avoid using deadly force by officers and on training focused on how to de-escalate the use of deadly force. To prevent possible excessive use of force incidents and to provide better services to the communities the recruits will be serving, law enforcement agencies and training facilities are incorporating human relations training specifically focused on understanding the cultural patterns and characteristics of the respective communities. Wrong perceptions and biases can contribute to excessive force applications toward minority and immigrant representatives. Including members of the community in the training process could have beneficial results.

Police officers interact with very diverse populations under unlimited variations of circumstances. These present strong challenges for use of force training. Therefore, officers need to be trained and practice rapid adjustment to accommodate a variety of different members of the public in a wide spectrum of circumstances. Communication skills training has to focus on balancing between gaining control (and compliance) and expressing empathy and maintaining public trust. Language problems may also represent an important training need. Communication skills should be an integral component of a comprehensive use-of-force training program.

To train law enforcement officers to make a decision to use lethal force is one of the most critical areas of police training. That is why firearms training is prevalent in the block of the use of force segment of basic training. According to the PERF survey the median number of hours for firearms training is 58 h nationwide in basic training, 93% of agencies provide in-service firearms training, and from all in-service training hours 18% go to firearm training (PERF, 2015). Most police departments only have firearms training about two times a year, averaging less than 15 h annually (Grossi, 2011). As a rule use of lethal training consist of classroom instruction of deadly force policy and procedures and other legal topics, shooting range practices, and scenario and simulator exercises. The courts continually indicated that firearms training needs to be relevant, realistic, and regular.

Shooting range exercises vary greatly among academies and agencies. Most state legislatures enacted acts requiring all law enforcement officers annually to complete a handgun qualification course from curricula based upon model standards established by the state POST. Recruits and officers usually practice target shooting with and without taking cover at a distance of 3, 7, 15, 25 yards, etc. Shooting range course are limited in scope. This course evaluates an officer's ability to perform basic shooting skills in a controlled setting and in a low-stress environment. Generally such exercises do not indicate whether officers have received recent, relevant, and realistic training necessary to perform their job. Police academy students qualify using a law enforcement handgun, duty belt, and holster as typically worn by patrol officers and issued or approved by their academy. Students must successfully qualify to pass the firearms unit exam. Academies maintain a record of the qualification attempt(s) of recruits.

There is a national consensus that the key to improving police-recruit training is to move from traditional classroom and static target shooting to more hands-on instruction by increasing the use of scenario-based training hours. Scenario based firearms training is going beyond the static and often limited range training models. Scenario-based training is giving an officer experience and exposure to real-life experience without facing the risk of deadly situations or serious injury. Use of force simulators provide an important training tool which allows transferring trained judgment and firearms skills from the classroom and the firing range to actual field encounters. Simulator training should not replace range training but is designed for stress intensity training, that can assist officers in improving their assessment/perception abilities and actions (Ross et al., 2012a).

Use of force training programs succeed if the law enforcement officers can demonstrate that they have mastered the skills taught. They should be able to apply the skills learned in the training facility or at an agency, and their performance must improve in a way that benefits the police department. Training evaluation is a systematic analysis of data that helps law enforcement administrators make an informed decision. The current practice is limited to evaluation of the single training event.

☐ Conclusion

Use of force prevention and training is the only panacea that leads to professionalism in this critical area of policing. Such an emphasis requires a change to the system that currently exists, with police administrators at all levels taking a greater responsibility for specific use of force prevention and training development according to modern standards. The focus for law enforcement administrators in use of force training should be promoting a need for all officers to receive training on the agency's use of force policy and procedures on a regular basis. Police departments are responsible to make sure that use of force training is consistent with policies and protocols. Law enforcement agencies should become learning institutions, capable of developing use of force training programs suited to their departmental and individual demands, continuously assessing training challenges and approaches.

☐ Cases cited

City of Canton, Ohio v. Harris, 1989. 489 U.S. 378, 109 S. Ct. 1197.
Graham v. Connor, 1989. 490 U.S. 386, 109 S. Ct. 18651989.
Monell v. New York Department of Social Services, 1978. 436 U.S. 658.
Zuchel v. City and County of Denver, Colorado, 1993. 997 F. 2d 730, 7th Cir.

☐ References

Alpert, G.P. and Walker, S. 2000. Police accountability and early warning systems: Developing policies and programs. *Justice Research and Policy*, 2(2), 59–72.

Arnspiger, B. and Bowers, G.A. 1996. Integrated use-of-force training program. Available online: https://www2.fbi.gov/publications/leb/1996/nov961.txt. Retrieved: November 26, 2015.

Ashley, S. 2003. Use of force simulation training: The key to risk reduction. Available online: http://www.sashley.com/SimulationTraining.htm. Retrieved: February 6, 2003.

Birzer, M. 2003. Learning theory as it applies to police training. In: M. Palmiotto and M. Dantzker (Eds.), *Policing and Training Issues* (pp. 89–114). Upper Saddle River, New Jersey: Prentice-Hall.

Brandl, S., Stroshine, M.S. and Frank, J. 2001. Who are the complaint-prone officers? An examination of the relationship between police officers' attributes, arrest activity, assignment, and citizens' complaints about excessive force. *Journal of Criminal Justice*, 29(6), 521–529.

IACP. 2012. Emerging use of force issues. Balancing public and officer safety. *Report from the International Association of Chiefs of Police/COPS Office Use of Force Symposium*. Office of Community Oriented Policing Services, U.S. Department of Justice. Washington, DC. Online: http://www.theiacp.org/portals/0/pdfs/emerginguseofforceissues041612.pdf.

Grossi, D. 2011. Police firearms training: How often should you be shooting? Available online: https://www.policeone.com/training/articles/3738401-Police-firearms-training-How-often-should-you-be-shooting/. Retrieved: November 5, 2015.

Hickman, M. 2006. Citizen complaints about police use of force. Bureau of Justice Statistics (BJS), US Department of Justice, Office of Justice Programs, USA. Available online: http://www.ncjrs.gov/App/publications/abstract.aspx?ID=210296.

Lersch, K.M. and Mieczowski, T. 1996. Who are the problem-prone officers? An analysis of citizen complaints. *American Journal of Police*, 15, 23–44.

Longsway, K. 2002. Men, women, and police excessive force: A tale of two genders. National Center for Women and Policing, April 2002.

Martinelli, T. 2015. Unconstitutional policing: Part 3–a failure to train is compensable liability. *Police Chief*, November 2015. http://www.policechiefmagazine.org/magazine/index.cfm?fuseaction=display&article_id=3947&issue_id=112015

McElvain, J. and Kposova, A. 2008. Police officer characteristics and the likelihood of using deadly force. *Criminal Justice and Behavior*, 35(4), pp. 505–521.

Newstrom, J. October 1993. Transfer of training. In: P.L. Caravaglia (Ed.). *How to Ensure Transfer of Training. Training and Development* (pp. 63–68). From http://arl.cni.org/training/ilcso/transfer.html. Retrieved November 26, 2002.

PERF. 2015. Re-engineering training on police use of force (August 2015). *Critical Issues in Policing Series*. Washington, DC: Police Executive Research Forum.

Paoline III, E. and Terrill, W. 2007. Police education, experience, and the use of force. *Criminal Justice and Behavior*, 34(2), 179–196.

Paoline III, E. A., Terrill, W. and Rossler M. T. 2015. Higher education, college degree major, and police occupational attitudes. *Journal of Criminal Justice Education*, 26(1), 49–73.

Rydberg, J. and W. Terrill. 2010. The effect of higher education on police behavior. *Police Quarterly*, 13(1), 92–120.

Ross, D., Murphy, R. and Hazlett, M. 2012a. Analyzing perceptions and misperceptions of police officers in lethal force virtual simulator scenarios. *Law Enforcement Executive Forum*, 12(3), 53–73.

Ross, D.L. 2005. A content analysis of the emerging trends in the use of non-lethal force research in policing. *Law Enforcement Executive Forum*, 5(1), 121–148.

Rothlein, S. 2015. Early intervention systems for law enforcement. *Public Agency Training Council*. Online: http://patc.com/weeklyarticles/intervention.shtml

Schlosser, M. and Gahan, M. 2015. Police use of force: A descriptive analysis of illinois police officers. *Law Enforcement Executive Forum*, 15(2), 1–12.

Sergevnin, V. and Ross, D. 2012. Police use-of-force policy and force training model: Best practice. *Law Enforcement Executive Forum*, 12(1), 139–146.

Stanard and Associates. 2015. *Public Safety Testing Products and Services Catalog.* Chicago, p. 3.

Walker, S. Milligan, S.O. and Berke, A. 2007. *Early Intervention Systems: A Guide for Law Enforcement Chief Executives*. Washington, DC: Police Executive Research Forum, U.S. Department of Justice, Office of Community Oriented Policing Services.

Williams, G.T. 1999. Reluctance to use deadly force. *FBI Law Enforcement Bulletin*, 68(10), 1.

Wittie, M. 2011. Police use of force. *PB & J*, 2(2). Online: http://www.wtamu. edu/webres/File/Academics/College%20of%20Education%20and%20 Social%20Sciences/Department%20of%20Political%20Science%20 and%20Criminal%20Justice/PBJ/2011/2n2_03Wittie.pdf.

CHAPTER

Conclusion

Michael J. Palmiotto

Use of force can be traced back to ancient times. Those in authority whether formal or informal have used force to control the behavior of their subjects. Formal governments or those not so formal governments maintained control of the people through the use of force. History is full of examples where either the military or some semi-military group was authorized to subject the people of the state to fall in line to the establishment.

Chapter 1 "Use of Force throughout History" has as a basis that throughout most of history formal law enforcement agencies did not exist. Even though formal law enforcement was nonexistent, order was necessary to have a functioning state. Governments, whether sophisticated or unsophisticated, maintain social control which may be associated with physical or coercive powers of those in authority.

Similar to today, early forms of policing in ancient times emphasized social and criminal control which can be traced to the family, tribe or clan which assumed responsibility for the safety of their members. The concept of "kin police" developed with the concept that an attack on one member of the group was an attack on the entire group. The members of the group enforced the law which was often inhumane and retaliatory. This could be considered an early example of excessive use of force.

Policing traced to ancient Egypt had responsibilities similar to modern day. The major empires of the ancient world—Babylonians, Assyrians, Egyptians, Greeks, and Romans all had systems to maintain order, a major responsibility of policing to this day. The acts of violence can be traced to ancient times as well as to the early decades of the twenty-first century. Information on the maintaining of order during ancient times is somewhat sketchy and informal. Throughout history those in authority have used force against those below them in status, power, and authority.

Chapter 2 "Police Use of Force" reviews the controversial issues connected with the legitimate and illegitimate authority of the police to use force. The illegal or unacceptable or excessive use of force has often been referred to as police brutality. The use of force by the police can be defined as occurring "any time the police attempt to have citizens act in a certain way." Incidents of police use of excessive force have included beating civil rights protestors, deliberating kicking and choking someone while making arrests, and unprovoked use of deadly force when attempting to control riots and disturbances. There are situations in which individual officers, a group of officers, or a large number of officers within the police department, thus pervading the culture of an entire police department, may carry out acts of excessive force.

Incidents of the "use of excessive force" by police officers, or "police brutality" can be traced to early times in police history. Some forms of "police brutality" have also been referred to as the "third degree," a term that came into vogue during the early decades of the twentieth century and refers to excessive force during the questioning of suspects. Apparently, the term "first degree" means the arrest, the "second degree" the transportation to a place of confinement, and the "third degree" the interrogation, which frequently meant brutality.

The third degree does not occur to the extent as it did in the early decades of the twentieth century but it does occasionally occur. Excessive force occurs not only in poorly managed departments but also in well managed departments. Although use of force occurs in police–citizen contacts, it rarely occurs. The use of force or threat of force takes place in only one percent of police encounters.

Chapter 3 "Use of Deadly Force" explains and defines deadly force, described as force capable of causing serious bodily injury or death. The police can only use deadly force to save their lives or another person's life. The concept of deadly force can be traced to the middle ages in England when all felony crimes were punishable by death. Under this concept it was not considered a serious offense for the police to kill a person who committed a felony. Under the American law today the only capital offense is first degree murder, the only felony that allows for the death penalty. When a police officer uses deadly force in an encounter with a citizen he is using power greater than a judge and jury.

The use of force and specifically deadly force has been an issue since the police began arming themselves. It became a major issue in the second decade of the twentieth century and is continuing through the early decades of the twenty-first century. Most states have laws describing deadly force and stating when deadly force can and cannot be used. The use of deadly force when perceived by the public can lead to demonstrations and riots.

Chapter 4 "Nonlethal Weapons and Technology" authored by Dr. Szde Yu reveals how nonlethal weapons and technology can be involved in use of police use of force against citizens. The police deal with dangerous criminals daily, and when under attack, they need to subdue the attacker by any means possible. The use of lethal weapons is justified by the police even if the criminal does not have a firearm, as long as the threat is imminent. The police need nonlethal weapons because at their discretion the officers may feel that nonlethal weapons can assist in subduing the offender without causing him much physical harm. When a police officer's life is not being threatened, then less than lethal options should be available as an alternative to guns. The term nonlethal weapons means weapons that are not meant to end a life. It does not mean that nonlethal weapons cannot inflict fatal wounds.

The chapter "Militarization of the Police" written by Laurence Armand French reveals how militarization can lead to excessive force by the police. French writes that part of the problem can be traced to the type of equipment available to law enforcement agencies, specifically the increased firepower of modern military-style weapons. The undercurrent of racial/ethnic, sectarian, and class biases that are inherent in a complex multi-cultural environment in the United States also leads to the problem. Add the proliferation of high capacity hand-guns and assault weapons within the general population, and the situation worsens. Although the United States has a long history of decentralized law enforcement, there exists a long history of a symbiotic relationship between the military and police enforcing U.S. laws.

Dr. French provides a brief history of the police-militarization connection from colonial days to our present day. In this section French provides information on the role of the military played in law enforcement. He also discusses the roles that various law enforcement agencies, such as the F.B.I. and U.S. Marshals played in law enforcement. The next section discussed by Professor French is the evolution of firearms and deadly force. The firearms evolution is traced from 1791, the era of the Second Amendment to the present day. The third section considers the civilian's military-authority and status. French considers that an interesting outcome of the militarization of law enforcement is the corresponding rank-status phenomenon. Larry French concludes with a discussion of various recommendations from U.S. Supreme Court decisions, Presidential Blue Ribbon Commissions, and legislation. The conclusion also reviews psychological factors and the mental suitability of law enforcement personnel.

Chapter 6 "Racial Profiling: The Intersection of Race and Policing" written by Dr. Michael L. Birzer takes a critical look at racial profiling. His chapter is divided into five categories: the introduction covers the fractured history, the underpinning of race, and the second section specifically deals with racial profiling which is further subdivided into emotional and affective, symbolic vehicle, nature of violation, normative experience, and race and place. The third section discusses solving a complex problem with subsections on training, fostering mutual respect, professional motorist contacts, building and sustaining community coalitions, communication and community oriented policing.

Professor Birzer provides an excellent background on racism in America and the profiling of blacks and Hispanics in America. He provides detailed cases of minorities receiving rude and abusive treatment from the police. Dr. Birzer suggests that courtesy and a respectful treatment of minorities during police stops would go a long way in improving the attitudes of blacks and Hispanics towards the police. There is ample proof that racial profiling does occur and stopping someone based on their race or ethical heritage is prejudicial. The police could solve many of their problems with minorities if they had legitimate reasons for stopping and providing an explanation on why people have been stopped.

The seventh chapter "Understanding the Law of Police Uses of Force to Arrest," was authored by Professor Alison Brown. This chapter describes what law is in layman terms, so that a non-lawyer can comprehend what law is all about. A discussion of prosecuting excessive force under state criminal codes is thoroughly discussed. This section explains what common-law is and how it led to statutory law. Also reviewed is the use of force defense. The landmark case of *Tennessee v. Gardner* pertaining to the use of deadly force is carefully reviewed.

Professor Brown reviews the prosecution of excessive force under federal law. This section discusses federal criminality for excessive force used in an arrest that arises from federal statutory law. The elements pertaining to federal law are explained. The 1983 federal statutory pertains to state law enforcement officers while the Bivens cases refers to federal law enforcement officers. Both the 1983 law and Bivens are laws that cover cases when law is used by law enforcement officers to violate the rights of citizens. Law enforcement officers can be prosecuted for violating the civil rights of citizens.

Chapter 8 "Psychological and Social Factors in the Use of Force" was written by Dr. Jodie Beeson, a psychologist. She traces the role psychologists play in dealing with the police and the use of force back to the early 1900s. She reviews the 1960s, a period of turmoil when the role of the psychologist substantially increased. Federal governmental agencies were interested in professionalization of the police. Eventually, pre-employment tests to assess fitness of candidates became an acceptable practice. Dr. Beeson reviews personality and individual characteristics which could lead to excessive force. The impact of social factors on use of force decisions are discussed along with cognitive decision-making factors. This chapter provides a good overview as to why some police officers may be prone to use excessive force.

Dr. Carolyn Speer Schmidt authored Chapter 9 "Police Violence, Public Response: The Public Gets What It Tolerates." She advocates that the political impact of police violence can be proportioned to the larger societal view of violent acts being either reasonable or unreasonable. Public perception can be divided with whites tending to view police violence as justified and racial and ethnic minorities, especially African-Americans, viewing such acts as injustices. Since older, better educated whites have a higher rate of voting than younger less well-educated minorities, the impact of whites is greater on public policy in the United States.

The last chapter of this book "Prevention and Training," was written by Drs. Vladimir A. Sergevnin and Darrell L. Ross. The authors initiate their chapter with the idea that law enforcement personnel are constantly striving to promote and preserve a positive, moral image of their department. Due to controversial use of force incidents, the use of force phenomenon has moved into the public, academic, and even political spotlight. Nationwide efforts have been undertaken by law enforcement agencies to confront and reevaluate the use of force paradigm. Sergevin and Ross divide their chapter into several sections which they review. The sections include challenges of use of force training, recruiting, selecting, and evaluating training framework and limitations and training models and needs. The authors indicate that training should take place on three levels: the state level; the agency level; and at the individual level. These three levels are carefully explained.

The authors in their conclusion claim that use of force prevention and training may be the only approach to police professionalism. Further, all officers should be trained in their department's use of force policy and procedures. Police departments should become learning institutions in developing use of force training and prevention.

INDEX

NATO Divided,
NATO United

The Evolution of an Alliance

Lawrence S. Kaplan

PRAEGER

Westport, Connecticut
London

Library of Congress Cataloging-in-Publication Data

Kaplan, Lawrence S.
  Nato divided, Nato united : the evolution of an alliance / Lawrence S. Kaplan
    p. cm.
  Includes bibliographical references and index.
  ISBN 0–275–98006–5 (alk. paper)—ISBN 0–275–98377–3 (pbk. : alk. paper)
  1. North Atlantic Treaty Organization.   2. United States—Foreign relations—Europe.
  3. Europe—Foreign relations—United States.   I. Title.
  JZ5930.K37   2004
  355'.031'091821—dc22   2004044381

British Library Cataloguing in Publication Data is available.

Library of Congress Catalog Card Numer: 2004044381
ISBN: 0–275–98006–5
       0–275–98377–3 (pbk.)

First published in 2004

Praeger Publishers, 88 Post Road West, Westport, CT 06881
An imprint of Greenwood Publishing Group, Inc.
www.praeger.com

The paper used in this book complies with the
Permanent Paper Standard issued by the National
Information Standards Organization (Z39.48–1984).

10   9   8   7   6   5   4   3   2   1

To Debbie, Josh, and Cris

Contents

Preface

NATO's (North Atlantic Treaty Organization) war against terrorism that had begun on 11 September 2001 inspired a brief spirit of unity in the alliance. Invoking Article 5 was a fitting response to the assault against the United States. But the spirit did not last long. Within a few weeks the old fissures within the alliance reemerged, threatening once again to dissolve an entity that had survived over half a century. In the first two generations of NATO's existence, the Cold War with the Soviet Union had been the major purpose of its existence. But since the dissolution of the Warsaw Pact and of the Russian empire itself, NATO has struggled to seek new raisons d'etre, and has succeeded to some degree in finding them in crisis management in Europe and in areas beyond the boundaries of the alliance. The absence of a traditional enemy to serve as a centripetal force, along with the recognition of the United States as the lone superpower, has placed a focus on internal troubles of the alliance that had been obscured in the past by the presence of a common enemy in Soviet-led Communism.

This book is a history of NATO that concentrates on the differences within the alliance, particularly between the United States and its European partners. Most studies of NATO have centered on the East–West conflict, on how NATO coped with and ultimately triumphed over its Communist adversary. Too little attention has been paid to West–West conflicts that arguably have been more frequent and often more bitter if not more dangerous than the struggle with the Soviet Union. Differences among the allies began with the formation of the alliance itself. Some of them were resolved over time; others persisted and remain in place more than 50 years later. Many of them related to "out-of-area" issues in which the Soviet Union was not involved or only peripherally concerned.

At the heart of the differences within NATO was the transatlantic gulf between the United States and its European partners created by the disparity in their respective resources and in their respective outlooks on the world. These differences are at the center of NATO's difficulties today. How the alliance managed the unequal relationship in the past may offer insights into the common ground the alliance partners can identify in the twenty-first century. If NATO is to survive, solutions will have to be found. This history places in the foreground issues that the Cold War had relegated to the background.

I want to express my gratitude to a few of the scholars who have influenced my thinking and my writing on NATO history. Charles G. Cogan has produced a series of important studies in Franco-American relations, and his recent book on "The Third Option" was particularly valuable to me in this project. Robert S. Jordan has been an early contributor to NATO historiography, notably in his insightful institutional studies of the offices of the secretary-general and supreme allied commander. Pierre Melandri's doctoral dissertation at the École Normale Supérieure on the United States and European unification from 1945 to 1954 was a pioneer effort in this field that influenced my approach to the subject. Frank Ninkovich has integrated diplomatic with intellectual history in his scholarly work. His survey on Germany and the United States after World War II made a deep impression on me. Stanley R. Sloan has been more than a "government" historian of NATO. His two books building on Harlan Cleveland's "transatlantic bargain" have illuminated the continuing significance of the alliance, and have helped mold my judgment of NATO's history. Of all the conferences that have been held on NATO's past, present, and future, none has produced more impressive results than Gustav Schmidt's monumental three-volume history of NATO.

In addition to the foregoing scholars, I should like to recall with gratitude, once again, individuals and institutions who have nurtured my studies: S. Victor Papacosma's Lyman L. Lemnitzer Center for NATO and European Union at Kent State University, my NATO history classes at Georgetown University, and Alfred Goldberg's Office of the Historian of the Office of the Secretary of Defense (OSD). I want to thank Dalton West and Carolyn Thorne of the OSD Historian's Office for supplying me with NATO information from contemporary news sources. I would add a special note of appreciation to Steven L. Rearden for his willingness to read my writings with good will and an expert eye. I have profited too from Stanley Kober's command of contemporary geopolitical relations. At the Brussels center for international studies of the University of Kent and at NATO headquarters, Jarrod Wiener, Nicholas Sherwen, and Jamie Shea have been constant supporters of my studies, as has Morris Honick, former SHAPE historian. My thanks to Marie Gallup, archival adviser to NATO, and to Jacqueline Pforr, librarian of the NATO Parliamentary Assembly, for their advice and assistance during my Fulbright stay in Brussels in 2002. I appreciate as well the editorial talents of Heather Ruland Staines, which have helped my morale as well as the contents of this book. And thanks, too, to Janice who finally agreed with my choice of a title.

Abbreviations

ABM	Antiballistic Missile
AFSouth	Allied Forces, South
ANF	Atlantic Nuclear Force
AWACS	Airborne Warning and Control System
CDE	Confidence-and-Security-Building Measures and Disarmament in Europe
CIS	Commonwealth of Independent States
CJTF	Combined Joint Task Force
CSCE	Conference on Security and Cooperation in Europe
DFEC	Defense Financial and Economic Committee
DPC	Defense Planning Committee
EDC	European Defense Community
EEC	European Economic Community
ERW	Enhanced-Radiation Weapon
EU	European Union
ICBM	Intercontinental Ballistic Missile
IFOR	Implementation Force
INF	Intermediate Range Nuclear Force
IRBM	Intermediate-Range Ballistic Missile
ISAF	International Security Assistance Force
KFOR	Allied Occupation Force in Kosovo
KLA	Kosovo Liberation Army
MAAG	Military Assistance Advisory Group
MBFR	Mutual Balanced Force Reduction Program
MLF	Multilateral Force

MPSB	Military Production and Supply Board
MRMBM	Medium-Range Mobile Ballistic Missile
MTDP	Medium Term Defense Plan
NACC	North Atlantic Coordinating Council
NATO	North Atlantic Treaty Organization
NPG	Nuclear Planning Group
NSC	National Security Council
OSCE	Organization for Security and Cooperation in Europe
OSD	Office of the Secretary of Defense
PfP	Partnership for Peace
RDF	Rapid Deployment Force
RRF	Rapid Reaction Force
SACEUR	Supreme Allied Commander, Europe
SACLANT	Supreme Allied Command, Atlantic
SALT	Strategic Arms Limitation Talks
SDI	Strategic Defense Initiative
SEATO	Southeast Asia Treaty Organization
SHAPE	Supreme Headquarters, Allied Powers, Europe
START	Strategic Arms Reduction Talks
TNF	Theater Nuclear Force
UN	United Nations
UNPROFOR	United Nations Protection Force
U.S.	United States
USSR	Union of Soviet Socialist Republics
WEU	Western European Union
WU	Western Union
WUDO	Western Union Defense Organization

1

NATO AND ARTICLE 5:
2001 AND 1949–1950

The savage attacks against the United States on 11 September 2001 marked a mile-stone in the long history of the Atlantic alliance. The terrorist destruction of the World Trade Center in New York City and partial destruction of the Pentagon in Vir-ginia, along with the failed assault against Washington targets, left over 3,000 dead in the ruins of the towers, in the corridors of the Pentagon, and in the fields of west-ern Pennsylvania. It also galvanized the Atlantic alliance. For the first time, Article 5 of the North Atlantic Treaty was invoked in defense of an ally under attack.

The invocation of Article 5 evoked memories of the difficult days of 1948 when that article was the subject of agonized debate among the framers of the treaty. For Europeans this was the most important product of the impending al-liance between America and Europe. For the first time since the termination of the Franco-American alliance in 1800, the United States, through this article, was abandoning its tradition of nonentanglement in European political and military af-fairs. If any member were attacked, it could be assured that the United States would respond differently from its responses in 1914 and 1939. The message was that an attack against one would be considered an attack against all; an attack against Paris or London would be considered the equivalent of an attack against New York or Chicago. The venerable American tradition of isolationism had been breached when the treaty was signed on 4 April 1949.

Or so it seemed. West European governments, worried about the threat of Communist subversion internally and Soviet aggression externally, had hoped that their efforts to unite under the Brussels Pact of March 1948 would have moved the United States to join the Western Union that the pact was creating. Their leaders recognized that the promise of economic aid under the Marshall Plan of 1947 could not succeed unless their countries felt politically and militarily secure. Only an American guarantee could serve this purpose, and such prominent statesmen as British Foreign Minister Ernest Bevin and French Foreign Minister Georges Bidault had consciously modeled their Western Union along the lines the United States had laid out in the Marshall Plan, namely, showing evidence of self-help in individual member nations and economic integration into a new European community.

It required more than a year of intense negotiations before Europe could satisfy America's requirements, and even then questions about the credibility of the American commitment remained unanswered. Although the United States had no doubts about the seriousness of Europe's plight in 1948, it was uncertain about the course it should take to address it. Simply joining a European alliance seemed too drastic a step given the nation's history. Secret meetings in the Pentagon in late March 1948 of American, British, and Canadian representatives resulted in a recognition that some form of security organization was necessary in light of the inability of the United Nations and the Western Union to provide security for the West.

But the Truman administration had to cope with more than opposition from the old isolationists who were a rapidly diminishing presence in American life after World War II. It had to consider the articulate reservations of the military establishment, which feared that an open-ended military commitment to Europe would extend the responsibilities of the armed forces beyond their capacity to fulfill them. Additionally, there was a gnawing suspicion that European allies would draw military supplies and equipment from the limited budget the government was willing to allocate to the armed forces. Arguably, the most inhibiting factor in America's hesitation was pressure from former isolationists now joined with former adversaries in the belief that the UN charter was the key to a new world order. Arthur H. Vandenberg, a former isolationist senator, displayed the zeal of a reformed drunkard when he demanded that any treaty with Europe would have to conform to the terms of the UN charter.

The Truman administration's caution about the extent of the nation's commitment to the defense of European allies was reflected primarily in the language of the treaty. It was no coincidence that the UN charter was connected to as many articles as possible—Articles 1, 5, 7, and 12—as well as to the preamble of the treaty that specifically endorsed the principles of the charter. This was to assure Congress and the American public that the treaty's purpose was not only to support the aims of the world organization but to conform with its restrictions as well.

The treaty's managers sought to portray the alliance as a regional organization under the auspices of the UN charter, even though an identification was literally impossible. A regional organization had an obligation to report its activities to the Security Council where the Soviet Union held a seat and veto power. If NATO were a regional organization under Chapter VII, Article 53, it would have lost its primary purpose, namely, to build a defense structure that would not be subject to Soviet interference. The assumption of its founding fathers was that NATO was needed to counter Soviet obstructionism in the United Nations. Ultimately, the only article in the UN charter that applied to the North Atlantic Treaty was Article 51—the right of individual and collective self-defense—which would have been operative independently of the charter. This subterfuge seemed necessary to win Senate ratification of the treaty.

The issue of UN identification was not the only evasive gesture taken by the treaty's framers. Even more glaring was the name of the new alliance—the "North Atlantic" Treaty Organization. By emphasizing the Atlantic character of the alliance, the United States was further distancing itself from the Western Union and placing it inside a traditional American context. As Secretary of State Dean Acheson asserted, Europe would be joining America, not vice versa, as the scope of the Monroe Doctrine was widened to embrace the eastern shores of the Atlantic. The ocean itself had shrunk to the size of the Caribbean Sea as a consequence of modern technology. Given this concern, the membership of Canada, and even of Iceland, assumed an importance in the composition of the alliance that they might not have had in other circumstances. Isolationism may have dissolved as a vibrant ideology but its memory lingered on. When the Senate finally accepted the treaty by a vote of 82 to 13, the minority led by Republican Senator Robert A. Taft, vainly sought to scrap a binding treaty in favor of extending unilaterally to the Europeans the putative protection of the Monroe Doctrine.

Insulating the treaty against isolationist critics, however, was not a preoccupation of the diplomats preparing the terms of the treaty in Washington in the summer of 1948. If the European delegates to the Washington conference had their choice, NATO would have consisted only of the United States, Canada, and the five signatories of the Brussels Treaty. Reluctantly they acceded to the admission of Norway, Denmark, and Iceland as stepping-stones across the Atlantic for the delivery of American military aid. Denmark's Greenland and Norway's control of the Norwegian Sea, along with the geographical position of Iceland, were vital transatlantic links. Similarly, Portugal's Azores made that nation an acceptable candidate despite its lack of a democratic government.

If Portugal under a dictatorship was an undesirable ally, Italy in the middle of the Mediterranean Sea was an equally unlikely member of an "Atlantic" alliance. Its presence as a charter member was a product of the combined influence of the United States, which valued Italy as integral to Europe's defense, and France, which wanted to counter the northern tilt the Scandinavian members would give to the organization. A further concession to France was the inclusion of the Algerian departments north of the Tropic of Cancer within NATO's boundaries. It was obvious that in creating an organization that claimed to distinguish itself from conventional alliances, the diplomats sweltering behind closed doors in the heat of a Washington summer engaged in conventional trade-offs.

But the heart of the negotiations lay in what Canadian diplomat Escott Reid called "the pledge." This was, of course, Article 5. Everything else was subordinate to this vital assurance in European eyes. It mattered little to Europeans what name was attached to the alliance, and although it mattered more that increasing the membership to 12 could lessen the value of American military aid, this too was a price worth paying. But concessions were palatable only if the core principle of the alliance remained intact. The appropriate language—again from a European perspective—was already available in Article 4 of the Brussels Treaty. It stated clearly and simply that an attack against one was an attack against all. That this language was unacceptable to the United States was the nub of the controversies over the terms of the treaty.

The problem over Article 5 remained unsettled at the end of the Washington meetings in September 1948. It was not to be settled before the presidential election of that year. Given the expectation that Governor Thomas E. Dewey, the Republican candidate, would defeat the incumbent in the presidential race, there had been no urgency—from an American perspective—about completing the text before this anticipated victory. The assumption was that a pro-treaty Republican would have less difficulty in winning ratification of the treaty than his predecessor would have had.

The surprise victory of President Harry S. Truman did not immediately advance the treaty's prospects. Not that the Democratic leadership was opposed; the isolationist wing of the Republican Party was more of a problem in this regard. The difficulty in the winter of 1949 derived from the arrival of a new leadership team in the State Department and Senate. The Democrats won control of the Senate, which meant that Tom Connally succeeded Arthur Vandenberg as chairman of the Senate Foreign Relations Committee. Dean Acheson replaced Robert Lovett as chief U.S. negotiator for the treaty. Both lacked their predecessors' familiarity with the details of the negotiations and the close working relationship between the administration and the Senate, even though they supported the need for a treaty. Personalities made a difference. Unlike Lovett who courted Vandenberg, Acheson considered him a windbag and treated him accordingly. He was, as Acheson once noted, the only person he knew who could strut while sitting down. Connally, jealous of Vandenberg's influence, was an equally difficult partner.

The upshot was a fresh look at the text, particularly at Article 5, which they felt needed a better choice of language to assure that military action would not be an automatic response to an attack against an ally. The constitutional process whereby Congress was vested with the power to declare war had to be respected. But an immediate reaction was precisely what the allies were demanding. It required the semantic agility of George Kennan, the father of the containment doctrine but a skeptic about its military dimension, to come up with a suitable compromise. Instead of the allies taking "forthwith such military or other action . . . as may be necessary," the adjective *military* was finessed by "including the use of armed force" to follow "such action as it deems necessary." Individual members were presumably free to fashion their response to an attack according to their respective national interests.

This was not an ideal solution but it was the best that the Europeans could get in 1949. What may have tipped the balance in favor of the American-oriented text was a recognition that the president's powers as commander-in-chief could evade, or at least dilute, the constitutional prerogatives of Congress. There were precedents sufficient to give the allies confidence in the credibility of the American commitment. President Woodrow Wilson in 1917 was able to bring the nation into World War I despite a strong isolationist pull against involvement. And, in the nineteenth century, President James K. Polk manipulated Congress into declaring war against Mexico by dispatching troops to a disputed territory in the expectation that the Mexican army would fire the first shots.

The unanticipated consequences of these tortuous negotiations emerged as ironies in 2001. The entire allied effort 50 years before had been to convert the United States into an active partner of Western Europe. Only through this linkage were the Europeans convinced that their publics would feel secure enough in the face of Communist hostility to take advantage of the economic aid offered under the Marshall Plan. The impact of Article 5 was psychological rather than military; the image of U.S. B-29s armed with atomic weapons in the air 24 hours a day was an illusion, but it was a comforting one to the European allies in 1949.

In 2001 it was the United States, not Western Europe, that was under attack, and the assistance of the allies was more psychological than military. The dispatch of five NATO AWACS (Airborne Warning and Control System) to patrol the Atlantic coast was a boost to American morale as much as it was an earnest of Europe's support. If there was no question about the allies mobilizing their armed forces once Article 5 was invoked, it was partly because this was not an appropriate response to the war against the al Qaeda terrorist network. Moreover, the careful text that the Americans had crafted in 1949 permitted a selective interpretation of how any ally should respond to an attack against another member. Opening air space, providing intelligence, and dispatching anti–chemical warfare teams were all legitimate ways of interpreting Article 5 in 2001.

From April through July 1949, the treaty was ratified by each of the member nations without difficulty. For the Europeans this process not only carried a sense of relief but was also a prelude to the activation of Article 3, which was a particular priority for France. This was the article that would offer U.S. military assistance to the alliance members under the rubric of "mutual" aid. So important was the perceived need for this aid that the Brussels core nations presented a laundry list of items to be supplied only one day after the signing ceremony in Washington. And so eager were the Europeans for military equipment that Article 3 seemed to have been almost as important to them as Article 5. In any event, their démarche discomfited the Truman administration, which felt that their requests were premature at the very least, and perhaps somewhat unseemly. It was as if the Europeans were too impatient in their zeal to take advantage of America's largesse.

Such was the American reaction; it was anything but premature to the allies. In anticipation of the completion of the North Atlantic Treaty, the Western Union's Defense Organization (WUDO) had established committees in the summer of 1948 with the express purpose of presenting their military needs to their future ally. This difference in perspective suggests that a transatlantic fissure developing at the onset of the alliance would expand into other areas over the years.

The Brussels Pact members did receive grants of military aid before the end of the year, but not until the administration and the Senate had attached conditions that did not conform with the spirit of the alliance. When Europeans banded together in 1947 to promote economic cooperation, their intention, spurred on by their American benefactor, was to break the old pattern of zero-sum relationships among the nations. But this was not the way the United States intended its military aid to be distributed in the Mutual Defense Assistance Act in October 1949. There was a bilateral dimension in "mutual" aid that the allies did not welcome but had to accept.

It took two months—from August to October—and some panic in the Senate over news of the Soviet detonation of an atomic device before the United States was prepared to release funds. Moreover, there were two conditions that the beneficiaries had to meet before the one billion dollars in military assistance would be granted. Both of them portended future difficulties in transatlantic relations that have never been fully resolved.

One of them involved the alliance's need to develop a strategic concept for potential military activity against an adversary. There was nothing unreasonable about this Senate demand. It conformed with the proceedings of the first North Atlantic Council meeting in September 1949 when regional planning groups were established under the aegis of its military units: the Defense Committee composed of defense ministers, the Military Committee represented by chiefs of staff of the member nations, and its Standing Group—the military leaders of Britain, France, and the United States—which would implement the plans of the Military Committee. The lesser allies could hardly object to this arrangement; they were well represented in the Military Committee and in the regional planning groups as well as in the Defense Financial and Economic Committee (DFEC) in Rome and the Military Production and Supply Board (MPSB) in London.

What displeased all the allies—the larger as well as the smaller—was the distribution of forces in the strategic concept. The role of strategic air strikes would be filled by the United States, tactical air by Britain, and ground troops by the other members of NATO. There was a logic to placing strategic air action in American hands, given the reality that only the United States possessed aircraft armed with atomic weapons. Nevertheless, the allies were discomfited by the recognition that they would serve as cannon fodder in the event of a Soviet attack. American airmen in the skies above the battle would be less subject to casualties than the European troops on the ground below. Echoes of dissent over this division of military labor could be found a half century later in Kosovo and Afghanistan.

While there were credible reasons behind the strategic concept, there was less understanding about the second caveat placed on military aid. The United States insisted on some form of reciprocation for the aid it was donating in the form of base rights on the territories, particularly in the colonial territories of the allies. The argument for such concessions, in Tunisia or Morocco, was that American air bases would serve the alliance and facilitate the military aid the nation had promised. If the sense of national sovereignty was offended, its abridgment could be rationalized.

It was more difficult for the European allies to accept the bilateral nature of the grants. The detailed arrangements of the dollars dispensed were made not by NATO as an organization but by an arrangement between the donor nation and the recipient. This bilateral approach was to ensure that the funds would be properly expended, but inevitably it created friction between the United States and its allies. The American missions in European capitals were intrusive. They were frequently too numerous. The Military Assistance Advisory Group (MAAG) in Oslo, for example, was larger than the entire Norwegian Foreign Office. In larger capitals, their diplomatic status smacked of imperial arrogance. The sensitive French insisted that "advisory" be removed from the title of the inspection mission, and the British insisted that military personnel wear civilian clothes. The aid missions were embarrassments to the European governments, even as they attempted to mitigate them. To add injury to insult, aid was slow in arriving and often inadequate to the country's perceived needs.

American insensitivity to European sensibilities was not confined to monitoring military aid. At the meeting of defense ministers in April 1950, Secretary of Defense Louis Johnson shocked and outraged his Dutch counterpart when he recommended, in the course of refining the strategic concept, that the Netherlands turn over its naval responsibilities to the British. The Dutch minister in turn surprised Johnson with the observation that Holland had a naval tradition equal to that of Great Britain, and in fact had swept the English ships from the English Channel in the seventeenth century. Nor were American leaders sufficiently sensitive to the fragility of Western Europe's efforts at economic recovery. Pressing the allies to expend more on their military defenses failed to take into account the jeopardy that diversion of finances might place on their economic recovery programs, which were embodied in the Marshall Plan. In brief, the American tradition of nonintervention may have been breached by the signing of the North Atlantic Treaty, but old habits of unilateralism died hard, and new assumptions of superiority based on prerogatives of power created an imbalance in the alliance that might have doomed it in its infancy.

What preserved NATO in that first year was a fitful recognition on the part of the United States that its behavior reflected serious shortcomings, and required a willingness to repair damages it had inflicted. For example, over the years, the Joint Chiefs of Staff had come up with scenarios on war with the Soviet Union.

The predominant one that they brought into the alliance was the impossibility of defending the European mainland from a Soviet ground attack. In their Short-Term Defense Plan, they postulated defense at the perimeters—the Pyrenees, the Suez, and the British Isles. From these bases NATO could mount an attack on Soviet Europe much as the allies of World War II did against Nazi Germany less than a decade before. To Europeans, a defense plan of this sort revived memories they would prefer to forget. Liberation after another enemy occupation was unacceptable. The populations of Europe, particularly of France, would opt for a pro-Communist neutralism rather than undergo the replication of World War II. The gloomy judgment in Paris was that the Americans would be liberating a corpse.

The United States understood and responded to this concern with a revised plan—the Medium Term Defense Plan (MDTP), which NATO adopted in the spring of 1950. The blanket of NATO responsibility would be extended to the Rhine. This was not a wholly satisfactory solution; it left the Netherlands, divided by the river, uncertain of the alliance's protection. Although it also excluded a divided Germany, the continuing presence of allied occupation forces, particularly American, was a source of at least temporary solace. The tensions between the senior and junior partners in the alliance underlay all NATO activities. The initiatives inevitably were the product of the American conception of the alliance's interests, and the Europeans for the most part had no choice but to comply with them. That the United States was sensible to some of their concerns when they were raised loudly enough helped lend an aura of success to NATO's first year.

2

IMPACT OF THE KOREAN WAR: 1950–1958

The unifying force in the beginning of NATO's history was the Korean War. Initially, it activated many of the doubts that American behavior had fed before 25 June 1950. Asia and the Pacific had been the traditional focus of American foreign policy; none of the elements of nonentanglement or of isolationism was attached to this part of the world. The United States had been a player in Asia throughout the nineteenth century, and it seemed probable to many European observers that the nation would turn its back on Europe and focus once again on Asia.

These fears proved to be groundless. Rather than retreat from Europe, American policymakers envisioned the North Korean invasion of South Korea as part of the global Communist assault against the West. The Truman administration assumed that Stalin had incited the North Koreans to test NATO's resolve. Although this proved to be an inaccurate reading of the complicated politics of the intra-Communist world, it was sufficient to equate a divided Germany with a divided Korea. If the Communists succeeded in controlling the Korean peninsula, they would then unleash the Communist forces of East Germany to attack West Germany. In this context, the United States not only led a coalition nominally under the auspices of the United Nations in defense of South Korea but felt it necessary to build up sufficient strength in Western Europe to cope with an anticipated Communist attack from the East. East Germany, like North Korea, would serve as Soviet surrogates. Rather than abandon NATO and Europe, the United States embraced the alliance and intended to fortify it and reshape it as a military organization.

Western Europeans should have been grateful for the American reaction, and up to a point they were. The Mutual Defense Assistance Act of 1949 had been renewed shortly before the outbreak of the Korean War, but with a minuscule increase in the amount of monetary contribution. In the summer of 1950, Congress added 4 billion new dollars to the support of Europe's military defenses. Gratifying though this show of support was, America's heightened awareness of Europe's vulnerability brought discomfort and confusion to the alliance. In increasing aid, the United States required its allies to assume a proportional burden. But this expectation raised the danger that additions to their military budgets would jeopardize the economic recovery that the Marshall Plan had fostered since 1948. The United States was asking too much of its allies. It could afford to put into effect the findings of National Security Council document NSC 68 that had advocated in the spring of 1950 a massive increase in the nation's defense budget to cope with an impending Soviet invasion. Before the Korean War, President Truman had been wavering over whether to accept this recommendation; after June 1950, the administration felt it could do no less. And the NATO allies who would bear the brunt of a Communist assault should do their share. The United States could afford this buildup; the allies could not.

But raising the level of military assistance and increasing defense budgets were minor elements in the changes NATO would undergo and in the traumas they could cause the allies. The Korean War transformed the alliance into a genuine military organization. Until June 1950, there were only the trappings of military underpinnings of NATO—military committees, regional planning groups, even a military production-and-supply board in London and a Defense Financial and Economic Committee in Rome. They were going through the motions of military preparation. There was little coordination among them; the extended spread of their locations suggested a political rather than a military justification for their presence. What mattered in the first year of NATO's history was the rubric of America's commitment that would shelter all its members. This permitted the Europeans to accept the difficult terms of that commitment.

The post-Korean environment brought some changes that the allies welcomed. Before the end of 1951, a year-and-a-half after the war began, NATO had a supreme allied command in Europe, headed by General Dwight D. Eisenhower, a supreme allied commander for the Atlantic, coherent military commands in Europe, and the impending admission of two new members—Greece and Turkey. In this period, plans were underway as well for a civilian secretary-general to replace the foreign and defense ministers who lacked the time to devote to NATO affairs. Their deputies lacked the authority to coordinate NATO activities efficiently in the Deputies' Council that had been established in May 1950. To give additional credibility to the military character of the alliance, the United States in the winter of 1951 agreed to dispatch four divisions to Europe not only as a deterrence against Soviet aggression but also as an earnest of NATO's ability to turn back a Soviet invasion.

If these reinforcements—political and military—had been the totality of NATO's transition, the allies could have managed the additional burdens on their economies. But in the process of enabling NATO to meet a Soviet military challenge, the United States created new divisions between itself and its allies. These involved, for the most part, the two major European powers, Britain and France, and to a lesser extent the smaller members, who felt excluded from the decision-making process.

BRITISH GRIEVANCES IN THE 1950s

British "Greeks" versus American "Romans"

Of all the allies, it was the United Kingdom that believed itself to be the most intimate partner of the United States. Foreign Minister Ernest Bevin had taken the initiative in pushing America out of its isolationism after the collapse of negotiations at the foreign ministers meeting with the Soviet Union in London in December 1947. In January 1948, his speech before Parliament advocated a union of European nations as evidence of their seriousness in breaking with their tradition of internecine conflict and demonstrating that Western Europe was ready for a political counterpart to the economic reconstruction sponsored by the Marshall Plan. His conception of the Brussels Pact two months later was to have the Western Union serve as a vehicle for the United States to join the new organization.

The Truman administration's endorsement of the Brussels Pact did not include American membership. But British hopes were buoyed by the subsequent Pentagon conversations with the United States and Canada in late March 1948 resulting in a confidential understanding that an Atlantic security organization would follow in the near future. It is worth noting that France was excluded from the Pentagon meetings on the grounds that Communist influence in its government precluded confidentiality. Ironically, it was the British mole, Donald Maclean, serving as the rapporteur of these and other meetings, that permitted the Soviets to know the inner workings behind the formation of the North Atlantic Treaty. British leadership in the ongoing negotiations in Washington and in the Western Union Defense Organization (WUDO), both moving simultaneously if not cooperatively in the summer of 1948, went unchallenged. Field Marshal Bernard Montgomery, not General Jean de Lattre de Tassigny, was chairman of WUDO's Commander-in-Chief Committee.

In this setting it is understandable that British leaders would identify a special relationship with the United States that would make the United Kingdom primus inter pares in Europe. Indeed, the sentiment prevailing in Britain in the 1950s, expressed by such political figures as Harold Macmillan and by British pundits of the distinction of Alistair Buchan, was that the British would serve civilization as Greeks to the American Romans. In other words, Britain may have lost an empire but not the wisdom, as in the case of Greek slaves, to guide the powerful and relatively ignorant Americans, the Romans of the twentieth century, in the ways of diplomacy

Bevin and his colleagues were mistaken. The Americans had no intention of serving as surrogates for the strong but immature Romans. Their leaders, tested in World War II, came to the conclusion that the Old World diplomats, especially those of Britain in the 1930s, had failed to deal with the Fascist menace successfully. Americans could do better and did not need the discredited diplomacy of Europe to manage the Communist threat. The British were the "Greeks" who had successively departed India, Greece, and Palestine in the years immediately preceding the Atlantic pact. No American statesman expressed the devaluation of British statecraft more succinctly than former Secretary of State Dean Acheson who outraged Britain in 1959 with a speech at West Point in which he observed that the British had lost an empire without finding a new mission. The "special" relationship obviously had its limits.

The limits of British influence over American foreign policy in NATO were evident early in the history of the alliance. The leadership Britain had exercised in 1948, when Britain was a key partner in the Pentagon conversations and when the Western Union's headquarters was in London, dimmed by 1952. NATO's headquarters was transferred from London to Paris under pressure from the American ally to appease the French partner. The transfer was not in the British interest. Similarly, Britain was frustrated by its inability to secure a major command as NATO was reorganized in 1951. That Britain with its long and distinguished naval tradition should have assumed that the Supreme Command of the Atlantic would be assigned to a British admiral was only logical, a counterpart to the American general as supreme commander in Europe. To the dismay of the British government, and particularly to the admiralty, the command went to an American, Admiral Lynde D. McCormick, with the headquarters in Norfolk, Virginia.

There was more frustration for Britain when it was denied a Mediterranean command, under Lord Louis Mountbatten in Malta, which might have had a standing only slightly inferior to that of Eisenhower's Supreme Allied Commander, Europe (SACEUR) in Paris. Instead of enjoying an autonomous role in the Mediterranean, Mountbatten was required to report to Eisenhower through the southern command headquarters in Naples, headed by an American admiral. The most that the British could salvage from a distribution of commands in 1951 was the assignment of the Channel Command, an obvious sop to British pride. It was also an accurate judgment of the disparity between the American and British military establishments.

The special relationship suffered further setbacks in NATO's first decade, but none was more humiliating than the American reaction to Britain's effort to retake the Suez Canal by force in 1956. Egypt and the canal were not within the scope of NATO's responsibility, as defined in Article 6 of the treaty. It became, however, one of many "out-of-area" problems that affected both U.S. relations with its allies and occasionally the survival of NATO itself. The colonial empires of NATO allies had presented problems in NATO's first generation involving Portugal, Britain, France, Belgium, and the Netherlands. In fact, even as the North Atlantic Treaty was being framed in the early spring of 1949, American demands that the Netherlands accede to Indonesian independence generated resentment in The Hague that could have kept the Dutch out of the alliance. Only the intervention of Britain's Bevin eased American pressure at that critical moment.

The Suez Debacle

The Egyptian dictator Gamal Abdel Nasser's nationalization of the Suez Canal was a more severe challenge to the alliance. In a bid for leadership in the Arab world as well as an assertion of Egyptian nationalism, Nasser took over an operation that had been built and controlled for almost a century by Britain and France. For the British, the canal was a vital link to what remained of their empire in Asia. The Eisenhower administration had appeared to share the concerns of the allies but when it came down to possible military action against Egypt, Secretary of State John Foster Dulles was evasive about the American position. He wanted to work within the framework of the UN charter to undo Nasser's seizure of the canal. Distrustful of Dulles's intentions, Britain and France joined with Israel in October 1956, without informing their American ally, to wrest the canal from Egypt. Israel, under constant threat of Egyptian aggression, successfully crossed the Sinai, defeating the Egyptian army as it moved swiftly toward the canal. The British and French naval invasion, however, stalled before it could retake it, allowing Egypt to appeal to the United Nations for support against aggression from two major NATO partners.

The result was the near destruction of the alliance as the United States sided with the Soviets to oppose the Suez operation. It was a painful moment for all the allies because the abortive invasion of Egypt coincided with Soviet suppression of the Hungarian revolt against the Warsaw Pact. Instead of condemning the Soviets' brutal actions in Hungary, NATO found itself on the defensive as the Communist world condemned the Anglo-French aggression against Egypt in the United Nations. Given the strong position of the United States on the illegal use of force, it felt compelled to join the Soviet adversary in the UN judgment against its NATO allies. America's condemnation was all the more galling because it spoiled an opportunity to place the Soviet Union on the dock before the bar of world opinion over its behavior in Hungary. Both Britain and France succumbed to this combined pressure and retreated from the canal. Not surprisingly, Israel, which had the most justification for striking at its Egyptian enemy, received the harshest treatment from the United Nations as it surrendered the security it had hoped to gain from occupying the Sinai.

Prime Minister Anthony Eden resigned under criticism from liberals critical of gunboat diplomacy and from conservatives critical of the failure of that form of diplomacy. Still, Eden's successor, Harold Macmillan, enjoyed a close relationship with President Eisenhower, stemming from the camaraderie of World War II, that helped repair the relationship between the two nations. A case may be made that the relationship, having survived the Suez crisis, was stronger at the end of the 1950s than it had been at the beginning of that decade. Despite periodic tensions, Anglo-American ties dating from World War II remained strong in such areas as intelligence and technology, symbolized by Britain's being granted access to nuclear information in 1958. Congress amended the 1946 McMahon Act, which had proscribed dissemination of nuclear information to all foreign nations. The ongoing challenge of the Soviet Union, emboldened by its success with Sputnik, the first earth satellite, in 1957, drew the United States closer to Britain, as did Chairman Nikita Khrushchev's efforts to drive the Western allies out of Berlin in 1958. Arguably, General Charles de Gaulle as president of the new Fifth Republic was another unifying force, given his opposition to the "Anglo-Saxon" domination of NATO. Whether these centripetal forces were sufficient to justify a meaningful "special relationship" remains open to question.

THE FRENCH MALAISE IN THE FOURTH REPUBLIC

There was similar ambivalence in France's attitude toward the senior partner. It was a complicated mix of appreciation for American leadership against the Soviet threat and potential German revival combined with resentment over a superior civilization's dependence on a parvenu nation's power to surmount the challenges of the postwar world. The respect was usually grudging, and gratitude rarely acknowledged. If France had to accept America's bounty, it wanted to be sure that American assistance would be used to make France the leader of the European allies.

The Treaty of Paris (1778) and the Treaty of Washington (1949)

A comparison between the Treaty of Paris in 1778 and the Treaty of Washington in 1949 may have some legitimacy. In both cases the lesser power was dependent on a great ally for its immediate future—in the American case, independence from Great Britain; in the French case, protection in an American-led alliance against both the Soviet Union and Germany. Although there were some obvious differences—the United States was an emerging nation, while France had been the premier power in Europe—the similarities in behavior were striking. Neither country gave suitable recognition to the contributions of the other. France's intervention was a critical factor in the success of the American Revolution. Yet the leaders of the new nation not only distrusted the senior ally but completed its treaty of independence without consulting France, and then sought to terminate the entangling alliance without consideration of the sacrifices the ancien régime had made on its behalf.

Something of this spirit prevailed in France's attitude toward the United States after World War II. If an alliance had to be made, France should be the primary recipient of American aid without regard to the sensibilities of the benefactor or of the other beneficiaries. It distrusted American motives much as the American revolutionary leaders had doubts about the beneficence of its French ally. They feared a secret plan to restore a French empire in America despite the French monarchy's disclaimers. Similarly, the French saw behind America's support an imperial design that justified France's lack of gratitude for U.S. aid.

Arguably, the most telling link between the French of the eighteenth century and the Americans of the twentieth century was the willingness of the senior partners in each circumstance to accept the distrust, the selfishness, and the ingratitude of the junior partners in the treaties. Two distinguished economists—Mancur Olson and Richard Zeckhouser—proposed an explanation for the willingness of the senior partners to accept the lack of support for a common policy by the junior partners. This lay primarily in the larger stake the greater power has in the purposes of the alliance. The lesser ally could often pursue its own national interests even when they conflicted with the general welfare of the alliance or even with the national interest of the senior partner. This was manifestly true in 1782 when the American peace commissioners in Paris made their own arrangements with Britain without informing their French benefactor. Rather than punishing the United States for this behavior, the French foreign minister accepted the treaty initialed by the Americans and even provided new loans to the young nation. The reason simply was that to abandon the treaty of alliance would encourage an undesirable Anglo-American rapprochement.

In the negotiations over the North Atlantic Treaty, French representatives insisted on measures that irritated the American partner. Initially, France opposed enlarging membership beyond the five Brussels Pact members. But when the United States insisted on including the Scandinavian countries, France reversed its objections to Italian membership, largely to redress the northern tilt Denmark and Norway would present to the alliance. It also secured the inclusion of France's Algerian departments north of the Tropic of Cancer within NATO under Article 6. This was not an addition that the United States wanted, but one it had to accept to satisfy the French constituency.

The ability of the lesser power to manipulate the greater was most visible in the aftermath of the Korean War. America's decision was to treat West Germany as a potential victim of Communist aggression in much the same way that it judged the war in Korea. Was Stalin testing America's ability to resist an invasion in a divided peninsula? The nation's response was to take no chances in the likely event that the North Korean invasion of South Korea was a proving ground for an East German invasion of the West, both orchestrated by the Soviet leader. Consequently, the United States demanded of its allies a buildup of their armed forces commensurate with the threat they faced but did so without sufficient recognition of the limits of their abilities to finance increases in their military establishments.

Yet this was not the core of France's reservations about American demands. Its primary concern was over the apparent need for NATO to accept German rearmament as a significant part of Western defense. From the American perspective this was a logical step. German resources were necessary for NATO to cope with a Soviet invasion that was anticipated as early as 1952, and certainly no later than 1954. For France, the prospect of Germans in uniform once again so soon after World War II was unacceptable no matter how vital the need of a rearmed Germany. Furthermore, the American demand for a German contribution seemed to be a repudiation of the many assurances American leaders had given on demilitarization as well as denazification of Germany.

The United States, France, and the European Defense Community

Other European allies, former victims of Nazi aggression, shared French uneasiness about the American demands, but it was France that articulated opposition at the New York meeting of the North Atlantic Council to what Secretary of Defense Louis Johnson had put into a "single package": namely, massive American aid in return for German troops. One French delegate called Johnson's proposal "the bomb in the Waldorf." The result initially was a stalemate at the New York meeting of the North Atlantic Council in September 1950. France could not accept a German military contribution to NATO even if the new Federal Republic formed in May 1949 was fully purged of Germany's Nazi past. The impasse was broken in the following month when a more flexible secretary of defense, General George C. Marshall, replaced the less experienced Louis Johnson. The latter's frosty relationship with Secretary of State Dean Acheson had been a source of friction within the Truman administration even before the outbreak of the Korean War. With Johnson's departure, the Acheson–Marshall partnership opened new opportunities for accommodation with France.

In this improved atmosphere Jean Monnet, a respected French economist and proven friend of the United States, proposed the Pleven Plan (named for the premier of France at the time) to place German troops at the service of NATO under safeguards that would appease the uneasy French. Under this plan, German soldiers would not serve as a separate national force, but would be placed in a European army in units no larger than that of a battalion. Monnet, a proponent of an

evolutionary approach to European unity, saw this arrangement as a military counterpart to the economic integration of Germany's and France's coal and steel production in the Schuman Plan of May 1950. His ultimate objective was the creation
of a united Europe in which the old enmities of France and Germany would be
permanently buried. The Pleven Plan would be a functional step toward his goal.

The initial American response was negative. The plan seemed unworkable
with Germans represented in only battalion strength. The compromise of the Spofford Plan, named for Charles Spofford, the U.S. chairman of NATO's Deputies
Council, raised the German membership from battalions to regimental combat
teams but did little to still American skepticism about both the viability of the plan
and France's reasons for advancing it. Acheson was convinced that it was a device
to postpone if not to negate the needed German contribution to Europe's defense.
Although his estimate was accurate, at least as far as the motives of the French
government were concerned, American reservations did not matter. The United
States had to accept the French terms—and more.

If German rearmament was the quid in the Franco-American relationship, the
re-creation of NATO as a military organization under a Supreme Allied Commander in Europe was the quo. German units available for the defense of Europe
would serve under the Supreme Commander, General Dwight D. Eisenhower, the
liberator of World War II. This was the price the French demanded for their concessions on Germany, and the Americans paid it at the Brussels meeting of the
North Atlantic Council in December 1950. It was at this session that NATO was
reorganized into a credible military entity. Over the following two months the
United States underscored its commitment to France's concerns by the agreement
of the U.S. Senate to dispatch four divisions to Europe. The American pledge had
been largely psychological until the winter of 1951. It became a military reality
under French pressure for a vehicle to contain a German contribution.

In the short run at least, the junior partner had achieved its goals at the ex-
pense of the senior. France had balked at German rearmament until the United
States had agreed to change the nature of its role in Europe. Its own modest concession was only on paper. It required a year-and-a-half of hard bargaining before
France would sign the treaty establishing the European Defense Community
(EDC) wherein the members of the Western Union, minus Britain, would join
West Germany and Italy in an integrated military establishment. The armies of its
members would serve under the aegis of the SACEUR. An elaborate governing
arrangement was put in place as part of the new community. It would contain an
executive authority, a council of ministers, and a court of justice. Although most of
the members of the EDC had reservations about one or more of its terms, they all
were prepared to ratify the EDC treaty with its 132 articles and associated protocols—except France, its originator.

It disturbed France that Great Britain did not intend to join the EDC. The
United Kingdom did sign protocols guaranteeing its association with the Euro-

peans in the event of a crisis. These promises were never strong enough to calm French fears of just what impact the 12 German divisions—out of 43 in the EDC force—would have on its own national security. France could never bring itself to ratify the treaty despite repeated assurance of British support.

Signed in May 1952, the treaty died at the hands of the French National Assembly in August 1954, two-and-a-quarter years later. In this interval, France identified new problems growing from fear of rising inferiority to the German military as the Indochina war absorbed its energies. The result could be loss of economic as well as military leadership. Equally important was the blow to French pride in the absorption of its army into a supranational force despite additional protocols that were added in 1953 to preserve the integrity of France's armed forces. Even these were not sufficient. When Premier Pierre Mendes-France pressed for one more protocol at an EDC conference in Brussels in August 1954 to assure passage in the National Assembly, it was one too many for the allies. If accepted, the supranational elements in the community would be removed, a veto would be introduced, and responsibility for collective European defense specifically assigned to the United States and Britain. They rejected the package of amendments and the National Assembly in turn terminated the EDC on a procedural maneuver without debate or vote. What was central to France's rejection was the dilution of French sovereignty implicit in the EDC.

Mendes-France himself may not have been opposed to ratification; his subsequent acceptance of the Federal Republic's admission into NATO by way of an enlarged Western European Union (WEU) suggests that he would have accepted German rearmament. The key to solving the German problem was the involvement of Britain in an enlarged Western European Union that would not only include West Germany but condition its membership on renouncing production of nuclear, biological, or chemical weapons and on placing its armed forces directly under the Supreme Headquarters, Allied Powers, Europe (SHAPE). These were the terms of the London and Paris agreements in the fall of 1954 that brought Germany into NATO in May 1955 through its membership in the WEU. The way was now reopened for the functional integration of Western Europe that Monnet began with the European Coal and Steel Community in 1950.

A new era of Franco-German cooperation had begun that would be further advanced in the Treaty of Rome in 1957 that created the European Economic Community (EEC). These developments should have been greeted with appreciation by the American partner. European integration was a long-standing objective of American statecraft. It ranked with the containment of Soviet Communism as a means of ending once and for all the internecine wars in Europe. In practical terms, a united Europe should be able to confront the Communist menace without the United States assuming the economic and military burdens of the post–World War II years. Yet the course of Europe's progress inspired considerable doubts in Washington, particularly because it seemed to be under the dubious auspices of France. From the outset, the Truman administration suspected that the Pleven Plan and the subsequent EDC were simple devices for France to increase the quantity and quality of American aid. But because there was no alternative to the French proposal as far as the German question was concerned, the Acheson State Department gave its support and eventually its enthusiasm for the EDC.

The Republican administration under President Eisenhower was even more supportive of the EDC than its predecessor had been. This was not because of a reevaluation of France's purposes behind the new community. Rather, it was largely a consequence of the weight the influential secretary of state, John Foster Dulles, exercised in favor of the EDC. He believed that harnessing German resources to NATO was the most effective way of preventing the revival of German militarism. In these expectations he fostered a close collaboration and friendship with the powerful German chancellor, Konrad Adenauer. The German leader was sensitive to the inferior role France wanted his country to play in the community. He had to fend off criticism from nationalists on the right, who feared that bending to French pressures would prevent recovery of territories lost to the Communist bloc, and neutralists on the left who feared that binding Germany to the West would either provoke Soviet retaliation or sacrifice an opportunity for reunification. What Adenauer wanted was recovery of German national dignity while tying the nation to the West in such a way that Germany would never again be a threat to world peace. In these goals he had the wholehearted support of Secretary of State Dulles.

Given the empathy of the U.S. State Department with the position of Adenauer's government, the early suspicions of France's intentions revived. As France stalled in its ratification of the EDC treaty, demanding more and more amendments, Dulles became increasingly impatient with French tactics. By 1953 the Eisenhower administration had become fully convinced that the EDC was the only practical route to German participation in Europe's defense if only France would overcome its objections. In a widely publicized speech in December 1953, the secretary of state threatened an "agonizing reappraisal" of America's support of France. Such a reappraisal could bypass France if the allies chose to allow German rearmament under a special defense agreement. American unhappiness did not stop with suggestions of collective NATO action. If France ultimately scuttled the EDC, Dulles seemed to be willing to make a bilateral alliance with Germany irrespective of French concerns. And in this prospect he had the full backing of the U.S. Senate, which, by a vote of 88 to 0, endorsed a German–American special arrangement.

When the worst scenario appeared to materialize in August 1954, Dulles's anger was directed against Mendes-France. He was willing to believe, for the moment at least, that Mendes had made a deal with the Soviets to kill the EDC in return for Soviet support for France's departure from Indochina. Although the French premier did not merit Dulles's distrust, the tense relations after the demise of the EDC placed the alliance itself in jeopardy. It was at this point that British

Foreign Minister Anthony Eden was credited with coming up with a device to use German resources and at the same time do so with France's concurrence.

Only one month after the French Assembly acted—or refused to act—a nine-power conference composed of the Western Union countries, Germany, Italy, the United States, and Canada met in London to resolve the problem. It had to be done outside NATO's institutional framework because German accession to NATO would have been impossible under the alliance's rules. Any one member could have stopped the process, and France might not have been the only ally to cast a veto. But by enlarging the Western Union to include Germany and Italy, France would have assurances that had been lacking before, namely, Britain's participation and the aforementioned restrictions on German military involvement. Here was the vehicle that permitted Germany to join the alliance with France's approval.

In these negotiations the United States played a minor role—at least on one level. It did not initiate the solution. In fact, it took Dulles some time to overcome his suspicions of Mendes-France's government and to realize that much of what he had wanted from the EDC would be available in the circuitous path to German membership in NATO. German troops would be in the service of NATO even though there would be no separate German military staff; unlike the forces of the other allies, Germans would be assigned to and deployed directly by SACEUR. Not until the winter of 1954–1955 did the secretary of state appreciate the steadfastness of Mendes-France in winning the National Assembly's reluctant approval of the Federal Republic's admission into NATO via the expanded Western European Union. The effort cost the premier his position.

The American role in the solution to the German question is still shrouded in some mystery. In the course of Mendes-France's visits to the United States in the 1960s, long after he was out of office, he was asked about Eden's initiative in formulating the London agreement, an initiative, incidentally, for which Harold Macmillan also claimed credit. Mendes-France responded that it was not a British idea; it came from France. The former premier said that Dulles was too angry with him to receive any new ideas from a French minister. Hence, he turned over the proposal to Eden in the expectation that a British sponsor would be more acceptable to the American partner. In so doing, Mendes-France disclosed that France was not opposed in principle to German membership in NATO; it was the terms of the EDC that were indigestible to the National Assembly.

Where then does the United States fit into this European picture? The course of events in the fall of 1954 suggest that the United States was an onlooker, a belated supporter of actions taken by its junior partners, largely because it had no choice. It seemed to have been just a single member of the Nine-Power Conference, not its dominant figure. Consequently, a prominent British scholar, Alan Milward, has judged that the United States was essentially irrelevant in the solution to the German problem. This was a European problem, solved by Europeans.

There is some validity to this argument. Certainly the passions manifested in the State Department and the Congress did not deflect France from its course against the EDC. Nor did the United States pick up the pieces afterward. Yet Europe was constantly looking over its shoulder as it worked its way out of the conflict between France's concern for security against revival of German power and the Federal Republic's concern for equality in the alliance. The Cold War remained a focus of all the allies despite hopes that Stalin's successors would ease East–West relations. Only the United States could ensure stability while the European allies wrestled with the Franco-German issues. Granted that Dulles was not the prime mover in the fall of 1954, if the United States had opposed the agreements leading West Germany's accession to NATO, the London and Paris agreements would not have succeeded. The American imprimatur was a necessity.

The United States, France, and Indochina

Of all the problems in Franco-American relations in the 1950s, Indochina was the most enduring obstacle to harmony between the two allies. The German problem did come to a conclusion in 1955 while Indochina, like other out-of-area issues plaguing NATO, festered in French consciousness into the next decade and beyond. There was no Jean Monnet to deflect American pressure. France felt itself a victim of American manipulation in Indochina when it abandoned the peninsula in the Geneva Conference of 1954.

Indochina was a NATO problem from the inception of the alliance. For France the alliance was a seeming lifesaver for its stake in Southeast Asia. When World War II ended there had been hopes both in Indochina and among its friends in the United States that an independent new nation would be established. France, on the other hand, was put off balance by American sympathy for anticolonial movements in Asia; President Franklin D. Roosevelt opposed French resumption of its colonial rule after Japan had been ousted and applauded the efforts of the popular nationalist leader, Ho Chi Minh, to remove French colonialism permanently from Indochina.

France resisted its ouster, asserting that it had eradicated colonialism by including the three associated Indochinese states—Vietnam, Laos, and Cambodia—in a French Union under their own ruler, Emperor Bao Dai. But the most compelling argument for France in its relations with the United States was the Communist label attached to Ho Chi Minh. As confrontations between the United States and the Soviet Union spread after World War II, the transformation of an anticolonial rebellion into a Communist drive for power resonated positively in the United States by the time NATO was formed.

France's success in winning American support for its war in Indochina was secured by its claim to be fighting a war against international Communism. This reasoning became all the more important when the Korean War placed the United States in a similar position. An equation was made between the war against Communism in northeastern Asia and the war against Communism in southeastern Asia, both orchestrated, it seemed, by the Soviet Union. What many Americans had considered a nationalist rebellion against French domination before 1950 became a partner of the Communist challenge to the West. France in its own way was attempting to resist the tide of Communist expansion much in the way the United States and the United Nations were resisting North Korea's invasion of South Korea.

The critical link between NATO and Indochina developed from France's derailing of American demands for a military buildup in Europe by claiming that its war in Indochina was serving the common cause. When the NATO allies at the Lisbon meeting of the North Atlantic Council in February 1952 agreed to raise 50 divisions in Europe, the United States made known its intention to provide $200 million in military equipment for use in Indochina. If there was any doubt about the equation of military aid to Indochina with France's participation in Europe's military effort, the State Department dispelled it by admitting that the United States had to be prepared to assume an increasing share of France's burden in Indochina. The reason was clear. If Washington did not help, the weapons the French would supply to the Indochina war would be at the expense of their NATO commitments, particularly to the EDC.

The connections between NATO and Indochina became more entangled when France used the meeting in Paris of the North Atlantic Council in December 1952 to make specific the intertwining of its struggle against Communism in Asia with NATO's in Europe. Under French pressure, the council passed a resolution proclaiming that the French campaign in Indochina was in "fullest harmony with the aims and ideals of the Atlantic Community" and so "deserved continuing support from the NATO Governments." It is worth noting that the United States in the Korean War never won—or asked for—this kind of NATO blessing, although it received passing mention in the resolution. That war, however, was in its last phases, and might have elicited negative reactions from the allies if it had not been conducted under the auspices of the United Nations.

Immediate increases in American military aid to the French forces in Indochina signified a practical application of the NATO resolution. But France had won only a pyrrhic victory in its successful exploitation of weakness in Europe and Asia. The end result of its war was a catastrophic defeat for France in the loss of its garrison in Dienbienphu in May 1954, consequent blaming of the United States for the disaster, and subsequent surrender of all Indochina at the Geneva Conference in July of that year. The two allies exchanged increasingly bitter charges. Having undertaken the supply of the French army in Indochina, American military advisers also offered advice and guidance on the assumption that France's difficulties stemmed from strategic as well as tactical errors. As French leaders boxed themselves in at a putatively impregnable stronghold like Dienbienbphu, they blamed Americans first with unacceptable interference with their campaigns, and then with failure to fulfill promises of sufficient military assistance. The American military team on the ground in turn concluded that the French generals' unwillingness to follow their advice led to their defeat.

A spate of mutual recriminations came after Dienbienphu. The atmosphere was clouded by the French accusation of betrayal when the United States refused to employ its nuclear weapons to help the beleaguered ally at its moment of crisis. If such a promise was made, it was so vague that it could be credibly denied. Such was the case. The chairman of the Joint Chiefs of Staff asserted that a commitment to the use of nuclear weapons was never made. France, in the judgment of the U.S. government, was responsible for its own plight. The French military in particular did not accept this denial, and the country's political leaders were convinced that American behavior at the Geneva Conference confirmed their belief that their ally purposely undermined French defense of Indochina.

It was obvious that the United States was the primary actor at Geneva in the effort to extract France from its plight in Indochina without conceding victory to the Communist adversary. To effect this result, the cooperation of the two Communist powers, the Soviet Union and the People's Republic of China, was required. The Soviets were willing to support the United States on this issue because they anticipated benefits from the dissolution of the EDC. Moreover, they, along with British representatives, would serve on a commission to observe compliance with the terms of the Geneva agreement, giving them a visible presence in Southeast Asia. China was less happy with the outcome of the conference but was pressed by the Soviets to accept it. From the American standpoint the results were positive. The victorious Viet Minh under Ho Chi Minh did not take over all Indochina. Laos and Cambodia became separate independent entities although Vietnam was divided at the seventeenth parallel; the northern half would become North Vietnam under the control of Ho Chi Minh. But south of that line an independent South Vietnam would decide for itself in a free election whether it would unite with the North.

It was France that felt slighted in these arrangements. The temporary new government of South Vietnam would be headed by a nationalist, Ngo Dinh Diem, who had a history of anticolonial and anti-French activities. In French eyes, Diem was an American surrogate, which confirmed their suspicions that the United States engineered their ouster from Southeast Asia in order to replace France as the "colonial" power in Vietnam. Although this interpretation may be written off as a species of paranoia, the subsequent history of Vietnam and the American relationship to the new state gave credibility to French accusations of collaboration with Diem. The promise of a free election was not realized, in good measure because the United States feared that Ho Chi Minh's popularity as a nationalist hero would have won over South Vietnam, creating a unified Vietnam on Communist terms.

To bolster South Vietnam against subversion from frustrated Communist supporters, the United States initiated the creation of the Southeast Asia Treaty Organization (SEATO), with Asian members drawn from Thailand, the Philippines, and Pakistan but also including an ambivalent France as well as the United States, the United Kingdom, Australia, and New Zealand. The professed mission of the new organization was to contain Communist expansion in Asia as NATO was doing in Europe, but without the integrated command organization the Atlantic alliance had assembled. But SEATO's most immediate function was to issue a protocol placing a vulnerable South Vietnam under its protection.

France would neither forget nor forgive American behavior in 1954. The Indochina trauma poisoned Franco-American relations in the Fourth Republic and provided a major justification for Charles de Gaulle's treatment of NATO in the next decade. For France, the Indochina humiliation at the hands of the United States was replicated at Suez in 1956. Unlike in Britain, there was no rapprochement with the United States after that debacle. Instead, there was an anticipation of further American animosity against French interests in the more sensitive area of Algeria in the late 1950s. The Algerian demand for independence was sparked by Indochina's success, even though Algeria, unlike the Associated States of Indochina, was integrated into metropolitan France. It did not escape French attention that there was an articulate lobby in the United States, with which such prominent figures as Senator John F. Kennedy was associated, that promoted an independent Algeria. The legacy of resentment carried over into the Gaullist years of the 1960s and beyond.

The Attitudes of Smaller Members

It is hardly surprising that the allies outside the leadership circle would nurse their own resentments; the Military Committee, for example, encompassed all the members except Iceland, but only Britain and France joined the United States in its Standing Group. And it was not just United States behavior that disturbed them. As early as the winter of 1948 when the Brussels Pact was in process, the Low Countries had to raise their voices to receive equal treatment from the British and French allies. But inevitably it was the United States that bore the brunt of their criticisms. Their complaint essentially centered on the failure of the senior partner to consult with the smaller nations in the alliance. Although NATO prided itself on its decision making by consensus, "the NATO method," consensus was reached either by unilateral actions or by confining consultation to the major powers. The smaller nations were left on the sidelines. To remedy this situation, the North Atlantic Council, in May 1956, established a committee of three foreign ministers from Italy, Canada, and Norway to advise the council on means of advancing cooperation within NATO to produce greater unity. The report of the Committee of Three in December of that year went no further than to ask the secretary-general to develop proposals that would implement their recommendations.

Coming as it did in the year of the Suez crisis, the discontents of the smaller nations received minimal attention at the time. Although their concerns about neglect were genuine, the Scandinavian countries had been able to leverage their influence from the beginning to act successfully against the preferences of the United States. They were important cogs in the U.S. plans for supplying Europe's defenses, and as such required concessions not given to other allies. Yet they entered the alliance negotiations at the end of the process, partly because of the reluctance of the core Brussels Pact signatories to enlarge the membership, partly because of the possibility of Denmark and Norway—with Sweden—entering into a Nordic Pact. Under Swedish leadership, this group counted on American assistance to make their defense plans viable. When the United States refused to accept the arrangement, Sweden opted for neutrality in the Cold War, leaving Norway and Denmark to join the Atlantic pact.

Norway with its historic ties to Britain was more anxious than Denmark to participate in NATO. The latter had a long tradition of neutrality, even though like Norway it saw that neutrality violated in World War II. Norway, however, was the one NATO ally in 1949 that had the Soviet Union as a neighbor, which intensified its awareness of potential Soviet aggression. In 1948, a provocative Soviet demand for a nonaggression pact with Norway had been a factor, along with the Communist coup in Prague, that accelerated the conclusion of the Brussels Pact. Still, there were significant reservations in Norway's and Denmark's adherence to the North Atlantic Treaty that earned them the name of "footnote" members.

Given Norway's northern border with the Soviet Union, the Norwegians wanted to be assured that no NATO troops would be stationed on their land except under threat of war. Until then all military exercises by the allies on Norwegian territory would be held 250 miles from the border. Denmark, less vulnerable to Soviet pressure, joined Norway in denying NATO the deployment of atomic weapons on its territory as it deferred to neutralist sentiments in its legislature. The United States did not welcome these footnotes, but had to accede to them as the price of Scandinavian participation in the alliance. As in the case of France in this period, the Olson–Zeckhouser thesis was applicable; the smaller nations with a different stake in the treaty forced the senior partner to permit a degree of independence it otherwise would not have granted.

Such freedom was not always in evidence. Another Scandinavian ally, Iceland—with a special isolationist tradition created by is location—caused a crisis when it attempted to follow its own path in 1956. Not that Iceland was unfamiliar with wartime exigencies. When Denmark was overrun by Nazi Germany in World War II, the United States occupied Iceland to keep it out of German control, but this was a special circumstance. In 1949 Iceland tried to write into the North Atlantic Treaty a neutral status if it became a member. Although this reservation was unacceptable to the United States, Iceland managed to extract an understanding that there would be no bases and no arms unless there was danger of invasion. The Korean War came to Iceland in the form of a defense agreement with the United States in May 1951. It stipulated that the United States would come to the aid of Iceland in accordance with its responsibilities under the North Atlantic Treaty and that Iceland would make available its defense facilities.

Under this arrangement the American military was based primarily in the area of the Keflavik airport in numbers that loomed large in a population of little more than 150,000. And when the Korean War wound down two years later, the U.S. forces became a ready target for a coalition of the liberal Progressive Party, the Communist Party, and the National Preservation Party that had won an impressive victory in the 1953 general election on the strength of its opposition to the U.S. defense forces in Iceland. In the next two years there was expectation that the United States might withdraw from its base at Kleflavik as the Cold War seemed to thaw under the leadership of Nikita Khrushchev. The Soviet decision to give up its naval base in Porkkala, Finland, provided an impetus for pressure to remove the Americans from the country. The rising discontent with the American presence conformed with the nation's historic isolation and present condition as the one ally in NATO without an army.

By June 1956, a coalition of Progressives, Social Democrats, and Communists took over the government and called for the implementation of a legislative resolution in March calling for the withdrawal of the United States military forces in Iceland. The State Department adopted a deceptively mild line in dealing with this challenge. Just two years before, Dulles had been prepared to take drastic measures against French intransigence over the EDC. In the case of Iceland, however, he appeared ready to accept the demand despite the obvious threat both a Communist-influenced government and the vulnerability of the North Atlantic sea lanes posed to the NATO defense posture in the North Atlantic.

Two significant factors lay behind the U.S. tolerance of Iceland's behavior in the summer and fall of 1956. One was a confidence that the departure of U.S. forces would have a damaging economic impact on the country, raising questions among those affected about the wisdom of its government's decision. A few weeks after the government reversed its position the U.S. International Co-Operation Administration announced a loan of $4 million. The other was the united stand of the NATO allies against withdrawal of American forces. Conscious of Soviet suppression of the Hungarian rebellion in October, Iceland changed its mind. The Suez crisis in 1956 gave special urgency to NATO's plea. Iceland's positive response and its rejection of the Communist role in its government was a relief to all the members.

Iceland's behavior suggests both the lengths and the limitations imposed on a small and, in this case, a very minor ally as it pursued its own interests. The limits and freedoms of all allies—large and small—were evident in the discontents of the 1950s. Each of the European members had its own grievances against American leadership in NATO, and each in its own way made them clear to the senior partner. At no time did any member consider disengagement from the alliance, even Iceland in 1956. The Cold War in the background always provided a check on transatlantic passions. The partners managed to work out most difficulties through "the NATO method" of consensus. And where difficulties appeared irreconcilable, they were bypassed in the hope they would dissipate in time. Tensions seemed highest not over conflicts of national interests but over perceptions of the weakening of the American pledge after Sputnik in 1957.

3

THE GAULLIST DECADE: 1958–1968

That General Charles de Gaulle as president of France under the new Fifth Republic was the leading European challenger to American primacy in NATO during the next decade is not open to doubt. His towering presence dominated Europe's relations with the United States, even as many of the European allies resented France's pretensions in this period. His rise to power from the ashes of the Fourth Republic coincided with the perception of American vulnerability to Soviet intercontinental ballistic missile attack generated by the successful launching of its earth satellite, Sputnik, in October 1957. It was a shock both to Americans and Europeans to experience a potential enemy flying the skies over their countries. Not even American efforts to demonstrate that its missile technology was actually more advanced than the Soviet counterpart or its quick dispatch of nuclear stockpiles to Europe were sufficient to erase the trauma caused by the Soviet exploit.

Until 1957, the United States had been considered invulnerable to any potential Soviet aggression. Unlike Europe's, its territory was beyond the adversary's range, and its promise under Article 5 to respond to an enemy assault credible. The Soviets could not touch the United States while the Soviet Union and its allies were restrained by U.S. nuclear power based in Europe. It was under this rubric that the NATO allies found a sense of security and achieved economic prosperity. They accepted an inferior role despite all their discontents over American control of the alliance. It is worth observing that the titles and authority of Supreme Allied Commanders were given to American leaders while the Europeans had to settle for the role of Secretary-General. The former were military figures, the latter civilian. Moreover, the generals were usually figures of international fame and influence. General Dwight D. Eisenhower and General Lauris Norstad often seemed to be the equals of European heads of government. The secretaries-general on the other hand were prominent figures, but usually only within their own nations. Lord Ismay (General Hastings Lionel Ismay), the first secretary-general, was a wartime aide of Winston Churchill; Paul-Henri Spaak and Dirk Stikker were political leaders in Belgium and the Netherlands, respectively, but not in the class of an Eisenhower.

European concession to American superiority was the pattern of the 1950s. Would the American commitment to its allies remain intact when the United States could be the object of an enemy attack by means of the new missiles? Repeatedly during his presidency de Gaulle answered this question negatively. It seemed illogical, he proclaimed, for any country to place the security of others, whether or not in an alliance, over its own. Would the United States consider an attack against Paris the equivalent of an attack against New York when New York was as exposed to enemy action? He never framed his question quite this baldly but the implications were always there. More specifically, he reminded the allies about America's interests in Asia and the Pacific being older and more constant than its involvement with Europe. The Vietnam War in which the United States was increasingly entangled was his case in point. Among its other instructive uses he cited it to question the wisdom as well as the geographical direction of American policy. Given doubts about the credibility of the U.S. commitment to Europe, de Gaulle saw France assuming the leadership in Europe that the United States had held in NATO's first decade.

FRANCE AS COLD WAR MEDIATOR

De Gaulle's actions in the 1960s proceeded on the assumption that the Soviet threat of aggression was seriously diminished. Although he considered the Soviet Union a nuclear power on a par with the United States and its intentions no less hostile to the West than it had been in the past, he recognized that it was no longer the expansionist state it had been a decade before. Its retreat from belligerence over Berlin in 1959 and again in 1961, along with its literal retreat from Cuba in the missile crisis of 1962, encouraged de Gaulle not only to equate the two superpowers in their relation to Europe but also to claim that a Europe under France's direction could play a significant role in mediating between the two. It was this claim that lay behind de Gaulle's assertion that France's arms were poised to counter challenges from every "azimuth."

It was unlikely that he genuinely considered the United States, given its history in NATO, posing the same kind of military threat as the Soviet Union. But his image of the two adversaries suggested more similarities than differences. An anecdote circulating in Europe in the 1960s referred to a dangerous world in which two Caliban monsters, in the Shakespearean image, required the civilizing functions of an Ariel to keep the peace. In this context the distinctions between the

United States and the Soviet Union disappear, and the European Ariel becomes the key to moderating if not terminating the Cold War. De Gaulle's France would be the center of a European order in which the nations would recognize Paris as the arbiter of Europe's interests. Europeans in general approved the implied flattery even if they might dispute the position of Paris as the capital of this new Europe.

De Gaulle moved gradually but inexorably toward his goals in carefully calibrated steps. The first was to confront the Anglo-Saxon powers with a plan for a triumvirate in which France would join the United States and the United Kingdom to direct NATO affairs. This would presumably correct a situation in which the "NATO method" of consensus on decisions had conferred too much authority on the smaller nations. It is not surprising that the United States and Britain rejected this proposal on the grounds that it would distort the nature of the alliance even if it improved its efficiency. Nor is it likely that de Gaulle was surprised at this reaction; it confirmed his judgment that NATO was a ward of Anglo-America and that France could not achieve equality under this arrangement. He justified rejection of British membership in the EEC in 1962 by his conviction that Britain would be America's Trojan horse in his projected European order.

The Force de Frappe

Having failed to win over the United States to his version of a reorganized NATO, de Gaulle moved to accelerate the development of nuclear independence through France's *force de frappe*. Although France's nuclear program originated in the frustrations of the Fourth Republic, it was an important gauntlet he was laying before the senior partner. The United States vigorously opposed the proliferation of nuclear weaponry, and made its views clear. In a major speech at the Athens meeting of the North Atlantic Council in May 1962, Secretary of Defense Robert McNamara antagonized both the British and the French by criticizing their pretensions to a nuclear capability, but it was the French force de frappe that he found the more unacceptable. From the American standpoint, no other NATO member should find it necessary to have nuclear weaponry; the U.S. nuclear arsenal was more than sufficient to serve all the others. Indivisibility of command was the key term in the secretary's lexicon to avoid conflicting strategies in preparing for a nuclear war. If competing nuclear forces operated independently, the results could be disastrous. Not only would small nuclear powers find building their arsenals expensive and prone to obsolescence but they would lack credibility as a deterrent. Understandably, de Gaulle believed that he was the target of McNamara's peroration.

France made it clear that it did not accept America's objections. Taking the offensive against the American case, French military intellectuals rejected the notion that France would be the Soviet's first victim in the event of a nuclear war, and that its small nuclear capability would be quickly wiped out in the event of a nuclear war. On the contrary, they suggested the prospect of destroying even a limited number of Soviet cities would serve as a force of dissuasion. National nuclear arms, no matter how small, would strengthen deterrence by instilling a sense of insecurity in the minds of a potential aggressor. What was really at issue in French eyes was a transparent American attempt to block France from achieving an element of equality with the United States in NATO and to undermine its leadership in Europe.

The Gaullists could also appeal to fellow Europeans by pointing out that the American insistence in adopting "flexible response" in place of "massive retaliation" against acts of Soviet aggression put the defense of Europe at risk. By keeping nuclear weaponry under sole American control, the United States intended to render it unusable as a weapon of war on the assumption that a nuclear war would be too destructive to initiate. Herein lay the reason for flexibility that would emphasize conventional forces to be used in the event. Only as a last resort would nuclear arms be activated.

France won considerable support from the allies by exposing this strategy as a betrayal of Europe. Given the territorial proximity of Warsaw Pact armies and the putative inadequacy of NATO ground troops, the only guarantee of European security lay in the deterrent power of a low nuclear threshold, not the high threshold urged by Secretary McNamara. De Gaulle was able to use the Soviet–American Limited Nuclear Test Ban Treaty of 1963 as proof of his argument. This was an example of the United States going over the heads of the allies to reduce nuclear arms, and in doing so reduce as well the deterrent function of the nuclear weapon. France and most of the allies were not reconciled to the alternative to nuclear weaponry that McNamara advocated in 1962, namely, building up conventional forces both to deter aggression and to defeat an attack if it occurred. Despite American claims to the contrary, such a buildup would be too expensive and probably futile in the face of Soviet conventional strength.

America's failure to impress the French on nuclear matters was only to be expected. Too much had been invested in the force de frappe to convince France to abandon its nuclear program. American opposition was simply another piece of evidence in the case against the hegemony of the transatlantic ally. France's independence of the United States required keeping is nuclear weapons outside NATO's integrated command.

France Leaves SHAPE

It was only a matter of an appropriate time before de Gaulle detached France from SHAPE. He had begun the process by signaling the Soviet Union that France would follow its own course when he removed the French fleet from the

Mediterranean theater in 1959. The slogan *Mediterranee aux Mediterraneens* (The Mediterranean for the Mediterraneans) was his assertion of French preeminence in the area as well as an assumption that the warships of both superpowers would be excluded from the sea. Four years later he removed the French Atlantic fleet from the Supreme Allied Command, Atlantic (SACLANT). In refusing to have France participate in "Fallex '66," NATO's annual military exercise, he seemed to have completed preparations for full withdrawal from the military structure of the alliance.

By the end of 1965, the time at last was ripe. The Cold War had sufficiently thawed for overtures to be made to the Soviets; the German neighbor had accepted France's leadership in Europe through a treaty of cooperation with Adenauer; and the Algerian war had been liquidated. In March 1966, de Gaulle sent a letter to President Lyndon B. Johnson requiring that all NATO commands on French territory be removed within a year's time and that all French personnel would leave their SHAPE posts. The deadline of a year for the United States to pack up its men and matériel and get out of France was insultingly short. But at the same time, the French made it clear that they would not denounce the alliance but would separate participation in the treaty from membership in its military organization.

There was shock and anger in Washington, although the former reaction was less understandable than the latter. The French president had supplied enough signals of his intentions to cushion the surprise when the final action was taken. In fact, American reaction was mixed. The most vehement protests came from such Francophiles as Undersecretary of State George Ball, who felt personally betrayed by France's behavior. He wanted to challenge the legality of de Gaulle's cancellation of agreements that provided for two years' notice before termination. If Ball could have had his way, the United States should retaliate by challenging the legality of the eviction from its bases in France and denying the French access to NATO intelligence sharing. With some bitterness he wondered if the French wanted to evict as well the bodies of American soldiers who had died in two World Wars. The most serious NATO riposte, however, was to remove not only the military headquarters from France but the political as well. NATO's new home was to be in Belgium.

Undoubtedly, France did do damage to NATO's defense capabilities in the short run. The sheer physical effort to transfer supply lines into Germany from an Atlantic route via France to North Sea ports in Germany was not only costly but disruptive. Yet it did not generate the kind of hostility that could have led to France's isolation if not ejection from the alliance. (There was no mechanism to throw out a member.) In fact, de Gaulle's posture, as pointed out in another context, always had admirers, particularly from Europeans who shared his resentments of American dominance. Diplomats, such as NATO's Secretary-General Manlio Brosio, had deep ties to France and were not anxious to move the office from Paris to Brussels. And ironically, Americans who, unlike Ball, were ordinarily hostile to French pretensions, welcomed de Gaulle's action as an occasion to reduce American oblig-ations and place greater responsibility on Europeans for the defense of their terri-tories. From another perspective, Secretary of Defense McNamara dismissed the military significance of French participation and saw an opportunity in its depar-ture to streamline the NATO defense system, making it more efficient and less costly. President Johnson himself accepted de Gaulle's decision with equanimity, at least publicly, on the grounds that the French president was not going to change his mind whatever arguments may be made.

The alliance survived the French challenge, partly because de Gaulle, his grand gestures notwithstanding, kept French forces in Germany, although not under NATO's provenance. He also kept French air space open to NATO aircraft. Moreover, France continued to be represented in every NATO military headquar-ters, although its representatives were identified as "missions" not "delegations." The French president had no intention of severing his ties with the alliance.

In retrospect, his challenge failed to discredit America's leadership of NATO. Success for his aspirations to replace the United States as the paramount influence in Europe depended on Germany as a junior partner. Up to a point the close links between de Gaulle and Adenauer, solemnized in the Franco-German treaty of co-operation in 1963, gave substance to French hopes. But although there was Ger-man dissatisfaction with America's management of the Berlin crisis in 1961 and with Secretary of Defense McNamara's preference for a high nuclear threshold of response to a Soviet attack, Germany was not prepared to substitute American leadership for a less credible French defense capability. Nor were the smaller allies comforted by the prospect of a Gaullist Europe.

In some respects NATO felt liberated by the departure of France from its mil-itary structure. That country was rarely in step with its allies. By absenting itself from the new SHAPE headquarters in Mons and from meetings of the Interna-tional Military Staff in Brussels (which had replaced the three-nation Standing Group in 1966), France freed the United States from having to deal with French obstructionism in the Defense Planning Committee. Its self-propelled removal from SHAPE also opened the way for a more harmonious collaboration between the United States and the smaller members of the alliance in the Nuclear Planning Group, established in the year France expelled NATO military bases from its soil.

SKYBOLT AND THE BRITISH TRAUMA

Of all America's partners in NATO, the United Kingdom should have been the most secure and most supportive. Amendments to the U.S. Atomic Energy Act of 1946 had ensured its role as a nuclear power, and the United States seemed pre-pared to make a distinction—if not a new, special relationship—between Britain and the Continent. But the nuclear issue would cast a pall over this relationship in the 1960s as it raised once again the issue that also agitated Germany and France: dependence on the United States for the nation's nuclear security. Each ally reacted to America's dominance in a different way, but none was more explosive than the Anglo-American wrangle over Skybolt in the early 1960s, at least not until de Gaulle's withdrawal of France from NATO's military command in 1966.

Prime Minister Harold Macmillan, like Churchill, the son of an American mother, was the archetype of a cultivated Briton who expected to use the more powerful but less sophisticated Americans to achieve British national ends. He had understood from his experiences in World War II that the best way to deal with Americans was to thrust them into the limelight while the British set the agenda in the background. Macmillan, however, was no cold-blooded Machiavellian. He genuinely respected the abilities of both Eisenhower and Kennedy and believed that his friendship with them, patronizing as its undertones might be, would serve the interests of both countries.

The Skybolt was to be an example of mutual advantage. It was an air-launched ballistic missile intended by the U.S. Air Force to be carried by strategic bombers. As such, it would be a competitor to the Navy's Polaris, the submarine-launched intermediate-range ballistic missile (IRBM), and would permit the Air Force to fit into the space age without surrendering its manned bombers. Begun in 1952, it was originally considered too far beyond the current state of the art to be developed, but after the technological breakthroughs in that decade, the Eisenhower administration approved its development as a weapons system in 1960, although without a commitment to its production.

Once this decision was made, none of the auguries boded well for the Skybolt. The Air Force dismissed the Army's and Navy's questions about feasibility and costs as the original estimation of $180 million rose to $391 million by mid-1961. The original operational date of May 1962 was stretched to October 1964. Given these problems, the Air Force had to contend with pressures from civilian as well as from military analysts to cancel the program. It resisted these pressures successfully at first, propelled by its eagerness to have under its own aegis a strategic IRBM capability comparable to the Navy's ability to launch a missile from a submarine.

What McNamara found as he entered office in 1961 was a weapons system that the Air Force celebrated as a two-state, solid-propellant missile delivering its warheads to a maximum distance of 1,000 nautical miles when launched from a B-52 or a British Vulcan bomber. The checkered history of Skybolt was not lost on McNamara, particularly that of its escalating costs. While he was skeptical about the Air Force's claims, Britain's enthusiasm for the weapon was a card the Air Force could play when it encountered pressure over costs and feasibility. Skybolt promised to answer Britain's growing problem of financing a credible independent deterrent as an alternative to the costly and obsolescent

Blue Streak, a liquid-fueled ballistic missile. Britain consequently canceled its missile in favor of purchasing the American weapon.

It should have been obvious that if this deterrent on which the British had placed high hopes were to be abandoned, the Kennedy administration would have to conduct extensive, careful political and military discussions with the Macmillan Cabinet before taking such a step. These did not take place. Instead, the relationship suffered from a lack of comprehension of just what commitments were made in the Eisenhower administration by both the British and the Americans. What would the British offer in exchange for benefits gained by their access to Skybolt technology, which they expected to acquire at little expense to their economy? Although they would contribute funds toward the development of the weapon, there were no charges for the research that would go into the program, according to an agreement signed between the U.S. Air Force and the British Ministry of Aviation in 1960.

In return for this largesse, Eisenhower had understood from a meeting with Macmillan that the United Kingdom would furnish berthing facilities for U.S. submarines on the Clyde River in Scotland. This was the president's understanding but unfortunately not the prime minister's; Macmillan was determined that the Holy Loch site not be regarded as a quid pro quo, and he even congratulated Defence Minister Harold Watkinson on managing to separate the two issues. Yet there was some ambiguity about the terms of the agreement when Macmillan noted in his memoirs that the Clyde was to be available as a Polaris base, and that Eisenhower had assured him access to the Polaris missile itself if necessary.

Britain succeeded in securing the promise of a new weapon system if Skybolt should fail to serve its purpose. This much emerged from the opacity of memoranda and the haze of an imperfectly remembered past. The ally achieved this commitment without a written guarantee of a U.S. base in Scotland.

Given McNamara's unhappiness with the absence of any British contribution to research and development costs of the Skybolt, it was hardly surprising that any political fallout in Britain from the cancellation of the weapon was not his primary concern. A string of failures of test launches in 1962, accompanied by misleading Air Force press releases about delivery schedules, increased his doubts about the feasibility of Skybolt. Conceivably, the secretary of defense might have been more tolerant of experimental failures if the costs had been more bearable. In the context of interservice rivalry at the Pentagon, the defects of the program weighed more heavily on the secretary's scale of priorities than the sensitivities of the British partner. The result was a decision to cancel the weapon system in November 1962.

The immediate consequence was anger and panic in London, even though McNamara did speak informally to his British counterpart about the decision. The British were appalled, and their press accused the United States of betrayal. Having abandoned their Blue Streak, they would be left without a credible nuclear deterrent, and were quick to suspect an American conspiracy to downgrade Britain's nuclear capability.

The Kennedy administration was initially perplexed over the British reaction. Neither the British defense minister nor the British ambassador in Washington had given indications of their distress over the loss of the Skybolt, perhaps out of traditional British sangfroid. There should have been greater appreciation of the British political culture than McNamara and his colleagues exhibited. British leaders felt themselves besieged by hostile forces, whether it was Dean Acheson proclaiming the end of the British empire or de Gaulle preparing to keep Britain out of the European Economic Community. But to McNamara British behavior was mystifying. He thought it was clear to them that problems with the program doomed the Skybolt, but if they wished to assume the costs they could continue its development. There was no excuse for Britain at any time in the Kennedy years not to recognize the American reservations about its future. Kennedy then was taken aback when Macmillan told him at the Nassau conference in December 1962 that Britain would not have cancelled the Blue Streak in favor of Skybolt unless there were an alternative missile system.

Ironically, the alternative was available, even if the willingness of the transatlantic partner to grant it was not appreciated at the time. The United States agreed to sell two Polaris submarines to Britain, each with 16 missiles. Here was a weapon system superior to the Skybolt that should have satisfied British aspirations as well as their concerns. The only ostensible drawback was the requirement that the British nuclear fleet would be assigned to NATO, a precedent that could be a model for a European nuclear force. But this restriction was not binding: the British could withdraw their nuclear force from NATO when they decided that their national interests were at stake.

There was no simple zero-sum balance in the Skybolt affair. If it was ultimately a British success, it had a limited scope. Macmillan gained a better weapons system, but with a price to be paid beyond the costs incidental to purchasing the Polaris missile. The Skybolt affair only reinforced de Gaulle's determination to pursue a separate path for France; this would have happened irrespective of the outcome at Nassau. Nor was it responsible for Britain's exclusion from the Common Market in 1963; this too was part of de Gaulle's grand plan. Rather, the incident underscored the decline of Britain as a world power and its consequent dependence on the United States for its "independent" nuclear deterrent.

For the United States the Skybolt fiasco offered a case study of a preventable mistake. Its origin lay in the absence of centralized control in the Pentagon that permitted the Air Force to make its own agenda without appropriate checks. McNamara deserved credit for canceling a failed program, but he did so without sufficient recognition of British pride. The president's offer of the Polaris missile came across as an impulsive gesture certain to complicate relations for both countries with their NATO partners, even though the Polaris substitute had been enmeshed in Eisenhower's negotiations with Macmillan. Without fully appeasing the British, the Polaris exchange accentuated the problem of how to deal with those members, particularly in view of the ambitions of West Germany, that did not possess nuclear weaponry. It helped solidify a Franco-German connection that might have had negative consequences for the United States.

There was another dimension to the Skybolt crisis that never rose above the surface of negotiations. This was the current of mutual suspicion that was a legacy of the Suez crisis, as historian Ronald Landa has observed. On the one side, Americans were wary of British duplicity, a fear of being manipulated; on the other, the British doubted the dependability of Americans, a fear of being abandoned in a crisis.

THE MULTILATERAL FORCE AND THE GERMAN PROBLEM

Although France's constant dissent from American positions in NATO was accepted as normal and Britain's distress over its junior partnership seemed under control after 1963, West Germany's Federal Republic posed increasingly pressing questions about America's nuclear stance. West Germany had been admitted into the alliance by the back door of the Western European Union, and one of the fees for membership was abjuring the acquisition of nuclear weapons. Dependence on the United States for its nuclear defense inevitably strained the relationship. More than other major powers, Germany was sensitive to any deviation from America's rigid nuclear policies of the 1950s.

German uneasiness was manifested in the wake of Sputnik's success in 1958 and in its concern over U.S. management of the Berlin crisis in 1961. When the Soviets threatened in 1958 and again in 1961 to turn over their control of East Berlin to the German Democratic Republic, they awakened German fears about the constancy of the American commitment to the ultimate reunification of Germany. If the United States, Britain, and France—the Western victors of World War II—accepted the legitimacy of East Germany, they would have violated the Federal Republic's reasons for embracing the Atlantic alliance.

The first Berlin crisis ended without resolution in the Eisenhower years but revived more dangerously as the Soviet leader, Nikita Khrushchev, tested young President Kennedy. What bothered the Germans was the contrast between the initial stridency of Kennedy's hard line on rebuffing the Soviets' demand in July 1961 and his seeming complacency in accepting the Berlin Wall that propped up the East German regime in the following month. Despite desultory challenges to East Germany's periodic claims of sovereignty over Berlin, the Kennedy administration appeared to buckle under Soviet intimidation. This was the perception of such leaders as Mayor Willy Brandt of West Berlin.

The second Berlin crisis underscored Germany's concerns about its position in the alliance. Adenauer continued to brood over the inadequate U.S. response to the building of the Berlin Wall. German dissatisfaction was exacerbated by American demands for raising conventional force levels and the concomitant elevation of the threshold of a nuclear response in the event of a Soviet attack. Underlying their reservations was a painful awareness of dependence on American nuclear missiles for defense of the nation. Increasingly, there was pressure in the Federal Republic for a more active voice in determining the use of nuclear weapons, particularly those stationed on German soil. Defense Minister Franz Josef Strauss displayed a Gaullist perspective when he implied that Europe needed its own deterrent in the event that the Soviets would threaten them but spare the United States in a deal over the heads of Europeans. Strauss was not alone in raising American concerns that the Federal Republic might follow a Gaullist if not a neutralist path over its perceived nuclear vulnerability.

Arguably, the fundamental purpose of the Multilateral Force (MLF) was to satisfy Germany's sensitivities over its lack of control over nuclear weaponry. The issue was the use of the weapon, not whether Germany would become a nuclear power in defiance of the agreements under which it entered NATO. In retrospect, there was a striking similarity in NATO's history between the European Defense Community (EDC) in the early 1950s and the Multilateral Force a decade later. Both were experiments in the integration of national forces that could have been powerful agents in advancing the cause of a United States of Europe, and both were intended to tap German resources in the service of NATO.

There were differences as well. The EDC would end the destructive rivalry between France and Germany, while the goal of the MLF was to undercut German ambitions for a national nuclear capability. By the 1960s the European Economic Community had facilitated Franco-German integration with considerable success. The issue of an independent German nuclear force did not exist in the 1960s. But in both cases the focus was on the role of Germany. The MLF was to give the Germans a sense of equality in the alliance by their possession of a European nuclear weapon, in company with the other allies.

As it developed in the transition from the Eisenhower to the Kennedy administration, the MLF would consist of 25 surface vessels with mixed-manned crews, carry 8 Polaris A-3 missiles with a range of more than 2,500 miles. This fleet would be assigned to the two supreme allied commands covering the Atlantic Ocean and the Mediterranean Sea. The key to its success was to be the joint ownership and custody of the nuclear weapon. German membership in this force was the critical factor not only because its participation would divert their attention from the British and French nuclear systems, but also—from an American perspective—would be a vehicle for pushing Germans and other allies into helping finance the MLF.

None of these plans materialized despite the hopes raised in the United States that the question of nuclear sharing would be solved. Part of the problem derived from the conflicting aspirations of the American authors of the MLF. Supreme Allied Commander Lauris Norstad offered a version that would make NATO itself a fourth nuclear power with its own land-based medium-range mobile ballistic missiles (MRMBMs) under the authority of the SACEUR. In some respects, this was a version of Kennan's dumbbell conception in the 1940s and of Kennedy's Grand Design in the 1960s, with its two transatlantic pillars undergirding the alliance.

The Norstad plan as such never had much chance of realization. Norstad himself as an Eisenhower acolyte was not a popular figure in the Kennedy circle. His reputation was not helped by his continuing support for a low nuclear threshold in the event of a Soviet attack at a time when McNamara was pressing Europe for a flexible response. And despite his considerable influence in Europe, neither France nor Britain was interested in promoting a European nuclear power unless in the former case France was its center. The British were still nursing hopes for invigorating its special relationship with the United States rather than with Europe; nor was Congress willing to abandon the McMahon Act, which denied to Europeans (except the British) access to American nuclear facilities. Only Germany warmed to the proposal, and this receptivity was enough to alarm other allies. Even if the Supreme Allied Commander was an American, the prospect of 15 fingers on the nuclear button was unacceptable to Congress.

An additional obstacle to Norstad's ambitions lay in a rival plan launched by the State Department almost simultaneously. A bipartisan group of Eurocentric officials, led by Robert Bowie, director of Eisenhower's Policy Planning Staff, saw in a multilateral force an opportunity not only to soothe German sensitivities by making the Federal Republic a partner in a European nuclear community but also to make the MLF into a stepping-stone toward an equal partnership with the United States. They won the sobriquet of "theologians" when these enthusiasts for European unification transformed the Norstad plan into an ideal that would realize the aims of the old EDC even as it lured France from the force de frappe, harnessed British energies—in the form of their aircraft—and neutralized German pressures for their own nuclear deterrent. Although the State Department plan was concocted in the Eisenhower administration, it won a fervent believer in the Kennedy years in the person of Undersecretary of State George Ball.

The MLF did take shape in the early 1960s in a maritime form in the aforementioned surface fleet with its jointly owned Polaris missiles. It progressed to the point of actually delivering one mixed-manned ship, but no more than one. The idea held some appeal to a practical manager such as McNamara who envisioned the MLF as a quick fix for a variety of NATO problems, not least of which was the German Gaullist question. His was a limited enthusiasm after the major allies did not warm to the plan. De Gaulle could not be lured out of the force de frappe and into a NATO force; the MLF to him was simply another weapon in America's effort to control Europe. Nor would Macmillan's Britain exchange its nuclear deterrent, limited though it was, for loss of identity inside the MLF. As the British prime minister once commented to Ball, "You don't expect our chaps to share grog with the Turks, do you?" Only the Germans welcomed the prospect, an attitude that created more problems than it solved. German access to weapons, no matter how carefully insulated, still could send tremors down European spines and agitate the Soviets as well.

The major drawback, however, was the implausibility of the MLF. There was a sleight of hand about its operation. The Europeans were invited to purchase the missile, but the warhead remained in American hands. In this context how meaningful was a "European" nuclear missile? Only the true believers in the Kennedy administration were convinced that it could work, and they did not include the secretary of defense or the national security advisor, McGeorge Bundy. The MLF was put on the back burner in the Johnson administration despite efforts of the "theologians" to revive the program.

The British made an apparent effort to keep it alive by proposing first an alternate MLF plan based on a nuclear force with American MRMBMs already in Europe and Britain's Polaris submarines joining an allied force of surface ships. This Atlantic Nuclear Force (ANF) would include an advisory group composed of France, Germany, and Italy to participate in conventional as well as nuclear planning. It was likely that the British initiative was to seek a way of scuttling the MLF without assuming any blame. In any event, the MLF was never formally disbanded; it just disappeared in 1965 in increasingly vague rhetoric. Neither the MLF nor the ANF appeared in NATO communiqués in that year. The muddled conception with its internal contradictions solved neither the German nor any other problem when France left the organization. The nuclear weapon was a continuing obstacle to transatlantic comity in the mid-1960s.

THE HARMEL INITIATIVE AND THE SMALLER MEMBERS

The failure of the MLF to resolve any of the transatlantic problems accentuated the need for some other means of satisfying Europe's sense of isolation from the decision-making process in NATO. It was the smaller allies who felt most distant from American planning. The larger members—Britain, France, and Germany—suffered frustrations in dealing with the United States, but at least they were the focus of American attention. Belgium and Denmark were not. Their constant complaint was the lack of consultation. This had been clearly expressed in the Wise Men's report in 1956, but it was not taken seriously. The Suez crisis drowned out their voices at this time. Conceivably, the MLF would have given them greater influence if it had materialized, but even this was questionable.

The departure of France from the integrated military structure along with the MLF's demise parenthetically had a positive effect on those countries that had felt ignored in the past. First, the absence of France at the table breathed new life into the Defense Planning Committee (DPC) that had been established in 1963 under the secretary-general to deal with military affairs. Similarly, with France out of the picture, the Standing Group in Washington, composed only of American, British, and French members, was replaced with an integrated International Military Staff in 1966, with headquarters in Brussels. This move did not guarantee the kind of consultation the allies wanted but at least it gave them seats at the table, an asset they did not enjoy in the Standing Group.

But the primary change benefiting the smaller nations derived from Secretary McNamara's initiative to extract from the moribund body of the MLF some form of nuclear sharing. Arguably, the most concrete by-product of the French departure was the creation of the Nuclear Planning Group (NPG) in 1966. What the MLF could not accomplish—supplying a NATO vehicle for sharing nuclear knowledge and nuclear decisions—the NPG did, up to a point. The new committee did not have the scope of the MLF, but its relatively modest aspirations offered a better chance for success. Its origins may be traced to McNamara's proposal made at a meeting of NATO defense ministers in Paris in May 1965, before France left the integrated command, to seek ways to have allies participate in nuclear planning, including the role of strategic forces. Not until France had left SHAPE in 1966 could the new policy be put into place.

As in the case of the MLF, there was an element of deception in the promotion of the NPG. The Johnson administration hoped to coax the allies into believing they were now fully involved in nuclear planning. Without the handicap of the MLF's high visibility, where the gap between promise and fulfillment was easily exposed, the NPG meetings indulged in generalities that could become specific in the future. The allies' ultimate acceptance of the strategy of "flexible response" was quickened by America's openness to consultation in 1967, even though the assignment of studies for their own sake often seemed to be the main order of business.

The fact that the United States did not share full information, let alone control, over nuclear weaponry was less important to the smaller members than American willingness to give them relative equality with the larger allies. This positive response to their demand for consultation made it easier for NATO to approve officially in December 1967 the doctrine of flexible response (MC [Military Committee] 14/3), raising the threshold of nuclear response, which the United States had been urging since the beginning of the Kennedy administration. NATO's acceptance signaled a renewal of faith in the American connection to Europe. If the allies—large and small—were still unwilling to spend the funds needed to support a major part of flexible response—an increase in conventional forces—they recognized at least the value of a graduated rather than an automatic response to Soviet provocation.

It is noteworthy that the North Atlantic Council's decision in favor of MC 14/3 accompanied the acceptance of the Harmel report on "The Future Tasks of the

Alliance." The Harmel initiative, too, was a by-product of France's departure from the organization as well as a measure of American responsiveness to the concerns of the smaller European members. When the Belgian Foreign Minister Pierre Harmel proposed a broad examination of the future tasks facing the alliance in December 1966, France was too distracted by the fallout from its disengagement to raise difficulties about a possible political reorientation of the alliance. But the meaning of the Harmel report signified more than the diminished role of France in the alliance; it represented, as did the NPG and the resuscitated DPC, the new authority of the smaller nations. The participants in the Harmel exercise were repeating the appeal of the Wise Men of 1956—Lester Pearson from Canada, Halvard Lange from Norway, and Gaetano Martini from Italy—who tried in vain to tell the larger powers that their voices should be heard. In 1967 their voices were heard and attended to.

The smaller allies won not just a vague promise of future consultation but a specific program that elevated détente to the level of defense as a major function of the alliance, The key statement in the Harmel report was its pronouncement that "military security and a policy of détente are not contradictory but complementary." This was a new approach to the Communist adversary that had implications the United States and its allies would not have anticipated at the beginning of the decade. One of them was the expectation that the Cold War was steadily waning, and the smaller nations led the alliance in asking members to recognize the change. In fact, de Gaulle himself, early in the 1960s, operated on the assumption that the Soviets were no more a danger to Europe than the United States. This was not quite the same as a mutual relaxation of tensions that characterized détente because the United States remained a benign presence in Europe from the perspective of the smaller powers; "defense," after all, was part of the Harmel promise, and this required continuing American support.

As important as any other question is why the United States accepted, if not embraced, the Harmel recommendations. More than just a wish to appease the smaller members accounted for its attitude. It did not represent a recognition that the Soviets had abandoned their expansionist ambitions, despite the assumptions of some of the European partners—large as well as small. American behavior at the end of the 1960s was a product of vulnerability, different from that at the beginning of the decade but just as important in the shaping of its relations with European partners in NATO. In 1960 the United States had to cope with Europe's fear that the Soviet mastery of intercontinental ballistic missiles would undermine America's credibility as defender of Europe. De Gaulle prospered at this time by stoking those fears, and the United States was forced to devote special effort, as in the MLF campaign, to restore Europe's faith in the transatlantic protector.

By 1968 Europe felt it could live with the Soviets and worried, often schizophrenically, about the rashness of American leadership that could have consequences for the European allies. This was demonstrated by the American absorption in Vietnam, creating a situation in which Europeans doubted the stability of American leadership and at the same time worried about the diversion of its energies in Southeast Asia to the detriment of its responsibilities in Europe. American impetuousness could threaten détente and its diversion of resources from Europe to Asia could threaten defense, the twin pillars of the Harmel report.

EUROPE AND THE VIETNAM WAR

The Vietnam War did not descend on NATO like a bolt from the blue. As noted, Indochina had been part of NATO's consciousness ever since France had equated its war against Communist insurgents with NATO's containment of Soviet expansion in Europe. Its link was not enough to prevent France's defeat in 1954 despite the extensive military assistance granted by the United States. And when the Republic of Vietnam replaced France's presence after the Geneva Conference, the United States was blamed for imposing its own puppet regime as part of America's imperial ambitions. From the Gaullist point of view Vietnam was a symbol of America's domination not only of Southeast Asia but of Europe as well.

De Gaulle's carefully planned withdrawal from NATO's military structure had its counterpart in France's efforts to intervene in the Vietnam conflict as South Vietnam descended into chaos after the overthrow of the Diem family in November 1963. He stepped up his campaign for a neutralist solution to the struggle between North and South Vietnam by supporting influential South Vietnamese military figures, former members of the French colonial establishment in Indochina, who pressed for this approach. If this objective had been reached, de Gaulle would have regarded it as suitable retribution for America's ouster of France from Indochina in 1954. But even though he failed to remove the United States from Vietnam, he could savor some Schadenfreude as he watched the Americans dig themselves deeply into the Vietnamese quagmire.

Given France's special ax to grind, it is important to learn how much influence de Gaulle's attitude had on other NATO allies. Certainly, his argument that America was not serving the alliance's interests by focusing its attention on Asia found some resonance in NATO circles. Moreover, there was a growing consensus in Europe that the Soviet Union, after failing to budge the United States from Berlin and succumbing to American demands in Cuba, was no longer the same order of danger to European security that it had been in the 1950s. Khrushchev's bellicose language masked his reluctance to push the West into war. A third Gaullist case against America carried less weight in the late 1960s than it would have early in the decade: that America's vulnerability to Soviet attack had impaired the credibility of the "pledge" of 1949.

Despite the alarms raised by France, the deliberations in NATO's political councils did not confirm France's charges, although there was some uneasiness expressed in the presses of most of the allies about the direction American policy was taking in Vietnam, particularly as the American presence in Vietnam increased exponentially after 1964. There was still a consensus in mid-decade that the Soviet Union and the People's Republic of China, either as partners or rivals, continued to be a threat to the West. Although there were occasional signs of concern about America devoting its energies in an area far removed from Europe, most member states continued to be aware that Communism was a global menace and that NATO should recognize its many dimensions.

If the United States was mentioned at all in the council's consideration of South Vietnam's struggle, it was in positive terms. As late as 1963 NATO's Expert Working Group on Southeast Asia credited American aid for the apparent improvement in the military situation. Secretary of State Dean Rusk spoke periodically of the progress, modest as it was, in U.S. efforts not only to help the Republic of Vietnam's army but also to develop a program of economic aid to the country's rural population. Such was the "strategic hamlet" concept that created fortified communities designed to remove the influence of Viet Cong forces and permit U.S. specialists to work with Vietnamese counterparts in supporting village-level health and public-works programs as well as in providing agricultural loans and honest administrators. Civic action could be more effective than military aid in winning over the peasantry to the side of the government. Not even the crisis at the end of the year, when a military coup left President Diem dead and the country in chaos, undermined their belief that the new leadership would reverse the damage done.

This optimism dissipated in mid-1964 as the Viet Cong grew in strength and a succession of Vietnamese generals proved incapable of maintaining a stable government capable of coping with the enemy. In May 1964, Secretary of State Rusk sounded an alarm, blaming both North Vietnam and China for the vigor of the Viet Cong insurgency. He wanted to ensure that the NATO allies recognized that Hanoi was specifically directing the operations in the south. France's Foreign Minister Maurice Couve de Murville used this occasion to express qualified sympathy for American difficulties in Vietnam and for Britain's in Malaysia, but he reminded his allies that France had endured these burdens in Indochina and Algeria for a longer period in the past. He implied that his country did not receive the understanding that the United States was now seeking.

The Americans did receive support for their efforts in Southeast Asia from NATO's Expert Working Group, which was composed of both larger nations such as Germany and France and smaller allies such as Belgium and the Netherlands. These observers were dispassionate in their estimates of the chances of South Vietnam to cope with internal unrest and external pressure. At the same time, they looked with approval on American military and economic assistance for its beneficial effects on the tactical situation. They represented majority opinion in the alliance that U.S. support of Vietnam served a NATO interest. The

containment of Communist expansion and the suppression of Communist subversion was a leitmotif of the alliance's views on Southeast Asia, at least until
the summer of 1964.

THE AFTERMATH OF TONKIN GULF

The Tonkin Gulf crisis in August 1964 marked a turning point in attitudes toward U.S. involvement in Vietnam. When North Vietnamese torpedoes attacked
one and arguably two American warships in August 1964, the United States responded with a Senate resolution empowering President Johnson to take all necessary measures to repel aggression. The way was opened for more than just a
massive increase in military aid to South Vietnam. The resolution led to the United
States taking over the conduct of the war from the incompetent South Vietnam
government. In this context the apparent consensus over American action dissolved. Rusk pleaded with the allies to express their support not with words but
with troops or supplies. At the very least those allies that had diplomatic relations
with China should chastise Beijing for its role in the war. Later in the decade Rusk
was reduced to pleading with the NATO allies to stop their shipping to North Vietnamese ports. There was increasing American irritation over the lack of European
backing of the United States as it expended its forces and resources in a war the
allies should support.

European leaders were initially sensitive to U.S. dissatisfaction with their behavior. In October 1965, Secretary-General Manlio Brosio warned a NATO Parliamentary Conference that a setback of the United States in Southeast Asia would
be a defeat for NATO. An American retreat or humiliating compromise in Vietnam
could have a domino effect on other areas in Asia and elsewhere. This was a sentiment that appealed to Presidents Kennedy and Johnson. Other allies recalled that
the United States was bearing the bulk of the military burden that might have been
shared by European members.

Although Europe seemed to be distancing itself from the conflict, two NATO
allies—Britain and the Netherlands—had reasons to be more empathic than their
colleagues. Both nations had experience with Communist-backed aggression in
their former colonies, Britain in Malaysia and the Netherlands in Indonesia.
British Defense Minister Denis Healey observed in December 1965 that the
United States—and Britain—carried a disproportionate share in the defense of the
free world outside Europe, and that the United States would soon have as many
troops in Vietnam as in western Europe.

Rather than responding sympathetically to this reality, many of the allies saw
it in a negative light, as a zero-sum situation in that more troops for Asia meant
fewer troops for Europe. Beneath the language of politesse (France excepted), a

sense of uneasiness pervaded NATO meetings and NATO publics in western Europe, propelled initially by vocal opposition among the Scandinavians in the summer of 1965. Their concern was over the American emphasis on military means to cope with the Viet Cong adversaries and their North Vietnamese patrons. They worried about the conflict escalating and expanding to encompass Europe and the Soviet Union. This concern spread to America's conduct in Vietnam that led to widespread suffering by innocent civilians. The Scandinavian allies in particular urged unconditional negotiations with the enemy given the assumption that there was no military solution. At the same time, they were skeptical about America's good faith, and doubted the sincerity of its professed intentions. The delegates reflected public opinion at home.

What triggered doubts in December 1965 were charges in the American press that the Viet Cong had put out peace feelers that the government had ignored in the middle of the nation's presidential campaign. This putative approach from the Communists apparently took place at a time when the United States was advertising its willingness to enter negotiations unconditionally. The criticism was made all the more significant in that it came at a time when the American forces in Vietnam were being rapidly expanded and when the air campaign against North Vietnam was striking a country that was not at war with the United States. Europeans as well as American antiwar critics recalled that one of the Gulf of Tonkin incidents in the year before may have been provoked by the U.S. naval intrusion into North Vietnam waters and the other may not have occurred at all.

If there was ambiguity about America's war in Southeast Asia on the part of Scandinavian members, there was none with respect to France's attitude. It was clear and hostile. The French representative at the NATO Parliamentarians' meeting in May 1965 condemned the United States for its systematic, large-scale military action north of the seventeenth parallel, observing that its unilateral steps were taken without allied consultation. The United States consequently damaged the alliance in the eyes of the nonaligned states and weakened the moral standing of the free world. British diplomats were particularly sensitive to the issue of consultation, and saw future trouble in precipitate action that was out of proportion to the provocations. As friends and defenders of the United States, they concurred with the French warning that Asians and Africans could regard NATO as a club for rich, white countries.

When some of the allies expressed reservations about France's open rejection of America's behavior in Vietnam, French officials were contemptuous of their colleagues in NATO for their passive support of the United States. Did the United States hesitate to voice its disapproval of French and British actions in the Suez crisis when they acted without informing Washington of their plans? The other members were hypocritical in silently opposing American involvement in Vietnam while France was frank in its criticism.

European silence certainly did not extend beyond 1965. And when they spoke out it was not because of collateral damage inflicted on the civilian population or because of any sympathy for the Viet Cong cause. Partly they were upset over the Johnson administration's inability to see the quagmire it was falling into. Europeans were primarily concerned that the United States was diverting energies and resources that should have been spent in Europe. The Americans claimed that its commitment to the South Vietnam government showed its fidelity to its obligations, which Europeans should appreciate. If the United States failed to support its allies in Southeast Asia, faith in American commitments to other parts of the would be undermined, emboldening Communists to throw up more challenges to the West. This argument was not convincing to most Europeans. They did not perceive fighting for Vietnam and fighting for Europe as comparable.

Before the major buildup of American troop strength in Vietnam, it was the Federal Republic, the most vulnerable of the European allies, that appeared the most understanding of American motives. German Foreign Minister Gerhard Schroeder feared that withdrawal or defeat of the United States in Vietnam would have an effect on the situation in Europe, comparable to the test of strength over Cuba in 1962 on the situation in Berlin. Recognition of Soviet intentions made it imperative for Germany to support a policy on Vietnam that would protect NATO allies against Communist efforts to extort concessions from the West in Southeast Asia through application of pressure in Europe.

German empathy with the American war in Vietnam, however, could not survive the realization that more American troops in Asia meant fewer American troops in Europe. In fact, the role of American troops in Europe had roots independent of the Vietnam War. From the beginning of his tenure as secretary of defense, McNamara was seeking ways of using the latest advances in technology to increase the efficiency of the American military contribution to Europe. He believed he found it in the "Exercise Big Lift," the dispatch of troops by air from the United States to American bases in Germany. It involved the airlifting of some 16,000 tank troops of the 2nd Armored Division to West Germany in more than 200 Air Force transport planes. Not only would the United States be able to provide rapid reinforcements in Europe when needed, but these divisions in reserve in the United States would also save expenditures that American forces in Europe imposed on the balance of payments.

But this program raised questions in Europe—particularly in Germany— whether the resulting U.S. flexibility would affect its forces in Europe. What could be sent quickly could be recalled just as quickly. It required assurances from McNamara that the exercise did not signify U.S. intentions to reduce the number of combat troops in Europe, and the U.S. member of the Military Committee in NATO tried to minimize the impact by noting that the Defense Department had been conducting this sort of exercise for many years. The allies, nonetheless, were not fully reassured. German General Adolf Heusinger, the Military Committee's chairman, responded that the capability of airlifting entire units across the Atlantic did not replace the need for combat-ready troops on the ground to oppose an attack from the outset.

If the troops issue was sensitive in 1963, it was all the more so two years later when questions were raised over the toll the redeployment of troops from Europe to Asia was taking on the status of Europe's defense. European journals expressed the widespread fear that President Johnson would have to call up specialists drawn from the European theater to supply forces in Vietnam. In the event they were replaced at all, the new units would lack the skills of those withdrawn. As for the growing transport capacity of U.S. forces, they suspected that no airlift could offer full equivalence to forces on the ground. However mobile the mobile strategic reserve may be, it would not have the same effect as uniforms on the streets of Europe.

It was this kind of speculation that inspired Senator Leverett Saltonstall of Massachusetts to proclaim in October 1965 that the war in Vietnam had not affected the strength of American forces in Europe. McNamara offered the same assurances at Senate hearings two months later when asked about plans to take troops out of Europe. He saw no reason for doing so on the grounds that such moves might send the wrong signals to the Soviet adversary. The stark realities of the war in Vietnam, however, compromised the credibility of this statement. United States forces grew from 59,000 on 30 June 1965 to 267, 500 a year later, an investment of manpower that had to affect American commitments to NATO.

The personnel were as specialized as the European press feared. The Army had to draw down highly skilled personnel from aviation maintenance, construction, and signal services; the Air Force had to yield four tactical reconnaissance and six tactical fighter squadrons totaling 7,000 men; and the Navy offered a Marine Corps battalion landing team from the Sixth Fleet. And this was only the beginning. By mid-1966, a substantial portion—up to two-thirds of the U.S. Air Force reconnaissance aircraft—would be removed from NATO assignments, along with 30,000 servicemen with critical skills.

The British delegation to NATO worried that the withdrawal of U.S. troops from Europe, even if only temporarily, would give the French military spokesman opportunity to make as much political capital as he could from these redeployment plans. For the Germans who had put a brave face in supporting American actions in Vietnam in the early 1960s, the implementation of plans to redeploy American troops from Germany to Vietnam was frightening. The most immediate fear was the danger to a population on the front line facing Warsaw Pact forces. The consequence was not only weakening NATO's defenses against a powerful enemy but the psychological damage to the German people if they conflated these reductions of U.S. forces with reduction of American concern for the survival of the Federal Republic.

Secretary McNamara was not impressed with Europe's negative reactions. He was able to rationalize the redeployment much in the way he approached France's withdrawal from the military structure. It would serve rather than harm the alliance by permitting a reorganization of supply and support units to offset the decrease in the numbers of troops in Germany. The reason behind his complacency rested once again in the greater efficiency of the forces in place, combined with a greater capability to deploy men quickly from the continental United States. There was little respect in the secretary's analysis of the defense of Europe for the sensibilities of the allies.

The issue became more acute in the later years of the decade. It required considerable effort on the part of McNamara's Pentagon to mask the effects of some 200,000 additional troops in Vietnam by March 1967 on the status of U.S. troops in Europe. The reduction of forces announced to the NATO allies in April 1967 involved 30,000 Army and 6,000 Air Force personnel. As a result of this drain, the Joint Chiefs of Staff increasingly voiced reservations about the ability of the military services to prosecute the war in Vietnam and at the same time maintain the American presence in Europe without calling up the reserves. The secretary and his civilian staff advisers felt this was unnecessary. Instead, individuals with critical military skills would continue to be withdrawn to Vietnam. The result was an inability of the United States to meet its NATO commitments. At the end of 1967, only one and one-third of the airborne divisions, instead of three reinforcing divisions, were available to NATO by M-day (mobilization day) plus 30.

The Vietnam War intensified divisions within the alliance without reaching the point of dissolution. A combination of factors limited the damage. The Soviets themselves provided some help unwittingly by their brutal destruction of the Czech reform government in 1968. At the same time, the Brezhnev Doctrine, justifying the suppression of any defection from the Soviet bloc, had only a temporary impact on NATO, even when it reminded the European partners of Soviet power. Many of the allies interpreted it as a sign that the Communist world had turned away from aggressive designs against the West, and confined their military action to their own allies. Moreover, by 1968 President Johnson appeared to be de-escalating the war in Vietnam as he moved toward peace negotiations with the North Vietnamese.

U.S. GRIEVANCES AGAINST EUROPE

Just as European resentment against the United States escalated over Vietnam, so did American anger at the lack of appreciation for the enormous burden Americans had assumed on behalf of the free world. The key to the American attitude lay in the concept of burden sharing. Why should the United States continue to shoulder the costs of defending Europe when most of the allies not only had recovered from the devastation of World War II but had achieved a level of prosperity that should have made it possible for them to lift some of the burden from the back of the transatlantic partner. Yet, on the one hand, they balked at increasing their conventional forces, preferring to rely on American troops to fill the gap. And, on the other hand, they persisted in opposing America's war against Communism in Southeast Asia. This stance struck U.S. senators as provocative ingratitude.

Vietnam was a breaking point for many American critics of NATO. It was the culmination of a long series of European offenses against the spirit—and the costs—of the common defense of the West. The nub of the issue was the imbalance of payments resulting from American expenditures of dollars in Europe, particularly in Germany. This grievance was manifest early in the Kennedy administration. A State Department aide-mémoire in February 1961 intended as a guide for American negotiations made it clear that "the deficit of the United States arises wholly from the common defense of the free world. Without these freely assumed obligations, the United States would now be running a heavy surplus in its commitments and actions in balance of payments." The United States was prepared to lean heavily on its allies to redress the balance of payments.

Germany was at the heart of the problem because of the relationship between the Deutsche mark and the dollar. With the U.S. military spending contributing almost $400 million annually to Bonn's foreign reserves, the time had come for reciprocity. This would include Germany's increasing its share of foreign aid to undeveloped parts of the world as well as to easing the defense burden in Europe. The proposed remedies involved greater purchases by Germany of U.S. military equipment and larger payments for maintaining U.S. facilities in Europe to offset U.S. expenditures.

The Berlin crisis of 1961, soon after Kennedy took office, aggravated the balance of payments. The rapid buildup of U.S. troop strength in Germany in the shadow of the Berlin Wall sharpened the differences between two allies. The Federal Republic could not resist American demands at a time when the United States had sent 40,000 additional troops to bolster NATO defenses in Germany. The simple fact of the United States expending its resources and manpower on behalf of a frightened Germany made efforts to lessen the financial burden all the more imperative.

The Germans had to concede, but not before they raised as many objections as they could. The economics minister was anxious that the Americans not exaggerate his country's wealth. The press was filled with articles, encouraged by the government, to blame the United States for the dollar crisis. They pointed to the sharp rise in the outflow of dollars through U.S. private investments abroad and implied that the source of the problem lay in tax privileges granted to American-owned multinational corporations such as General Motors and Firestone. Hence, they argued, it would be unfair for Germans to pay for U.S. corporate profits.

This reasoning failed to relieve Germans of American pressure. To soften the often blunt tones in the negotiations, the United States was willing to accept German purchases of U.S. equipment in place of specific dollar outlays. Direct sale of

U.S. tanks or airplanes would offer the least objectionable way of achieving results without offending German dignity. In October 1961 the Germans agreed to purchases ranging from armored troop carriers to rockets at a cost of $230 million. Coupled with earlier purchases, the figure in 1961 would reach approximately $500 million, increasing to $700 million in 1962. The successful offset agreement with Germany accelerated negotiations with other allies on whose territory the United States had installations that drained dollars.

Even as the secretary of defense displayed some satisfaction with the downward trend in the balance-of-payments deficit, he kept pressing the allies for more. In July 1962 he stated that he would seek $900 million more between 1963 and 1966 to liquidate the imbalance. McNamara had the enthusiastic backing of Congress. There never was a time when congressmen or the secretary of defense felt that the allies were contributing their fair share of the defense burden. When a new agreement was made with Germany for 1965 and 1966, the funds were not enough; the $1.350 billion was $30 million less than the Pentagon had estimated its costs in Germany would be in this period. As long as an imbalance of payments remained, there were threats emanating both from the administration and the Congress that if a more equitable sharing of costs were not forthcoming, America's contribution to Europe's defense would be in jeopardy.

The offset quarrels were essentially background noises, rumblings of discontent, but not loud enough to fray the transatlantic ties. The American military presence in Europe between 1961 and 1965 remained stable, aside from spikes in a moment of crisis; and the European partners did make efforts to accommodate the American demands. The situation changed dramatically in 1965 when the offset conflict with Germany meshed with the expansion of the Vietnam War.

Unhappy with Germany's unwillingness to meet full offset payments, McNamara threatened in June 1965 to reduce U.S. forces to match lower offset goals. He claimed that 30 percent of the increase in defense expenditures could be traced to the burden of the Vietnam War. When the State Department warned against unilateral action, he asserted that the Germans had brought this situation on themselves by refusing to change their position on the offset problem. The secretary of defense was not simply expressing a personal judgment. The Johnson administration, aside from the State Department, shared McNamara's impatience. Two senior administration officials had advised the president in November 1965 to dramatize the balance-of-payments problems as a means of raising Europe's consciousness of American sacrifices in Vietnam. If they would not contribute to the cause, at least the allies could minimize America's burden in Europe.

By mid-1966 the financial distress of the United States and the United Kingdom over the upkeep of their troops in Germany had reached a point at which the Americans and British claimed that they would keep their forces intact only if new arrangements were made. The Defense Department threatened a major increase in troop withdrawals from Europe unless Europe responded to American needs. The conflict was temporarily resolved through the establishment of a Trilateral Commission in 1967. State Department officials, always more attuned to European sensibilities than their counterparts in Defense, wanted to limit withdrawals to two or three brigades of only one army division, but McNamara wanted four brigades from two divisions.

The result was a compromise whereby the German Bundesbank would purchase $500 million in medium-term U.S. government bonds during fiscal year 1968 and promise not to convert their dollars into gold. The United States in turn scaled down its redeployment plans and pledged that security and not financial considerations would be the primary factor in determining U.S. force levels in Europe. The allies agreed to accept the principle—and expansion—of dual basing that had begun with the Big Lift in 1963. The agreement in April 1967 relieved tensions at the diplomatic level, but did not satisfy a growing public demand, fueled by the failing military campaign in Vietnam, for more equitable burden sharing from the allies. The reaction of the Senate majority leader, Mike Mansfield of Montana, to the trilateral compromise itself reflected continued dissatisfaction with the conduct of the allies. Senator Mansfield scorned the arrangement allowing Germans to purchase special U.S. government securities, claiming that Germany would be winning new profits from their loans that would make a mockery of the compromise.

The truce over the offset issue did not, in fact, affect the larger American complaint, namely, the anomaly of the United States maintaining over 300,000 troops in defense of a Europe that could do more to defend itself while sending as many—and more—personnel to wage a war in Vietnam without European support. Inevitably, there would be outcries in the press and in the Congress to redress this imbalance. Secretary of Defense McNamara's selective redeployments were not sufficient for many senators. In August 1963 Mansfield gathered 43 sponsors to introduce the first of many subsequent resolutions calling for substantial reductions of the U.S. presence in Europe unless the allies increased their defense expenditures. Mansfield obviously was not a lonely voice, although his objections extended back to the early 1960s. The senators' concerns, however, were not identical. For some, the main issue was the money drain; for others it was the persistent complaint about unfair burdens; and for still others, it was the lack of European understanding of the stakes in the Vietnam War.

Mansfield's resolutions were just that: an expression of discontent without expecting to alter America's role in Europe. In the next year, however, Senator Stuart Symington of Missouri, introduced an amendment to the annual defense procurement bill that would have prohibited the use of funds to support more than 50,000 U.S. troops in Europe. Unless successfully vetoed, this amendment would have the force of law and would have affected the viability of NATO's defenses in Europe. Symington's action was intended to show the growing impatience of Congress with European behavior. But like Mansfield's resolutions, it was basically a warning, not a prelude to America's departure from Europe. Symington withdrew his amendment on the same day. Neither Mansfield nor Symington had any wish to weaken NATO in the face of the Soviet adversary.

In one respect the Mansfield and Symington maneuvers reflected the ongoing importance of NATO to American leaders. They wanted to get their message across without damage to the defense capabilities of the alliance. The Warsaw bloc's suppression of Czechoslovakia's attempts to liberalize its system in 1968 was a sobering reminder—more to the United States than to its allies—that defense preparations were still necessary.

Nonetheless, the accumulation of grievances on both sides of the Atlantic could have had more damaging effects on the survival of the alliance than was inflicted by America's diversion of men and matériel from Europe to Vietnam. If NATO surmounted these challenges it was largely because neither Europeans nor Americans wished for a divorce. Nor did they want to use the provision in the North Atlantic Treaty—Article 13—that would allow any member to depart legally after 20 years. Although there was recognition—more on the European than on the American side—that the Soviet menace was not what it had been at the beginning of the decade, there was also recognition that the détente sought by the Harmel report was not yet achieved.

The Czech crisis of 1968 had a centripetal effect in reminding the allies of their raison d'être. It reduced American pressure for further reductions of their troop level in Europe but did not eradicate frustration with the behavior of the European partners. A Senate report in October 1968 admitted that the invasion and occupation of Czechoslovakia by the Warsaw bloc armies were profoundly disturbing. Given the unsettled conditions in Europe following the invasion, the report concluded that the time was not propitious for substantial reductions of U.S. forces. But it also quoted McNamara's statement at the North Atlantic Council's December meeting in which he agreed that although there should be no major diminution of U.S. strength in Europe, the Europeans bore a responsibility to meet the balance-of-payments deficit created by America's contributions to Europe's defense.

The issues that divided the allies throughout the 1960s—the balance of payments that so disturbed Americans, European suspicions that the American war in Vietnam was diluting its commitments to NATO, and America's conviction that Europe lacked empathy for its sacrifices in Southeast Asia—persisted. But despite all the transatlantic alarums, the United States remained in Europe in substantial numbers at the end of the decade. In 1961 U.S. military personnel totaled 373,000; in 1969 the figure was still well over 300,000—316,000 after the years of McNamara's efforts to redeploy troops not only to satisfy pressing needs in Vietnam but also to further his hopes to reorganize the military structure of the alliance. By early 1968 he had left office, with the U.S. NATO military in Europe largely intact. If there were substantial changes since 1961, they were caused less by the secretary of defense's policies than by the actions of the president of France.

There were both similarities and differences between the transatlantic tensions at the beginning of the decade and those at the end of the decade. In both periods Europeans had doubts about their American partner. In 1961 they centered on the aftermath of Sputnik with concomitant fears that the new vulnerability of the United States to Soviet intercontinental ballistic missiles would jeopardize the American pledge to its partners under Article 5 of the treaty. Soviet power never seemed more formidable. At the end of the decade, Europeans still had doubts about their main ally, but on different grounds. After the Vietnam debacle, doubts centered on the shortcomings of American leadership. The Soviet adversary was no longer the behemoth it had been in the past; its blinking over Berlin and Cuba had reduced its menace and convinced most Europeans that the East and West could coexist in relative peace. This was the message of the Harmel agreement, and the Czech crisis, shocking as it was at the time, was indeed a momentary scare. The Soviets had taken care to assure the West that their actions were directed internally not externally. Détente was derailed only temporarily.

What was superficially surprising was that the United States appeared prepared to accept détente in 1968. The explanation lies in the troubles in Vietnam. Unlike the Korean War, Vietnam did not transform NATO. Nor did it destroy the organization. It induced the United States to follow the European path of détente with the Warsaw bloc less because of a new belief that the Soviet threat had dissipated than because of a need to disentangle itself from Southeast Asia. Détente with the Soviet Union was a means of securing this objective although, unlike its allies, the United States had fewer illusions about Communism's ultimate objective.

4

DÉTENTE AND ITS
LIMITATIONS: 1968–1980

Détente was the driving force in the first half of the 1970s not only in the relationship between NATO and the Warsaw Pact but also in the more complicated ties between the United States and its European allies. The term itself was neutral; it meant simply relaxation of tensions. But when applied to international politics at the end of the 1960s, it was fraught with ideological content. For the United States it meant an opportunity to extricate itself from the quagmire of Vietnam without equating détente with an abandonment of Soviet ambitions for a Communist world order. At the same time, it was an implicit recognition of equality in the military power of both superpowers, a fact of international life that the United States would have to live with. For the Europeans, détente was far more expansive and implied far more optimism than the American version. There was a sense of normality in their outlook on the Warsaw bloc; the Eastern Europeans seemingly were no different in their wish for coexistence than the Western Europeans. In investing different meanings to détente, the transatlantic allies almost guaranteed the generation of friction.

Détente on one level symbolized the equality of NATO and the Warsaw Pact. In recognizing the power of the Soviet bloc, reinforced by its decisive action against Czechoslovakia in 1968, Europeans gave it a respectability it had not enjoyed in the first 15 years of its existence. NATO communiqués in the 1970s, unlike those of the 1960s, routinely discussed relations with the Warsaw Pact. An annex to the December meeting of the North Atlantic Council gave lip service to the "defense" aspect of the Harmel report but emphasized the role of détente in the broader context of the alliance's basic purposes. The communiqué looked forward to détente's success in negotiations between NATO and the Warsaw Pact.

The language of this annex connoted another meaning of détente: the decline of American authority in NATO circles. It was not that the United States was now dispensable as the senior ally. It was that the combination of a more reasonable Soviet adversary and a perception of American weakness in the Vietnam War encouraged an independence among the Europeans that had not been possible in the first two decades of NATO's history. This new sense of European empowerment was reflected in the actions, sponsored primarily by the smaller partners, to flesh out the promise of the Harmel initiative. In effect, "defense" was to be submerged under "détente."

It produced immediate results. The Eurogroup formed in 1968 was an entity in which smaller powers would be heard, a forum for harmonizing European views on major political or strategic questions. Its purpose, outlined in the "Reykjavik signal" at the North Atlantic Council's meeting in Iceland in 1968, was to set in motion confidence-building measures with the Warsaw Pact by a Declaration on Mutual and Balanced Force Reductions.

The United States was not a major player in these proceedings. Yet, it collaborated in every phase of the changing posture of NATO even as American leaders differed with their European colleagues over the meaning of détente. There was little faith in the State Department or in the Pentagon that the Soviets regarded détente in the way the European allies did. The major explanation then for America's relative quiescence in 1968 was the impact of the Vietnam War. The conflict had absorbed the nation's energies and more of its troops than were stationed in Europe; it had led McNamara to leave office in 1967, belatedly recognizing that the war could not be won; and rising opposition at home destroyed President Johnson's hopes for a second term in the White House in 1968. Europe's role as America's primary ally appeared to diminish as Asian concerns predominated. When NATO did intrude into the nation's consciousness, it was usually as an irritant both because of the allies' opposition to the U.S. war and because they continued to demand more money and manpower than the alliance seemed to merit in that year. The Soviets exacerbated America's annoyance with its allies by its conscious efforts to avoid confrontation with NATO during the Czech crisis.

DÉTENTE'S MANIFESTATIONS

Britain and the EEC

From 1968 to the middle of the 1970s, the Harmel spirit seemed to dominate the alliance. Accommodation was in the wind once the Czech crisis had been put aside. It took a number of forms. After its heavy-handed advocacy of Britain's membership in the European Common Market, the United States stood back as

Britain successfully negotiated its entry into the economic community in 1973. De Gaulle had died in 1970 and the successor government, while Gaullist, was less strident in its anti-American stance and more open to a British association. The Conservative British government under Prime Minister Edward Heath in turn appeared more anxious in this period to cultivate ties with the Continent than with its transatlantic partner. In fact, Henry Kissinger, national security advisor to President Richard Nixon, regarded him as the most indifferent of all British leaders to the American connection. He showed no sign of any interest in promoting the special relationship. Heath remembered with resentment the Suez debacle and admired many aspects of the Gaullist vision of Europe. Unlike his predecessors, the prime minister made no effort to meet with Nixon after his defeat of Harold Wilson in 1970. The distance the British prime minister placed between himself and the president did not signify a major breach; there were close connections at lower levels of government. But it did reflect the Zeitgeist of the time when Europe was seeking via détente to impress its own views on NATO.

There was little resistance to this British drift on the part of the United States. Although not irrelevant, Britain was no more important politically than Germany to American leaders at the end of the decade. It had failed to give sufficient support on Vietnam, and the devaluation of the pound in 1967 suggested that Britain had failed as well to sustain itself as a major player on the global scene. Not least among the obstacles to promotion of a closer relationship was American irritation over British moralizing about Vietnam. When the My Lai massacre was uncovered, the House of Commons expressed its shock on discovering the depth of American brutality.

Ostpolitik

Similarly, the United States was an uncomfortable but passive witness to Chancellor Willy Brandt's new policies toward East Germany. Ever since the Federal Republic had been established there was fierce resistance, supported by the United States, to recognition of the German Democratic Republic. This position was the basis of the Hallstein Doctrine, which pledged to break diplomatic relations with any government that recognized the Communist government of East Germany. The Berlin crises of 1958 and 1961, when the Soviets threatened to make a separate peace treaty with its client regime, signified the dangers that the hostile East German government posed to the West.

But in the changing environment of East–West relations at the end of the 1960s, a new chancellor, Social Democratic leader Willy Brandt, initiated Ostpolitik in a major break with the German past. It was also a species of détente, in keeping with the mood of the European allies. By opening ties with East Germany, he was tacitly accepting a reality that Adenauer and his successors had denied: the apparent permanence of a divided Germany. He was also responding to the reality that Germany's allies were giving only lip service to the concept of German unification. Europe's—and America's—acceptance of the Berlin Wall drove Brandt to try a new approach to German foreign policy.

Ironically, the coolest response to economic political connections with the Warsaw bloc came from East Germany. Its leaders suffered from an inferiority complex toward their more powerful western kin and felt that their role as the most advanced of the Communist allies would be lessened if West German connections with the Soviet world flourished. The Soviets, on the other hand, welcomed Brandt's approach as an opportunity to win an agreement that would keep West Berlin outside the Federal Republic. Even more important to the Soviets was West Germany's willingness to respect the Yalta boundaries that incorporated parts of prewar Germany into Poland and to acknowledge the permanence of the Oder-Niesse line. These concessions became treaties in 1970 and 1971. A four-power accord on Berlin was signed in September 1971 followed by agreements between East and West Germany. In May 1972 the Federal Republic signed treaties with Poland and the Soviet Union.

The American reaction to the transformation of German foreign policy was mixed. On one level the new foreign policy team of Nixon and Kissinger admired Brandt's courage in finding a way for the Federal Republic to live with a partitioned Germany, and even to profit from the division. They recognized that unification was impossible—outside an unlikely and suicidal war with the Warsaw bloc. In the context of the rising spirit of détente, West Germany could be a magnet for Communist Europe. An improved standard of living for East Germans, increase of trade with the Soviet Union and its satellites, and the freer flow of travel and exchanges between East and West could blur the dividing lines between the blocs. In the long run, then, the Brandt policy was intended to achieve German unity rather than perpetuate division, with Germany as the kind of European leader that de Gaulle's France had aspired to become.

These were worthy goals from the American perspective, up to a point. On the other hand, the Nixon administration nourished some doubts about Brandt's—and particularly his close confidant, Egon Bahr's—adherence to the Atlantic alliance. Brandt had made no secret of his disillusionment about the allies' hesitations over the Berlin Wall and, consequently, over the future of West Berlin itself. Would a flourishing new relationship with the Warsaw bloc loosen or even destroy the Federal Republic's relationship with the West? But the outcome might not be an assertion of a potentially dangerous German nationalism manifested in a withdrawal from NATO; the ties were too strong for such a break. A more likely result could be a neutralist Germany, long sought by the Soviet Union, by which West Germany's entanglement with the Warsaw bloc would become so intimate that Brandt or his successors could not be counted on to support the United States in a future crisis between NATO and the Soviet Union. And could this dependence sway other European members to separate themselves from the United States at critical moments?

These nightmares did not prevent the United States from suppressing its misgivings and supporting Ostpolitik. There really was very little choice. Détente with the Soviets was too strong a sentiment to frustrate even if Nixon and Kissinger genuinely wanted to kill Brandt's rapprochement with the East. They could take satisfaction in the agreements to safeguard the integrity of West Berlin. They were also appreciative of a consequence that would remove once and for all the kinds of tensions growing out of a promise of German unification. Moreover, détente between Germany and the East cleared the way for new arrangements between the United States and the Soviet Union. Nixon and Kissinger were determined to profit as best they could from the discomfiting fact that American weakness permitted allies to make their own agreements with the Communist world. The United States itself would have to make concessions to the Soviet Union in recognition both of its military strength and of pressures from allies, but these concessions would also involve Soviet concessions as well.

The Nixon Doctrine

The dilemma facing American policymakers in the Nixon administration was how to counter Europe's seeming rush to accommodation with the Warsaw bloc and at the same time use détente as a means of both renewing ties with Europe and deriving advantages from a new relationship with the Soviet Union. The Nixon Doctrine on the surface was a means of extricating the United States from the Vietnam War by turning over its conduct to the Vietnamese themselves, although with the blessings and material support of the United States. The doctrine was purposely entwined with the Vietnamization of the war, as Henry Kissinger presented it in the journal *Foreign Affairs* before entering government service as presidential adviser in 1969. The president restated this theme in his visit to Guam in the spring of that year.

The role of the NATO allies was a major element in the doctrine. Kissinger himself had a long record of engagement with European issues, from his doctoral dissertation at Harvard on the Congress of Vienna to his perceptive analysis of NATO in *The Troubled Partnership*, published in 1965. In this study he considered a genuine transatlantic partnership with Europe to be vital to the success of the alliance. He emphasized the importance of European unity as a prerequisite to NATO's coherence in the future, and urged the United States to promote its connections for the sake of its own national interest.

Although the Kennedy–Johnson years had witnessed some softening of the rigidities of John Foster Dulles's stewardship in the Eisenhower administration, NATO's military structure remained intact, and the strident tones of anti-Communist rhetoric rang more loudly under Kennedy than they had under his predecessor. During the Johnson administration NATO seemed to have been consigned, at least in Nixon's judgment, to a form of limbo attended to after the Vietnam War ended. Because the war did not end during Johnson's administration, Nixon and Kissinger believed that inattention to NATO's concerns and consequent European resentment damaged the transatlantic relationship.

The Nixon Doctrine was to signal both the end of the Vietnam War and the end of America's diversion of its energies and resources away from the European arena. The identification of NATO as the first priority in American foreign relations should have won a warm reception from the European allies. The alliance should have been reinvigorated by America's response to European concerns. Indeed, as presidential candidate, Nixon had lashed out at the Johnson administration for dismissing NATO, for not even mentioning it in his State of the Union Address in 1968. It was time, he declared, to pay more attention to the European partners, to lecture them less and listen to them more.

As president, he made a point of visiting Europe a month after this inauguration to dramatize his desire for greater consultation. Beyond this spirit of cooperation he promised to present a plan to move from crisis management to crisis prevention to an era of cooperation. This commitment applied not only to relations within the alliance but also to relations with the Soviet bloc.

Mutual Balanced Force Reductions Program and Conference on Security and Cooperation in Europe

The Mutual Balanced Force Reductions Program (MBFR), introduced in the same year as the Nixon Doctrine, was a product of the confluence of America's interest in accommodating Europe's drive toward terminating the Cold War and the nation's need for its own accommodation to Soviet power. If there was a balance of terror achieved through the parity of NATO's and the Warsaw Pact's military machines, this should be an occasion to give meaning to détente by reducing the numbers of troops on the front lines of Europe. The allies pushed for rapid action in East–West negotiations for troop reductions and for inhibiting development of mutually destructive weaponry. The Harmel report itself made these objectives clear with its plans for "studying disarmament and practical arms control measures, including the possibility of balanced force reductions." Three years later, at the North Atlantic Council meeting in Rome, NATO placed emphasis on adequate verification and controls to ensure agreements made under MBFR.

The United States did not lag behind its European colleagues in celebrating the virtues of MBFR. Senators such as Mike Mansfield praised the effort for its potential effect in reducing American manpower in Europe as well as for alleviating the always-emotional balance-of-payments issue. The reason the Nixon administration embraced the program had little to do with the potential end of the Cold War and much to do with diminishing the Soviet superiority in ground forces, hence the emphasis on "balanced" force reductions. The Warsaw Pact organization would be required to reduce far more troops than would the Western allies.

It was the Soviets who resisted the MBFR, ignoring the North Atlantic Council's approaches as long as they could without alienating the Europeans. The Soviets were ready enough to have NATO forces reduced. This was a long-standing Communist goal. By "NATO forces" they meant removal of American forces altogether from Europe. Ideally, the Soviets wished to deal only with the Europeans not as a part of a NATO bloc but as individual nations sharing the European continent with them. By finally consenting to meet with NATO representatives in Vienna in 1973, they temporarily gave up their intention to exclude the United States from the negotiations or to exclude NATO as a bargaining agent.

The MBFR talks opened in Vienna in 1972 and proceeded at a snail's pace through the 1970s. A basic problem with these negotiations was the virtual impossibility of genuine parity. The United States hoped for an asymmetrical reduction of forces with the larger Warsaw Pact armies making proportionately larger reductions. The problem of parity was further complicated by the geographical proximity of the Soviet Union to central Europe compared with the distance of American forces from their home base. Inevitably, the Soviet conception of parity was a reduction of an equal number of troops from both sides, whereas the United States recommended less than half be withdrawn from the West.

Neither proposal had any chance of satisfying either party, and this stalemate suited Soviet objectives. Its interest was in the convening of a Conference on Security and Cooperation in Europe (CSCE) that opened in Vienna in 1973 and ultimately produced the Helsinki Agreement two years later. This agreement presumably allowed the kind of freedoms for the peoples of the Warsaw bloc that were taken for granted in the West. They turned out to be empty concessions. More important to the Soviet Union was the aura of legitimacy the Helsinki Agreement gave to the Soviet role in Eastern Europe. Just as Ostpolitik led to German acceptance of the Yalta decisions, the CSCE was the path to NATO and U.S. recognition of a seemingly permanent division of Europe. This was a direction détente was taking the NATO alliance.

In the many negotiations in the early 1970s, the United States was uncomfortable with the eagerness of its European partners to embrace these manifestations of détente. Senate leaders in particular were worried about the subordination of defense to détente in the translation of the Harmel report into reality. The ongoing MBFR talks increasingly sensitized Congress to the realities of Soviet military power in conventional weaponry and, conversely, NATO's weaknesses in troops and armaments. Rather than endorsing the expectations of Senators Mansfield and Symington, the prospect of successful talks could undermine NATO's military position in Europe. A cut of 100,000 U.S. troops, even if balanced against a much larger reduction in Warsaw Pact forces, could destabilize the political as well as military posture of the organization. There would be nothing "mutual" or "balanced" in an American rush to achieve force reductions while burdened with the war in Vietnam.

Despite reservations about Europe's enthusiasm for MBFR and CSCE, the Nixon administration repeatedly gave evidence of its concern for NATO in ways that should have been unmistakable to Europeans. The revival of the Mansfield resolutions in the U.S. Senate after the shock of the Warsaw bloc intervention in Czechoslovakia had worn off put the issue of American troop withdrawal from Europe in focus once again, even more seriously than in the Johnson years. It was not surprising that the American public's increasing disillusionment with the Vietnam War would spill over into the NATO arena. Nixon's carefully crafted plans to turn over the conduct of the war in Vietnam to the Vietnamese did not bring a quick end to American involvement. On the contrary, the expansion of the war into Cambodia in 1970 intensified American anger with the Nixon administration. Europe's seeming insensitivity to America's agony over Vietnam made Europe one of the targets of this mood. While the dollar was weakening as a consequence of the war, the economies of the Western allies were flourishing and currencies were strengthening at America's expense.

The Nixon administration held firm against the rising demands for sharp troop reductions in Europe, asserting that the United States would not reduce its forces unless there was reciprocal action through the MBFR on the part of the Soviet adversary. Any unilateral action, it feared, would create a military imbalance that might induce the Warsaw bloc to risk provocations it would otherwise avoid. It would also generate doubts among allies once again about the steadfastness of American commitments to NATO.

This was not simply a rhetorical gesture in support of the alliance. The Nixon position was tested in 1971 when Senator Mansfield mounted a more powerful challenge than he had made in the 1960s. Unlike the resolutions in the past, which were simply signals of dissatisfaction, he attached an amendment to a bill extending the Selective Service Act requiring that U.S. forces in Europe be halved to 150,000 troops. If successful, this would become law and not just the sense of the Senate. To counter the popularity of this amendment, the administration mobilized former NATO supreme allied commanders Alfred M. Gruenther, Lauris Norstad, and Lyman L. Lemnitzer, along with such veteran Democrats as Dean Acheson and George Ball, to express their opposition to the Mansfield amendment. Nixon also won the endorsement of former President Johnson who agreed that drastic reduction of troop strength would be dangerous to the mission of the alliance. The amendment was defeated in the Senate by a substantial majority, 61 to 36, but the administration's attention to the danger was a measure of its determination to give primacy to Europe in America's foreign relations.

At the same time that it was staving off the Mansfield threat, the Nixon administration was helping Europe by maintaining a low profile on matters that in the past would have provoked American objections, privately if not publicly. The acute French pundit, Raymond Aron, observed the "ostentatious silence" of Americans on Britain's latest attempt in 1972 to enter the Common Market. It was in striking contrast to the heavy-handed advocacy that damaged rather than served the British cause during the de Gaulle years. Similarly, as noted, the United States chose not to speak out against the Ostpolitik of Chancellor Brandt despite serious reservations about the terms the Soviets might demand in return for improved relations with the Federal Republic. The United States confined its public interest in the accords to those facets that directly related to its own position in Berlin. This discreet behavior appeared to confirm the Nixon Doctrine's resolution to support Europeans' management of their own affairs in ways they regarded appropriate without American interference.

DISILLUSIONMENT WITH DÉTENTE

U.S. "Unilateralism"

The result should have been a more harmonious transatlantic relationship in the 1970s than in the 1960s. Such was not the case. In retrospect, Nixon and Kissinger received little credit from the European allies for their low profile on internal European affairs or even for their firm championship of the American military presence in Europe in the face of vocal domestic opposition. A primary factor in European reservations about the Nixon policies was suspicion of hidden agendas within the Nixon Doctrine. Was the doctrine a mask concealing American weakness? Vietnamization of the war was seen as the real reason for America's interest in détente. It provided an exit from an unwinnable situation. Given this perception, it was likely that America's reduction of commitments abroad would touch Europe as well, no matter what priority the Nixon Doctrine assigned its NATO relations. The drive for a modus vivendi with the Soviet Union could be an admission of inferiority in the competition with the Soviet Union, in which European interests might be sacrificed. If partial disengagement from one part of the world was a reaction not only to failure in Vietnam but a concession to domestic opposition to costs in Europe as well as in Asia, the administration would have to walk a fine line to maintain its credibility with the allies.

That this credibility was in doubt was raised by the obvious linkage between American economic and foreign policy manifested in new measures in 1971 to shore up the weakened dollar. The issue of financial implications of the cost of American military investments abroad had always been a major theme in the demands for Europe to share the burdens more equitably. Nixon may have stopped the latest Mansfield amendment but he sanctioned suspension of the convertibility of the dollar in August 1971. A 10 percent surcharge imposed on all imports shocked the European members, partly by its unilateral application and partly because of the confession of weakness it demonstrated in what had been a bastion of stability for a generation.

The American justification for its defense of the dollar was not surprising; the dollar gap of the 1960s continued to worsen under the burden of massive military expenses in Europe and the unresolved conflict in Southeast Asia. The outcome was the devaluation of the dollar in 1971 and, with it, the apparent end of the policy of trade liberalization as protectionist sentiment burgeoned in the United States. The impact of a cheaper dollar on European producers was sharp and immediate. The European Economic Community, an object of American benevolence in its formative years, was no help in mediating with the United States. Indeed, a major source of Secretary of the Treasury John Connally's animus against Europe was the preferential trade agreements, especially in agricultural products, that discriminated against American competitors. Europe's potential as an economic rival of the United States was a dimension in the relationship that American leaders had neglected to observe in the 1960s.

The Connally initiative was short-lived. An agreement signed at the Smithsonian Institution in Washington before the end of 1971 established a floating exchange rate system that helped restore, temporarily at least, equilibrium to the international system. There was a return to the status quo in that the surcharge was lifted and the troop levels of Europeans and Americans in Europe remained in place. But psychological damage to the Nixon Doctrine could not be undone. The Treasury Department's action contradicted the new spirit of cooperation that the administration was nourishing. Bringing the dollar gap to the fore through devaluation reminded the partners that America's domination of much of Europe's market from automobiles to soft drinks siphoned a constant stream of dollars back to the home bases of the American multinational companies.

Annoying as the economic gauntlet was that the United States laid down to Europeans, a more disturbing element in the transatlantic relationship in the 1970s was a new spike in their doubts about the strengths of America's commitment to Europe's security. Granted that the thrust of détente signified a diminished fear of Soviet aggression, Europeans still lived next to a superpower equipped with large conventional forces as well as an impressive nuclear capability. In this context the American presence on the front lines remained a vital counterweight. But from the inception of the Nixon Doctrine there was a suspicion abroad that the U.S. drive for détente with the Soviet Union was a confession of weakness in Europe as well as in Vietnam. If "Vietnamization" of the hot war in Asia was a euphemism for abandonment of an Asian ally, then a unilateral approach to the Warsaw bloc might lead to the "Europeanization" of NATO's defense in the Cold War. Reducing

America's global commitments undertaken in the old Truman Doctrine might be accomplished by sacrificing the interests of the European allies.

The American embrace of the Strategic Arms Limitation Talks (SALT) fed anxieties about the fraudulence of the Nixon Doctrine's putative elevation of NATO Europe as the first priority in America's foreign relations. The doctrine in this light was a sinister way of making a virtue out of weakness by retaining the presumption of leadership while reducing obligations to its allies. Even more distressing was the entrance of the United States into a bilateral relationship with the Soviet adversary outside the NATO framework. Superficially, negotiations with the enemy, as evidenced in Ostpolitik and in MBFR, should have been a positive sign of a more stable life in Europe. Such was the objective of those initiatives. And it should be noted that Ostpolitik was as much a unilateral action by West Germany as SALT was by the United States.

In many ways the time was right for a mutual effort to reduce strategic nuclear weaponry on both sides of the Iron Curtain. The Soviets had achieved essential parity with the United States in nuclear intercontinental ballistic missiles (ICBMs) and had an interest in inhibiting another offensive-weapons cycle. For the United States, the ending of its nuclear superiority made the Nixon administration all the more sensitive to the perils of mutual destruction if the nuclear arms race were not reversed.

There were two other factors in play from an American standpoint. One was the rising opposition in Congress to a further arms buildup, fueled by disillusionment over the Vietnam War. A second was the opportunity, in a new bilateral relationship with the Soviets, according to Secretary of State Henry Kissinger (as of 1973), to link SALT and other arrangements to Soviet concessions to American interests, not least of which would be Soviet backing for American policies in Southeast Asia.

The upshot of these mutual considerations was an agreement between the two nations in 1972 to limit permanently their deployment of antiballistic missile systems (ABMs) to no more than two sites, 1,300 kilometers apart and to no more than 200 missiles. For the first time in history, as Kissinger observed with some exaggeration, two great powers built their future security on the vulnerability of their defenses. But what attracted Europe's attention was its exclusion from the proceedings.

The allies foresaw danger in the SALT agreements of 1972 from the differing interpretations of just what were strategic weapons. Although the substance of the talks devolved on the limitations on strategic weapons that could hit either the Soviet Union or the United States, the definition of which weapons were strategic affected the European allies directly. Although the United States insisted that only intercontinental missiles should be classified as strategic, this was not the Soviet position. Any weapon that could strike the Soviet homeland was its definition of a strategic weapon. This meant that such nuclear IRBMs deployed in Europe would be considered "strategic" and subject to regulation under the SALT agreement. Because Soviet IRBMs aimed against European targets would be "tactical" and hence excluded from SALT, the resulting asymmetry became an understandable concern for the partners.

The lack of a strong American protest confirmed Europe's perception that SALT served the Soviets and signified American insensitivity to its security. If this were the product of bilateral negotiations without European collaboration, the Nixon Doctrine would be more than a fraud; it would be a betrayal of the alliance. Europe's uneasiness was compounded by the continuing American pressure to build up NATO's ground forces on the familiar assumption, dating back to the Mc-Namara era, that nuclear weapons could not provide the deterrence it had provided in the 1950s. From the allied perspective, the product of such a buildup not only would be unreasonably costly but could never match the array of conventional forces the Warsaw bloc could muster. The American argument that in reality the better equipped NATO forces were more than a match for their Communist counterparts was no more persuasive in the 1970s than it had been when McNamara had presented it in the 1960s.

The efforts of American officials to calm these fears did not dispel the ongoing uneasiness in Europe about the direction the United States was following under Nixon and Secretary of State Kissinger. Their doctrine seemed to have been wholly discredited at the very time that the president's second term in office was about to be terminated by the Watergate scandal.

"The Year of Europe" and the Yom Kippur War

It was obvious to Kissinger that there was greater need to repair linkages within NATO than there was to establish new ones with the Soviet Union—not that Europeans disagreed with the key platform of the Nixon Doctrine. They felt they deserved the equality the United States had professed to give them. A uniting Europe under the aegis of the European Economic Community seemed to promise a new transatlantic relationship. The population of the EEC was 260 million in 1973, as opposed to 210 million in the United States, and 249 million in the Soviet Union. The community's gross national product was almost twice that of the Soviet Union and only 20 percent less than that of the senior partner. The impulse toward détente was essentially a European project, and it implied a normality in international relations that portended a lessening of the importance of the American connection to Europe's future.

But with all the gains accumulated by a more confident Europe, there still was no United States of Europe ready to assume the military responsibilities the United States of America had borne over the first quarter-century of NATO's history, and there was little prospect of such an entity coming into being in the foreseeable future. The EEC had no means of raising its own armies or of exacting taxes to pay for them. And despite a modest nuclear capability in its British and

French components, there was no movement toward developing a credible nuclear force of its own. The role of the NATO superpower was still indispensable in dealing with the Warsaw bloc controlled by the Soviet Union. As long as European defense rested on the flexible-response doctrine the allies had reluctantly accepted in 1967, they would remain dependent on the American presence in Europe.

European frustration over this continuing inferiority, joined with doubts about the reliability of the American ally, induced Kissinger to proclaim 1973 as the "Year of Europe" in a speech at the Waldorf Astoria hotel in New York on 25 April of that year. The speech highlighted America's intention to reinvigorate the Atlantic alliance. A new Atlantic Charter dedicated to a transatlantic collaboration would deal with defense, trade, and energy issues. In essence, the Year of Europe would perform what the Nixon Doctrine failed to resolve, proof of America's devotion to its European allies.

The attempt was doomed to failure. Europe's reaction was cynical. Kissinger's speech was delivered just as Watergate was beginning to shake the foundations of the Nixon administration. Shortly after Kissinger made his grand gesture, the president was forced to dismiss his key aides to calm the rising storm over the rifling of Democratic Party records at the Watergate complex and the subsequent efforts to cover up the administration's involvement. The scandal that forced Nixon out office left Kissinger with more power than he had enjoyed in the first administration. It was understandable, then, that European observers would wonder if the proposed Atlantic Charter was just an attempt to divert attention from the ongoing Watergate troubles. They might even speculate that the ambitious Kissinger may have envisioned himself as a latter-day Roosevelt or Churchill.

But it was more than Watergate that derailed the Year of Europe. The proposal was awkwardly presented without sufficient consultation at home or abroad. Kissinger's overtures contained many of the elements that had contributed to Europe's suspicions from the beginning of the Nixon years. Few judgments could have angered Europeans more in his message than the observation that "[t]he United States has global interests and responsibilities. Our European allies have regional interests." The arrogant tone and language grated on European sensibilities and served to accentuate rather than narrow the gap separating America from Europe.

Not all the difficulties arising from the speech derived from Kissinger's lordly manner or from his assumptions about Europe's role in the world. Some of them were the product of the allies' own pretensions. The disarray in the Nixon administration encouraged them to deprecate American leadership in the alliance even as they refused to accept any diminution of America's military contribution to Europe's defense. The mood in the United States was resentful. Although the Vietnam War was winding down in 1973, the Senate and public at large were reminded of the lack of support western Europe had given to the war against the common Communist adversary. Although the Mansfield resolutions were no longer on the table, congressional cutbacks of military aid, along with Watergate-inspired restrictions on the president's power to conduct war, inevitably would bring on new versions of the old resolutions.

Grievances on both sides of the Atlantic burst open in an out-of-area issue, the Arab–Israeli war in October 1973. As was the case in 1956—the Middle East, an external conflict—triggered a destructive centrifugal movement that threatened to destroy the alliance. Former Assistant Secretary of State Eugene V. Rostow believed that the crisis the war created in NATO was more serious than earlier flashpoints in Korea, Cuba, or Berlin. Whether the Soviets intended to use the war to drive the United States out of the eastern Mediterranean is arguable. What is beyond question was the depth of American anger at Europe's distancing itself from its major ally. The allies quickly embraced the Arab cause, including Egypt's assault against Israeli forces in the Sinai. When American military aid to Israel was rushed to the scene, the NATO partners denied the use of their territories and air space. Portugal was the reluctant exception. Although there was no NATO obligation to provide staging areas for transshipment of supplies, as Portugal did in the Azores, Europe's hostility to America's role in this crisis contained political and economic undertones that were more significant than a pro-Arab bias.

The latter was certainly a factor as NATO members carefully nurtured their special relations with Arab powers, France with Algeria, Italy with Libya, Greece with Egypt. Support for the Egyptian assault was a cheap price to pay for the economic benefits Arab connections provided. Their economies were more dependent on Middle Eastern oil than was America's, a situation they felt Americans did not appreciate sufficiently. Given the American presence on the North Atlantic Council, they could not express this sentiment clearly in this setting. The EEC, however, in which the United States was not represented, issued a communiqué in the midst of the war endorsing the Arab interpretation of UN Security Council Resolution 242 requiring Israeli evacuation of all territory captured in the 1967 war. In effect, the Europeans gave their blessing to the concerted Egyptian–Syrian attack against Israel.

A political factor was also in play. Europeans saw America's support of Israel in the conflict as a typical example of its disregard for European interests. Convinced that pandering to the Jewish lobby was at the heart of the American response, they blamed domestic politics for policies pursued at their expense. Confronting the United States over a Middle East issue was an opportunity to express discontent with a host of other American policies. Secretary of State Kissinger concluded that the Yom Kippur War released the allies from restraints that had prevented them earlier from fully venting their displeasure with their inferior position in the alliance.

This attitude received no sympathy from American public opinion. The war, after all, pushed the United States to the brink of a military confrontation with the Soviet Union, Egypt's principal arms supplier. When the reinforced Israeli forces crossed the west bank of the Suez Canal, the Soviets threatened to intervene on behalf of the besieged Egyptian Third Army. They could not afford another humiliating defeat of a fractious client that would leave their reputation in tatters in the Arab world. At the same time that Kissinger's shrewd diplomacy marginalized Soviet influence in the area, he placed limits on the extent of the Israeli victory. The United States was the paramount power in the Middle East by the end of the decade.

As these events unfolded, Europe's behavior was more than just an annoyance to the Nixon administration. To the Congress and public at large, it was nothing less than outrageous. The Europeans not only had deserted their senior ally in the crisis but also profited from an oil embargo that the Arab producers mounted against the United States for its support of Israel.

Congress had already made its resentment felt by means of the Jackson–Nunn amendment, a rider to a vital military appropriations bill. The bill became a law that required the president to reduce U.S. forces in Europe by the same percentage that Europeans failed to offset American costs in the balance of payments. This was not an unfamiliar congressional response to European offenses, but even before the outbreak of the war, emotions had been raised to the point of giving teeth to what had been warning resolutions. The president underscored the nation's feelings when he asserted in March 1974 that the allies "cannot have it both ways. They cannot have United States cooperation on the security front and proceed to have confrontation and even hostility on the economic and political fronts."

Small wonder, then, as the twenty-fifth anniversary of the North Atlantic Treaty approached, predictions of an early demise of the alliance surfaced again. A Gallup poll disclosed that internationalist views in 1974 had dropped to the lowest figure since 1945. Only 48 percent of those polled approved the use of force to help western Europe in a crisis. Another measure of the alliance's distress was the equality that the *NATO Review* reluctantly gave to the "Downs" in an essay on "Twenty-Five Years of Ups and Downs." Nevertheless, the editor remembered that NATO was always in one state of disarray or another, and if it had survived the rancor of the Suez crisis in 1956, the shock of the Berlin Wall in 1961, and the high tensions following de Gaulle's expulsion order in 1966, it would also outlive the bitterness on both sides of the Atlantic in the wake of the Arab–Israeli war in 1973. Détente had not yet run its course, even if the Year of Europe had such a brief shelf life. The NATO allies continued to keep détente alive in the mid-1970s.

Cyprus and the Greek–Turkish Imbroglio, 1974

The twenty-fifth anniversary of the signing of the treaty was also the occasion of an explosion of violence between two NATO allies. Conflict between Greece and Turkey had historic roots in the Ottoman empire, and its manifestation over the newly independent island of Cyprus was hardly a surprise. More surprising was their anger against the United States, the nation that had been a patron of both countries since the announcement of the Truman Doctrine in 1947. Each ally asserted that America had used its powerful influence to favor its rival's cause.

Hostility between Greeks and Turks, always deeper among the weaker Greeks, lay beneath the surface of the fragile spirit of cooperation that developed in the 1930s because both countries wanted to avoid entanglements with the great powers that had hindered their national ambitions in the past. World War II temporarily shattered this cooperation when the belligerents exploited Greece and Turkey in that war. But fear of Communism brought them together again when Greece fought a civil war against domestic Communists and Turkey endured enormous pressure from its Soviet neighbor for both maritime and territorial concessions. The United States was their patron in their successful resistance because Americans fulfilled the promise of the Truman Doctrine with funds and arms. As a result of this experience, Greece and Turkey were joint suitors for membership in the Atlantic alliance in 1949. That neither nation was anywhere near the Atlantic did not matter; Italy, after all, was a signatory. Both countries felt that its confrontation with Communist aggression deserved recognition, and feared that without the embrace of NATO the Communist menace might rise again.

Their arguments had not been persuasive in 1949. Only after the outbreak of the Korean War and the militarization of the alliance under SHAPE was their application revisited. The perceived need for NATO to secure its southeastern flank against a potential Soviet attack and the prospect of acquiring troops, particularly from Turkish divisions, changed their status. Against the better judgments of the northern allies, the United States led the way to bring Greece and Turkey into NATO at the Lisbon meeting of the North Atlantic Council in February 1952. For a brief time there was even a Balkan Pact that embraced Communist Yugoslavia, as well as Greece and Turkey, out of a common fear of Soviet aggression. This pact dissolved in the mid-1950s when the Soviets appeared ready for a rapprochement with Yugoslavia while the Greek and Turkish members revived their mutual suspicions, particularly over Cyprus, even as they remained in NATO.

Centuries of antagonism made Turkey, not the Soviet Union, the primary threat to the Greeks; Russia in the nineteenth century had been considered the protector of Greeks and the enemy of Turks. Although Turkey was more conscious of the Soviet danger, it nourished grievances against Greek influence in the United States and Greek claims over the air and sea space around the Greek islands in the Aegean Sea. It was the island of Cyprus, with a population 80 percent Greek and about 20 percent Turkish that was the scene of a serious crisis in the mid-1970s. As long as Britain had remained sovereign over the island, an uneasy coexistence prevailed. But Greek Cypriot pressure for enosis with the mother country and Turkish Cypriot agitation for protection from Turkey had accelerated Britain's willingness to give up the control that it had exercised since 1978. As in India and Palestine over a decade before, the widespread terrorism between the two communities created more problems than the Cypriots could handle.

Given that Greece and Turkey were both NATO members, Secretary-General Lord Ismay attempted to mediate in the late 1950s. His successor, Paul-Henri Spaak, proposed a federal arrangement with separate Greek and Turkish legislatures advising a British governor. It, too, failed, and Cyprus became independent in 1960. Under the terms of independence, Greece, Turkey, and Britain were to have special rights in Cyprus. The British would retain two bases and the two Balkan powers would keep a small force on the island—950 personnel for Greece, and 650 for Turkey. Essentially, the Spaak plan allowed the majority Greek Cypriots to control the government under President Archbishop Makarios, but with special protections for the Turkish minority intended to promote internal harmony and eliminate obstacles to NATO's objectives. These elaborate precautions failed. Archbishop Makarios chafed under unwieldy regulations that guaranteed the Turkish Cypriots a larger share of governance than the size of its population warranted. He made plans to curb the minority's role in government. The result was violence between the two communities.

Until 1964, the United States had kept a relatively low profile in Cyprus. But it was always conscious of the dangers a Greek–Turkish conflict could inflict on NATO's defense structure in the eastern Mediterranean. Makarios was instinctively anti-American, identifying himself with the Third World and susceptible to Soviet effort to pose as the champion of anticolonialism. He was also a believer in a unitary state, with minimal liberties for the Turkish minority. Although he did not support union with Greece, his attitude toward Britain and the United States meshed with Greece's feelings about its victimization by the great powers.

Turkey, neighbor to the Soviet Union and concerned about Soviet aggressive intentions, normally enjoyed warmer relations with the United States, but events in the 1960s and 1970s loosened these ties. There was a sense of betrayal in Turkey when the United States removed its medium-range missiles from its emplacements, without consultation, as part of the Soviet–American resolution of the Cuban missile crisis in 1962. Two years later President Lyndon B. Johnson used harsh language in warning Turkey that if its intervention in Cyprus with U.S.-supplied military weapons brought on a Soviet attack, NATO would reconsider its military obligation to respond to an attack against Turkey under Article 5 of the North Atlantic Treaty. These actions raised doubts about the reliability of the American commitment and made the Turks as susceptible as Greeks to Soviet efforts to weaken their ties to NATO.

This was the background of the major crisis in 1974 when Makarios was overthrown by supporters of the dictatorial Greek junta in Athens and replaced by an unscrupulous agent of the new ruling colonels intent on securing Cyprus's enosis with the mother country. Ironically, Turkish Cypriots preferred the authoritarian Makarios to the outlaw regime that ousted him as an opponent to union with

Greece. Fearful of the fate of Turkish Cypriots in this new situation, Turkey ignored the warnings of 1964 and invaded the island. Three days after the Turkish invasion, the Greek junta fell and was replaced by a civilian government that was powerless to repel the Turkish assault.

What Athens could do was vent its frustrations on NATO and the United States. The Konstantine Karamanlis government that succeeded the dictatorship could withdraw from the NATO military structure, in the manner of France's departure in 1966, because it could not take on the Turkish military. Secretary of State Kissinger personified in Greek eyes a conspiracy that had been behind the coup in Cyprus and behind the bellicose Turkish response. An articulate and influential Greek lobby in Washington worked to focus American attention on the betrayal of its Greek ally. That Greek public opinion turned against the United States was hardly surprising; the American ally had been a prime supporter of the colonels' dictatorship. All Greek factions could agree that once again Greece suffered for its dependency on friends willing to sacrifice Greek national interests in a crisis.

There was some merit in this charge. Although American public opinion traditionally and sentimentally had been pro-Greek since the time of the Greek war of independence, the U.S. military placed a higher value on the military strength and the seemingly consistent anti-Soviet cast of Turkey. It was Turkey's military potential and strategic location straddling the Dardanelles that made the Turkish partnership more valuable than its Greek rival. A consequence of this gap between the two countries was the apportioning of military aid on a de facto 7 to 10 ratio: for every $7 granted to Greece prior to the invasion of Cyprus, Turkey was to receive $10.

Yet Kissinger fared little better over Cyprus with the presumably favored Turks than he did with the Greeks. Under congressional pressure, the United States placed an embargo on transfers of military equipment to Turkey in February 1975. The threat uttered by President Johnson in 1964 materialized 10 years later. Turkey was as mystified as it was angered by the American punitive action. Turkey's purpose in intervening in Cyprus was to protect the Turkish minority from persecution by the more numerous Greek Cypriots, and its American ally either did not understand the motives or was excessively influenced by pro-Greek public sentiment in the United States. As a result, Turkey suspended U.S. operations at Turkish military bases in 1975.

The Cyprus crisis that left 40 percent of the island under Turkish control precipitated the departure of one ally from the military structure of the alliance and the equivalent action on the part of the other ally in NATO. The United States was blamed for withholding its blessing from either side, and so earned the enmity of both. This clash between two NATO allies left the carefully constructed defense arrangements in the eastern Mediterranean in shambles. It was the continuing presence of the powerful American Sixth Fleet that provided NATO's shield in the last half of the 1970s. The Soviets were the beneficiaries as both Turks and Greeks warmed their relations with the putative Communist enemy, and there was little NATO or the United States could do to solve the Greek–Turkish imbroglio.

Still, there was no permanent break in the alliance or in U.S. relations with either power. The onset of a Soviet intervention in Afghanistan in 1979 made Turkey more appreciative of the American ally, and willing to come to some compromises with the Greeks. Greece agreed to reintegrate into NATO's military structure in 1980, less because of any revived fears of Soviet aggression and more out of concern that Turkey would benefit from America's renewed military aid at its expense as long as it stayed outside SHAPE's command. Fairly or not, the United States was the scapegoat for Greece's and Turkey's frustrations. But as with Iceland in 1956 and with France (de facto), the two countries felt they had no choice but to remain under the aegis of the transatlantic partner.

THE END OF DÉTENTE?: 1974–1976

The lure of détente dominated both sides of the Atlantic in the 1970s. Although the motives may have been different, the goal was the same: de-escalation of tensions that permitted the United States to extricate itself from Vietnam and that permitted the European allies to believe that the Cold War was ending. No such expectation animated Kissinger's foreign policy. Given the fall of the Nixon administration in 1974, the secretary of state became the dominant figure in fashioning American foreign policy, and he saw in détente an opportunity to restrain the aggressive impulses of the Soviet Union by pursuing "linkage" in place of confrontation. Europeans distrusted Kissinger's motives in seeking détente, even as the NATO partners pressed in concert for the MBFR process. Alistair Buchan, an authoritative British analyst of NATO affairs, suspected that the MBFR program would become a mask for the administration's appeasement of Senator Mansfield and a cover for dangerous unilateral reductions of American troop strength in Europe.

Although this strain of anti-American sentiment persisted among the allies, its virulence decreased as the Vietnam War ended and as American troops remained in place during the Ford administration. Yet an uneasy sense of stagnation pervaded the alliance, stimulated perhaps by the absence of the kind of crises that roiled NATO in the 1960s. The MBFR negotiations made little progress in Vienna. Even if the Soviets were seriously interested in a "balanced" reduction of conventional forces, the problem of achieving a balance seemed insoluble when the Warsaw Pact armies were at NATO's doorstep while the American ally's main forces were across the Atlantic—its European outreach was relatively small and more tenuously perched. The MBFR negotiations stretched out with one unproductive round of talks following another.

The allies' disillusionment was compounded by the rapid progress of the CSCE. Those negotiations, begun at the same time as the MBFR's, yielded the successful Helsinki agreements in 1975, meeting the goals of the Warsaw bloc by legitimizing the Yalta boundaries of 1945. So anxious were the Soviets to convene the CSCE that their agreement to talk about force reductions in Vienna appears in retrospect to have been lip service in return for the genuine service the allies rendered in Helsinki.

Less than a year after the Helsinki accords had been signed, the idea of détente became an albatross around Kissinger's neck. The word itself disappeared from official papers when President Gerald R. Ford decided that its French origin was too imprecise in English to transmit its proper meaning. Détente's disappearance in 1976 symbolized how far Kissinger had fallen from the public esteem he had enjoyed in 1974. For a time—in the last months before Nixon fled Washington in disgrace, one step ahead of impeachment—the secretary of state was the most important figure in the U.S. government. This was the period when his shuttle diplomacy in the Middle East extracted as much of a victory for American influence abroad as could be expected under the existing adverse circumstances. His successful projection of American power obscured his failure to prevent the demise of South Vietnam in 1975.

President Ford, a lackluster Michigan congressman, earnest and honest, had been catapulted into the vice presidency and then the presidency in 1974 without benefit of electoral provenance. Untutored in the intricacies of foreign affairs, he initially placed the management of foreign relations entirely in the hands of his secretary of state, who continued to serve as adviser for national security. But Kissinger was unable to win the triumphs he had achieved under Nixon. His descent from Olympus was rapid. It was also probably inevitable. The Vietnam experience damaged him as it had damaged every leader connected with that debacle. His Nobel Peace Prize notwithstanding, he was blamed not only for widening that war by the invasion of Cambodia but also for the deceptions that accompanied it and for the ultimate collapse of South Vietnam itself. The Turkish invasion of Cyprus was laid at his door, as was the support the United States had given to the Greek dictatorship in the past. Turkey was only slightly less upset with American policy in the Ford years, and American policy meant Kissinger's. When Greeks and Turks could not reach each other, they struck out at NATO and at its leader. Kissinger's reputation suffered.

From the other end of the Mediterranean, NATO faced a new worry. Just three months before the Turkish invasion of Cyprus, a military coup in Portugal ended the Antonio de Oliveira Salazar dictatorship that had been solidly pro-NATO and anti-Communist. Even though the new government pledged loyalty to the alliance, it took a sharp turn to the left. Communist influence seemed to predominate just at a time when "Euro-Communism" in France and Italy sought to present a new and moderate Communist system willing to live with the West, even with NATO. Kissinger and Ford feared for the future of the southern flank of the alliance if a Communist government should be elected. Even those European leaders disposed to criticize the United States at every opportunity were taken aback by this possibility.

There was some recognition that Soviet behavior, and not just Kissinger's Machiavellian diplomacy, helped to undo détente. Most of the allies tried to put the best face possible on obvious Soviet efforts to manipulate the process to their own advantage, whether by stalling on the MBFR negotiations or by exploiting one "basket" of the Helsinki agreement and ignoring another on human rights. Nevertheless, the weight of blame fell more heavily on the secretary of state.

The reaction against President Nixon's abuse of power in the Vietnam War was itself a factor in limiting Kissinger's freedom of action. Bowing to the anti-military mood of Congress, the Nixon and Ford administrations presided over annual cuts in defense requests from 1969 to 1976 on the average of $6.7 billion a year and a decrease in the defense-spending percentage of the gross government expenditures from 40.8 percent in fiscal year 1970 to 24.3 percent in fiscal year 1977.

The reduction in U.S. defense spending was not a problem as such for the European allies; they had set their hopes on détente facilitating reductions in their military budgets. What was disturbing was their recognition that arms control agreements promoted by the United States were not simply satisfying by-products of détente but a confession of military weakness on the part of the United States. The agreements not only recognized Soviet nuclear parity but also the impossibility of winning over a post–Watergate Congress to reverse this course if it became necessary. The allies' ambivalence on this subject was intensified by the obstacles uncovered in the evolution of détente.

American liberals joined with their European counterparts in deploring the amorality of the Kissinger policies in Greece, Vietnam, and southwest Africa. They were not as ready as former Undersecretary of State George Ball to lump the CSCE agreements into the same category. Ball damned the Helsinki accords as submission to the logic of the Brezhnev Doctrine, which had been the Soviet justification for the overthrow of the Prague government in 1968. The West had legitimized Communist control of eastern Europe. The American right wing took up this theme and made it part of Governor Ronald Reagan's campaign for the Republican presidential nomination in 1976. Reagan failed in that year, but he pushed the Ford campaign to distance itself from Kissinger's authority by having the National Security Council removed from his jurisdiction. It was at this point that the president also distanced himself from détente.

Kissinger's approach had failed. "Linkage" was not working. Détente in the Soviet lexicon did not encompass activities in the Third World. The Ford administration looked with dismay but without influence on Cuban surrogates in southwest Africa spreading Communism in the former Portuguese territory of Angola.

Nor did any mutual understanding between the superpowers inhibit massive Soviet intervention in northeast Africa when Somalia fell into the Soviet camp.

The outlawing of détente from American foreign policy did not lead to an immediate revival of the Cold War in Europe. Both the American and NATO moods required continued searching for modes of coexistence with the Warsaw bloc. Even though Kissinger had set himself up for a fall by overselling the American version of détente, it still had an appeal for Europeans, and under a different label for Americans, too, in 1976 and beyond. Although the European allies were suspicious of superpower deals in SALT negotiations and were worried about Communist tactics in Portugal, France, and Italy, they had no wish to see the Cold War reinvigorated. Europeans felt that normalization of economic and cultural relations with eastern Europe depended in the long run on the survival of détente between East and West.

EUROPE AND THE CARTER INITIATIVES

The successful presidential candidacy of Governor Jimmy Carter of Georgia offered a welcome change for the NATO allies. As with every president, Carter entered office determined to distinguish himself from his predecessors, and immediately did so. An outsider to the Democratic Party, President Carter had won a reputation for honesty and efficiency as governor of Georgia. A born-again Christian, he intended to apply moral principles to foreign relations in a manner that would contrast sharply with Nixon's or Kissinger's. Equally important was his conception of a seamless world in which every issue was interconnected. By this example, the United States would exhibit to the world that moral power could serve mankind. There would be none of the manipulation of power that had characterized American policy in the recent past.

A successful peanut farmer and an engineer educated at the U.S. Naval Academy, he fitted into no clear mold beyond a vague idealism tinged with populism. It is unlikely that he would have made his way to the White House if the Vietnam War had not turned the nation against the Washington establishment. Hardworking and intelligent, he was also obsessive to a fault about detail. Whether these qualities were sufficient guarantees for success in the management of foreign relations was quickly tested.

His troubles grew out of a lack of experience in foreign affairs that was reflected in his choices of secretary of state and national security advisor. Secretary of State Cyrus Vance, a veteran of the McNamara Pentagon, embraced the president's wish to change the nature of America's foreign policy objectives. Rather than dwell on the Cold War confrontation with the Soviet bloc or even on the slow and uncertain steps toward détente, Carter intended to reorient the direction of

American foreign policy from East–West to North–South problems. Following his moral compass, the president saw the source of future instability in the world arising from the inequality of wealth and resources between the First World and the Third World. In this reformulation of policy, the conflict with the Second World should be quickly liquidated as an impediment to the more pressing issues facing Latin America, the Middle East, and South Asia. Nuclear weaponry in this context should be removed from the relationship with the Warsaw bloc as soon as possible. The rule of law should govern international relations.

Carter's inexperience in foreign affairs accounted for allowing his grand design to be translated into action by two able but conflicting personalities. His national security advisor was Zbigniew Brzezinski. A Harvard-educated professor of government at Columbia University, Brzezinski was knowledgeable and articulate about the problems of a multipolar world. With his European background and slight but impressive Polish accent he could not help but be compared with Henry Kissinger. Although he professed to share Carter's abhorrence of the former secretary's method of diplomacy, his deep suspicions of the Soviet role in eastern Europe colored his advice to the president and tended to keep East–West relations at the top of the administration's agenda.

Brzezinski's approach conflicted with Secretary of State Cyrus Vance's and led to divisions within the administration's foreign-policy establishment that were never bridged. Where Vance promoted a program based on the centrality of arms reduction and cooperation with the Soviets in easing tensions in the Third World, Brzezinski saw a Soviet arms buildup and the need to counter Communist initiatives through traditional power relationships. Although rivalry between the secretary of state and the national security advisor was hardly a new phenomenon in Washington, former presidents usually resolved it by clearly designating the preeminent spokesman for foreign affairs. In Carter's case, his disposition to be involved in all aspects of government, combined with an inability to make firm decisions in favor of one or another of his advisers, made for confusion about America's position on NATO interests among the European allies.

Given their discontent with Kissinger's manipulative behavior toward Europe, there should have been widespread rejoicing over the arrival of an American leader who spoke of normality in relations with the Soviet Union even if he did not use the term *détente*. His genuine devotion to North–South problems and to moral solutions in international relations seemed to evoke the finest of American traditions, particularly in their contrast with the putative realism of the Nixon years. Perhaps in another time and in other circumstances this would have been the case. But Carter was burdened by European partners such as Premier Valéry Giscard d'Estaing of France and Chancellor Helmut Schmidt of Germany, who saw not the ideals but the inconsistent positions of Carter's advisers and the distance between the pronouncements from the White House and the threatening Soviet military buildup in Europe.

If Nixon and Kissinger had been too overbearing in their dealings with the allies, Carter and Vance by contrast were too casual in their relationship. Confident in the rightness of their approach, they simply assumed that Europeans would follow the American lead. Free from the inordinate fear of Communism and the Soviet Union, as the president noted in a speech at Notre Dame University, NATO should no longer adopt the erroneous practices of its adversary at the expense of the West's own values and principles. And on the assumption that the Soviets would share the new approach the United States was advocating, Carter plunged ahead with proposals two months after his inauguration for deep cuts in the still incomplete SALT II accords on further limiting deployment of strategic weapons. A public and humiliating rejection of this initiative did not deter the administration from canceling the production of the costly B-1 strategic bomber on the grounds that the existing B-52s could perform the same functions at much lower cost.

These actions in the early months of the Carter administration unsettled the allies. They were well aware that although there were relatively few increases in the number of NATO forces, the number of Warsaw Pact forces rose dramatically. In the years 1971 to 1976, a period of declining NATO defense budgets, Soviet military spending increased by 4 to 5 percent annually. This was the situation at a time when the new administration pledged to cut U.S. military spending by $5 to $7 billion four days after taking office. Rather than seeing in the Carter actions a more principled as well as a more rapid approach to détente, the allies feared that a naïve American president was engaging in unilateral disarmament, ultimately at Europe's expense. By contrast, the Kissinger policy of hard-nosed linkage in dealing with the Soviet Union, flawed though it was, seemed in retrospect more appealing to the allies.

The United States did make an effort to respond to Europe's concerns by asking each NATO partner to accept a 3 percent increase for national defense budgets. Because this was at least a specific response to a growing crisis that the Carter administration had not previously recognized, the North Atlantic Council responded positively to this challenge, particularly when it addressed IRBMs, but Europeans wanted more, realizing that even a 3 percent solution would not produce results that would match the formidable Soviet military machine in this period. The continued presence of more than 300,000 U.S. troops in Europe provided significant but insufficient reassurance to nervous allies.

THE NEUTRON BOMB FIASCO

Germany's Chancellor Helmut Schmidt was Carter's most articulate challenger. He was suspicious of the soft human rights approach of Secretary Vance, which he regarded as a diversion from the appropriate agendas of the alliance. And he was personally hostile to National Security Advisor Brzezinski, whose aggressive anti-Soviet stance may have contained anti-German components. But it was the open conflict over the development of an enhanced-radiation weapon (ERW), popularly known as the neutron bomb, that raised the differences with the Carter administration to almost crisis proportions. Enhanced-radiation warheads had been under development for almost two decades and had been on the NATO agenda since 1973. Its achievement was an ability to destroy enemy concentrations without the kind of damage to the environment that existing battlefield nuclear weapons would inflict. The warhead, mounted on a short-range missile such as the Lance, would produce radiation sufficient to kill enemy tanks and troops without the blast and heat caused by other nuclear weapons emitting an equivalent amount of radiation.

The neutron bomb was ready for deployment in 1977. Chancellor Schmidt recognized its value in deterring aggression but he wanted the United States to assume the burden of responsibility. He had domestic opposition to a weapon that would be used exclusively on German soil even if the buildings in the area of the killing fields would be spared radiation contamination. Carter let him down. Although the president saw in the neutron bomb a means of redressing the imbalance in ground forces between NATO and the Warsaw bloc at a reasonable cost to all the allies, he had to face a storm of criticism from a variety of domestic groups—from those who felt that its use would revive the possibility of winning a nuclear war to those who called it "the ultimate capitalist weapon," designed to kill people but spare property. This cry was echoed and expanded on by Soviet propaganda. It left Carter in a quandary that he solved in 1978 by deferring production of the bomb.

Although Carter's conscience may have been relieved by the decision, Schmidt was outraged. He regarded the president's waffling as a betrayal of faith. But Schmidt's own caution may have inhibited Carter. He and other allied leaders had sent confusing signals to the United States. They wanted the bomb as a bargaining chip in dealing with the Soviet Union, but they refused to offer their territories as sites for the bomb's deployment. Blame for the failure of the ERW deserved to be shared, although it was Carter's image as leader of the alliance that was damaged. The allies were all too eager to find in the administration's diplomacy weakness that the Soviets would exploit, such as negotiations in SALT II that could result in banning the American use of cruise missiles.

SS-20s VERSUS CRUISE MISSILES

In the wake of the neutron debacle, the issue of the cruise missile assumed greater significance for Europeans than it might have had otherwise. Once again the issue was trust in America's commitment, and the medium-range missile was a test case. They knew that the Soviets regarded (or pretended to regard) any missile that could reach their territory as a strategic weapon open to removal in SALT negotiations. What exacerbated the allies' fears was the Soviet deployment, beginning in 1977, of SS-20 missiles targeted on western Europe. The weapon contained a triple warhead, was mobile, and was capable of being launched in a few minutes. The Carter administration knew of its lethal potential, but instead of seeking to ban its use by the Soviets, it made sure in SALT talks that it would not be converted into an intercontinental missile aimed at the United States. This success on the part of American negotiators did nothing to soothe European feelings. Was America turning its back on its allies? Europe's cities remained vulnerable to the SS-20.

Chancellor Schmidt raised the European alarm. At a highly visible forum, London's International Institute for Strategic Studies, he spoke sharply against the path American foreign policy was taking. While the United States preached the virtues of increasing defense expenditures on the European allies to build up conventional forces, it downplayed the possibilities inherent in a major weapon that, unlike infantry, could deal with the SS-20 threat. Moreover, it appeared willing to entertain the Soviet proposal to block transfer of strategic weapons to other states. This proposal was embedded in SALT II, signed in 1979 but never ratified. From a European perspective the cruise missile, although not mentioned in the address, would be removed from the American arsenal, and NATO Europe would be left defenseless against the Soviet adversary. The speech in effect was a stinging rebuke of American policy and behavior, calling into question the whole issue of U.S. strategic nuclear guarantee.

The alarm raised by the German chancellor was shared throughout Europe. There was no question that the United States had to renew its assurances to the allies, and the surest route would be a decision to deploy the new ground-launched cruise missile equipped with the ability to navigate at treetop level and to strike its targets with little margin for error. It was relatively cheap to produce. Unlike the ballistic missile, it was slow, taking hours rather than minutes to reach its objectives, but its small size and mobility, particularly its capacity for evasion, compensated for its lack of speed. In 1978 the modernized Pershing II missile was included in NATO plans, replacing the Pershing IA missiles in Germany with a weapon capable of reaching Soviet targets, and with a flight time of only 6 to 12 minutes The allies seized on both missiles as NATO's antidote to the SS-20, and the Carter administration had no choice but to go along with their allies, if only to redeem its credibility as leader of the alliance.

In fact, the American establishment—military and civilian alike—never saw the SS-20 as a threat to the strategic balance between NATO and the Warsaw bloc. The cruise and Pershing missiles, if employed, would be a segment of the broad American deterrent that encompassed land-based and sea-based intercontinental nuclear ballistic missiles. The Minuteman ballistic-missile silos in the American Midwest and the submarines armed with Polaris missiles made intermediate-range cruise missiles located in Europe unnecessary. But given the level of anxiety exhibited by the allies, the American partner had to show its empathy, and to do so by taking the SS-20 threat as seriously as its European allies did. Secretary Vance successfully convinced them that nothing in the SALT II negotiations would inhibit the deployment of missiles to counter the SS-20s.

Driven by the need for action, NATO leaders agreed to a plan that would couple the deployment of IRBMs in Europe with negotiations for mutual limits on long-range-theater nuclear systems. At a special meeting of foreign and defense ministers in December 1979, the High Level Group, formed in 1977 under the Nuclear Planning Group, proposed the deployment of 464 ground-launched missiles—160 in Britain, 112 in Italy, 96 in Germany, and 48 each in the Low Countries. In addition, 108 Pershing missiles would be included, replacing the older Pershing missiles already in Germany. The fact that the SS-20s were being installed at a rate of one a week by 1979 intensified the urgency of counteractions. This distribution of weaponry had political as well as military implications. Vital to the success of deployment were the requirements that NATO powers share responsibility for deploying weapons on their own soil.

There was sufficient precedent for this dual-track initiative. After all, missiles had been placed in Europe since the 1960s and were due for replacement, and the hope for de-escalation of the nuclear arms race was a continuing inspiration for the ongoing SALT negotiations. At a special meeting in Brussels in December 1979, NATO's foreign and defense ministers emphasized that the dual-track approach would further the course of arms control and détente in the 1980s. As in the Harmel report, détente would be facilitated by the deployment of the new missiles. The carrot of détente would accompany the stick of missile deployments.

The dual-track initiative should have been a turning point in Carter's relations with the European allies. It seemed to respond to most of the irritants in the transatlantic relationship. It reaffirmed America's commitment to the defense of Europe by identifying once again America's stake in Europe's security; it alleviated Europe's dread of the Soviet nuclear weapon by a counterweapon that could strike deep into Warsaw Pact territory; and it underscored the relevance of the Harmel spirit by its embrace of arms control. These accomplishments should have fashioned a legacy that elevated Carter's reputation above those of his two most recent predecessors. He had come to grips with the rising Soviet power in a way that satisfied the European partners without relinquishing his support of détente. Unlike his predecessors, the allies recognized a genuine, if naïve, commitment to arms control.

IRAN AND AFGHANISTAN

The dual-track approach was certainly a milestone in NATO's history. It influenced the events of the 1980s but failed to change Carter's image as an indecisive bumbler in foreign affairs. Two external events diminished what should have been an impressive record of accomplishment in his dealings with allies. Both occurred in 1979, the year of the dual initiative, and cast the planned deployments into the background. The Iranian revolution against the Shah and against America's role in his regime broke out three weeks before the dual-track decision. Student militants aroused by religious leaders took 53 Americans hostage, most of whom were not released until Reagan took office in 1981. It was a humiliating experience for the nation, made all the worse by bungled attempts to free the prisoners. The Shah's Iran, a keystone in Nixon's and Kissinger's Middle East policy, became a millstone for Carter's. It revived Europe's perception of an inept leader.

The second crisis was the Soviet invasion of Afghanistan. Unlike the Iran debacle, the United States acted vigorously and with some success to check the Communist overthrow of an insufficiently pliant Communist regime in Kabul. Washington was alarmed, fearing that the true Soviet objective was not Afghanistan but the Persian Gulf's oil resources. Brzezinski identified "an arc of crisis" from the Horn of Africa through the Middle East to the Persian Gulf, which required immediate allied attention. The United States led the way with the Carter Doctrine, calling for a joint task force—the Rapid Deployment Force (RDF)—in March 1980 to reinforce the claim that any attempt by an outside force to gain control of the Persian Gulf region would be considered an attack against America's vital interests. NATO responded with the Defense Planning Committee (DPC) urging allied coordination of out-of-area deployment of forces. Scenarios envisaging Iranian conquest of the Middle East and the overthrow of moderate Arab regimes by Moslem extremists were not confined to American planners.

But this show of American resolve did little to restore Carter's credibility as a strong leader of the alliance. His reactions were too spasmodic, and too often overshot their mark. Trade sanctions against the Soviet Union or the American boycott of the 1980 Olympic Games in Moscow suggested to Europeans that the Americans took the invasion more seriously than they did, once the initial shock was over and the limits of Soviet intentions made clearer. From a European perspective, the United States paid too much attention to an out-of-area issue and too little attention to other concerns of its allies. The Afghanistan invasion should not be an occasion, according to Chancellor Schmidt, to jeopardize the delicate negotiations between NATO Europe and the Soviet Union for a multibillion-dollar plan to build a natural gas pipeline from Siberia to the West. Although Americans were hostile to this rapprochement with the Soviets, Europeans rationalized that Afghanistan had long been a Soviet preserve, and the regime that precipitated the invasion was itself Communist. Carter was conducting his foreign policy without considering its impact on the allies. Only the new Conservative British prime minister, Margaret Thatcher, gave full backing to his hard line against the Soviet Union.

Carter lost the presidency in the election of 1980, but it was unlikely that NATO relations were at the heart of his difficulties. His handling of the Iranian hostage situation occupied a larger space among the American electorate. Nor was his seemingly impulsive veering from moral suasion in foreign relations to an aggressive stance against the Soviets the source of his domestic troubles; his critics felt he had not gone far enough in either direction. But was Europe's rhetoric excessive? It was America's revived awareness of a Soviet threat that relieved the allies' fears sufficiently for them to relax the timetable for deploying cruise missiles and to pursue new economic relations with the Warsaw bloc. His indecisiveness may have subjected him to the contempt of his allies, but the Carter presidency's support of NATO, appreciated or not, was a factor in the continuing relevance of the transatlantic relationship.

5

ENDING THE COLD WAR:
1980–1990

REAGAN AND THE "EVIL EMPIRE"

The election of Ronald Reagan to the presidency in 1980 offers a study in contrast with his predecessor. Carter entered the White House with a vision of a world free from the Cold War competition between the East and West, in which the North would use its energies and resources to lift the economies and polities of the South. Reagan had a simpler vision of a world divided between good and evil, and identified himself and his nation as standing without reservations against the Soviet evil empire. Carter was a master of details, but with a plodding rhetorical style that reflected a pessimistic nature. Reagan was the supreme communicator with an affable manner and simple solutions to problems of government—foreign or domestic. Carter immersed himself in the minutiae of government and vacillated over decisions; Reagan left details to his aides; in fact, most of the major issues of his administration were left to his staff. But he had no hesitation about making firm decisions, whether or not he understood their implications.

Europeans might have appreciated the positions Reagan was ready to show the world. He agreed that America had suffered from some reverses, as in Vietnam and Iran. But it suffered most from lack of firm leadership of the free world, leaving a gap that he proposed to fill. His administration would stand up to the Soviet Union and revive an unambiguous primacy in the alliance that had been absent under his predecessor. It was a strong message delivered with the verve and polish of the Hollywood actor that he once was. Given the malaise associated with Carter's presidency, there was a sense in Europe that any change would be a change for the better. But, in the Aesopian image, European allies soon wondered if they had exchanged King Log for King Stork as leader of the alliance.

Conflict with European goals inevitably followed from the American perception, strengthened under Reagan, that détente was truly dead, and that the Soviets could be dealt with only from a position of strength. Without giving appropriate recognition to the infrastructure the Carter administration had established for the modernization of America's defenses, this president gave his blessing to a massive buildup, raising the level the United States spent on defense from approximately 5.5 percent of its gross national product in 1980 to more than 7 percent four years later. There was little faith in the arms control promise that won over Europeans in 1979.

The rhetoric was hyperbolic in the view of the allies, but parts of the message resonated well in western Europe. Given the scare the Soviets had inspired with the SS-20 missiles, the clear promise of a firm nuclear guarantee was heartening. Carter was never convincing in this regard. The Reagan administration was equally staunch about the continuing presence of American troops in Europe. The allies not only appreciated the commitment, backed up with stronger reinforcement capabilities, but also the lack of pressure on them to increase their own contributions of conventional forces. The Europeans were not even willing to honor the 3 percent increase in their defense budgets that was mandated in the Carter administration.

This appreciation, however, had distinct limits. Just nine days after his inauguration, the new president frightened his European allies with charges that Soviet leaders reserved "the right to commit any crime, to lie, to cheat, to achieve their immoral ends." This bloodcurdling language was hard to overlook when officials in the Reagan administration seemed to believe in winning a nuclear war as well as in surviving one. A deputy undersecretary of defense for strategic nuclear forces envisioned a scenario in which citizens would "dig a hole, cover it with a couple of doors, and then throw three feet of dirt on top. With a sufficient supply of shovels, everyone's going to make it." This was not the kind of advice the European allies wanted to hear. No matter how disturbing the SS-20s were to their sense of security, and no matter how much they deplored Soviet actions in Afghanistan in 1979 or in Poland in 1981, they had to share a continent with the Soviet Union and its Warsaw Pact allies. Détente could not be permanently scrapped.

A major element in the survival of détente for Europeans was potential economic benefits from trade relations. Europeans had never shared the American conviction, going back to the Mutual Defense Assistance Control Act of 1951 that would cancel military aid to those allies who did not comply with the U.S. embargo on strategic items to the Soviet Union. This act assumed that trade restrictions against the Soviet bloc could defeat the Communists in the long run. Carter's cancellation of American participation in the Olympic Games in Moscow and the imposition of a grain embargo on the Soviet Union in the wake of the Afghanistan invasion in 1979 were not welcome events in Europe. When Reagan discontinued the grain embargo on assuming office, transatlantic critics saw only appeasement of American farmers deprived of a large market. Their suspicions were confirmed when martial law was imposed in Poland in 1981. The administration's response then was to apply sanctions not only against Poland, but also against its patron, the Soviet Union, on the assumption that economic retaliation might bring down Communism as well as benefit U.S. business interests.

Although there certainly was sympathy for Poland's resistance, just as there was revulsion against the Soviet invasion of Afghanistan, the more prevalent sentiment was that the United States was overreacting in both instances, and again at the expense of Europeans. This sense of grievance intensified when the Reagan administration suspended oil and gas technology sales to the Soviet Union to put teeth into sanctions. This action prohibited the export of technology manufactured by subsidiaries of American companies in Europe. The Reagan decision affected a planned pipeline from the Soviet Union to western Europe designed to carry natural gas to the West. This apparently thoughtless, automatic response to Soviet behavior did not sit well with the allies. Regulating European companies because of their American connections smacked of extraterritoriality, or at least an infringement on European sovereignty. The Europeans refused to abide by the American regulations, and prevailed after five months of wrangling with the United States.

THE UNITED STATES, NATO, AND THE FALKLANDS CRISIS, 1982

The hard-nosed anti-Soviet rhetoric—and policy that implemented it—led to new conflicts between Europeans and Americans. If Carter's perceived waffling over Soviet challenges distressed European leaders, Reagan's firmness itself created problems of perception. Allies who had begged America to respond to the SS-20s now wondered whether the response was too harsh and would generate a dangerous backlash from the Soviets. Such was the reaction of Chancellor Helmut Schmidt, the leading European opponent of Carter's policies.

But on balance, the Reagan position won more appreciation than his predecessor's principled efforts to balance an arms buildup with renewed efforts at accommodation with the Warsaw bloc. This was partly due to the arrival of new leadership in Britain and Germany. In both countries strong conservative governments under Margaret Thatcher and Helmut Kohl, in Britain and Germany respectively, displaced socialist administrations with records of hostility to the United States. The new leaders welcomed the firm positions and the forceful language that President Reagan offered and viewed American leadership more benignly than their predecessors had. In both cases, but particularly with respect to Thatcher,

Reagan established bonds that had not been seen in NATO since Eisenhower and Macmillan, or Dulles and Adenauer, were in office 20 years earlier. Thatcher and Kohl shared with Reagan concerns over Soviet behavior, whether in Afghanistan or in Europe, where Soviet missiles menaced western European targets.

A crisis in the South Atlantic arose in 1982 that cemented relations between Reagan and Thatcher and resuscitated the special relationship that had lapsed under the Conservative Prime Minister Edward Heath and the Labour leader James Callaghan. It was all the more intense because the clash between Britain and Argentina over the Falkland Islands was also a clash between America's old attachment to the Monroe Doctrine, which expressed opposition to European influence or control in the Western Hemisphere, and its new loyalty to the North Atlantic Treaty. In April 1982, the Argentine dictatorship attempted to occupy the Falklands, islands that the British had colonized in 1832. Both nations claimed the territory, which Argentina called the Malvinas. Its seizure of the islands was a demonstration of nationalist sentiment on the part of the country's dictatorship, which expected that this outpost, with its handful of occupants, would not be contested. Argentina, after all, had what some Americans considered a defensible case. In 1965 it had brought the Falklands issue to the United Nations, which sponsored what turned out to be unproductive negotiations between the two parties. Using the 150th anniversary of Britain's control of the islands as an occasion to demand its cession, the ruling junta took military action after Britain rejected its ultimatum.

When Britain responded with warships and an expeditionary force to aid the handful of shepherds and farmers, the United States faced a dilemma. If it did not support Argentina's actions, it risked antagonizing Latin American friends as well as arousing Americans around the banner of the Monroe Doctrine. On the other hand, if it turned its back on the British ally, the Atlantic alliance could be in jeopardy. Here was a clear-cut case of a new tradition confronting an old one.

Ultimately, the British ties prevailed, but not without considerable turmoil in Washington. The crisis over the Falklands was one of the factors that cost Secretary of State Alexander Haig his post. A strong supporter of London, Haig argued vigorously against Argentina's invasion of islands inhabited by British citizens. They were few in number, but the principle involved was important enough to inspire Britain to strike back at the aggressor. Secretary Haig recognized the "spirit of the Blitz" in Britain's dispatch of a task force of 100 ships and 28,000 men to retake the Falklands. He preferred to cast himself in the role of an honest broker, but when a choice had to be made, it was clearly with Britain. This brought Haig into conflict with Jeanne Kirkpatrick, U.S. ambassador to the United Nations, who feared the loss of solidarity with Latin America if the United States sided with Britain. A reawakening of Latin American nationalism as a consequence of the British action could damage American interests. Her choice would be to back Argentina.

An undercurrent in the dispute between Haig and Kirkpatrick was an Anglophobia reminiscent of American sentiment in the nineteenth century, during which

Britain represented all that was wrong with the Old World. One influential senator, Jesse Helms, a North Carolina Republican, supported Kirkpatrick's position, asserting that there was ample evidence that U.S. munitions were being shipped to Britain to kill Argentine soldiers. He was correct; the United States did provide military assistance to Britain in the name of alliance solidarity as well as in opposition to aggression. It is worth noting that of the 80 senators voting, Helms was the lone dissenter against a Senate resolution supporting Britain.

The Falklands were located in the South Atlantic, outside the boundaries of NATO's responsibilities, but the European allies joined the United States in expressing their unity on behalf of their British partner. It was a fragile unity, however, although the fragility was not the responsibility of the United States. If the war had not been concluded with a quick British victory, Italy might have wavered in its loyalty, given the large Italian population of Argentina. Additionally, the Socialist governments of France and Germany, although understanding the validity of the British action, worried about their constituencies' perception of an anticolonialist war in the Third World. The European allies might have complained—but did not—that NATO resources in the form of British naval forces were being diverted from their mission to serve one member's national interest. The upshot of the Falklands crisis was an affirmation of the solidity of the Atlantic alliance. It was also an opportunity for an expression of a transatlantic unity that was too frequently conspicuous by its absence.

TROUBLES OVER NUCLEAR ARMS, 1982–1983

Transatlantic comity inevitably was a transient phenomenon. There were too many competing forces separating Reagan's America from Europe for it to last. Yet the Anglo-American cooperation in the Falklands war consolidated a personal alliance between Prime Minister Thatcher and President Reagan that ameliorated tensions throughout the 1980s. The arrival of Helmut Kohl to power in 1972, replacing Socialist Helmut Schmidt, was another source of comfort to American policymakers. He shared with the Socialist president François Mitterand a skepticism about Soviet policies toward the West, as evidenced by the support France gave to Germany's decision to deploy the American cruise missiles in 1983. The commitment, as has been noted, was made in the dual-track decision of 1979, but the activation of the policy took four years to complete. The delay gave an opportunity for protests to develop, but there was no alternative; the missiles were not ready for deployment in 1979. Thatcher's Britain along with Kohl's Germany stood firmly behind the decision, and put the lives of their governments at risk in their nations' respective elections in 1983.

Although Thatcher and Kohl retained their offices, and the deployment of the cruise and Pershing II missiles proceeded as planned, these successes were accompanied by a wave of protest in Europe against the perceived American manipulation of the alliance. Reagan's entourage was part of the problem. When Secretary of State Alexander Haig, former supreme allied commander in Europe, was forced out of office, the administration seemingly dismissed the one American leader Europeans felt they could count on. His successor, George Shultz, a respected economist and former secretary of labor under Nixon, was inexperienced in foreign affairs and left room for more hawkish figures to direct the administration's foreign policy.

Reagan's anti-Communist rhetoric was translated by the European Left into a prelude to war against the Warsaw bloc. The formerly centrist Socialist parties of Britain and Germany had been radicalized in the 1980s, moving not merely toward opposition to the Atlantic alliance but to identifying the United States rather than the Soviet Union as the enemy of Europe. They found evidence of American imperialism in all parts of the world. In Africa, the United States supported the reactionary rebels in Angola against the pro-Communists who liberated the country from Portuguese colonialism; American money in Latin America backed the corrupt remnants of Anastasio Somoza's dictatorship against the Sandinistas seeking liberation from American domination. Only in Asia were there European objections to Soviet actions in Afghanistan, and even here the emotions expended against American imperialism in Latin America and Africa were deeper than those directed against Soviet intervention in Afghanistan. Critics concentrated on American rather than Soviet misbehavior.

Hostility to mighty America imposing its power on lesser nations was never confined to the radical left or to pacifists. The governments of the major European nations, allies of the United States, made their feelings heard in the UN Security Council in concert with the Soviet Union. The United States invaded tiny Grenada in 1983 to overthrow a Communist-controlled government charged with spreading Castro's doctrine in Central America. This military action evoked a UN Security Council resolution "deeply deploring" the intervention as a "flagrant violation of international law." The vote to condemn the United States won 11 votes in favor of the resolution, and among them were the NATO allies France and the Netherlands. Britain abstained. Only an American veto prevented adoption of the resolution.

The most powerful demonstration of opposition to the United States—and by extension, NATO itself—was over the ultimate deployment of cruise and Pershing II missiles in Germany and Britain in 1983. Mass protests in both countries preceded the elections, and they included pacifist and religious groups as well as Communist and pro-Communist elements. Many, but not all, of the demonstrations were orchestrated by Moscow. Communist arguments turned on the provocative nature of the missiles, with their ability to strike at the Soviet homeland. Peace demonstrators dwelled on the possibilities of a nuclear holocaust resulting from missile deployment. Few opponents were willing to look at the Soviet role in raising the level of fear in Europe.

Socialist newspapers in Belgium were convinced that even if the British and Germans accepted the American weapons, their country and the Netherlands would reject them. Shortly after the elections ratifying deployment of the American missiles in Germany and Britain, the Low Countries accepted them on their soil. Soviet intimidation that accompanied protests united rather than divided the alliance over this issue. The success of the Conservative governments at the polls in Britain and Germany affirmed NATO solidarity both over the extent of the Soviet threat embodied in the SS-20s and over the need for cruise and Pershing missiles to counter them.

If the deployment of missiles signaled a centripetal force in transatlantic relations, the lack of progress in arms control—the other half of the dual-track decision of 1979—was a centrifugal element that had preceded and followed the NATO decisions on deployment. There was gratitude among the allies for the steadfast opposition of the Reagan administration to Soviet pressure in Europe and at the same time dismay at America's disinterest, bordering on cynicism, in working toward arms reduction, nuclear or conventional, with the Soviet adversary. Whereas Europeans valued the American presence in Europe and appreciated its willingness to confront Moscow with cruise missiles, they were uncomfortable with the belligerence that accompanied its stance on arms negotiations.

There was reason enough for doubting the good faith of the Soviets. The stalling over a rational and balanced conventional force reduction had gone on for almost a decade before Reagan came to Washington. And the CSCE's success in the Helsinki agreements in 1975 only accentuated the selective application of its "baskets" to the advantage of the Soviet Union. It is hardly surprising that hard-liners in the new administration, such as Secretary of Defense Caspar Weinberger and Richard Perle, assistant secretary of defense for international affairs, dominated the scene. They were devoted advocates of a massive new military buildup and did their best to separate arms control from rearmament.

Their way of managing both was to place the burden of intransigency on the Soviets. Among the many efforts to manipulate suspicious Europeans was a semantic device to reassure allies while hewing to a strong line. The Theater Nuclear Force (TNF), which seemed to dissociate Europe's nuclear defense from America's, was replaced with the Intermediate-Range Nuclear Force (INF) as a more acceptable rubric for American missiles in Europe. The term *theater* could be construed as dissociating America from Europe.

Another approach to calming European tensions was the introduction in 1982 of Strategic Arms Reduction Talks (START) to replace the moribund SALT. The latter dealt only with "limitations" on nuclear arms, whereas President Reagan seemingly took a bolder step in asking for talks on "reduction" of nuclear arms. Rather than seeking an agreement that would do no more than codify and marginally influence the growth of strategic forces, the United States would make a proposal for substantial and verifiable reductions.

Instead of demonstrating solidarity with Europe's aspirations, the American offers appeared cosmetic and insincere. The director of the Arms Control and Disarmament Agency was an ardent opponent of both arms control and disarmament. Kenneth Adelman and his colleagues were convinced that U.S. security would be best guaranteed through unilateral action on strategic nuclear matters. START was consequently translated into a mock quid pro quo with the Soviets under the name of "zero option." If the Soviets would dismantle all their intermediate-range missiles, the United States would not deploy its 572 cruise and Pershing missiles. Superficially, this was as equitable and advantageous as any European ally would want. But in reality it was irrational to expect the Soviets, who already had their weapons in position, to give up their SS-20s in return for Americans giving up missiles that had not yet been deployed.

The immediate reaction abroad to the START proposals was not hostile. There was hope that this was a negotiating ploy, a first step in a compromise that would serve all parties. This was not the intention of the hawkish circle around the president, and not even the efforts of Paul Nitze, a former hawk himself, could make progress on START either through public diplomacy or through back-channel arrangements. Europeans were increasingly worried about American, not Soviet, inflexibility, and these worries even affected such champions of the American partnership as British Prime Minister Margaret Thatcher and West German Chancellor Helmut Kohl. They recognized the impossibility of securing a zero option in intermediate-range nuclear missiles in Europe, and hoped for a less ambitious agenda.

Paul Nitze, the chief American negotiator in Geneva, essentially agreed with the European critics, but his was almost a lone voice on this issue in the Reagan administration. But even if there had been a moderate response, the Soviets had no intention of moving toward a compromise. When the NATO allies finally accepted deployment of the cruise and Pershing missiles, the Soviets carried out their threat to walk away from the negotiating table in Geneva.

East–West relations had descended to levels not seen since the Cuban and Berlin crises of the 1960s. And West–West relations suffered as well, as European fears of American insensitivity to their vulnerabilities surfaced once again.

EUROPE AND "STAR WARS," 1983–1984

The Strategic Defense Initiative (SDI) will never shake the sobriquet of "Star Wars" because of its association with President Reagan. This former Hollywood actor and a devoted film watcher had been enchanted by the pyrotechnics in the film of that name, in which intergalactic warfare was conducted by what looked like space-based laser weapons. These appealed not only to his sense of drama but also to an ideal of a world made safe from nuclear war. But to European allies, the juxtaposition of this apparent streak of idealism with a fiery speech denouncing the Soviet Union as "the evil empire" in early March 1983, just two weeks before his Star Wars proposal, was confusing. It cast a shadow on the claim that by providing a perfect safety shield against an enemy attack, it would end the nuclear arms race as well as eliminate American vulnerability to intercontinental ballistic missiles. How serious was the president? What implication did his new enthusiasm have for the defense of the alliance?

This was ostensibly a plan to make nuclear war obsolete. The nuclear arms competition was "a sad commentary on the human condition." It would be far better, Reagan asserted in a speech on 23 March 1983, "to save lives than to avenge them." The president did talk with advisers, but his inspiration for this new direction in military policy came from the distinguished physicist Edward Teller who convinced him of the feasibility as well as the desirability of the new strategic initiative. Reagan was intrigued by the image of 50-foot-long bolts of high-energy electrons destroying any ICBM at nearly the speed of light—ultimate impregnability of America's defense system was the objective, to be achieved within the foreseeable future. But this was never the sole function of the SDI. Rather, the hope it opened in the future was a world free from nuclear nightmares.

Questions about the SDI immediately arose. Some skeptics recognized that it would require years, even decades, before the technology necessary to produce the miracle weapon would be available. Other skeptics with a hard-line, anti-Communist agenda saw in Star Wars a means of destroying the Soviet empire. It was not just that no Soviet missile could ever strike at the American continent, and so return Soviet power to the pre-Sputnik era; the advanced technology that the SDI would require would be too costly for the Soviets to develop, with consequent damage to their economy if they would make the attempt.

That the Warsaw bloc would not appreciate the benefits of the SDI was hardly surprising. But the transatlantic allies were no more welcoming than NATO's adversaries. There were three major concerns in the reactions of European allies. First, they worried that American technology would be advanced at Europe's expense, exacerbating the growing divide between the United States and Europe over their respective military capabilities. New consortiums of European defense industries had difficulty competing with their American counterparts. Even if the fruits of the SDI would not materialize until the distant future, there would be economic by-products of the research that would leave Europeans at a disadvantage in world markets. The Reagan administration did offer subcontracts that would engage allies in the enterprise, but it would be obvious that these entrepreneurs would not be the prime beneficiaries of the SDI's development. Second, Europeans wondered what effect the new venture would have on the Soviets. It was possible that it would only stimulate them to come up with new means to cope with America's future impregnable defense system. Even if the future was distant, energy in the present would be expended to expand their offensive capabilities. It was likely that the Soviet Union could always build new missiles that would over-come any defensive shield. Instead of enhancing the security of the West, SDI could make the East–West competition more dangerous than it had been since the crises of the early 1960s.

Disturbing as these scenarios were, a third element was the most serious issue between the United States and its partners. SDI could undermine the credibility of NATO's nuclear strategy that had been in place for over a decade. It was built on the principle of mutual assured destruction, a concept that McNamara had pro-moted in the Kennedy and Johnson administrations. It assumed that no defense was possible against a nuclear attack without an unacceptable loss of lives on both sides. Mutual vulnerability would be a deterrent against a strike. Such was the phi-losophy behind the ABM agreement signed by the United States and the Soviet Union in 1972. Although it applied essentially to intercontinental missiles, the ABM Treaty was a major milestone in the expansion of détente. It symbolized sta-bility between the superpowers that the allies valued even as they demanded other assurances with respect to IRBMs. Embarking on the Star Wars project intended to shield America—and presumably those allies willing to join—against a nuclear attack would make the ABM Treaty meaningless.

There was still another caveat about the SDI. It occurred inevitably to Euro-peans that a successful SDI would make NATO itself meaningless and useless to the American partners. If the United States had a perfect defense against a nuclear attack, it would not need a European involvement. Once again the cry of America decoupling itself from Europe was heard in the West. Would it lead to the with-drawal of U.S. troops from Europe and the abandonment of Article 5, leaving west-ern Europe prey to the ambitions of its Soviet neighbor? The suspension of IRBM arms control talks in 1983 contributed to the insecurity that the SDI inspired.

Continuing American dissatisfaction with Europe's reluctance to share more of the burden in conventional arms also played a role in raising tensions in the alliance as the SDI was preoccupying the Reagan administration. This was a familiar charge, but when it surfaced again in 1984 under the name of the Nunn–Roth amendment to the fiscal-year 1985 Defense Department budget, it struck a partic-ularly harsh chord among the allies. Its main author, Senator Sam Nunn of Georgia, was known to be one of the nation's strongest NATO supporters, and his putative jump into what had been the Mansfield camp of the 1960s appeared to be a power-ful signal of widespread American discontent with the allies. He proposed to man-date troop reductions in Europe by almost one-third unless the European members met the target commitment of 3 percent per annum real increase in defense expen-ditures. There was no countering the fact that while the United States since 1980 was more than doubling the minimum requirement approved by the North Atlantic Council, most European nations were failing to meet it.

The Nunn initiative shocked Europeans. German Foreign Minister Hans-Dietrich Genscher acted for his European colleagues by rushing to Washington to repair the damage. He need not have troubled. The amendment was a one-day phenomenon in the United States, intended only as a sign of American displeasure with Europe's role in NATO's defense. On the next day, the Senate replaced the amendment with a toothless resolution urging greater troop contribution that carried no specific threat. The Nunn action did not create a substantive change in European contributions, but it did jolt the allies into remembering that the American troop presence in the alliance was still a necessary and very visible entity on European soil.

The allies' reaction to the Nunn amendment reflected a sense of malaise that afflicted NATO in these years. A delegation from NATO headquarters made a point of asking at a conference on the Mediterranean theater in Italy in the spring of 1993 if the Lemnitzer Center for NATO Studies at Kent State University would serve as host for a team of NATO speakers. They feared an anti-NATO backlash from students prepared to abandon Europe and the alliance. The NATO team did not gather sufficient funds to make its tour in 1983. If it had done so, it might have been disappointed as well as relieved by their findings. The reasons for relief would have derived from the absence of any groundswell of revulsion against Europe on American campuses over the deployment of American missiles. At the same time, they might have been disappointed over the relative disinterest in European affairs and the lack of knowledge about the alliance. But if there was apathy in the universities, it seemed to signify a relationship with the outside world in the same way that abstention from European affairs had been the norm before World War II. NATO was accepted as a given in American foreign relations; apathy was not to be equated with antipathy.

TRANSATLANTIC COOPERATION IN THE MID-1980s

Instead of heightening transatlantic tensions, the outcome of the Nunn amendment was a reassuring signal of the continuing American commitment to Europe, whatever the status of SDI might be. When a group of distinguished American diplomats, including George Kennan, Robert McNamara, and McGeorge Bundy, issued a widely publicized call for "no first use" of nuclear weapons in 1982, the Reagan administration rejected it outright on the grounds that acceptance would deprive NATO of a vital deterrent. Despite the clamor for arms control, the allies welcomed the American action. Deterrence remained dependent on the potential of a nuclear response to Soviet aggression, as NATO's ultimate solidarity vis-à-vis the SS-20s attested.

SHAPE planners made a special point at this time of noting, as SACEUR Bernard Rogers did in 1984, that emerging technologies were being incorporated into NATO's defense structure. These would enhance the effectiveness of conventional forces, which in turn adopted new tactics to deter or defeat an assailant. Such measures as "follow-on forces attack"—striking at the Warsaw Pact forces behind front lines in the event of war—was a means of raising the nuclear threshold as well as giving heart to Europe's faith in the deterrent power of ground troops. The European allies may have been reluctant to increase their contribution of conventional forces, but they recognized and fitfully appreciated the efforts their senior partner was doing in their stead. And they had a right to remind the United States that despite the disappointing level of defense spending, the allies provided approximately 75 percent of NATO's readily available ground forces in Europe, 75 percent of the tanks, 65 percent of the air forces, and 60 percent of the naval vessels. The percentages were obviously higher when French forces were added to the list. The United States occasionally recognized these services, but never to the extent the allies felt they deserved.

Where successful transatlantic collaboration did take place in the mid-1980s was, ironically, in the Third World, largely on an informal basis. It was ironic because the most visible transatlantic conflicts had been out of area, in such places as Cuba, where the allies failed to follow America's lead in shunning Castro, and in Vietnam, where the United States appeared to divert its resources and attention away from NATO. Yet in the world outside NATO, member nations acting individually served the common interest in situations in which the United States could not intervene. The approach was usually through an informal distribution of responsibilities—witness French activity in Francophone Africa to defeat Soviet initiatives generally and specifically to repel Libyan aggression against Chad. Arguably, the most impressive service was performed by Italy, which took the leadership in helping liberate Malta from its Libyan-influenced leader Dom Mintoff in 1984. Neither the United States nor Britain would have been an acceptable partner to protect this important Mediterranean island from hostile powers. Lesser powers such as Italy and uncertain allies such as France found opportunities to move Third World nations out of the Soviet orbit more effectively than a show of NATO solidarity or American power might have managed.

THE GORBACHEV FACTOR, 1985–

The fast-changing leadership in the Soviet Union generated new fears of the adversary's intentions. Within a period of 16 months, three septuagenarian Soviet leaders led the nation, each molded by the attitudes of the Cold War and none prepared to change the status quo. Leonid Brezhnev had controlled the Politburo for over 18 years when he died on 10 November 1982. His successor, Yuri Andropov, a veteran of the KGB, was said to lean toward some reforms in the Soviet system before his death in February 1984. But it was under his leadership that the Soviet delegation walked out of the Geneva negotiations. Konstantin Chernenko was in no better health than Andropov; he barely survived a year in office, and had no more to offer than his predecessor to resumption of serious talks with the West. These old men were beset by problems with coping with the U.S. missile deployment and with the implications of the SDI. But their health and idées fixes about relations with the United States assured only the continuation of stasis. There were no actions on the part of either superpower to give comfort to the European NATO allies in this period.

The accession to power of the 55-year-old Mikhail Gorbachev as general secretary of the Central Committee of the Communist Party on 11 March 1985 might have portended an extension of the negative approach of the three men who preceded him. As a protégé of Andropov, he fitted the image of a younger version of his mentor. But the image would have been misleading. Conceivably, the reforms that the ailing Andropov wished to impose on the Soviet system were the inspiration for the opening and reconstruction (glasnost and perestroika) that marked the Gorbachev years in office. Whether this was their source or not, they became the leitmotifs of Gorbachev's policies from 1985 to the end of the Cold War. What he wanted in domestic policy was never fully clear; it centered on de-emphasizing funds for military ends and redirecting them to other uses in the Soviet economy. It was clear enough, however, that his intentions were not to overturn the system and adopt Western capitalism, but to strengthen it to cope better with the economic power of the West. In foreign policy his means seemed to have been as candid as his objectives, namely, to end the Cold War that was so costly to the nation's well-being, and to reintegrate the Soviet Union into what he called "a common European home."

These objectives were just what the European allies had been seeking ever since détente had been on their agenda. That the United States may be left out of this "home" was a problem because it would raise questions about the future of NATO itself. Nor was it axiomatic that the Gorbachev opening guaranteed an end to the Cold War. Could the Soviets now be trusted as new partners?

Inevitably, this question agitated the hawkish members of the Reagan team. Weinberger's Pentagon remained skeptical of a sudden Soviet conversion, and was uncomfortable with the Soviet leader's proposal of a Reagan–Gorbachev summit in Geneva that would take place in November 1985. But unlike their role in Reagan's first term in office, they were less influential in the second; Shultz's more accommodating State Department had taken their place, with Paul Nitze in the lead. The president was impressed with Gorbachev's return of Soviet delegates to Geneva to discuss new arms control negotiations that encompassed space systems, strategic nuclear forces, and INF issues. Reagan's rhetoric and attitude toward Communism had softened. A year before Gorbachev arrived on the scene, the president had addressed the 34-nation Stockholm Conference on Confidence-and-Security-Building Measures and Disarmament in Europe (CDE), at which he spoke of a new dialogue with the Soviet Union, and in February 1985, just a month before the formal announcement of succession in Moscow, the *NATO Review*, the alliance's official organ, featured a photograph of a broadly smiling Secretary of State George Shultz shaking hands with a more constrained Soviet Foreign Minister Andrei Gromyko, a veteran spokesman of the Soviet Cold War against the West. The caption above the photograph read that new negotiations were to begin. The photo opportunity would not have been possible without the support of the president.

THE REYKJAVIK GAMBIT, 1986

Gorbachev showed by the end of 1985 that he was more than willing to respond to Reagan's initiatives and, indeed, to assume leadership himself in reducing the levels of nuclear weaponry. The Geneva Summit meeting between the two leaders in November 1985 was the occasion for him to assert his interest in a 50 percent reduction in nuclear arms. Fascinated European observers were not wholly relieved by this aspiration. There was no specific common understanding about whether this reduction would apply to strategic arms, to intermediate-range weapons, or to space systems. Nor was there any sign of advances in the long-standing negotiations on MBFR negotiations in Vienna toward a verifiable agreement for Warsaw Pact–NATO reduction of ground forces. The allies had a right to wonder how a generalized, 50 percent cut in nuclear forces would affect their security, particularly if it would be a bilateral Soviet–American arrangement produced without their involvement.

Yet the momentum that had been building toward constructive relations in 1985 accelerated in 1986. It was embodied in the agreement of the two leaders to visit each other's respective countries in the near future as well as in the conclusions of the Stockholm conference. The CDE required mandatory notification and observation of military activities throughout Europe, from the Atlantic to the Urals. These measures would apply to all of Soviet Europe, and not just the 250-kilometer-wide strip along the USSR (Union of Soviet Socialist Republics) western border (as under the Helsinki Final Agreement of 1975). There would be no right of refusal of on-the-spot verification inspections.

These events provided the psychological infrastructure for the meeting of Reagan and Gorbachev in Reykjavik, Iceland, in October 1986. There the subtexts of Gorbachev's policies became apparent, to the consternation of the European allies. His immediate goal was to undercut the American commitment to the SDI, an objective that Europeans for their own reasons did not find objectionable. Recognizing that it was unlikely there would be any breakthrough along conventional diplomatic lines, Gorbachev went directly to the president himself, presumably to sign an interim agreement on the INF that would leave some missiles in Europe. The SDI was not part of the agenda. At the last minute, he offered instead a grand compromise on both offensive and defensive weapons to an unwary Reagan. The Soviet premier's proposal was to have both sides get rid of all nuclear weapons rather than dicker over piecemeal arrangements. This was a "classic bait-and-switch operation," as *Time* journalist Strobe Talbott called it, a way of eliminating the troublesome SDI without admitting this purpose. The SDI, after all, was a nuclear instrument. If removing the SDI would be the end result of the Reykjavik meeting, the European allies would have been relieved. But the removal of all nuclear weapons was another matter; this would include both strategic and intermediate-range nuclear missiles that would strip Europe of protection from the Soviet ICBMS and force NATO to rely on conventional forces alone against the Warsaw bloc.

The president initially saw none of these implications. He had enjoyed his encounter with Gorbachev in Geneva, and was pleased to continue the colloquy in Reykjavik, approximately halfway between Moscow and Washington. Confident in his powers of persuasion, he felt he could bring the Soviet leader around to recognizing that the SDI would be of benefit to both countries. His advisers were less sanguine about these prospects. The week before the meeting, Rozanne Ridgway, assistant secretary of state in charge of European affairs, tried to discourage excessive expectations when she informed Congress that this was essentially a preparatory meeting, an opportunity for private and informal talks, in anticipation of Gorbachev's visit to the United States.

The State Department was justified in its uneasiness over the meeting in Iceland. American diplomats feared that an aging president, never educated in the arcane arts of diplomacy, would be maneuvered by the younger man into making arrangements that would damage the nation's security and throw relations with the European allies into turmoil. The initiative behind closed doors appeared to have been Gorbachev's when he pressed Reagan to respect the ABM Treaty of 1972 and to accept an interpretation of that treaty that would prohibit development of the SDI outside of laboratory research. Fortunately, from the perspective of its partisans, the president would not yield to the Soviet views on the SDI.

What disturbed Europeans was less the president's intransigence over the SDI than his apparently impulsive counterproposal to eliminate, within 10 years, not just intermediate-range nuclear missiles but all missiles and, as Senator Sam Nunn observed, "everything else, including bombs." It was as if the Soviets had finally taken up the zero option proposal of 1982 and carried it to an extreme, which, if implemented, would have removed U.S. nuclear presence from Europe. Richard Perle and other hawkish American critics thought at the time that the 1982 proposal was so skewed against Soviet interests that it would never be accepted. In fact, the zero-zero option was what Gorbachev specifically endorsed, with Reagan, for the moment at least, joining in enthusiastically. Only the SDI stood in the president's way of achieving the zero-zero option. The prospect of removing all nuclear weapons from the NATO arsenal while keeping alive only the SDI would accelerate the pace of America's decoupling itself from Europe.

Reagan's State Department was almost as shocked as the allies at the cavalier way in which the president was ready to cast off nuclear defenses. Although the White House quickly rephrased Reagan's statements to take the sting out of its implications, Europeans were not wholly calmed by the communiqué applauding the meeting's effort on behalf of balanced reduction of conventional forces without addressing their concerns.

EUROPE AND THE INF AGREEMENT OF 1987

Despite the apparent standoff at Reykjavik over Star Wars, the Soviets continued their campaign to reduce both strategic and medium-range nuclear weapons, and found an increasingly receptive partner in Washington. The Reykjavik meeting brought to the surface an issue that would be picked up later: a 50 percent reduction of strategic missiles over a 10-year period. The meeting also opened the way for an INF treaty signed in Washington on 8 December 1987. This agreement would remove 470 of the Soviet INF missiles (SS-20s, SS-4s, and SS-5s) and 429 of the American cruise and Pershing II missiles. For the first time, there would be machinery in place to enforce compliance. A key element was the establishment of a force of 200 inspectors, 200 monitors, and 200 aircrew members from each side to verify the phased reductions over a 13-year period. The signing of this treaty seemed to testify to the success of NATO's linkage of defense preparations with a peaceful détente.

On another level, however, the INF Treaty raised a host of questions about the future of the alliance that could have led to its dissolution if its members failed to respond to the new challenges. Former SACEUR General Bernard Rogers feared that western Europe was "on the slippery slope of denuclearization," a prospect that alarmed many of the European allies. The 1987 INF Treaty seemed to give credence to concerns about the United States turning away from its allies. Like the abortive Reykjavik discussions the year before, the two superpowers could be on the verge of working out their own détente at the expense of the NATO allies. These possibilities poisoned the atmosphere despite the genuine success the treaty had achieved in minimizing the SS-20 threat that had hung over the European allies. This outcome would lose its luster if the end product of these efforts toward de-escalating East–West tensions should be the removal of American troops as well as American missiles from Europe.

A species of schizophrenia characterized the European reaction to the changing environment in the Soviet Union. On the one hand there was some disbelief in the sincerity and durability of the Gorbachev reforms, but if they were credible, what effect would they have on relations with the transatlantic ally? If NATO, empowered by the American presence in Europe, should dissolve, would this be in the interest of the European allies? No matter how much friction there had been between America and Europe, Europeans recognized that their freedom to oppose American leadership derived from a knowledge that the United States remained a firm ally. After 40 years of dependency, standing alone could present troublesome scenarios.

At the same time, there was a sense of triumph in the West. This emotion was hardly surprising as the allies watched Gorbachev's policies tearing down the barriers that had been built up between East and West for more than a generation. Not only was there unilateral Soviet reduction in conventional forces to match reductions in nuclear weaponry, there was also the loosening of controls over the Warsaw Pact allies. When the first multicandidate elections in an open contest in March 1989 rebuffed official Communist Party candidates for the Congress of Peoples' Deputies in the Soviet Union, the floodgates were opened in Poland and Hungary and Czechoslovakia and Romania. Glasnost had reached the Warsaw bloc, leading to the overthrow of its Communist regimes in each of these nations. Gorbachev unwittingly and unwillingly had opened a Pandora's box to let out the repressed passions of nationalism and anti-Communism.

In this new world, Europeans could be excused if they believed that America was less necessary to their lives than in the past. A presentiment of European unity was in the air, propelled by the growing power of the European Economic Community. For half a generation, since the *Wirtschaftswunder* of the 1960s, Europe had the potential of equaling, if not surpassing, both the United States and the Soviet Union in economic power. Its population was larger than both superpowers, and two of its members had nuclear capabilities that could serve a potential United States of Europe. There was reason to anticipate the flowering of a genuine third force in the Western Union in the 1990s.

As events rapidly unfolded in the wake of the INF Treaty of 1987, NATO itself was confined to the sidelines by Gorbachev's initiatives, and remained a step or more behind the Soviets, without a clear sense of the changes that were convulsing the Warsaw bloc. Its leaders were concerned that the European public might be lulled into complacency by Gorbachev's style. Although reductions in conventional armaments were welcome, particularly if they were asymmetrical, the European partners continued to worry about the nuclear dimension. They saw no evidence of arms reductions in the Soviet modernization program even as large cuts in nuclear warheads were projected for the near future.

To cope with a potential danger that a new generation of Soviet nuclear weaponry might inflict, SACEUR General John Galvin advocated the deployment of an improved short-range nuclear missile. But instead of welcoming NATO's plans to modernize the reduced tactical nuclear weaponry in Europe, Germans balked at the prospect. Whereas the Lance missile might be more efficient as a battlefield weapon, it would strike only forces in Europe, most notably in Germany, if it were deployed. At another time, when the Soviet words and actions were more threatening, these misgivings would have been muted. But proposing more advanced weaponry at a time when Gorbachev was delivering on his promise to forge a new relationship with the West seemed needlessly provocative. The increasing German opposition to the acquisition of new short-range missiles was part of a more general complaint against NATO maneuvers—tanks that chewed up arable land and planes that generated unbearable noise pollution. Sacrifices that would be bearable in times of peril now were unacceptable. Understandably, Chancellor Kohl urged postponement of a decision until after the next German elections.

Here was the dilemma. Although NATO recognized the importance of maintaining and even strengthening the organization's defense posture, there remained a residue of distrust of Soviet intentions. General Galvin noted in May 1989 that since March 1985, when Gorbachev took power, the Soviets continued to expand production of tanks and artillery. Such reductions in conventional forces that Gorbachev announced at the United Nations in December 1988 would make at best only a modest dent on their offensive capabilities. Uneasiness about Soviet objectives was shared by the leadership on both sides of the Atlantic. Were the Soviets just offering a variation of the old plans to lull Europe into inaction and to drive the United States out of Europe?

Yet public opinion in the member nations necessitated a response to the adversary's deepening of détente. An American counterpart to the Soviet peace offensive took forms that disturbed Europeans. From the right wing came the charge that the lack of support given by the allies to the common cause should induce the United States to leave the alliance and encourage Europeans to make their own security arrangements. Two familiar themes that seemed receptive to many Americans were the unfair sharing of the defense burden, and the potential but still untapped strength of an almost-but-not-united-enough Europe. Voices of pundits from the left wing in the United States were equally loud in urging withdrawal. The United States, in their view, should use its good offices to demilitarize the Continent because the Soviet threat was no longer valid. They agreed with the Green Party in Germany and the radical wing of the Labour Party in Britain that the United States military presence in Europe was an obstacle to peace. It was apparent as NATO celebrated its fortieth anniversary that the alliance could be in greater danger from Soviet benevolence than the malevolence displayed in the past.

THE CHALLENGE OF GERMAN REUNIFICATION, 1989–1990

As the Cold War lurched into its final phase, the transatlantic problems within the alliance assumed new forms. The dissolution of the Soviet Union and the Warsaw Pact in 1991 should have terminated most of the conflicts in the organization.

It did not; in fact, for a variety of reasons, the end of the East–West rivalry served to intensify West–West differences. But before the final collapse of the Communist empire, the reunification of Germany opened a new schism in the West, along less-familiar but not altogether new lines. The unification of Germany in the wake of the loosening of Soviet controls over its allies, symbolized by the razing of the Berlin Wall in November 1989, brought the United States and Germany together in opposition—often sotto voce—to Britain and France.

It would not be the first time that the United States took stances with respect to Germany that created intra-European conflict. It was American pressure for a German contribution to the alliance in the wake of the Korean War that produced France's defensive Pleven Plan. And when the resulting EDC failed in 1954, the United States threatened to make a bilateral treaty with Germany at the expense of France. As noted earlier, these were examples of transatlantic conflict but they were also symptoms of division within Europe itself. In 1989 the issue was even more volatile because the possibility of reunification was so unexpected. Its reality forced the allies to come to grips with an outcome that none had anticipated—that the Soviet Union would actually release East Germany from its grip and permit Germans the freedom to choose their own government. This, after all, was what NATO presumably had been seeking since the 1950s and had been the reason for Chancellor Adenauer to throw West Germany into the arms of NATO.

Whether the rapid breakdown of authority in the Warsaw bloc was a result of the Soviets' inability to match America's expensive military expansion or a result of a Gorbachev plan that got out of hand is a debatable question. What is not at issue is that Gorbachev's tacit approval of political reforms in Poland in April 1989 led to the election of a non-Communist government in Poland by August. The urge to oust the Communist regimes in the Warsaw bloc now seemed to be irresistible as well as contagious. Between September and December, Hungary, Czechoslovakia, Bulgaria, and Romania had removed their Communist leaders, by free elections in Czechoslovakia, by violence in Romania.

But it was East Germany, the German Democratic Republic, the most important member of the Soviet bloc, that quickened the end of the Communist empire. A domino effect was in process when Hungary opened its western border in September, permitting thousands of East Germans to cross freely to the West. When Gorbachev urged reforms a month later, popular demonstrations forced the replacement of Erich Honecker, a symbol of the Brezhnev era, and two months later were responsible for tearing down the Berlin Wall, a symbol of the Khrushchev era. The road to German unification was cleared of its major obstacles. The dismantling of the Wall was the most striking signal that the end was approaching. What was apparent to so much of Europe—in the West as well as in the East—took longer to reach American leaders: that the Cold War was indeed in the final throes of dissolution and that the Wall's destruction was the end product of changes taking place throughout the Warsaw bloc.

But a vital by-product of the changed environment was incorporation of East Germany into the Federal Republic in 1990, less than a year after the Wall had fallen. Although this was a logical position of the last falling domino, it still elicited surprise and shock among both NATO allies and the Soviet adversary. The rhetoric of unification notwithstanding, few outside Germany believed that it was possible in their lifetime. A revealing moment occurred in September 1989, at a meeting in Brussels of future leaders of NATO, under the auspices of the NATO Information Directorate. At one session, a young British member of Parliament asked a German general from SHAPE what kind of thinking were he and his colleagues doing about German reunification. Recognizing that this was a mischievous question, he gave a supercilious reply, saying with a wide grin that they were doing as little thinking as possible. The possibility was too far-fetched. This meeting took place just six weeks before the Wall was dismantled, to the surprise of the NATO establishment. At the Brussels conference, the expectation was that the modernization of the Lance missile would be the most pressing NATO issue in the year ahead.

There was always a question about the desirability as well as the possibility of a single Germany. Doubters included German leaders as well as those from their allies. Adenauer's devotion to the principle had been suspect. His more enduring goal was incorporation of the Federal Republic into the West as a means of burying an ugly past. As a Catholic Rhinelander, he identified East Germany with Prussia and Protestantism, which were outside his vision of the future, despite his political rhetoric. Nor was Brandt's accommodation with the Warsaw bloc a support for unification. Ostpolitik accepted the reality of two German states. These German sentiments were seconded by many in the West, particularly in France, who were worried about the direction a strong, populous, ambitious Germany would take. The carefully crafted relationship with Adenauer's Germany was intended to maintain France's seniority in the partnership. Uniting the Germanies threatened to reverse the roles and revive fears that had been repressed for a generation. Britain may have lacked the memories and defeat that afflicted France, but Britain had its own long memory of opposing the dominance of any single Continental power.

The idea of two separate Germanies appealed as well to the Soviet Union. Like France, it had vivid memories of two world wars involving a powerful, united Germany. Not only would the Communist German Democratic Republic be a bulwark of the Warsaw bloc, but it would inhibit the ambitions of the Federal Republic. The disassembling of the Wall and the wild celebrations that event inspired among Germans jolted all their neighbors into a recognition that they were more comfortable with the status quo than with the prospect of a unified German state. As historian Frank Ninkovich observed, "after the bacchanal in the streets of Berlin came sober morning-after thoughts in Western capitals."

There was no cheering in Paris and London, and there was some puzzlement in Washington. Although events went too fast for President George H. W. Bush,

American leaders shared none of the visceral dread that afflicted their European allies. The American role in the rapid envelopment of East Germany into the West within a year of the fall of the Wall attested to a significant difference between America and Europe. Bush was certainly willing to join the British and French as well as the Soviets in trying to slow the momentum of reunification, but he lacked the emotional baggage carried by European victims of German occupation. It was this relative objectivity on the part of the United States that facilitated Chancellor Helmut Kohl's rejection of a confederation of East and West Germany in favor of absorption of the Communist state into a greater Germany.

Anglo-French resistance to immediate incorporation of East Germany into an enlarged Federal Republic was more than matched by open Soviet opposition. Gorbachev undoubtedly underestimated the momentum the removal of the Wall would have on German aspirations. Soviet leaders became concerned a bit belatedly about the ramifications of Kohl's plans for "federation" that would emerge from his proposal of binational commissions to arrange the process. The Soviets recognized that settled boundaries could be scrambled, including commitments under the Helsinki agreements. Their allies in the Warsaw bloc would be affected psychologically as well as politically, and their assets in East Germany, including the enclave of Kaliningrad, might come under review. Not least among Soviet worries was the question of East Germany becoming a part of NATO after unification. Gorbachev turned against the unifying process in the months following the opening of the Wall, and he had quiet support from Germany's NATO neighbors.

If British and French reservations were not blatant, they were not invisible. President François Mitterand of France, miffed that Kohl had not consulted him before announcing his plans, visited East Germany and the Soviet Union, presumably to check their sentiments. The French president spoke of deepening rather than widening the European Community, a not-too-subtle objection to impending change. Prime Minister Margaret Thatcher wondered about an excessively powerful new Germany and its impact on Europe. Only in the United States were both public opinion and the administration supportive of rapid reintegration, although with recognition that it should be accompanied by assurances of a united Germany's attachment to NATO and the West.

What forced the hand of all the interested parties was the disintegration of the German Democratic Republic. Where East Germany would go was a vital question. A neutral, united Germany outside NATO was not a prospect its western neighbors, or even some of the Warsaw bloc associates, would welcome. The answer was to anchor Germany inside NATO, in the manner of the Federal Republic in 1955, with promises to the Soviets that NATO forces would not move into East Germany. Additionally, generous financial arrangements would be made to facilitate the withdrawal of Soviet troops from Germany. To advance the process, Secretary of State James A. Baker proposed what was called the "2+4" approach. The "2" referred to the two Germanies that would settle internal issues between themselves; the "4" were the most interested and most influential nations—the former occupying powers that would determine the new Germany's place in Europe.

Again, the demands of East Germans for immediate incorporation undid the timetable that NATO and the Soviets would have preferred. The waiting period via a confederation of the two German states fell by the wayside. Gorbachev tried to stem the tide with a proposal in June of a five-year transition period in which the two Germanies would retain their alliance obligations. He failed. The momentum for reunification was too strong to resist—by the West as well as by the East. Neither the "2" nor the "4" could prevent Chancellor Kohl from winning his objective; the most that Gorbachev's plan could achieve was to ratify the termination of the remnants of the Four-Power occupation rights in Germany. A united Germany would stay in NATO and Soviet forces would leave gradually over a four-year period, after which German troops under NATO auspices would be stationed in the East. As compensation to the Soviets, Germany would bear the costs of their military withdrawal. Limits would be placed on German forces in the form of reduced size of the Bundeswehr and a pledge that neither non-German NATO troops nor nuclear weapons would be located in the former East Germany. After the East German legislature voted to join the West in August, a formal treaty of unification was signed in August 1990. Behind the scenes, the United States support heartened Chancellor Kohl's drive for reunification. His success seemed to validate NATO's mission to contain (and ultimately overturn) the Communist East and to integrate a unified Germany into the democratic West.

The Cold War ended in NATO's forty-first year. For a brief moment the allies could savor the sense that they had prevailed over the Soviet adversary while maintaining its own coherence. Granted that the unity was precarious, and that examples of friction were more numerous than those of harmony, they were able to keep their differences within the NATO family. Whether the alliance could survive after the demise of the Soviet Union and the Warsaw Pact remained open to question. But unlike the Warsaw Pact, it had a future in the last decade of the twentieth century. Would the end of the Cold War destroy NATO's raison d'être? Was it only the existence of a common adversary in the Soviet Communist regime that maintained allied cohesion despite the many challenges over almost two generations? If so, the future of NATO in the post–Cold War era would be in doubt.

6

SEEKING NEW MISSIONS: 1990–2000

TOWARD A NEW STRATEGIC CONCEPT

The domino effect that Gorbachev set in motion in 1985 finally came to rest in 1991, and in that interval Germany was reunited, the Warsaw bloc was disbanded, and the Soviet Union itself imploded. The Baltic republics regained the independence they had lost in 1940, and the Commonwealth of Independent States (CIS) replaced the Union of Soviet Socialist Republics (USSR). The difference between the two entities was that the USSR was controlled from its center in Moscow, while Russia in the CIS was just one of several loosely associated independent nations. These dramatic changes left the United States as the sole superpower.

But where did they leave NATO? And what implication did these changes have for the United States and its European allies in NATO? For a brief moment, celebrated by the euphoric predictions of U.S. State Department official Francis Fukuyama, the world appeared to be witnessing not just the end of the Cold War but the end of history itself. The success of the West in the long contest with Communism would mean the universal acceptance of Western democracy as the final form of government for all nations. This putative cancellation of the Hegelian dialectic encountered too many obstacles to be credible, but even if it was never more than a passing aspiration, it called attention to the future of NATO. Without the Soviet menace to serve as a unifying glue, there seemed ample reason to recommend its dissolution.

This was not idle speculation. At a meeting of the North Atlantic Council in London in June 1990, pro forma recognition was given to the military capabilities the Soviet Union possessed even as the council's communiqué proclaimed the substantial decrease in military risks. But more attention was paid to the Conference on the Security and Cooperation in Europe (CSCE) as "a central element in the construction of a new Europe." Given a membership that embraced both the United States and the Soviet Union as well as 34 European and Asian countries, it is understandable if some thought was given to the CSCE as a "framework for far-reaching reforms and stability" in Europe. If NATO remained essentially an entity dedicated to the defeat of Communism and the containment of Soviet expansionism, it could be replaced by an organization more suited to the changing international environment.

The CSCE was not the only vehicle considered in place of an obsolescent NATO. A reinvigorated United Nations to which the framers of the alliance had paid lip service might also make NATO unnecessary. Because the reformed Soviet Union was no longer the source of automatic vetoes in the Security Council, it was possible for the United Nations to revive its charter's Article 47, which established a Military Staff Committee to assist the Security Council's military requirements. Unlike the doomed League of Nations, the United Nations would have military contingents to give teeth to its resolutions. But as long as the Cold War was in process, there was no prospect of this committee serving as an agent for collective security of the member nations. With the end of the Cold War in sight in 1990, the Soviets might be inclined to take on a more positive role in the Security Council.

NATO AND THE GULF WAR

The moribund Soviet Union reluctantly acquiesced in the Security Council to the Gulf War that ignited in the winter of 1991 after an aggressive Iraq occupied neighboring Kuwait. But the United Nations was in no position to use the Military Staff Committee even if the United States had supported it. Only one organization could manage a successful military action against a country that threatened the oil resources of the Middle East and, in particular, the survival of Saudi Arabia. Only NATO with its forces centered in Europe and with its own stake in a stable Middle East could do this. In December 1990, both the North Atlantic Council's Defense Planning Committee and its foreign ministers, meeting in a ministerial session in Brussels, praised UN resolutions calling for the withdrawal from Kuwait and for all NATO members to "further support this continuing effort, in line with evolving requirements."

It is noteworthy that the recommendations for each member to provide support did not signify that the American-led war against Iraq in 1991 was a NATO effort any more than it was a UN operation. The UN resolutions were a useful diplomatic screen for U.S. defense of its own interests, and putatively of NATO's as well. But beyond this aid, the idea of giving meaning to Article 47 of the UN charter was never seriously considered. The Joint Chiefs of Staff would have objected to subordinating U.S. contingents to a UN command in 1991 no matter how the composition of the Security Council had changed.

But a NATO command could have been a different matter. Although Article 5 would not have been applicable, the allies might have converted the coalition into a NATO operation under the rubric of Article 4 of the North Atlantic Treaty, which authorized consultation "together whenever, in the opinion of any of them, the territorial integrity, political independence or security of any of the Parties is threatened." NATO intervention in the Persian Gulf would have required a broad construction of that article, but "security" involved protection of oil resources and the potential spread of Iraqi aggression to the neighboring nation, Turkey. The "out-of-area"—beyond the specific territorial limits of Article 6—was an arena in which NATO might have acted under a formula the allies had accepted in 1982 at a Bonn summit meeting at which they agreed not only to consult on out-of-area deployment but also to compensate the United States for the costs it would incur. But while the allies sought justification for its survival in the post–Cold War era and found a common cause in their opposition to Iraq's invasion of Kuwait, they could not bring themselves to embrace common action in a specifically NATO context. Articles 4 and 6 lacked the credibility of Article 5.

The Persian Gulf War in the winter of 1991 then was an American war conducted from Washington, not from Brussels. Yet it was also a coalition of the willing (most of them members of the alliance) blessed by the UN Security Council. Twelve of the 16 NATO allies provided forces to the coalition. The United States was able to draw on the military infrastructure NATO had created over the years. Britain and France dispatched troops to the Gulf while other allies facilitated the transit of U.S. aircraft through their logistical support. In the course of the buildup and the subsequent rapid victory over Iraq, the kinds of transatlantic tensions that had been visible during much of the Cold War were in abeyance. France may not have returned to the SHAPE military fold but its ground troops were present in the assault against Iraq.

The one openly dissenting voice in this crisis was Germany's, and it was expressed over the possible invocation of Article 5 if Iraq attacked neighboring Turkey. Its initial reaction was to assert that the nation would not be bound by its treaty obligations if Turkey were attacked. Germany's justification for its stance on the application of Article 5 was that U.S. use of Turkish bases to strike Iraq could be construed as a provocation that relieved that government from having to aid Turkey if Iraq retaliated. An unstated reason for German reluctance to join the allies stemmed from concern that the Soviets might back away from ratifying the treaty unifying East and West Germany if they were offended by Bonn's joining its allies in an operation the Soviets had accepted so reluctantly. But before the war ended, a German air squadron was dispatched to Turkey as part of NATO's support of their Turkish ally.

The triumph of the coalition over Saddam Hussein's forces had a centripetal effect on allied unity. Frictions between America and Europe seemed a relic of the past as the allies were energized by their victory. The Defense Planning Committee and the Nuclear Planning Group, meeting in Brussels in May 1991, not only welcomed the success of the coalition forces in the Gulf War but gave credit to the alliance for the air and naval forces deployed to the Persian Gulf to deter a potential attack on its members. This celebratory note did not change the reality of a war in which NATO allies functioned outside the control of the alliance's military structure. But NATO's virtual representation in the Gulf War reinvigorated the alliance and pointed to roles it might occupy in the future. In other words, a case may be made for the war serving as a life preserver for the alliance.

RAPID REACTION FORCE VERSUS EUROCORPS

Two immediate changes flowed directly from the experience in the Persian Gulf, and both posed problems for transatlantic comity. One of them arose in May 1991 when NATO defense ministers unveiled a plan for managing future military crises with smaller forces. The allies would establish a multinational rapid-reaction corps composed of four divisions based in Germany under British command. Although personnel would be drawn from Germany, the Low Countries, Italy, Greece, Spain, and possibly Turkey, its core rested on Anglo-American collaboration. The United States would provide tactical airlift and sealift transportation for the corps and two of the four divisions would be British. The other two would consist of an Italian division supplemented by Greek and Turkish support, and a mixed division with Dutch, Belgian, German, and British elements. In the initial stage of a crisis, a mobile unit of 5,000 troops would respond within 72 hours. The corps' rapid mobility was expected to compensate for reduced numbers of troops. These forces would be augmented by contributions from all willing members and would include U.S. Reserve and National Guard units that could be dispatched over a period of weeks. The Rapid Reaction Force (RRF) would be under British command and headquartered in London. The implications in these deliberations involved out-of-area operations that sought to anticipate and forestall crises of the order that Iraq had created in that year.

Although these plans not only reflected the crisis of 1991, they were by extension identifying a mission the alliance might follow in the post–Cold War era. But a major obstacle stood in their way—the obvious dominance of the Anglo-Saxon members in the Rapid Reaction Force. Other allies were given a minor place in the force, and France in particular was left out entirely. This omission was not inadvertent. The concept of an RRF was a product of NATO's Defense Planning Committee (DPC) and the Nuclear Planning Group (NPG), two bodies in which France was not represented. Inevitably, the combination of an unequal distribution of power in the new force with the exclusion of France revived some of the transatlantic tensions that had been lessened by the impending implosion of the Soviet Union and dissolution of the Warsaw Pact.

These activities sparked France's initiative in establishing a Franco-German counter to the British-led force. Germany's Chancellor Helmut Kohl was almost as uncomfortable with the prospect of serving under a British command as President François Mitterand was. Their response was to create a "Eurocorps," building on the Franco-German brigade that had been in progress since 1987. This brigade symbolized the Franco-German rapprochement that had been solemnized in the Elysée Treaty of 1963, fashioned by Charles de Gaulle and Konrad Adenauer. Ultimately this force would consist of 35,000 personnel when it gathered contributions from other Western European Union (WEU) powers.

The multinational model that France would not accept under NATO auspices advanced in October 1991 under the rubric of the WEU. Given France's ambiguous position in NATO over the past generation, it was hardly surprising that it would support a rival program to effect the same objective of managing small-scale, out-of-area problems affecting European security, but under French leadership. Unstated but nevertheless a factor in the French initiative was that country's felt need to be assured that the German military would be more securely anchored in a French-dominated corps than in the more loosely knit NATO context. Less understandable was the German rationale for membership in both forces, one inside NATO, the other outside. Germany rationalized the apparent contradiction by claiming that the Eurocorps was necessary to justify maintaining a French military presence in Germany. Not least among the reasons for its identification with the French approach was the major role Germany would play in the Eurocorps, as opposed to the lesser assignment in the RRF. A subtext for American consumption was Germany's potential service as the middle man between NATO and the WEU, using its influence to bring France closer to NATO.

NATO'S ROME SUMMIT AND THE EUROPEAN UNION'S MAASTRICHT SUMMIT

French leadership was evident in the transformation of the European Community into the European Union (EU) at a summit meeting of European powers in Maastricht in December 1991, two months after the formation of the Eurocorps. Out of this gathering emerged the promise of a common foreign and security policy, using the WEU as its instrument. Although the path to the objective of a European defense identity was not clear, the idea of the WEU as an arm of the EU was a signal of European independence of the United States, and perhaps of NATO itself.

Divorce from NATO was not the stated purpose of the Maastricht summit's plans; the defense capabilities of an independent Europe were still too far in the future. On the surface, the new European treaty noted that the EU's policy "shall not prejudice the specific character of the security and defense policy of certain member states and shall respect the obligations of certain member states under the North Atlantic Treaty and be compatible with the common security and defense policy established under that framework." Such was the labored language that papered over a major rift between America and Europe, a separation that had precedents in the Cold War.

The caution that the Maastricht meeting displayed may be traced to the work of the major NATO summit meeting following the end of the Cold War in Rome in November 1991, at which the allies implemented the agreement made in London in July 1990 to "transform the alliance to reflect the new, more promising era in Europe." It was here that the allies determined that potential dangers lurking in the wreckage of the Soviet empire—ethnic strife in the new republics, a counterrevolutionary coup in the Russian Federation, territorial disputes between former members of the Warsaw Pact—meant that NATO would have a different function from its role in the Cold War. The organization would be the crisis manager in the event of new threats that could emanate not from "calculated aggression against the territory of the Allies, but rather from the consequences of instabilities." The scope of NATO's concerns extended, as the text of the communiqué made clear, to the "Southern Mediterranean and the Middle East."

How to translate the new strategic concept into reality was a question that was asked by NATO supporters as well as by its foes. Could it presage new American pressures for disengagement from Europe? This was not just casual speculation. Without intending this objective, a successful evolution of the new European Union into a genuine United States of Europe, as envisioned by its leaders in Brussels, would threaten NATO at its most elemental level. There would be no need for an Atlantic alliance, with or without the Americans, if Europe developed defense capabilities sufficient to take care of its own security. The political expectations were as exciting as the economic prospects when the European Union at Maastricht pressed for the removal of the WEU headquarters from London to Brussels to strengthen the links between the two institutions. Implicit in all the activities relating to the EU in the 1990s was the lowering of NATO's profile in Europe's future.

The apparent success of a unifying Europe under Franco-German auspices resonated across the Atlantic in a number of ways. Least surprising was the reduction of the size of U.S. forces in Europe. The Bush administration fought a losing battle with Congress to keep the number of troops in Europe at 250,000. The reduction bottomed out at 100,000 by the middle of the decade. At that figure, the Congressional Research Service report estimated that the United States could barely manage to field a medium-sized army corps, and below 50,000 the Joint

Chiefs of Staff anticipated that the military could make noncombat contributions through peacekeeping and humanitarian aid, but not much more.

Why not leave Europe to the Europeans, given the limited functions drastically reduced American forces would have in these circumstances? This question became critical in February 1962 when Canada announced that it would close all its bases and pull its combat forces out of Europe by the end of 1994. Europeans recognized that Canada's decision might well foreshadow an American departure, and both actions could be done without consultations with their partners beforehand. If no military threat was visible in Europe's future, it was understandable if the United States should depart from Europe—and from NATO.

The European allies in the EU had decidedly mixed feelings about an American abandonment of Europe. There were lively suspicions at the time of the Maastricht meeting that the United States was conspiring to undercut the development of a separate European defense force. Attention was paid at the WEU assembly in the winter of 1992 to a Pentagon paper, subsequently modified, that asserted America's intention to ensure that no rival superpower be allowed to challenge the preeminence of the United States in the post–Cold War era. A potentially powerful Europe could become that superpower rival. Europe's resentment of American hegemony might have gone to the extreme of preempting America's disengagement by disengaging itself from the United States—and from NATO.

Despite the renewal of transatlantic tensions, the new strategic concept crafted in the Rome meeting of the North Atlantic Council pointed the way to a détente between Europe and America. The new emphasis on crisis management provided room for Europe to make its own special contribution in a Franco-German–led corps within the NATO context. Europe was not ready to divest itself of American power, and the United States was not ready to turn its back on the role it had occupied for almost two generations. Americans were too hasty in dismissing the Eurocorps as a convenient means of removing Europe from American domination. And Europeans exaggerated the sense that Americans assumed a sovereign right to maintain the same controls they had held in Europe since the darkest days of the Cold War. NATO and the WEU, America and Europe, needed each other if there was to be stability in Europe.

There was no guarantee of security against the threat of crises that might arise in the years ahead. The unstable status of the successor nations to the defunct Soviet Union was sufficient of itself to make both NATO and the United States remain vital partners in Europe. A North Atlantic Coordinating Council (NACC) was established in 1991 to foster cooperation with the former members of the Soviet empire, creating an "interlocking network" to deal with all aspects of defense issues as well as with managing conversion of defense production to civilian purposes. Promotion of a close relationship with Russia reflected the NATO partners' concerns about the nuclear power remaining in the East and the dangers they might pose in the hands of dissidents in the new Russia. An abortive coup against Gorbachev in August 1991 that led to the formal dissolution of the Soviet Union in the following month gave credence to the worry about instability in the region and, by the same token, increased reliance on the United States as the comforting arm of NATO.

THE BOSNIAN CHALLENGE

The breakdown of the Yugoslav Federation in July 1991 should have been an occasion for the Eurocorps or a revitalized WEU to display its ability to manage crises beyond NATO's borders. The Balkan civil war was also an opportunity for NATO to give meaning to its crisis management intentions. Yugoslavia's instability could directly affect the security of the European allies under Article 4 if its war spread north to Hungary or east to Turkey, or led to a flood of refugees into western Europe.

The Serbian leader Slobodan Milosevic precipitated the crisis by refusing to recognize the secession of Croatia from Yugoslavia after Slovenia's declaration of independence. He then engaged in a limited war on the pretext of protecting the Serbian minority in Croatia. Conflict spread to Bosnia-Herzegovina where a mixed population of Serbs, Croats, and Muslims provided a setting for warring Croats and Serbs to seek annexation of their nationals at the expense of the Muslim population. The resulting bloodshed accompanied by ethnic cleansing aroused cries for international intervention, particularly as the horrors of war were displayed on television screens.

Arguably, the distinctions between aggressor and victim in Croatia were sufficiently blurred to make NATO's hesitation to intervene understandable. This was not the case in Bosnia in 1992, where a strong Serbian minority, armed and supported by the Serb-dominated Yugoslav army, seized all the territory it could manage from a country with a Muslim plurality. Milosevic's aim was to create a Greater Serbia in territory formerly occupied by Muslims. The Croats too were victims of Yugoslav aggression as they tried to stem the attacking Serb forces, presumably in collaboration with the Muslims. But the Croatian role in the war was suspect. It had plans for annexing territory from Bosnia-Herzogovina.

Although the Milosevic campaign was just the kind of challenge the Rome meeting had identified for NATO, it was even more appropriate that Europeans should take the initiative in meeting it. The war was in their own backyard, with more at stake, it seemed, for EU members than for the distant United States. It was all the more appropriate because it was German pressure that induced the EU to recognize Croatia and Slovenia as independent states. Germany's objective was to encourage a Western orientation on the part of those two former Yugoslav republics, and to reap economic advantages from its relations in an area that had once been in the German orbit.

From the U.S. perspective, the troubles emanating from Serbia's military efforts to subjugate Croatia, if not Slovenia, were European, not American, problems. This was the message Secretary of State James A. Baker delivered to the European allies in 1992 when he observed that "We don't have a dog in this fight." Unlike the Persian Gulf, there were no natural resources on which the West was dependent; the national interest of the United States did not seem to hang on the outcome of the Balkan war. Conditions for a surgical strike that could win a victory at minimal cost were not present, as they had been in the Persian Gulf the year before. The heavily armed Yugoslav army fighting in mountainous terrain could wreak havoc on an invader, just as Tito's Partisans were able to inflict on the Nazis in World War II. To the Bush administration the Bosnian war was an opportunity for Europeans to demonstrate their ability to act independently of the United States, in the spirit of the Maastricht summit.

The allies failed to respond in an effective manner. The carnage in Bosnia escalated in 1992. Germany applied strict construction to the constitutional bars against military action outside the boundaries of NATO. The British and French preferred to regard the Bosnian conflict as a civil war in which neither side was blameless. Although recognizing the aggressive designs of the Serbian leaders, the European partners saw their primary role as helping the United Nations maintain a neutral presence, supporting innocent civilians to cope with damages inflicted by the warring parties. The Security Council denounced Serbian aggression and the UN secretary-general dispatched peacekeeping teams. The NATO allies hoped that the good offices of UN representative Cyrus Vance, joined by the EU representative, David Owen, could bring the belligerents to the peace table. The United Nations itself was not prepared in 1992 to conduct a war against the Serbs to enforce its resolutions.

Gradually and unwillingly the United States found itself drawn into the Balkan conflict. There was anger against Europeans who encouraged the breakup of Yugoslavia and then stood passively by as Milosevic's well-armed forces committed atrocities against the relatively defenseless Bosnian Muslims. These were reported in gory detail by the international press, and the hapless victims were visible on every television screen. The European approach through a United Nations Protection Force (UNPROFOR) proved powerless to protect civilians; its humanitarian objectives dwindled to an effort to protect just its humanitarian convoys.

As the war raged on, the new administration of President Bill Clinton, which had made a more active support of the Muslims a campaign pledge in the presidential race, looked for ways to increase American involvement without placing American lives at risk. The initial response was to employ U.S. planes under NATO auspices flying at high altitudes to drop food and supplies to starving Muslims. These air drops, however, were not only too modest and too frequently wide of the mark, but they also sent the wrong signal to the Serbs. The actions suggested timidity rather than boldness.

When the United Nations in 1993 requested that NATO draw up a detailed plan for implementing a no-fly zone barring Serb aircraft over Bosnia, the United States believed it had a solution to stop Serb aggression without embroiling the nation in ground warfare. A collaboration between NATO and the United Nations would give the international organization the benefits of the infrastructure NATO had built over the decades and at the same time legitimize the new NATO mission of maintaining stability in Europe.

But would this synergy be realized? And if it were, would it be in time to preserve Bosnia from being absorbed into a Greater Serbia? In mid-1993, as NATO entered its forty-fifth year, there was no clear answer. France was uncomfortable with being part of a NATO force unless it was indisputably under UN command. Britain's lightly armed peacekeeping contingent in Bosnia was vulnerable to Serb retaliation. Outside the Security Council, Germany paid more attention to its growing internal problems than to the ongoing crisis it helped ignite. As long as there was uncertainty about German military forces participating in a conflict beyond NATO's borders, NATO capabilities would be severely strained. As for the senior NATO partner, the United States remained fearful of being pulled into a quagmire. If it had to contribute to a NATO force, it would only be after all the parties had agreed to a peaceful resolution of their differences.

It seemed that Europeans and Americans had not been so divided since the Suez debacle of 1956. Although Americans pointed to Europe's unwillingness to take charge of a matter in its own neighborhood, Europeans refused to accept lectures from a country that would not provide troops for the UN mission. At most, American pilots would patrol skies high above the fighting on the ground where vulnerable Europeans, not Americans, would suffer casualties. Reluctantly, the allies accepted in principle the use of airpower to enforce UN safe zones, but then did little to make the threat of armed intervention credible to the Serbs. The principle of consensus in NATO, that seemed workable if Article 5 of the North Atlantic Treaty were involved, did not work as American authority dwindled and Europe failed to take up the leadership that the United States seemed to abdicate. Article 4 was too vague to bring cohesion to the alliance. Neither the Franco-led Eurocorps nor the British-led Rapid Reaction Force (both paper entities) was prepared to take action to stop the carnage in the Balkans.

Superficially, the problem in 1993 lay with the role of the United Nations, which the allies wished to use as a cover for their own inaction. The reason may be traced to the Gulf War, when the United Nations gave its sanction to the war against Saddam Hussein. The United Nations served NATO by blunting potential criticism with its blessing. Although the Gulf War was not a NATO operation, there were enough NATO allies engaged to offer that impression to the world at large.

But what worked in Iraq was a dismal failure in the Balkans. The allies' inability to act in harmony undermined NATO's self-proclaimed mission to preserve stability in Europe by managing its crises, although the United Nations once again provided a fig leaf for NATO action. The televised scenes of ethnic cleansing gnawed at the consciences of NATO allies and inspired UN Security Council Resolution 781 in December 1992 that banned all flights over Bosnia not approved by the United Nations. Although the allies vetoed U.S. recommendations to shoot down violators of the resolution, they did accept U.S. AWACS aircraft as monitors and did provide peacekeepers under UN auspices "for the first time" in NATO's history, as the NATO communiqué of December 1992 observed. There was no better example of the message from the Rome meeting in 1991 than the plight of Bosnia where the threat arose not from "calculated aggression against the territory of the Allies but rather from the adverse consequences of instabilities." NATO instead made a travesty of its mission by failing to implement its no-fly zones. The confused lines of communication between the United Nations and NATO inhibited decisive actions and encouraged Serbian aggression. The British and French were unwilling to jeopardize their peacekeeping forces in Bosnia by provoking Milosevic's forces. They appeared ambivalent as well about supporting the territorial integrity of Bosnia.

As the war intensified in 1993, the position of the new Clinton administration was in sharp contrast to that of the European partners. If they could have activated one or more of the European security organizations that had been projected in 1991 and 1992, it would have fitted the Clinton agenda in which domestic issues were its first priority. The allies not only resisted American pressures but articulated their own grievances against the senior partner for its unwillingness to station its own troops as part of the UN peacekeeping force. The most that the United States could extract from its allies was an agreement in March 1994 on a pact to create a Muslim–Croat federation in Bosnia and, a month later, to establish a "Contact Group" that included the United States, Britain, France, Germany, Russia, and Italy.

Actually, NATO had used U.S. airpower against Serb positions in Bosnia with apparent effect in February 1994 when international outrage over deaths from Serb artillery in a crowded Sarajevo marketplace temporarily united the allies. This strike was intentionally only a warning, and it succeeded in suspending Serb attacks for the moment. But when the Serb leadership recognized the extent of the disarray between the United Nations and NATO and between America and Europe, subsequent air strikes lost even symbolic value. The Bosnian Serbs rejected the "contact group's" division of the nation with impunity. Not even the putative influence of Milosevic or his Russian ally made a difference.

Despite the acrimonious transatlantic divide over the Balkans, the war was regional, not continental or global. There were countervailing forces against the American wish to stay aloof from the conflict and Europe's wish to maintain an exclusively humanitarian presence in Bosnia. There was room for compromise over the Bosnian tragedy without wholly abandoning the victims of that conflict. The United States refrained from a unilateral lifting of the arms embargo and Europeans moved toward enforcing access to protected zones under UN auspices. The Clinton administration offer in December 1994 to supply up to 25,000 troops to help extricate, if necessary, UN peacekeepers reflected an effort toward accommodation with its European partners that was not present earlier. And Britain's and France's intention to provide more effective lines of communication and supply to their forces in Bosnia was an earnest of their new resolve. The election of Jacques Chirac as successor to President François Mitterand in May 1995 seemed to indicate more vigorous European activity, particularly after Bosnian Serbs humiliated France by holding French troops temporarily hostage. France pressed Britain and the Netherlands in June 1995 to invigorate the role of UNPROFOR.

This new sense of purpose notwithstanding, the fact remained that there was no "NATO method" to deal with Bosnia. The United Nations, which NATO had hoped would solve their problems, stood in the alliance's way. Although the United Nations had asked for more NATO help after the marketplace bombing in February 1994, the international organization imposed a "dual-key" requirement before military operations could take place. NATO's SACEUR held only one of the keys.

NATO's and the UN's stasis in the Balkans ended in the summer of 1995 but only after a brutal Serb attack against one of the UN-protected enclaves in Srebrenica that led to a massacre of presumably protected civilians. Almost as horrifying to the West was the spectacle of Dutch UNPROFOR peacekeepers who witnessed the scene but were too lightly armed to intervene. Pressure to react with more than the spasm of activity that followed the marketplace killings in Sarajevo in February 1994 reached the breaking point when a Serb mortar attack on 30 August 1995 killed 38 people, again in a Sarajevo marketplace. This brought on massive NATO air strikes over a 22-day period that not only removed the heavy weapons from the heights overlooking the city, but also pushed the warring combatants to the negotiating table. The allies were aided by a vigorous Croat assault that resulted in their occupation of a large swath of Bosnian Serb territory. After the Serb siege of Sarajevo was broken, Milosevic saw no alternative for his country and his Bosnian Serb clients but to position himself as a peace broker at a conference in Dayton, Ohio, under U.S. auspices.

When the Dayton agreements were initiated in November 1995, the United Nations was conspicuous by its absence. Its limited contribution to peace efforts was an unarmed police force to monitor Bosnian police and, even in this limited sphere, NATO had to intervene. Yet the successful campaign was more an American than a NATO accomplishment. Although the North Atlantic Council congratulated itself in its communiqué of 5 December, welcoming "the agreement initialed in Dayton for peace in Bosnia and Herzegovina," the Dayton agreements were largely the work of Assistant Secretary of State Richard C. Holbrooke, the chief U.S. negotiator in Bosnia. They were not a council action. The fact that the meeting of Croat, Muslim, and Serb leaders took place in a midwestern American city conveyed a message to the European allies.

The success of the Bosnian mission momentarily alleviated the friction between the United States and its allies. Britain and France were well represented in the operation, with 14,000 and 10,000 troops respectively, although American dominance was evidenced in the airpower it displayed. When the Implementation Force (IFOR) was established, Bosnia was divided into three sectors in which troops from the United States, Britain, and France would take responsibility for keeping order. NATO's informal involvement was not confined to the three major allies. A fourth leading member, Germany, whose constitutional restrictions and memories of a shameful past had hitherto limited its involvement in the Balkans, sent some 5,000 noncombat personnel to the NATO command, and later included combat troops in its mission. Smaller allies, such as Belgium and Spain, were also present, and Italy served as a major staging area for NATO—and U.S.—forces. Considerable credit for NATO's continuing commitment to peace in Bosnia belonged to SACEUR General Wesley K. Clark, who had been deeply involved in working out the Dayton agreements.

Such success as NATO had in keeping the lid on violence in Bosnia arguably has obscured the ability of the allies to collaborate under the SACEUR in a major military operation. "Operation Joint Endeavor," as IFOR was labeled in 1996, also benefited from many non-NATO countries that participated in the operation. They were members, however, of the Partnership for Peace (PfP) program created at the Brussels meeting of the North Atlantic Council in January 1994. Eighteen nations, ranging from former members of the Warsaw Pact to current members of the Arab League, sent troops to serve under the NATO command. But the most important contribution to the peacekeeping effort came from Russia, a traditional ally of Serbia, that nevertheless dispatched an airborne brigade to Bosnia. In deference to Russian pride, its brigade nominally had an autonomous status, but in reality was under NATO command in an American-administered sector.

THE EUROPEAN UNION AND THE COMBINED JOINT TASK FORCE

Although the EU failed in a test of its ability to manage the Balkan crisis, the Brussels summit of 1994 did open the way not only for new partners but also for a division of labor between America and Europe in crisis management. This was the establishment of the Combined Joint Task Force (CJTF). "Combined" meant that two or more military services would be involved, and "joint" meant that two or more NATO members would contribute to the task force. The very linking of such loaded terms as "combined" and "joint" evoked expectations that a meaningful solution had been found to resolve the conflicting interests of a uniting Europe and the United States. Even the term *task force* raised expectations; it implied a limited operation in the post–Cold War era, in which NATO's power could be carefully concentrated on contingencies of all kinds, inside or outside NATO boundaries.

The problem with the CJTF was how to activate it without also accentuating the differences between the European and American conceptions of the task force's assets. When the North Atlantic Council bestowed its blessings on the CJTF in 1994, it noted that the military capabilities of the WEU and NATO would be "separable but not separate." Although it was no trouble for the allies to declare that a task force would not be separate from the organization, translating "separable" into a meaningful form was more problematic. This issue during the Bosnian operation was theoretical. Although the tensions in the summer of 1995 should have been the occasion for Europeans to mount a CJTF, it was unable to act. The trouble at this point was not with its mechanics; the CJTF offered a genuine means of fulfilling the European partners' aspiration to manage crises of greater concern to them than to the American partner. Rather, it was the lack of will on the part of European leaders that inhibited them in the Bosnian war.

The peacekeeping mission following the Dayton agreements was another occasion for Europeans to use the CJTF. The United States, uncomfortable with its role in the IFOR, created to maintain the uneasy peace secured at Dayton, was anxious to leave most of the responsibility to the allies. IFOR was terminated in December 1996, to be replaced by a Stabilization Force (SFOR) with the American contingent reduced from 20,000 to 8,000. Still, this was more than the United States wanted. Why not use this opportunity to place the CJTF front and center, as the North Atlantic Council recommended in June of that year? The WEU could use NATO facilities to command an all-European force in an SFOR context. The development of a European Security and Defense Identity (ESDI) to be transformed into a Common Foreign and Security Policy (CFSP) was a by-product of the Brussels summit in 1994 and should have prospered in an environment in which Europe, not America, was the primary actor. But the European agencies failed once again to take up the challenge. There were too many questions about the composition of the CJTF that were not answered, most notably, which ally would command the force.

For France in particular, the existence of the CJTF was both an opportunity to exercise its influence and a symbol of European inferiority. On the one hand, it opened an opportunity for France to participate in and lead a European force separable but not separate from NATO without having to return to NATO's integrated command. On the other hand, the Bosnian experience displayed the inability of the Europeans to use the CJTF. U.S. airpower under NATO command dominated the action against Serbia. Chirac's response to this impasse was to reprise a position France had taken in the Gulf War of 1991 supporting the American operation informally as a willing ally. France had participated in the denial of Bosnian air space to Serbian planes. It recognized that more intimate relations with NATO, and particularly with the United States, were necessary for influence in out-of-area problems as well as for potential access to the technology that lay behind America's domination of the alliance. With Bosnian independence achieved, France and Britain would be major actors in the peacekeeping mission and presumably in a position to strengthen their authority in the alliance. To accelerate this process, France announced that it would return to NATO's international Military Staff in Brussels and participate in meetings of NATO defense ministers. It appeared that France in 1995 was on a path to rejoin SHAPE in Casteau in 1996.

France did not pursue this path, and its decision touched on the continuing problem of transatlantic relations. How much freedom European countries would have to use NATO assets without being subjected to NATO control was the nub of the issue. The United States was more than willing to have Europeans fulfill their ESDI aspirations without American involvement as long as it was understood that the WEU or the EU directly would be responsible to the SACEUR. The Americans also understood that their facilities—from sophisticated communications to airlift providers—would revert to NATO once the particular operation was terminated.

This was not the French interpretation of the CJTF. For them, and other Europeans, the ESDI would function with NATO resources but not with NATO supervision. The argument turned not just on their ability to function freely but also on their need to free themselves from dependence on the United States. France as Europe's leader in this search found solutions in either elevating a European to the position of SACEUR or, if this was not acceptable, replacing the American commander of Allied Forces, South (AFSouth) in Naples with a European. The United States refused to accept either of these propositions. The senior partner was no more willing to cede overall command in Europe in 1996 than it had been willing to have a British admiral as SACLANT in 1951. The consequence was the termination of what seemed to have been progressive steps in France's full reintegration into NATO's military structure.

By the time of the Madrid summit in 1997, when NATO agreed to enlarge its membership by the admission of Poland, the Czech Republic, and Hungary, the French government suspected that American pressure for enlargement was not just the result of politicians wooing ethnic lobbies in the United States or of liberals seeking to erase the stain of the Yalta concessions to the Soviets in 1945 by bringing former Warsaw Pact countries into the Western fold. Some Europeans sensed an American plot to subvert European military autonomy by conferring membership on countries presumably more subservient, or at least more receptive, to American wishes. Resentment over America's seeming disregard for European sensibilities helps explain France's futile championship of Romania's candidacy for membership at the Madrid meeting.

NATO, THE EUROPEAN UNION, AND THE KOSOVO CRISIS

The blocking of European plans for the CJTF and the tilting of NATO's composition with the adherence of pro-American East Europeans stimulated France to seek new approaches to free Europe from American control. One avenue was to formalize what had been in the works for much of the decade, the incorporation of the WEU as the military arm of the EU. As long as Britain under Prime Minister Tony Blair continued to oppose Franco-German efforts to create a European defense entity that could duplicate NATO's, the EU's military progress was limited. Britain, the key American ally in Europe, was wary about undermining NATO's authority.

The expanding turmoil in the Balkans, however, was a major factor in affecting Britain's disposition toward the continental allies. It underscored the dilemma facing Europeans by the continuing reluctance of America to commit ground troops when Europe itself was not equipped to fulfill that mission. Without signaling any intention of weakening the special Anglo-American relationship, Blair took the initiative in 1998 to bring British military power into the European Union, thereby giving substance to European assertions of autonomy. Given Britain's unwillingness to participate in the monetary union that was to be consummated in 2000, involving the nation more closely in defense of the EU would be proof of its affiliation with a united Europe. Blair envisioned Britain as a bridge between Europe and America.

This was not an original idea. Britain in the past had often considered itself as a transatlantic interpreter, with the expectation that its special relations with both America and Europe would enhance its own authority in NATO. Only rarely were its expectations met. But in 1998 France appreciated the new British attitude. It opened an opportunity to breathe life into the ESDI at a time when Serbia was abusing the Albanian population in its Kosovo province. At St. Malo in December of that year Britain and France spoke to the common defense of Europe, and advanced the prospect of the WEU becoming the official arm of the EU, an outcome made final in November 2000. The Franco-British joint summit was intended to implement Europe's Common Foreign and Security Policy by granting to the EU, in the words of the communiqué, "the capacity for autonomous action, backed up by credible military forces, the means to use them and a readiness to do so, in order to respond to international crises." The other European allies welcomed the St. Malo declaration as much for its psychic value as for the actual changes it would make in the defense capabilities of the European Union.

U.S. reaction was less welcoming. Inevitably, questions would arise in Washington over what effect an energized European defense force would have on NATO, particularly after the EU had won the allegiance of Britain with its nuclear arms and its experience in out-of-area operations. At the very least the merger of the WEU with the EU could lead to duplication of resources, of commands, and of functions. The end product of a competitive European military force could be the decoupling of America from its transatlantic allies. In brief, if Europeans persisted in demanding NATO assets without NATO provenance, the United States, which controlled the resources the WEU needed, could withdraw from the alliance.

This was a scenario that no member wanted, including France. No European partner was prepared to supply the funds needed to make their ESDI truly independent of the United States. But despite their reluctance or inability to match NATO's capabilities, the European allies had been carrying the manpower burden of peacekeeping in Bosnia while the size of the American contingent was being drastically reduced. If there were to be future actions against Milosevic, Europeans would provide the force on the ground while Americans once again would supply airpower. Under these circumstances resulting casualties would be largely European.

Just as Bosnia offered a challenge that Serbia's European neighbors could not meet, so the Kosovo province of Serbia offered a second challenge—and encountered the same frustrations. Milosevic may have lost in Bosnia and Croatia, but he was determined to suppress the Kosovar Albanians' aspirations for autonomy, if not independence, from Serbia. In light of Serbia's historic roots in Kosovo, it was not surprising that the Serbian dictator would try to compensate his losses by ensuring control of the Kosovo province at any cost. Revolt had been brewing there since its autonomous status had been revoked in 1989 and, by 1998, had produced the Kosovo Liberation Army (KLA) with its objective of winning full freedom from Serbian rule. The scene replicated some of the horrors inflicted on Bosnia six years before as 250,000 refugees fled into Albania and Macedonia.

Once again the NATO allies and the European Union tried to stop the carnage, and once again they turned to the United Nations for moral if not physical support. Neither an arms embargo nor a call for a cease-fire and withdrawal of Serbian forces from Kosovo impressed Milosevic. Nevertheless, the European allies had a stake in resolving this crisis that was more compelling than in 1992. They had thousands of troops on the ground in neighboring Bosnia who would be vulnerable to Serbian retaliation in the event of a war over Kosovo. Transatlantic divisions inevitably would be more acute if the United States confined its role to airpower.

Given Serbia's repeated violations of an agreement Ambassador Holbrooke had made with Milosevic for partial withdrawal of Serbian troops, it appeared likely in the winter of 1999 that NATO might have to apply force. Unlike military actions in Iraq and Bosnia, the war against Serbia that began on 24 March 1999 was exclusively a NATO affair, justified under Article 4 of the North Atlantic Treaty. Its command center was in Casteau under SACEUR General Wesley K. Clark.

NATO's last-minute efforts in March 1999 at Rambouillet to reach a binding settlement between the Serbs and the KLA ended without a signed agreement. Milosevic was bent on continuing his ethnic cleansing, and an increasing number of Albanians were demanding a referendum on independence. Assured of a Russian veto in the UN Security Council and confident of his ability to manipulate uneasy allies, Milosevic resisted granting NATO forces access to all of Yugoslavia. He assumed that no ground troops would be engaged in any action against Serbia.

He was partly right. The allies initially ruled out a ground campaign. The United States was convinced that an air campaign would bring Milsosevic down in less than a week. This was also the fervent hope of the North Atlantic Council. They were mistaken. Instead of surrendering, Milosevic accelerated his ethnic cleansing, dispatching more troops across the border and terrorizing more Kosovar Albanians into flight. He was counting on conflicts within the NATO establishment and the diplomatic support of Russia to survive the assault. He expected to wait out the air attacks until the allies lost their nerve. With NATO's fiftieth anniversary summit just four weeks away, the Serbs appeared to conclude that they could win merely by standing still.

General Clark recognized the possibility of such an outcome as he observed that airpower by itself was no guarantee of success. But whether bombing Yugoslavia was the right strategy or not, the allies feared that failure to act in light of NATO's repeated threats would have destroyed the alliance's credibility. The nightly television images of Albanian refugees driven out of Kosovo made it impossible for NATO to back away from its objective, despite misjudgments about Milsosevic's staying power. The outcome was a 78-day war that found the SACEUR in the middle of conflicts with both his masters in the Pentagon and the civilian leaders in the North Atlantic Council. Clark was caught between the U.S. wish to intensify air strikes in and around Belgrade and the European anxiety to limit the strikes to Serb forces attacking ethnic Albanians. The war uncovered all the weaknesses implicit in decisions made by committee but with responsibilities laid on the shoulders of a single commander. General Clark could not carry out his mission without submitting his plans to two superior entities—the Department of Defense in Washington, represented by the secretary and the chairman of the Joint Chiefs of Staff, and by the member nations of the alliance in the North Atlantic Council.

From the outset, the SACEUR recognized the importance of ground forces, or at least the threat of deploying ground troops, to complement airpower. But both President Clinton and Secretary-General Javier Solana had made it clear that the campaign was to be conducted solely by air. Clark did request Army Apache attack helicopters to hunt down Serb forces inside Kosovo. Although he never won approval for the deployment of ground forces, he had the support of Britain to send a signal that a ground invasion might develop. It was likely that the perceived likelihood of an eventual ground operation, combined with the aggressiveness of the Kosovo Liberation Army as well as the diplomatic pressure from Russia, persuaded Milosevic to lay down his arms. This does not mean that airpower had failed; the belated assaults on the vital centers of Belgrade aided in the final outcome.

THE IMPACT OF THE KOSOVO WAR

The lesson in this conflict derived from the command-and-control failure caused by decisions made not by military leaders in Casteau but by a NATO body in Brussels—and, for different reasons—by the Joint Chiefs of Staff in the Pentagon. A war by committee could be a disaster. Every member nation had reasons to avoid the kind of action that might have won the war in March as early as the optimists had predicted. The Clinton administration's initial adamancy about ground war had its origins in the political repercussions that would follow from soldiers returning home in body bags. But they might have moved earlier to the British position had not the European allies been so opposed to an invasion. Greece would have faced strong domestic protest if troops and equipment were dispatched to Kosovo through the port of Thessaloniki. More than 90 percent of the country even opposed an air campaign, with the Greek Orthodox Church a major element in generating opposition. German support was also tenuous, with the Green Party in the governing coalition bitterly divided over the air campaign. The possibility of German troops being dispatched to the Balkans once again evoked ugly memories of their role in World War II. A NATO ground operation might have toppled the coalition.

As the war continued without apparent success, France and Canada spoke of reviving diplomacy while Italy raised the prospect of a bombing moratorium as an incentive for Milosevic to abandon his Kosovo policies. In May, Chancellor Gerhard Schroeder threatened to exercise Germany's veto in the North Atlantic Council to block a ground war in Kosovo.

The ending of the war in June sidelined this particular problem but transatlantic collaboration in the air war had revealed new fault lines between the United States and its European allies. The trouble did not arise from lack of European involvement. Every one of the 19 member nations officially supported "Operation Allied Force," opening where applicable their air space and offering bases for the allied air forces. A Rand study of European contributions to the Kosovo campaign observed that 13 countries provided military aircraft, with Britain and France using precision-guided weapons as well. Germany's stance on ground forces notwithstanding, the German air force flew over 600 sorties in the effort to suppress enemy air defenses, employing reconnaissance drones for intelligence tasks. Although Italy was the third largest contributor to the NATO operation, its most valuable support was its air bases.

This exercise in coalition warfare might have been an example of NATO collaboration at its best. Instead, the war exposed fissures in the transatlantic relationship that had been evident in the Gulf and Bosnian crises but without the traumatic effect its revelation had in the Kosovo war. Just how far ahead of its European allies the United States was in military research and development, in advanced weaponry and intelligence-gathering systems, became painfully obvious in 1999. Since the end of the Cold War, European governments had slashed their defense budgets, and had been reluctant to transform standing armies into more flexible units designed to handle such situations as Kosovo presented. They turned down opportunities to buy at bargain prices the U.S. air-to-ground surveillance system. Disputes over cost sharing aborted France's and Germany's plans to build a satellite reconnaissance system and heavy-lift air transport planes that would have given them some measure of equality with the United States military.

That the United States dominated the air war was undeniable; it deployed most of the aircraft, flew most of the missions, and provided the bulk of the air-lift capabilities. Small wonder that the disproportionate presence of America in the Balkans bred resentment among the partners. American unwillingness to share sensitive information exacerbated their sense of grievance. Targeting data and battle-damage assessments were denied to the allies for fear that such information would be quickly leaked. With some justice, the French could complain that France was not the only ally that did not subordinate its military to the integrated command.

Although there was no clear-cut demonstration of European discontent over its inferior position in the Kosovo war, the Allied Occupation Force in Kosovo (KFOR) did provide an occasion for an outburst against American military leadership that was usually sublimated in other forums. British Lieutenant General Sir Michael Jackson, commander of the Allied Command Rapid Reaction Corps in the immediate aftermath of the war, openly defied the SACEUR's attempt to prevent the Russians (who had agreed to serve in an American sector of Kosovo) from occupying the Pristina airfield without authorization. He was not going to risk a conflict with Russia, whatever American instructions might require. This was a small European victory but, like the contributions of Europeans to KFOR, Jackson's stand represented Europe's push for independence from U.S. control.

The experience in Kosovo had political implications as well. The European Union meeting in Cologne in early June shortly before the end of the Kosovo campaign reaffirmed in stronger language than used earlier its determination to achieve the capacity for autonomous action, although "without prejudice to actions by NATO." To underscore the seriousness of its intentions, the EU formally announced that it would not only absorb the functions of the WEU, but would also create a new office, the High Representative for Common Foreign and Security Policy under the leadership of Javier Solana, the retiring secretary-general of NATO. Solana's appointment, to take effect in October 1999, symbolized the EU's concrete steps toward autonomy while maintaining its links to NATO. By December the EU announced plans to create a European rapid-reaction force of 50,000 to 60,000 troops, to be deployed within 60 days of a crisis. When mobilized, this new force would be able to conduct operations that hitherto had been dependent on U.S. support. Such was the impact of the Kosovo War on the European allies.

This 6-month whirlwind of EU activities met with considerable skepticism in the United States. It raised the familiar question of duplication. What was NATO, and especially its senior partner, to make of these new obligations the EU was undertaking? When both the U.S. House of Representatives and the Senate expressed alarm in November at the direction the EU was following, the Europeans meeting in Helsinki in December 1999 made an effort to defuse the tensions by reaffirming the centrality of NATO, and assuring Americans that the new rapid-reaction force would be used only in situations in which NATO chose not to be involved.

Credibility of the EU plans was still at stake at the end of the decade. Historian Charles Cogan has identified three options for out-of-area operations as they were presented by France's defense minister at Georgetown University in February 2000. The first has been the pattern in Bosnia and Kosovo when NATO, primarily with American assets, led the way. The second would be an EU initiative wherein NATO assets would be borrowed, subject to some NATO monitoring, under the direction of the European Deputy SACEUR in his role as a SHAPE official. Although this arrangement might create awkward situations in which the gray areas between NATO and EU responsibilities may generate mutual irritation, it did meet the U.S. conception of the ESDI in action. But a third option, inspired by France, assumed that NATO would remove itself from the scene in favor of a European chain of command employing only European resources. Granted that this was a theoretical situation, it did disturb British and German allies. One direction it could logically take was a European action in conflict with U.S. objectives, a direction that could lead to the dissolution of the alliance. This was not the scenario France envisioned. Rather, the third option would be the logical outcome of Europe assuming responsibilities commensurate with its potential political and economic power. The United States and France at last would be equal partners.

In one sense, an air of unreality pervaded the notion of an effective European rapid deployment of substantial numbers of troops drawn from the EU members. Despite all the pronouncements emerging from EU summits in 1999 and 2000, no serious efforts had been made to evaluate the cost emanating from a defense buildup. The record in 2000 showed that defense expenditures by European NATO countries continued to decline—by 6.7 percent between 1999 and 2000. Was there any evidence of a turnaround in defense spending? On research and development alone, European spending remained about one-quarter of that spent by the United States and the gap appeared likely to increase in the future unless a drastic change took place in EU priorities.

Still another problem should be noted, which the European allies have not addressed except in the most superficial terms. Who would lead the new European force? The only answer to date was the Deputy SACEUR, always a European in the history of SHAPE. But if this officer functioned outside the NATO framework, or even within it under a different hat, would there be dissention within European ranks over the nationality of this commander? The only time Europeans had to face this question was in 1948 when the Western Union Defense Organization (WUDO), created under the Brussels Pact, established a host of military committees. These were earnests of their commitment to self-defense, demonstrating to the United States when the North Atlantic Treaty was being framed that the future European allies could cooperate in military as well as economic matters. Some of these committees were later integrated into NATO, but one committee was never adopted by NATO. This was the Commander-in-Chiefs Committee that presumably would manage any military operation. There was no single commander because both the British and French generals wanted the command. Lord Montgomery won the contest with General de Lattre de Tassigny, but the name of the committee on which they sat suggests problems that would arise if WUDO had to be tested. Would a similar contest over which national would lead the force be in store for the EU?

These questions have not been answered. When one delegate to a Paris conference in June 2001, celebrating the new ties between the WEU and the EU, raised these questions, he was greeted with an embarrassed silence. On the European side, optimism for the moment overwhelmed experience. Because the Deputy SACEUR was invariably a European, presumably he would take command of an EU force. On the American side there was both doubt about the ability of Europeans to achieve a third option and a resentment over their interest in doing so.

Despite all the tensions displayed in allied actions in the Balkans, the post–military operations have been the scene of genuine sharing of responsibilities. America's daunting superiority in weaponry, particularly in the air, was not sufficient to manage affairs on the ground after hostilities ended. Here Europeans had a preponderance of troops, both in the Bosnian SFOR and the Kosovo KFOR. There was mutual dependence in every Balkan peacekeeping situation that belied the transatlantic split. More than NATO personnel were involved; the United Nations authorized its own mission to facilitate the return of Kosovo refugees, and the Organization for Security and Cooperation in Europe (OSCE) succeeding CSCE, participated in the training of judges and police officers. A year after the Kosovo War began, Eurocorps under the command of a Spanish general took charge of KFOR, even as KFOR itself reported to SACEUR, and through him to the North Atlantic Council in Brussels. De facto cooperation between the EU and NATO on the ground did not preclude differences among the allies but they were managed under conditions of relative equality, unlike relations between Washington and Brussels, or Washington and Paris.

As NATO entered the new millennium, the transatlantic relationship could be considered in terms of *plus ça change, plus c'est la même chosè* (the more things changes, the more they stay the same). Almost from the inception of the alliance, Europeans have sought to get out from under American domination and chafed at their inability to free themselves. The Soviet menace was a unifying factor for the first 40 years but their subsequent unwillingness to come to grips with the costs of a viable European defense system helps to explain a continuing dependence on U.S. military power. That the 1990s witnessed the creation of the EU and a common currency in the euro may be an earnest of a future in which the dormant strength of a united Europe would establish a genuine second pillar of NATO—or make NATO itself irrelevant. Until that time, it seemed in 2000 that America's presence as a European power continued to be a necessary engine for the management of out-of-area crises.

7

INTO THE NEW MILLENNIUM

NATO in 2000

The new millennium more accurately should be identified with the year 2001 than 2000, but from a NATO perspective, particularly in transatlantic relations, the year did not matter much. On both sides of the Atlantic familiar complaints were heard. Europeans were resentful over American unwillingness to maintain their troops on the ground in Bosnia, Kosovo, and in neighboring Macedonia. Of the 65,000 military personnel in the Balkans, only 11,400 were from the United States; in Kosovo only 5,900 out of 37,000. The allies were providing peacekeepers not only through NATO but through their contributions in the OSCE and the United Nations. They received little credit from the senior partner.

On the contrary, the politics of an American presidential election year inevitably exacerbated relations as both parties exerted themselves to chastise the European allies for continuing to exploit American generosity. The Senate had some difficulty in May 2000 striking down legislation that would have imposed a deadline for the departure of all U.S. forces in Kosovo. Congressmen in the House of Representatives in the spirit of the Mansfield resolutions pressed for reductions of troops unless the allies assumed a greater share of the burden. In October 2000, the Republican presidential candidate, George W. Bush, recommended the complete removal of U.S. forces from the Balkans. The general tenor of his campaign embodied a criticism of the overactive foreign policy of President Clinton and suggested a retreat to a more modest view of America's role in the world.

The former governor of Texas had little experience with Europe and even less interest in remedying this condition. His first foreign visits as president were to Mexico and Canada, two American neighbors he seemed to value more highly than he did the European allies. His first visit to Europe was not until June 2001, when he had an opportunity to evaluate relations with Britain and France. These visits were not successes. The Bush administration had sent signals that were bound to antagonize the allies. At a time when concerns about global warming had aroused most nations, the United States chose to refrain from endorsing the Kyoto Protocol on global warming, which Bush's predecessor had accepted. Europeans found the grounds for rejection to be specious, namely, that there was insufficient evidence that global warming was a threat to the planet. Moreover, the administration objected to the absence of restraints on pollution emitted by developing nations.

If this had been an isolated act, it would have agitated the allies, but when combined with a unilateral approach to other multinational programs, the transatlantic partners grew alarmed at the behavior of the United States. American opposition in 2002 to the European-backed International Criminal Court was symptomatic of the Bush approach. Although the court was designed to serve as a forum to try individuals charged with genocide and crimes against humanity, the United States saw it as a vehicle to single out Americans vulnerable to politically motivated prosecutions. It was not that a fear of neo-isolationism animated the allies; America was not going to withdraw into its shell. On the contrary, the superpower had military resources that not even the combined forces of the world could match, and appeared to feel that NATO was essentially irrelevant. The Bush presidency was not to be bound by its ties to the allies.

It is likely that no matter how amenable the United States might have been to European interests in the first nine months of the Bush administration, the impulse for European unity, with the United States as the implicit adversary, would have progressed under its own steam.

ARTICLE 5 AND THE DEFENSE OF AMERICA

The terrorist assault on the World Trade Center and the Pentagon on 11 September 2001 transformed the transatlantic relationship overnight, with an afterglow that lasted through the fall of that year. NATO's rally to the defense of its senior partner under the rubric of Article 5 of the North Atlantic Treaty appeared to revitalize the North Atlantic Treaty and give it a relevance it had lacked before. For the first time in its long history, the member nations had invoked the mantra that an attack against one was an attack against all, and the nation so attacked was not a vulnerable European ally, but the superpower itself.

There are two ironies in NATO's response that should be noted: first, the reversal of the initial purpose of the treaty in 1949, which was the protection of defenseless western Europe by the powerful United States; and second, the purposely elliptical language of Article 5, designed by American policymakers to allow the United States to choose its own terms of engagement if a member nation were attacked. The escape mechanisms built into the article could have been exploited by Europeans to water down their support of the embattled transatlantic partner. They were not used.

The immediate reactions of both NATO and the European Union were instantaneous and supportive, reflecting the emotions of their constituent peoples. One day after the attacks, the North Atlantic Council responded to Secretary of State Colin Powell's assertion that the terrorists' actions were nothing less than a declaration of war against democracy by formally setting Article 5 in motion. The European Union, so frequently at odds with the United States, was equally strong in its professions of readiness to assist with every means at its disposal. NATO's former Secretary-General Javier Solana, now the EU foreign policy chief, pointed out that terrorism, which had afflicted European nations as internal problems (witness the Basques in Spain, the Red Brigade in Italy, the IRA in Britain), was now an international problem and a grave threat to NATO.

These sentiments were repeated by every ally, but none was more vocal than Britain Prime Minister Tony Blair. When Afghanistan was targeted as the headquarters of Osama bin Laden's al Qaeda, Blair was even more insistent than President Bush in demanding full-scale war against the Taliban in Afghanistan. Britain was not alone in its verbal support. Canada, Germany, and France also pledged forces for the operation against Afghanistan.

To implement Article 5, NATO allies took such steps as intelligence sharing, increased security of U.S. facilities on their territories, overnight clearances of U.S. and allied aircraft, and access for the United States to ports and airfields in all member nations for operations against terrorism. Impressive as these offers were, they were dwarfed by specific actions that matched their words. The most spectacular was NATO's dispatch of five AWACS (Airborne Warning and Control System) to patrol the eastern coastline of the United States. NATO's AWACS force, based in Geilenkirchen, Germany, was NATO's only multinational aviation unit, and was composed of airmen from 12 member nations, including the United States. They were intended to replace the U.S. AWACS fleet now required for service in the war zones of Afghanistan and for patrols over Iraq. Whether this gesture was a necessary part of the common war effort was immaterial. Europe's deployment of planes to American shores may be considered the equivalent to the psychological stimulus of the stationing of American troops in Europe in the early days of the Cold War. It contained both symbol and substance.

THE LIMITS OF CONSENSUS

The wave of good feeling toward America based on the empathy that Europe extended to a shocked nation inevitably subsided. There would have been softening, if not abandonment, of solidarity in the war against terrorism if the military campaign against the Taliban in the fall of 2001 had bogged down or if civilian casualties had reached an intolerable level. The definition of "intolerable" would vary, of course, from country to country and from party to party. The Green parties of Europe began to express their reservations about military action almost as soon as the American assault against al Qaeda bases began in November 2001. Less than a week after the destruction of the World Trade Center towers and only a few days after *Le Monde* declared that "We are all Americans" now, France's premier Lionel Jospin cautioned that his country would not automatically support the war in Afghanistan. The U.S. president increased European uneasiness in December when he sought greater defense expenditures from the allies as well as a promise of support if the war against terrorism should spread to other rogue nations.

Ironically, however, it was the American rejection of European military involvement in the Afghanistan campaign that annoyed Europeans at the same time that American leaders were pressing for the allies' help. The issue devolved on the command and control of the military operation. One advantage of the loose construction of Article 5 that the United States had imposed on its allies in 1949 was the freedom of the members to interpret according to their own judgments. Some members would be more active than others in executing their roles under Article 5. To energize public opinion in their countries, French and German officials offered to do more than the ancillary provision of intelligence information and rooting out of terrorist cells; they were ready to send military forces to join with the United States in combat against the Taliban.

This offer met mixed reactions in the United States, which served to exacerbate tensions. While invigorating the NATO partnership was heartening on one level, on another, the European offers appeared to be a devious way for them to exercise leverage over military operations in Afghanistan. Granted, military cooperation could mobilize European public opinion in favor of the war, an outcome welcome to the U.S. military. Less welcome were memories of command and control problems with alliance partners in previous crises. NATO's war over Kosovo less than three years before had witnessed the confusion that usually characterizes divided authority. The United States feared that anything more than a token contribution from the European allies would lead to interference with the American conduct of the war.

The campaign against al Qaeda and its Taliban hosts was run from MacDill Air Force base in Tampa, Florida, without reference to SHAPE or to the civilian authorities in Brussels. General Tommy Franks, operating out of the Central Command in Florida, controlled the air war. There were problems coordinating actions with CIA operatives on the scene in Afghanistan as well as differences between Franks and the Pentagon. But the rifts that developed after air operations began were not as debilitating as those the SACEUR had endured in Kosovo in 1999. The successes of the Northern Alliance and other anti-Taliban forces in taking control of most of the country in the first two weeks of November were due in large measure to a successful command-and-control arrangement overseen by the U.S. Central Command thousands of miles from the scene.

American reservations about allied involvement were understandable, particularly because much of the assistance given was seen as cosmetic. Even the touted British partnership, activated on the day after the attacks against New York and Washington, amounted to little more than a firing of a few missiles. Would French or German forces have made a positive difference in the outcome of the war? It was obvious to Europeans and Americans alike that there was little they could add to the firepower, intelligence gathering, and communications network that the United States had brought to bear in support of the Northern Alliance forces and those of the Pashtun opponents of the Taliban in southern Afghanistan.

EUROPE'S CONTRIBUTIONS IN AFGHANISTAN

If the United States held reservations about the interposition of unnecessary allied assets, the Europeans themselves were conflicted over their position on the war. Germany underwent a major debate over the dispatch of some 3,900 troops to Afghanistan. It turned on the symbolic importance of German soldiers engaging in combat for the first time since World War II, and almost undid the uneasy alliance between Social Democrats and the Green Party in the Bundestag.

The opposition to the war in the German peace camp was shared in varying degrees by all the major allies. Their governments recognized limitations placed by public opinion. At a time when Italy's Silvio Berlusconi was offering 2,700 service personnel as well as an aircraft carrier to ensure an Italian military presence in the war against terrorism, more than 240 sports figures—from racing car drivers to football players—signed a petition on 7 November asking for a halt to the bombing and aid to civilian victims. There was also an assumption among the European publics, more cautiously expressed by their leaders, that the American war, with its collateral damage, would lead to a dangerous alienation of the Muslim world. Moreover, there was a question of how far afield the war on terrorism would carry NATO. If it encompassed Iraq and Syria, it could not only stretch resources excessively, but also harm economic interests in the Middle East.

These caveats notwithstanding, the European allies stood behind the United States in the Afghanistan campaign, and the United States in turn accepted allied aid in the region. Europeans wanted to have a voice in the conduct of the ongoing war on terrorism, while the Americans wished to avoid a sense of isolation in conducting the assault against the Taliban. The differences, for the moment, were reconcilable as 2001 came to a close.

The problems confronting the European–American relationship, particularly the ability of the EU to maintain a military establishment independent of the U.S.-dominated NATO remained unsolved; the anticipated 60,000-strong EU Rapid Reaction Force was no closer to realization in December 2001 than it had been prior to 9/11, and for the same reason that had plagued the European military in the past: the lack of funds. In October 2001, less than three months before the euro was to become the concrete symbol of European unity, the allies remained unwilling to reduce their expensive social security systems in favor of enlarged defense budgets. George Robertson, NATO's secretary-general, observed that the United States was proposing to spend $328.9 billion on defense in 2002, while France was projecting $35.5 billion, Britain $34.9 billion, and Germany $21.7 billion for the same period. These figures help explain why the war against al Qaeda in the fall of 2001 was essentially an American war.

Distressing as these figures were to European defense ministers, their implications were not necessarily harmful to the survival of the Atlantic alliance. No matter how annoying the lagging European defense efforts were to the Bush administration and no matter how dismissive the U.S. military establishment was of European capabilities as active partners, the allies had roles to play in the mobilization against international terrorism, and even in the specific arena of Afghanistan. In the immediate aftermath of 9/11, the strident unilateralism that had marked the Bush administration on such issues as global warming was considerably subdued.

American misgivings about European interference in the conduct of the war were misplaced. Although their contributions were too modest to permit the North Atlantic Council the authority it was able to exercise in the Kosovo campaign, the allies filled gaps in equipment and personnel that Americans appreciated. The support they extended to the United States in the wake of the first American missile attacks against the Taliban on 4 November was consistent with the earlier dispatch of NATO AWACS to patrol the Atlantic coast. Germany's 3,900 personnel were designed to serve carefully targeted needs in response to American requests. These included some 250 troops to evacuate wounded, 500 more for air and matériel transport, and up to 800 soldiers to operate specially equipped armored vehicles capable of checking terrain for nuclear, biological, and chemical contamination.

Central Europeans, as new members of NATO, displayed a special readiness to provide immediate help to the U.S. war effort. Poland offered an elite command unit, and the Czech Republic an anti–chemical weapons component that had detected traces of nerve gas in the Saudi desert during the Gulf War. Not surprisingly, the more recent NATO allies felt a responsibility to show their fidelity to the nation that had championed their admission to the alliance so vigorously. Unlike some of the older allies, they did not attach conditions to their aid, and conspicuously refrained from interfering in the U.S. management of the campaign.

These modest additions to the U.S. arsenal in Afghanistan would fit comfortably into a vision of NATO projected by planners in the Pentagon under the leadership of Secretary of Defense Donald Rumsfeld and Deputy Secretary Paul Wolfowitz. It evoked a pattern of behavior as old as the treaty itself. Under the first strategic concept promulgated in January 1950, the United States would supply the strategic airpower while the European members would provide ground forces, a lesser role. Secretary of Defense Louis Johnson underscored the inferior position of the smaller allies two months later at an early meeting of the Defense Committee when he proposed the merger of the Dutch navy with the British navy. Secretary of State Colin Powell seemingly envisioned a different role for the European allies, an approach that would confer more equality among those nations engaged in a common struggle against terrorism and threats of mass destruction.

IMPACT OF BUSH'S STATE OF THE UNION ADDRESS, 2002

Transatlantic frictions were fired up once again early in 2002 when the president seemingly followed the Pentagon line in his State of the Union address. Its focus was not on shared NATO responsibilities for the war against al Qaeda or on appreciation for allied contributions to peacekeeping in the Balkans, or on their collaboration in building a post-Taliban Afghanistan. There was little recognition that the European allies provided 85 percent of NATO forces in the Balkans and approximately half the personnel in Afghanistan. Rather, the speech appeared to revive a unilateral approach to the world based on a superpower's prerogative that had been soft-pedaled in the course of the campaign against the Taliban.

The president's language was harsh as he spoke of an "axis of evil" that embraced Iraq, Iran, and North Korea. These rogue nations with their potential for mass destruction did not exactly remove al Qaeda from the list of enemies but it did reduce both its visibility and putatively its threat to the United States and its allies. The shift in the nation's objectives may have been more apparent than real. Rumsfeld's Pentagon had targeted Iraq ever since 11 September 2001, and had assumed that close links existed between Saddam Hussein and Osama bin Laden's network. But the tone of the president's language suggested that this was an American action that Europe should support whether or not it was consulted.

Frictions between America and Europe worsened in 2002 as resentment against American unilateralism, identified as the arrogance of a superpower, manifested itself in the form of rising anti-Americanism throughout western Europe. Some of the conflicts were familiar and inevitable, particularly in the economic sphere. Special interests in the United States provided the incentive to set up new barriers to protect America's steel industry, which had its counterpart in the agricultural policy of the EU. But there was an edge to the economic rivalry that was less apparent in the past. The decision of the EU to exclude genetically engineered food products imported from the United States was more than a measure to protect the health of Europe's citizens; it was a declaration of Europe's independence and a promise of future economic power that would successfully challenge America's past supremacy. One French analyst speculated that decline of the American empire would come from its future loss of economic hegemony despite its dominant military power. This assumption of a united Europe, with both population and resources superior to those of the United States, aroused American anxiety once again over having created a Frankenstein monster through long-standing encouragement of European unity.

But Europe's concern at this time was deeper than America's, as it witnessed the Bush administration reverting to the unilateral behavior exemplified in 2001 by rejection of the Kyoto approach to global warming. The United States seemed now to go out of its way to provoke the allies—as well as its former adversary, Russia—by pressing ahead with ballistic missile defense (formerly the Strategic Defense Initiative). To revive what many on both sides of the Atlantic regarded as a futile attempt to insulate America from a ballistic nuclear attack, the Pentagon emphasized the dangers from rogue regimes, such as North Korea, rather than fear of revival of a threat from a revanchist Russia, but Russia was a central figure in the U.S. effort, by virtue of the Anti-Ballistic Missile Treaty of 1972. U.S. officials asserted that the 30-year-old treaty, which had imposed severe limitations on missile defense installations, had lost its meaning with the end of the Cold War, and that it should be scrapped. If the administration's plans for Star Wars redivivus could materialize, the treaty would have to be voided. Although the new comity between East and West should have made this change a matter of course, it evoked protests among the allies and the Russians over the abandonment of one of the pillars of nuclear stability. The United States was moving ahead, irrespective of European objections.

Arguably, the American position on the International Criminal Court, the pride of the European Union, was even more irritating to Europeans than the withdrawal from the ABM Treaty obligations. The court was intended to deal with individuals charged with genocide or crimes against humanity. Crimes in the Balkans and Rwanda understandably aroused Europeans and Americans alike to seek new means to deter future Milosevics. But the United States was adamant in its refusal to have its nationals subject to the authority of this court. The Bush administration's opposition was based on the fear that Americans could be singled out unfairly in politically motivated prosecutions. The global presence of representatives of the superpower would provide an easy target for governments hostile to the United States. The administration consequently has asked for and received waiver agreements from a number of allied nations that would exempt Americans from the jurisdiction of the new court. This pressure in turn has antagonized the European Union, whose foreign ministers in August 2002 attempted to keep its members from signing any agreement that would allow an American exemption. To the EU, the American stance smacked of an imperial behavior that seemed to characterize the attitude of the Bush administration, while the administration berated the EU for its insensitivity to the problems of the superpower.

THE IRAQ QUANDARY

The most prominent transatlantic rift in the early twenty-first century has been over how NATO should deal with Saddam Hussein's Iraq. Throughout 2002, the Bush administration, led by its Pentagon planners, had linked Saddam Hussein with the terrorist network of al Qaeda. Although proof of a clear link has not been clearly made, Iraq fitted the image of a rogue nation, part of the "axis of evil," justifying the doctrine of "preemption" which also surfaced in 2002. The United States and its allies should strike down terrorists before they could strike, as the Islamic fanatics did on 9/11, and as Saddam Hussein may be preparing to do with biological and chemical as well as nuclear weapons.

The shifting emphasis from al Qaeda to Iraq in the war on terrorism opened a schism in the alliance that worsened when the United States prepared for war with a coalition of the willing, or alone if necessary. Perhaps the unilateral stance was even preferable to some officials on the assumption that a Europe unwilling to raise its defense budgets would only be a drag on the American effort. The superpower could take on the Iraqi dictator on its own. Weaker than it had been at the time of the Gulf War, Iraq was an easier and more manageable target than the elusive al Qaeda. Skeptical Europeans—along with some skeptical Americans—deprecated the Bush administration's rush toward war on a variety of grounds. Was the United States acting to gain control of Iraqi oil, or to complete what Bush *père* failed to do in 1991, or to display a presidential leadership that would ensure Republican victory in the 2002 elections, or to divert American—and the world's—attention from the failure to rout the al Qaeda network? Or was it a display of a superpower's ability to go its own way and expect its allies to follow?

European allies, aided by elements of the Bush administration, including Secretary of State Colin Powell, tempered the president's drive for immediate and unilateral action, if not his intemperate language, to work through the United Nations, even as he and the administration's hawks continued to say that they would not be bound by UN decisions. That Saddam Hussein was a persistent threat to stability in the Middle East was no more in question than his violation of UN resolutions since the end of the 1991 Gulf War. The allies recognized this challenge by an ultimatum to Iraq in November 2002 to accept intrusive inspections of weapons of mass destruction or face the consequences of war. Secretary Powell crafted this arrangement in a way that brought France, Russia, and China into agreement at the Security Council.

The apparent victory of diplomacy over military action only papered over divisions between the United States and the United Kingdom on the one side and France and Germany on the other. The old NATO adversaries, Russia and China, were quietly opposed to an American war, but remained in the background as NATO allies separated over the wisdom of a forceful overthrow of Saddam Hussein. France and Germany had placed their faith in the inspection teams that the Security Council had dispatched to discover if the Iraqis still possessed weapons of mass destruction; the United States and Britain were convinced of the futility of the mission, no matter how much more intrusive it would be compared with the failed inspections in the 1990s. The suspicion of many in the West and most in the Muslim world was that the United States had predetermined the failed outcome of the inspections and only wanted to use the United Nations as a cover for its invasion. President Bush's insistence that the United States was justified if necessary to wage war unilaterally was sufficient proof for critics to doubt America's good faith in accepting inspections while engaged in a military buildup on Iraq's borders.

Anger over American behavior manifested itself on the European street, and could be found in the editorials of most newspapers. Germany vied with France to display its independence of the United States. European resentment over American pressure to participate in a war against Iraq was fueled by their claim that the United States was supporting an aggressive and destructive Israeli war against Palestinians. Speaking through the European Union, they asserted that the plight of Palestine took priority over Iraq's transgressions.

Popular opposition to an American-led war was grist for Chancellor Gerhard Schroeder's election campaign in 2002 when he promised that under no circumstances would Germany provide troops or aid in the war effort whether or not a member, such as Turkey, might be attacked. In a sense, this was a reprise of a posture held in 1991. But in 2002, antiwar and anti-American sentiments went deeper. There was a truculence implicit in Schroeder's behavior that announced Germany's freedom from its habitual deference to America. World War II was long past, and so was the feeling of gratitude for the sustenance American provided the fledgling democracy. Schroeder talked about a "German way" that resonated with voters unhappy with the American hegemony. But it also had echoes of a German *Weltanschauung* that could awaken memories of a "German way" under the Third Reich.

Problems with a newly assertive Germany, however, were on the back burner in 2002. Europe's attention at this time was on the American threat of a preemptive war against Iraq and its demands for allied compliance. The Franco-German connection was solidified by a common anti-American posture, shared by the majority of European public opinion. This division was manifested in the inability of the North Atlantic Council to reach a consensus over an American request for support in the event of war. Even more divisive than refusing to back the American ally was the reluctance of France and Germany to guarantee solidarity with Turkey if it were attacked by its Iraqi neighbor.

American officials' responses to European dissent were often provocative, particularly when they accused the French and Germans of the kind of weakness that led to Munich. Secretary of State Colin Powell suggested at one point that his French counterpart suffered from the "vapors." Secretary of Defense Donald Rumsfeld went even further, suggesting that the two countries and their followers in the West represented "Old Europe." The NATO that had expanded in 1999 and again in 2002 had become the new Europe, which was composed of allies more understanding and more appreciative of American leadership. The Iraq issue conceivably could have been the rock on which the Atlantic alliance might split in two, or collapse altogether.

RUSSIA AS NATO UNIFIER?

Still, there were centripetal factors that weighed against the breakup of the Atlantic alliance. Some of them stemmed from ongoing transatlantic cooperation that has coexisted with the tensions of the last decade. No matter how badly the European allies mismanaged the Bosnian crisis and subsequently hampered the conduct of the Kosovo campaign, their role after each of these conflicts was vital to the peacekeeping process. Their numbers far exceeded those of the United States whose contributions to IFOR and KFOR in the last half of the 1990s steadily dwindled. Europeans picked up a burden that was more appropriately theirs. None of the military operations led by the United States was solely an American affair. In a similar way, although the war against the Taliban was managed from the United States, the postwar rebuilding of Afghanistan was shared by the allies. Even as Germany figuratively thumbed its nose at America over Iraq, it sought to rebuild bridges with the United States by assuming the cochairmanship in February 2003 with the Netherlands of the International Security Assistance Force in Kabul, replacing Turkish leadership in that city.

Europeans have been supportive as well in the war against al Qaeda, and not simply as a service to the superpower. Their own security was at stake because Europe appeared to be a target of the terrorist network and certainly the site of terrorist conspiracies. Here was an example of a war in which transatlantic allies could find a common foe and could respect the mission of Article 5. It is worth noting that high among the criticisms of U.S. policy toward Iraq was the European complaint about diversion of energy and resources from the primary enemy, the al Qaeda terrorists. Granted that Islamic fundamentalists have found safer havens in western Europe than they have in the United States, credit should be given to those allies whose investigators have been increasingly active in rooting out terrorist networks as vigorously and, arguably, even more effectively than their American counterparts.

A conspicuous example of transatlantic collaboration was evident in NATO's deft handling of its relations with Russia. As the alliance moved closer to Russian borders, there was visceral anxiety on the part of that nation's leadership. First the admission of Hungary, the Czech Republic, and particularly Poland in 1997 aroused opposition and awakened visceral fears of NATO as a hostile entity. NATO in turn attempted to soothe Russian nerves and undercut a nationalist backlash by signing a "Founding Act" in 1997 promoting cooperation and security between the Atlantic alliance and the Russian Federation. There was an expectation of close cooperation on matters of mutual concern, summed up in the mantra that the Russians would have a voice but not a veto in NATO affairs. A weakened Russia under volatile President Boris Yeltsin had little choice but to accept this promise of good intentions on the part of the West.

But the increasing pressure from other remnants of the Warsaw Pact put new strains on the relationship with a Russia under the leadership of a stronger president, Vladimir Putin. Admission of the Baltic nations to the Atlantic alliance was even more delicate than the membership of Poland; Lithuania, Latvia, and Estonia had been part of the Soviet Union, and their inclusion in NATO was perceived as especially insulting to an ascendant Russia. NATO attempted to assuage Russia's feelings by scrapping the Founding Act of 1997, which turned out to give the Russians neither a voice nor a veto. It was as meaningless as the North Atlantic Coordinating Council, established in 1991, or the Partnership for Peace, established in 1994, as vehicles to give Russians an active voice in NATO affairs without offering membership itself. Actually, the efforts of the 1990s did bear fruit, as seen in Russia's intervention with Serbia's Milosevic to help end the Kosovo War and in its participation in subsequent peacekeeping in that Serbian province. But because a new enlargement was in process in 2002, something more was needed. NATO rose to the occasion by establishing a NATO–Russia Council that enlisted Russia as an equal partner in NATO decision making when such vital issues as combating terrorism was on the agenda. Whether this new arrangement will succeed remains to be seen.

The outreach to Russia over the past decade has been a collective effort, lacking the transatlantic tensions found elsewhere in the NATO community. The United States arguably was the prime mover in both moving NATO eastward and in winning Russian acquiescence in the process. It was important for all the allies to appreciate the benefits of that nation's compliance, given its vocal opposition in the past and given nationalist unrest in the present. Why Russia complied with only murmurs of dissent lies in part in its need for a close Western connection to ensure the future of its capitalist economy.

The war on terrorism is another element in the relationship with the United States; the Chechen conflict has made Russia as conscious of the terrorist menace as the United States has been since 9/11. President Putin could also count on his personal relations with President Bush to minimize criticism of the brutal campaign against Chechen rebels. These factors have paid dividends for American foreign relations in what had been a pro forma Russian opposition to American policy on Iraq until it joined France and Germany in 2003 to oppose armed intervention.

Yet there should have been some reservations on the part of NATO, and certainly on the part of the United States, about their connections to Putin's Russia. The Russian president's continuing campaign against a free press, his tolerance of still-rampant corruption, and an ongoing willingness to allow Russian support for Iran's nuclear program, suggest limits to a permanent Western link with Russia, more from the American than European perspective. Russia remains a country possessing a still powerful nuclear capability under a regime that may not have fully reconciled to its lesser role in world affairs. Putin has shown a disposition as well to play off Europeans against Americans without tipping his hand about where Russia's future allegiance will be. Whether or not there is an irredentist spirit alive and active in the former Soviet Union, Russia has the potential of raising one more obstacle to a harmonious transatlantic relationship in the future.

THE SIGNIFICANCE OF THE PRAGUE SUMMIT

The NATO summit in Prague in November 2002 centered on the admission of seven new nations into the alliance in April 2004. That the presence of 26 as opposed to 19 members will tilt the balance in Europe away from the West to the East is moot. Certainly, the former Warsaw bloc members in the alliance have a more positive view of the United States than the older allies, but even if their presence does not reduce the level of anti-American sentiment, the adherence of seven new allies in the immediate future heralded a number of changes in the character of the organization.

First, it becomes apparent that the tradition of consensus may have limited value in the future; the community is too large to have decisions based on unanimity. One nation's dissent can undo a decision accepted by the other allies. Although there has always been an informal recognition that some members were more equal than others, NATO in the future may have to use a formal weighted system of decision making in which the larger powers have a greater voice than the smaller.

Turkey's invocation of Article 4 in February 2003, asking for consultation in light of Iraq's potential threat to its security, focused attention on the initial refusal of France, Germany, and Belgium to dispatch AWACS and Patriot missiles for its protection. The dissident members' reason centered on the destabilizing effect of war preparation on the success of continued UN inspections of Iraq's arsenal of weapons of mass destruction. This challenge could signal the formal end of the "NATO method" of consensus. In February 2003, the potential damage to the alliance, however, was sufficient to close ranks behind Turkey, although it should be noted that Belgium's and Germany's decision to withdraw their objections was made in the Defense Planning Committee on which France has not sat since 1966.

A second change was more explicit, although less explosive. The council at its Prague meeting agreed to expand its scope to encompass the globe. "Out-of-area" is the world at large, as long as terrorism is a threat to the organization's members. Without identifying any particular region or country, the NATO leaders promised at Prague "to meet the challenges to the security of our forces, populations, and territory, from wherever they may come." NATO's reach would extend to Pakistan, Indonesia, and the Philippines. As an earnest of these intentions, NATO in August 2003 officially took over the peacekeeping functions of the International Security Assistance Force (ISAF) in Afghanistan. It is noteworthy that the first goal expressed in January 2004 by Jaap de Hoop Sheffer, Lord Robertson's successor as secretary-general, was to expand the NATO-led peacekeeping force in Afghanistan as part of NATO's war against terrorism. When the NATO summit meeting convenes in Instanbul in June 2004, the United States hopes to have the alliance extend military cooperation with the Islamic world. A NATO role in Iraq would be an important part of the expanded mission.

A hesitant start had begun in the fall of 2003 when NATO was to provide logistical help to a Polish-led division of some 9,000 international troops in Iraq. The NATO presence, however, would be significant only when French and German forces participate in the peacekeeping operation. Their absence, understandable in the tense European–American relations stemming from the war against Iraq, nevertheless inspired a Senate resolution in July 2003 urging the president to seek help from NATO to reduce U.S. military presence in that country. As Senator Joseph R. Biden of Delaware, the author of the resolution, noted about the daily attacks against American soldiers in Iraq: "I don't want every kid blown up at a checkpoint being an American soldier. This is the world's problem. Not just ours." Rather belatedly, the Bush administration came to recognize the need for alliance support, but not on the terms the French and Germans demanded. If they or others such as India and Japan joined the United States, the NATO flag would have to be flown under a UN umbrella. The United States was not yet prepared to turn over a share of authority that would follow UN authorization of multinational intervention in Iraq, but as the difficulties over establishing an Iraqi government mounted in the winter of 2004, the United States was more inclined to seek UN help in legitimizing plans for a new democratic Iraq. In this context, NATO supporters such as Senator Biden recommended, in the summer and fall of 2003, that the administration of a post–Saddam Iraq be placed under a NATO command. It would then have the authority of a Security Council mandate, as most of the allies have wanted, and yet through SHAPE be under the operational command of an American general who would report to the North Atlantic Council.

Actually, NATO had made Iraq an out-of-area responsibility in 1991. Even though that "coalition of the willing" was not formally under the North Atlantic Council's provenance, the attack was led by the United States and NATO allies essentially comprised the coalition in 1991. It was obvious that the new members lacked the military capabilities of the senior allies, but it was equally obvious that there was no need in 2003 for addition of large numbers of divisions. The "niche" capabilities, such as those provided by the Poles and Czechs in assault against the Taliban in Afghanistan, could serve the alliance in future crises.

Yet more conventional military forces were recognized as necessary, not in the numbers that confronted the Soviets a generation ago, but in the form of a relatively small force quickly mobilized and quickly deployed to a troubled area. The North Atlantic Council at Prague created a NATO Rapid Response Force, 21,000 strong, to be operational by 2004. Although the communiqué emphasized its close relations with the EU, it also exposed fissures between the two organizations that mirrored the larger divisions between the United States and its major continental allies. The primary problem stemmed from the putative competition between the projected NATO Rapid Response Force and the EU counterpart, projected originally to have 60,000 troops available by 2003. This was as unrealistic—and unnecessary—an aspiration as was the short-lived decision in April 2003 of Luxembourg, Belgium, France, and Germany to establish a headquarters for non-NATO operations.

Why such an EU force was needed has been a subject of controversy since the Franco-German brigade morphed into the Eurocorps, and then merged with the Western European Union when the EU absorbed that organization. A military identity was important for the EU's sense of its rising power, particularly if it was to contest American hegemony successfully. But conflict was not necessarily a by-product of the EU–NATO relationship. The EU has the capability, anticipated in the CJTF proposal in 1994, of complementing NATO objectives. An example of cooperation were plans in 2004 for the transfer of NATO peacekeeping operations in Macedonia to the EU.

What hampers the EU—and undermines the integrity of its rapid-reaction force—has been its continuing unwillingness to invest funds in the military budgets of its members. NATO's Secretary-General Robertson repeatedly had urged injecting monies into their military establishments if they were to catch up with the technological advances of the United States. Europeans were spending an average of only 2 percent of their gross domestic products, down from 3.2 percent in 1989. The United States spent some 6 percent in 1989, which declined to 3 percent. Both figures in 1989 reflected Cold War budgets, but Europe's inability or unwillingness to do more forecloses opportunities to win equality with the United States. Instead, there was mounting resentment in Europe over U.S. superiority and its reluctance to share NATO assets with the allies. Correspondingly, the United

States was irritated over Europe's demands for sharing while refusing to carry its share of the burden, a familiar American refrain.

The transatlantic division over Iraq actually was only the most dramatic occasion for an open break that had been in the making since the end of the Cold War. The EU under Franco-German domination was flexing its muscles in challenging the hegemony of the American "hyperpower" (to use a current French term). France in particular opposed the United States at every opportunity. Its threatened veto at the UN Security Council in March 2003 of any resolution authorizing the use of force for the removal of Saddam Hussein symbolized the depth of European alienation from America. President Bush's bellicose language seemingly reflected values and views alien to the newly unified Europe. The war against Iraq that followed the deadlock in the Security Council further estranged France and Germany, and particularly the publics of even those NATO governments that accepted American leadership in the successful effort to remove Saddam Hussein from power.

Given the sharp exchanges over Iraq in the winter and spring of 2003, it was hardly surprising to find speculation once again about NATO being at the point of dissolution. Or, if it survives, it might be a rump Atlantic alliance of central and eastern European countries along with Italy and the Iberian countries as partners of the Anglo-Americans. France and Germany might still lead the EU, but even here, the admission of more East European countries could dilute a Franco-German condominium. The end product may be a return to the fractured West of pre–World War II, with the United States permanently following a path of unilateralism.

But termination of the transatlantic alliance is not inevitable. Tensions and frictions were built into NATO by virtue of a free association of its component parts. The presence of the United States as a centerpiece of the alliance is important for the very military strength that many of its members deplore. NATO is the only international organization with a military capability, and American participation has provided Europe with a relative freedom from having to pay for its own defense system. Beyond this economic benefit is an unstated concern that without the United States, a resurgent Russia, still a nuclear power, might disturb the stability of the West once again.

Even more submerged is an understanding that the United States in NATO stands as a counterweight to Germany. Germany, not France, would be the dominant force in Europe if America withdrew. Despite its genuine democratic credentials, the chancellor's evocation of a "German way" would have a more sinister resonance without the United States in Europe.

As for the American partner, a retreat into isolationism would have dangerous ramifications for the superpower. A chaotic Europe would be as damaging to America's well-being as it was between the world wars of the twentieth century. The European Union without a symbiotic relationship with NATO would be as open to fratricidal conflict as the Brussels Pact powers were in 1948 when they had trouble deciding which nationality would take the leadership. Equally important, the United States cannot manage world affairs alone. The partnership with the allies has been vital if not always respected for the services they have provided in the Balkans and Afghanistan, as well as for the support the United States seeks from Europe in a reconstructed Iraq. Granted the ongoing frustrations on both sides of the Atlantic, there is a mutual dependence that has kept the alliance together in the past and should continue to do so in the future. What is needed is mutual respect for the role each ally plays, and a civilized rhetoric when tempers flare.

IN RETROSPECT

The North Atlantic Treaty was formed in 1949 to correct the inability of the United Nations to provide the security the West had expected after the havoc of World War II. The Atlantic alliance drew its strength from a perceived need to contain the Communist threat to the Western democracies and to facilitate the political and economic integration of a divided Europe. The implosion of the Soviet Union, the dissolution of the Warsaw Pact, and the rise of the European Union at the end of the twentieth century were tributes to the success of a common transatlantic effort.

Yet no year in the Cold War had passed without revelations of strains between the United States and its European allies; some were minor, others serious. In most of the conflicts, Europe stood relatively united against perceived acts of discrimination or neglect, of insensitivity, or of intimidation committed by the senior partner. On occasions, frictions within Europe itself manifested themselves, between France and most of its allies in 1966, and between Greece and Turkey in 1974 (although the United States was a principal player in both these controversies). There were instances, too, in which European governments lined up with the United States against their own citizens, as in the their support of deploying cruise missiles in the 1980s. But for the most part, Europeans could and did display common grievances against the United States, and were ever ready to display them. The numerous congressional resolutions urging troop withdrawal from Europe suggested an American counterpart to Europe's grievances.

Yet the transatlantic bonds were never severed. Greece did remove itself from NATO's military structure, but not permanently. France did not return to the military fold, but made sure that its military was closely connected to SHAPE's command centers. In the headquarters of AFSouth in Naples, for example, a French "mission" was intimately involved in NATO planning. The nomenclature did not matter; the intimacy did. For political reasons, France has remained outside the integrated military structure, but its hostility to American leadership had never been as virulent as it was under de Gaulle. Britain has always chafed at its assignment as a junior partner in NATO, but its dissatisfactions, expressed in the Suez adventure of 1956 and in the Skybolt confrontation of 1962, never rose to the breaking point.

The United States, for its part, growled regularly over its sense of unfair distribution of the military and financial burdens of the alliance, but its bark was always sharper than its bite. None of the many Senate resolutions contemplating withdrawal of American troops from Europe was implemented. As long as the Cold War was in force, the United States maintained a strong military presence on the Continent, and continued to remain in place in a post–Cold War Europe, although in reduced numbers.

Arguably, the most compelling sign of transatlantic solidarity has been the allies' silence over terminating membership in the alliance. Under Article 13 of the North Atlantic Treaty, any member could "cease to be a Party one year after its notice of denunciation." No member has chosen to take advantage of this way out of the alliance. The danger in the future, however, lies less in the likelihood of an abrupt dissolution than in the possibility of NATO becoming as irrelevant as the League of Nations was in the 1930s if America and Europe fail to share the responsibilities of crisis management beyond the boundaries of the alliance.

Bibliographical Essay

In its 55-year history, NATO has been the subject of analyses in all its many facets. Aside from studies of the technical aspects of the organization, almost every monograph touched in one way or another on the transatlantic relationship of the Old World with the New World of America with Europe. Consequently, my list inevitably is as arbitrary as it is limited. It consists only of book-length monographs that have influenced my approach to this project.

The linkages were never more clearly demonstrated than in the protracted debate over the framing of the treaty. The problem of fabricating an American identity with Europe was the primary purpose of the alliance's founders, and with the success of this effort there developed strains that persisted into the twenty-first century. The most important contribution to an understanding of the origins of the alliance arguably was provided by the Canadian statesman Escott Reid, *Time of Fear and Hope: The Making of the North Atlantic Treaty* (Toronto: McClellan and Stewart, 1977), a member of the Canadian delegation at the Washington treaty talks in 1948. Nicholas Henderson, second secretary to the British embassy in Washington in that year, provided not only an account of the proceedings but also of the tripartite talks in March 1948 that preceded the negotiations as well as a useful description of the dramatis personae in *The Birth of NATO* (Boulder, CO: Westview Press, 1963). Dean Acheson presented a U.S. perspective in his authoritative, if often sardonic, *Present at the Creation: My Years in the State Department* (New York: Norton, 1969). On NATO's twenty-fifth anniversary, the official *NATO Review* published commentaries of observers from all 12 members of the alliance who were also "present at the creation." These brief pieces were intended to celebrate their national contributions to the treaty process, and were subsequently published by Andre de

Staercke et al., *NATO's Anxious Birth: The Prophetic Vision of the 1940s* (New York: St. Martin's Press, 1985).

For secondary accounts of the origins of the treaty, see, in particular, Timothy P. Ireland, *Creating the Entangling Alliance: The Origins of the North Atlantic Alliance* (Westport, CT: Greenwood Press, 1981); Lawrence S. Kaplan, *A Community of Interests* (Washington, DC: Government Printing Office, 1980) and *The United States and NATO: The Formative Years* (Lexington: University Press of Kentucky, 1984); John Baylis, *The Diplomacy of Pragmatism: Britain and the Formation of NATO, 1942–1949* (Kent, OH: Kent State University Press, 1993); E. Timothy Smith, *Opposition Beyond the Water's Edge: Liberal Internationalists, Pacifists and Containment* (Westport, CT: Greenwood Press, 1999).

As noted in Chapter 2, the transatlantic relationship was under strain in the 1950s even though—and often because—the European partners were so dependent at this time on U.S. military strength. Lord Ismay, *NATO—The First Five Years* (Paris: NATO, 1954), saw the evolution of the organization from his perch as the first secretary-general. An important work raising questions about the challenges facing the United States in its support of Europe was Klaus Knorr, ed., *NATO and American Security* (Princeton: Princeton University Press, 1959). The Chatham House Study Group, *Atlantic Alliance: NATO's Role in the Free World* (London: Royal Institute of International Affairs, 1952), raised the problem from a British perspective of reconciling European integration with the Atlantic Community. Mary Margaret Ball, *NATO and the European Union Movement* (New York: Praeger, 1959), examined the impact of the developing European Union on NATO and the United States in the 1950s. Edgar Furniss, *France, Troubled Ally: De Gaulle's Heritage and Prospects* (New York: Harper & Bros., 1960), explored the sources of France's difficulties with the American partner at the end of the decade. Karl W. Deutsch and Lewis J. Edinger, *Germany Rejoins the Powers* (Stanford, CA: Stanford University Press, 1959), showed how the Federal Republic's membership in NATO resolved a major source of tension in the mid-1950s.

Transatlantic relations grew more tense in the 1960s because Europeans felt more secure after the resolution of the Berlin and Cuban crises. Robert E. Osgood's *NATO: The Entangling Alliance* (Chicago: University of Chicago Press, 1963) was the first major scholarly work to place the transatlantic conflict over nuclear weapons into a historical context; Henry A. Kissinger, *The Troubled Partnership: A Reappraisal of the Atlantic Alliance* (New York: McGraw-Hill, 1965), urged the United States to help make the European allies genuine partners in light of a changing relationship, as did German statesman Kurt Birrenbach, *The Future of the Atlantic Community; Toward European–American Partnership* (New York: Praeger, 1963); Ronald Steel, *The End of the Alliance: America and the Future of Europe* (New York: Viking, 1964), had a different point of view; the increasing vulnerability of the United States made the "pledge" of 1949 invalid. William T. R.

Fox and Annette B. Fox, *NATO and the Range of American Choice* (New York: Columbia University Press, 1967), saw NATO as a valuable instrument of U.S. foreign policy in applying diplomatic pressure on its allies. David Calleo, *The Atlantic Fantasy: The U.S., NATO, and Europe* (Baltimore: Johns Hopkins University Press, 1970), agreed with the Foxes' judgment but with a pejorative spin: he saw NATO as a means of dominating Europe. France's opposition to America's hegemony was dramatized in the 1960s by its withdrawal from NATO's military structure. A measured presentation of the French view may be found in Andre Beaufre's *NATO and Europe* (London: Faber and Faber, 1967). John Newhouse, *De Gaulle and the Anglo-Saxons* (London: Andre Deutsch, 1970), discussed the consequences of France's actions. Richard Kugler, *The Great Strategy Debate: NATO's Evolution in the 1960s* (Santa Monica, CA: Rand Corporation, 1991), explained the fundamental transatlantic differences over nuclear and conventional defense in those years. Harlan Cleveland, *NATO: The Transatlantic Bargain* (New York: Harper & Row, 1970), head of the U.S. delegation to NATO in the late 1960s, was more optimistic about the future of the alliance. Thomas A. Schwartz, *Lyndon B. Johnson and Europe: In the Shadow of Vietnam* (Cambridge, MA: Harvard University Press, 2003), writing a generation later, contrasted failure in Asia with relative success in Europe.

Détente and disillusionment characterized much of the spirit of the 1970s. The title of James Chace and Earl Ravenal, eds., *Atlantis Lost: US–European Relations after the Cold War* (New York: New York University Press, 1976) signaled the disappointment of its contributors over the state of the alliance in mid-decade. Simon Serfaty, *Fading Partnership: America and Europe after 30 Years* (New York: Praeger, 1979), was particularly critical of the Nixon–Kissinger NATO policies. Agryris Andrianapoulous, *Western Europe in Kissinger's Global Strategy* (London: Macmillan, 1986), followed the logic of Kissinger's linkage of economic and security issues. Karl Kaiser, *Europe and the United States: The Future of the Relationship* (Washington, DC: Columbia Books, 1973), offered a European perspective on the relationship in the Nixon years. Physicist Samuel T. Cohen, *The Neutron Bomb: Political, Technological, and Military Issues* (Cambridge, MA: Institute for Foreign Policy Analysis, 1978), defended the use of the neutron bomb, one of the most controversial issues in the Carter administration. Sherri L. Wasserman, *The Neutron Bomb Controversy: A Study in Alliance Politics* (New York: Praeger, 1983), was critical of Carter's management of the controversy. Philip H. Tresize, *The Atlantic Connection: Prospects, Problems, and Policies* (Washington, DC: Brookings Institution, 1975), found resiliency in NATO relations but urged pragmatic rather than grand designs for the future.

The 1980s witnessed both new transatlantic crises and the winding down of the Cold War. Both developments received considerable scholarly attention. The significance of nuclear politics may be seen in such important studies in the 1980s as Lawrence Freedman's *The Evolution of Nuclear Strategy* (New York: St.

Martin's Press, 1981; David N. Schwartz's *NATO's Nuclear Dilemmas* (Washingon, DC: Brookings Institution, 1983); and Richard W. Stevenson's *The Rise and Fall of Détente: Relaxation of Tension in U.S.–Soviet Relations* (Urbana: University of Illinois Press, 1985). Josef Joffe, *The Limited Partnership: Europe, the United States, and the Burdens of the Alliance* (Cambridge, MA: Ballinger, 1987), an influential German journalist who emphasized the presence of the United States as a unifying force in NATO, and Robert A. Levine, *NATO: Subjective Alliance: The Debate over the Future* (Santa Monica, CA: RAND Corporation, 1988), categorized the many debates over the functions of NATO in the 1980s. John Palmer, *Europe Without America?: The Crisis in Atlantic Relations* (Oxford: Oxford University Press, 1987), worried that the fractious transatlantic relationship in the Reagan administration could destroy NATO. Geoffrey Lee Williams and Alan Lee Williams, *The European Defense Initiative: Europe's Bid for Equality* (London: Macmillan, 1986), advocated the Europeanization of NATO as a means of maintaining European support of the alliance; and Melvyn B. Krauss, *How NATO Weakens the West* (New York: Simon and Schuster, 1986), presented a neoconservative American view that the United States should leave Europe to the Europeans. Gregory F. Treverton opposed this solution with his *Making the Alliance Work: The United States and Western Europe* (London: Macmillan, 1985). Writing during the Gorbachev era, Lawrence S. Kaplan, *NATO and the United States: The Enduring Alliance* (Boston: Twayne, 1988), claimed that NATO retained its role as guarantor of transatlantic security.

The end of the Cold War and the implosion of the Soviet empire removed the major centripetal force uniting the allies. The result of these changes was a sharpening of the divisions within the alliance, portending, as many feared, the dissolution of NATO in the 1990s. Werner Bauwens and Luc Reychler, eds., *The Art of Conflict Resolution* (London: Brassey's, 1994), concentrated on the means of settling conflicts in the post–Cold War era. Jeffrey Simon, ed., *NATO: The Challenge of Change* (Washington, DC: National Defense University Press, 1993), recommended that the alliance make European stability a major raison d'être. Sean Kay, *NATO and the Future of Europe* (Lanham, MD: Rowman & Littlefield, 1998), raised problems associated with the enlargement program of the 1990s. James M. Goldgeier, *Not Whether but When: The U.S. Decision to Enlarge NATO* (Washington, DC: Brookings Institution Press, 1999), and Ronald D. Asmus, *Opening NATO's Door: How the Alliance Remade Itself for a New Era* (New York: Columbia University Press, 2002), explained why expanding NATO into eastern Europe would strengthen the alliance. The case against enlargement was made by Michael Mandelbaum in his *Dawn of Peace in Europe* (New York: Twentieth Century Fund Press, 1996). For some scholars such as Ted Galen Carpenter, *A Search for Enemies: American Alliances after the Cold War* (Washington, DC: Cato Institute, 1992), NATO, has outlived its usefulness and should disband. Joseph Nye, *Bound to Lead: The Changing Nature of American Power* (New York: Basic Books,

1990), was convinced that as the only superpower, the United States had an oblig-ation to lead in maintaining the security of Europe. A promise of transatlantic equality was presented in Charles G. Cogan's *The Third Option: The Emancipation of European Defense, 1989–2000* (Westport, CT: Praeger, 2001).

The events following 9/11 have exacerbated tensions between America and Europe, most notably over how to deal with Saddam Hussein's Iraq. On the one side, there has been a spate of articles and books criticizing Europe for its failure to accept American leadership in the war against terrorism, as in Robert Kagan, *Of Policy and Power: America and Europe in the New World Order* (New York: Knopf, 2003), who castigated Europe for its weakness in the face of global threats. A mirror image of the current transatlantic feud was Emmanuel Todd, *Apres l'em-pire: Essai sur le de composition du systeme americaine* (Paris: Editions Galli-mard, 2002), who foresaw Europe's future challenge to America through economic rather than military power. Andrew Bacevich, *American Empire: The Realities and Consequences of United States Diplomacy* (Cambridge, MA: Harvard University Press, 2002) and Charles Kupchan, *The End of the American Era: U.S. Foreign Policy and Geopolitics of the Twenty-first Century* (New York: Knopf, 2002), shared some of Todd's expectations without his biases.

More optimistic speculations about the future of transatlantic relations were offered in David S. Yost's *NATO Transformed: The Alliance's New Roles in Inter-national Security* (Washington, DC: United States Institute for Peace Press, 1998); Wallace J. Thies's *Friendly Rivals: Bargaining and Burden-Shifting in NATO* (Ar-monk, NY: M.E. Sharpe, Inc., 2002); and Stanley R. Sloan's *NATO, the European Union, and the Atlantic Community: The Transatlantic Bargain Reconsidered* (Lanham, MD: Rowman & Littlefield, 2003).

Index

About the Author

LAWRENCE S. KAPLAN is University Professor Emeritus of History and Director Emeritus of the Lyman L. Lemnitzer Center for NATO and European Union Studies at Kent State University. He is currently Adjunct Professor of History at Georgetown University.